Letters of the Brownings to George Barrett

LETTERS OF THE BROWNINGS TO GEORGE BARRETT

EDITED BY PAUL LANDIS WITH THE ASSISTANCE OF RONALD E. FREEMAN

UNIVERSITY OF ILLINOIS PRESS, URBANA, 1958

PREFACE

The letters here published constitute the larger and by far the most important part of a collection of Browning papers purchased in 1950 by the University of Illinois. The whole body of material is described, fully but with some errors, in a catalogue: *Elizabeth Barrett Browning, Unpublished Correspondence*, etc., Maggs Bros. Ltd., 1937. All the papers are now in the University Library in Urbana.

During the time when these letters were being edited, Professor Freeman was an Assistant in English at the University of Illinois. It would be neither possible nor desirable to make any specific separation of our joint efforts except to absolve him from all responsibility for the opinions of the editor. In the endless task of checking and rechecking the script of the letters and the discovery from slight clues of hidden information his assistance was painstaking, resourceful, and, above all, enthusiastic.

The difficulties presented by reading and transcribing the letters were no different from and probably less troublesome than those generally attendant upon such activities. Both Elizabeth and Robert normally wrote a clear hand, though hers was delicate and often minute, chiefly when she felt forced to use the flap of the envelope or to revert to the top of the first page to complete her remarks. The early letters from Torquay, written during her severe illness, are characterized by vagrant lines and cramped and twisted words, but all have proved decipherable except in a few cases when the sheet or envelope has been torn. Consequently, few conjectures have been required and all have been noted.

Punctuation presented a more perplexing problem, and perhaps a word should be said in explanation of the practice in the text. For better or for worse, it was decided to reproduce the original as nearly as that could be done in print. The object was to preserve the spontaneous and headlong character of the style, especially Elizabeth's. She wrote in sentences, but sentences which grew as she wrote, and often she was clearly less concerned with the stop than with the flow from one statement to another. Dashes and dots, therefore, often served her better and more readily than periods and semicolons. When dots occur within the text of the letters, they do *not* indicate omissions. Nothing has been omitted. For the same reason ampersands and abbreviations have been retained, even to Elizabeth's habit of placing the apostrophe between the two parts of the word rather than over the omitted letter; e.g., *w^{d}nt, is'nt*. Words and phrases underlined one, two, and three times in the original correspondence have been represented here by italic, small capital, and full capital letters. Moreover, since none of these letters was written for publication and all were addressed within the family, consistency must not be expected, even in idiosyncrasy.

The spelling, also, of the original has been retained, and only those lapses which seemed most likely to be interpreted as misprints have been noted. Here again Elizabeth is the chief offender, recalling often her charge to Robert in her third letter to him to take no thought "for your badd speling (nor for mine)."

The primary object of the notes is to acquaint the reader insofar as possible with persons and places whose names were familiar to the correspondents. No claim is made for the intrinsic importance of much of this information. Many are the people who float into a vague immortality solely because their names have been caught in the current of more famous lives, and, without identification, they sometimes achieve a disproportionate importance through the irritation of ignorance. It is the misfortune of editors that the effort to identify these is usually in inverse ratio to the importance of the information. Others — and there are many in these letters — have their own place in history, but its location has been dimmed by time and change. If any reader find himself annoyed because the notes are too full or patronizing of his knowledge, let him recall that such were not included for him, but for others. A few notes, it must be admitted, owe their presence chiefly to the fact that it interested the editor to write them.

The work of editing has been much facilitated by that of numerous Browning biographers and editors published during the past several years. Although we have leaned heavily upon these distinguished colleagues, it seems unnecessary to name them here since each, we hope, has received appropriate credit in each specific instance. May they all realize the gratitude with which their work was utilized.

Among the many here in Urbana whose knowledge and encouragement have been at our disposal it is a pleasure to single out Miss Isabelle Grant, Rare Book Room Librarian, and Miss Rachel Anderson, Assistant Editor of the University Press, in gratitude to both for their cheerful patience as well as their help, and to Miss Anderson especially for her careful reading of the proof and her intelligent suggestions so courteously given. Thanks also are due and are here gratefully given to Mrs. R. F. Freeman for her work in the preparation of the Index.

Finally and fundamentally, our thanks are due to Professor Gordon Ray, Vice-President and Provost of the University, at whose instigation, when he was Head of the English Department, the collection was purchased and who accorded to the editor the privilege of dealing with the letters, and to Professor Donald Jackson, Editor of the University Press, under whose direction the book was produced.

CONTENTS

INTRODUCTION

"And then the biographer is parsimonious of her letters, — which always tell a story of life better than the best abstract of it, elaborated by the cold hands of another — "

letter 13, p. 72

I

Volumes of the Brownings' letters accumulate as interest in their poetry wanes. To turn that sentence around would infer something more than the truth and yet, in Robert's case at least, something not altogether false. At any rate there can be no doubt about either fact. The *New Letters* of Knickerbocker and De-Vane, McAleer's *Dearest Isa*, Miss Miller's *Elizabeth Barrett to Miss Mitford*, and Miss McCarthy's *Elizabeth Barrett to Mr. Boyd* have all appeared within the past six years in addition to a biography of each poet, each based chiefly upon their letters. Yet lately when the writer was introduced — to speak upon another subject — as a student of Browning, the master of ceremonies interpolated, "Does anybody read Browning anymore?" And Professor Mario Praz remarked to him with what seemed like mild regret that he could find nothing of Mrs. Browning's worth including in his anthology of English poetry. Both comments are excessively derogatory, but it must be admitted that the hundredth anniversary of *Men and Women* and *Aurora Leigh* finds the former with fewer readers than at any time in the last eighty years, and the latter no more likely to be reissued than at any time since its twenty-second edition appeared in 1892. Whatever inference is to be drawn from these circumstances, one is clear: the interest in the poets themselves has at the present writing survived the interest in their poetry.

This interest in the Brownings as persons rests, of course, upon the fact that they were "people of importance in their own time." If they had not written original and distinguished poetry, no one would have bothered to collect and publish their letters. Still, even the most fervent of their literary admirers must admit the permanent interest which attaches to the circumstances of their lives: Miss Barrett's illness, her virtual incarceration in Wimpole Street, the strange courtship ending in the romantic elopement, the fantastic severity of Mr. Barrett's reaction, and the fifteen happy years of marriage framed by *Sonnets from the Portuguese* and the "Lyric love, half angel and half bird" dedication to *The Ring and the Book*. All this has made of the two poets the hero and heroine of the kind of romance which men have always imagined and seldom met with outside fiction. Robert and Elizabeth Browning have become in themselves the truth of poetry.

Moreover, their story has in it elements which sustain the interest and curiosity of a generation which likes to think of itself as unromantic. For the heart of the Browning story is the family of the Barrett, and the Barretts afford a more challenging invitation to psychoanalysis than even the Brontës.

At first glance the eight sons and three daughters of Edward

Moulton-Barrett present simply a group, one of whom was certainly very close to genius, while the others display a mediocrity verging upon dullness. But as one grows better acquainted with them, one becomes aware first of the extreme family solidarity extending to countless aunts and uncles and cousins and reaching across the years and the sea to the planter Barretts of Jamaica. Then one comes to realize that the members of this closely knit clan were possessed of a passionate spirit of personal independence. They hung together while they stood separately. They were anxious for each other's approval, but they felt no compulsion to agree. Presently the details become clearer, such as an intense religious fervor, manifesting itself in different ways, but always without anything suggesting spiritual exaltation; conformity with Victorian decorum without prudery or hypocrisy; the detachment of conscious family pride without any touch of snobbery or tolerance of privilege. Dominating this family is the tremendous figure of "Papa" who appears not only in the gloom of his silence, his dark obsessions, his apparent heartlessness and actual cruelty, but also in the glow of his children's affection, his friends' respect, and his own meticulous regard for the privacy of those whose lives he ruled with such exacting severity. Altogether it may be said that if the interest in Robert Browning's poetry should fade as far as that in his wife's already has, the "Family of the Barrett" will assure him a permanent place in the imagination of men.

II

The letters which constitute this volume are unique in the body of Browning correspondence in that they furnish the most complete and continuous record of Browning-Barrett relations. The Browning-Barrett correspondence previously published consists of Elizabeth's letters to her sisters with some scattered notes of Robert's, also to Arabella and Henrietta. These are filled with details of both families, their friends and their activities, but, unfortunately, they begin only after the marriage and end with Mrs. Browning's death. Moreover they are sisterly letters, narrow in scope and filled with talk, often surprisingly interesting, of health and weather and clothes and the bright sayings of children, especially Penini.

All the letters which follow here were written to Mrs. Browning's brother, George. Although there are only eighty-eight in all, they cover a period of fifty-one years from 1838 to 1889. Fifty-eight were written by Elizabeth, the first shortly after her arrival in Torquay in 1838, and the last two months before her death, June 29, 1861. Thirty were written by Robert, starting — with the exception of a few short notes — with Mrs. Browning's death and continuing until two months before his own, December 12, 1889. It is no disparagement to the rest to say that two of the series stand out as moving human documents: Letter 39, which Mrs. Browning left behind her at 50 Wimpole Street to announce to a startled family her marriage and departure; and Letter 62, in which Robert describes to the same brother her death and burial in Florence fifteen years later. There are two wide gaps, one in each series of letters. That between Letters 39 and 40 represents the years (1846-51) between the elopement and the reconciliation with George when the Brownings first returned to England. For the gap in Robert's letters (1882-87) no explanation suggests itself, and conjecture is pointless except to remark that there is no evidence of a break of any kind between them, and there is every reason to believe that the correspondence continued. It is clear, certainly, that George did not keep all the letters he received. Nevertheless, he did preserve many of his sister's letters from the age of twenty-one on, and to whatever degree he acceded to Robert's desire for privacy, he did not sacrifice all of his letters on that altar.

George Barrett, in full George Goodin Moulton-Barrett, need not delay us long in his own person. His sole claim to general interest derives from his sister and her husband. George was ten years younger than Elizabeth, but after their brother Edward's death in 1840, he was the one of all the family to whom she turned and in whom she confided. A slightly older brother, Charles John (Storm), is often referred to in these letters with great affection, but his extreme timidity, a reflection, doubtless, of his stammering, kept him from assuming the family leadership to which his age entitled him. The letters begin just about the time George was "gazetted" a barrister of the Inner Temple. He had been graduated meritoriously from the University of Glasgow and, after his admission to the bar, he served for years on the Oxford Circuit. It cannot be said that he ever achieved distinction in the practice of law or, indeed, that he desired to. He retired from active practice in 1860 (Letter 52) at the age of 44 and lived, traveling much, until 1895. He never married. His sister's early letters are filled with good-natured but thoroughly sincere disparagement of law and the legal profession. They are also full of hope, encouragement, and faith in his ultimate success in that, to her, disreputable calling. But by 1853 she writes, on hearing of his having been named in the House of Commons: "I do earnestly hope that after all this uphill work, this walking in bogs (called the law) you will get soon upon smoother ground – You have done well & uprightly in life, — which is certain good, let what will, come of it" (Letter 44).

One gathers at first that George was, on the whole, rather a stuffy person. Certainly he aligned himself with British policy in the Crimean War and the struggles to unify Italy, a policy for which his sister had no respect whatever. Certainly also, he had no respect for her infatuation with Swedenborgianism and spiritualism, and Elizabeth had as little regard for what seemed to her his oldfogeyism. The letters concerning the settlement deed indicate that with George the cautious lawyer always kept the upper hand. He seems to have been somewhat blundering in his forthrightness of speech in a family which while abhoring deception required the constant exercise of tact. Perhaps it was this characteristic along with the rigid Barrett code of right that so soon discouraged him with the law. When George was to meet Browning for the first time at a dinner party, November 21, 1845, Elizabeth undertook to brief Robert about him: "He is good and true, honest and kind, but a little over-grave and reasonable, as I and my sisters complain continually. The great Law lime-kiln dries human souls all to one colour — and he is an industrious reader among law books and knows a great deal about them, I have heard from persons who can judge; but with a sacrifice of impulsiveness and liberty of spirit, which *I* should regret for him if he sat on the Woolsack even."[1] After the dinner Browning reported: "I like him very much and mean to get a friend in him."[2] He does not appear to have been a particularly sensitive or at all a literary person. Nevertheless he associated with Talfourd and Venables and even Tennyson. Elizabeth writes familiarly to him about her poetry and once at least commends his reading of it aloud. He gives her presents of Ben Jonson and Beaumont and Fletcher while warning her — the boy of 21 to the sister of 32 — against their indecencies. He sided — and harshly — with "Papa" in cutting off Elizabeth after her marriage; yet five years later the reconciliation was easy, complete, affectionate, and permanent. Still, in spite of this restored intimacy and many pleading invitations, George never visited the Brownings in Italy, although he traveled much and actually went to Florence not long after Robert had left. He reported on the monument to Robert, who never saw it, and on his own initiative had marble busts made of his sister and her husband. He must have destroyed or lost many letters; he certainly sent some to Robert and some to Pen; yet he did not destroy precisely those letters which Robert wished suppressed. He remains, like most of the Barretts, an enigma, and becomes eventually a fascinating one. For us, however, the significant fact is that he was a Barrett and a brother.

Elizabeth's letters to George contain much of that same domestic matter which fills those addressed to her sisters, but in different proportion, mingled with comments on politics and society more calculated to catch the interest of the barrister. On subjects about which she is conscious of their disagreement she states her position with wit and firmness and sometimes with

---

[1] *Letters of R. B. and E. B. B.,* I, p. 288.
[2] *Letters of R. B. and E. B. B.,* I, p. 292.

scorn, but always with the confidence that disagreement, honestly maintained, on matters of belief cannot affect the firm foundation of love between them — almost, one might say, as man to man. However general and public the subject discussed, the letters always remain personal.

In the case of Robert's letters the personal character is even more marked — partly because it is missing in most of his other published letters. The relationship between Browning and George Barrett was not at all that between a poet and an admirer or even an interested reader; nor was George the kind of social intimate to whom Browning could chatter about their enormous circle of mutual acquaintances, mostly undistinguished people. Yet the relationship was close and genuinely affectionate. George was the brother of Browning's wife and the uncle of his son — the "one useful brother" Browning characterized him to Isa Blagden — and a lawyer besides. To him Browning could and did turn for unofficial legal advice, and to him the widowed father could voice his concern for the memory of the marvelous woman whose love they shared and for the future of the boy, so charming, so disappointing, and finally so "completely satisfactory." These letters are, in fact, precisely the sort which Browning made every effort to suppress. They deal entirely with his private personality even when the subject is his published work.

If the personal character of these letters serves to set them somewhat apart from the rest of Browning correspondence, it also emphasizes the fundamental difference in character between "the immortal lovers." For difference there was in spite of the indestructible perfection of their love. It is a little pathetic to see how commentators and biographers, searching desperately for anything that will break the monotonous perfection of this romance, emphasize the differences of opinion on Napoleon III and spiritualism. Lately Pen's curls and fancy clothes have become a serious point of disagreement, in spite of the fact that they were not at all extraordinary on a little boy in Italy in the eighteen-fifties. Certainly Browning cut the curls directly after Mrs. Browning's death, but there is no evidence that he did so with any profound satisfaction in having at last escaped from the domination of his wife. He was taking Pen to England. No, the real difference between Robert Browning and Elizabeth Barrett was one of personality. Although it colored everything they said and did, it was not a source of irritation, and neither was altogether aware of it. It is the difference between *How Do I Love Thee?* and *One Word More.*

Of Mrs. Browning it may be said that in her the woman, the poet, and the wife of the poet are all one; each phase affects the others, both enhances and limits them, but does not alter them. Between Robert Browning, the person, however, and Robert Browning, the poet, there is a cleavage so sharp that it invites misinterpretation as a contradiction. Both aspects operate upon the *manifestations* of Robert Browning, the husband of the poet, so that this aspect of the man is clear only at moments. Generally the image is clouded by the person and colored by the imagination of the poet. The dichotomy was, of course, sharpened by the almost thirty years he lived to remember her. A basic expression of this difference between the Brownings, and one emphasized by these letters, is the difference in their attitudes toward public interest in their personalities.

Robert's attitude is well known. He was possessed of an almost pathological antipathy to any public prying into his private life, and he considered almost any curiosity "prying." The letters to George contain many expressions of this passion for privacy and frequent indications that he had come to attribute the same attitude to his wife. That he could honestly do so is testimony both to his extraordinary confidence in himself and to his sense of the complete harmony between himself and his wife. For Elizabeth's letters express no such feeling at all. Apropos of Harriet Martineau's "anathema against all printers" of her letters, Elizabeth wrote in February, 1846: "I, for my part, value letters . . . as the most vital part of biography. . . . And if her principle were carried out, there would be an end! Death would be deader from henceforth. Also it is a wrong and selfish principle . . . because we should all be ready to say that if the secrets of our daily lives and inner souls may instruct other surviving souls, let them be open to men hereafter, even as they are to God now.

Dust to dust, and soul-secrets to humanity — there are natural heirs to all these things. Not that I do not understand the shrinking back from the idea of publicity on any terms — not that I would not myself destroy papers of mine which were sacred to *me* for personal reasons — but then I never would call this natural weakness, virtue — nor would I, as a teacher of the public, announce it and attempt to justify it as an example to other minds and acts, I hope."[3]

The comment quoted at the head of this introduction was made by Elizabeth Barrett in 1841 (Letter 13) on the biography of the unhappy Letitia Landon, now forgotten. It indicates an objective curiosity and a candid frankness which were no part of her husband's nature. Robert was not curious about people. He preferred to speculate about them and then to analyze the result of his speculation. As a matter of fact, he seems generally and on principle to be as reluctant to read the letters of others as to suffer anyone to read his. When in later letters Elizabeth objects to being "anatomized" in public, it is only on the grounds that she is not yet dead. Robert, it is true, takes the same position in Letter 83, but with characteristic equivocation. "You will believe me," he writes, "it is not for my own memory, once safe out of this gossip-loving and scandal-hungry world, that I am at all apprehensive." But the very next sentence runs: "Two years ago, I spent more than a week in destroying my own letters to my family,— from my earliest days up to the death of my father they had all been preserved." Nevertheless he could not bring himself to destroy his wife's letters — except for one sort.

Later in the letter quoted above he says categorically: "The unhappy letters which concern spiritualism I wish with all my heart could be eliminated from those out of my hands, and burnt forthwith,— as they ought to be." Of these letters he was ashamed. The opinions expressed in them were not his responsibility, and frankness did not demand of him that the picture of Mrs. Browning presented to the public include anything which *he* considered folly. Fortunately George did not burn all of them.

[3] *Letters of R. B. and E. B. B.*, I, p. 481.

Now, unquestionably there is a great deal of patent foolishness in Mrs. Browning's letters about spiritualism. But the woman who wrote them was no fool. The arguments she presents to her skeptical brother are intelligent; the evidence, unhappily, is weak. Mrs. Browning wanted to believe. The intensity of her desire was due, certainly in part, to the memories of her brother Edward and the circumstances of his death. Her firm religious convictions, her genuine affection for particular people, the current wave of spiritualism, and her avid interest in the changing world in which she lived furnished an environment favorable to the growth of her belief. Perhaps the fact that she lived so long so close to death encouraged it, for no one could ever say that Elizabeth Barrett Browning lived "in the shadow of death," but always on the threshold. At any rate her letters to George concerning spiritualism, however credulous, by their sharpness, their humor, and their scorn of stubborn resistance to the new, confirm her claim, in an early letter to Robert, that he would find her "on the whole an honest *man*." Naturally she would not be ashamed of her own belief, but it is hard to imagine her wanting to suppress Robert's expression of a belief honestly held, because *she* was ashamed for *him*. Nowhere in all that Browning has written about his wife is there a statement comparable for frankness to hers in Letter 57: "Agreed that Robert will probably survive me,— agreed even, on my side, that he may remarry . . being a man . . nay 'being subject to like passions' as other men, he *may* commit some faint show of bigamy — who knows? But what is absolutely impossible for him is that under any temptation or stress of passion, he *could* sacrifice what belongs to Peni to another. . . . He has that exaggerated idea of virtues connected with money, which distinguishes the man from the woman. . . . He is far more capable of committing murder, than of the slightest approach to pecuniary indelicacy."

One of Browning's favorite ideas, developed at length in many poems, is the difference between man and woman in the matter of love. His wife, too, recognized a difference, but her "'being subject to the same passions' as other men" is much more clear-eyed than the involved speculations of *Any Wife to Any Hus-*

band with her sophistry about the Titian Venus. In fact the difference is more implied than expressed in Mrs. Browning's statement, and it is characteristic of her that the difference which she emphasizes between the man and the woman is the "exaggerated idea of virtues connected with money." The men in her family were characterized by an almost quixotic attitude toward what they considered to be financial obligations. It is not that she would have condoned either sharpness or dishonesty in money matters. She simply refused to consider them of first importance. So far Robert could agree with her — ideally — but practically he could never bring himself to agree with her that any circumstances could exist in which the immediate payment of a debt might not be the deciding criterion. The sad little letter (49) which records her final failure to see Hyères shows both Brownings in agreement on the good sense of going the cheaper way, but leaves no doubt as to which one cast the weight of both on the side of thrift. "We've had a whole day of disagreeable — 'Shall I? Shant I? — ought I? — oughtnt I? — would you? — wouldn't you? –' and now the doubting's over to the hoping's disadvantage." Robert, the poet, could write hundreds of lines celebrating the glory, even the wisdom, of spontaneous action in utter disregard of circumstances, but the man took the cautious path.

There is no question here of commendation or blame. Certainly in financial matters, at least, in the light of their slender income, it was fortunate that one of the Brownings was a meticulous accountant. The point is that Mrs. Browning was all of a piece. There was nothing about her of thought or act that she felt the necessity of hiding. The moon of *One Word More* with its private face represents Mrs. Browning, but the figure is her husband's. It was he who exclaimed:

> God be thanked, the meanest of his creatures
> Boasts two soul-sides, one to face the world with,
> One to show a woman when he loves her!

And then, because he recognized the confusion, he added:

> This I say of me, but think of you, Love!

Of him it was true; of her it was his idea. *One Word More* is a
striking and sincere poem, but it is both more and less than a
love poem. Browning, for once, announces that he is speaking in
his own person, but in him the person and the husband must
speak through the poet. One cannot help feeling that the poet's
idea is original and ingenious, and that his major interest rests
there. It is founded upon a "fact" of the sort which if not true
destroys the validity of the thought, and the "fact" is at best a
legend. Even in the authority for the legend the psychology is the
reverse of that in the poem. Dante says that while he was "drawing the figures of angels," he got the idea of "putting words into
rhyme, to be an anniversary poem to her [Beatrice]." The development elaborates the poet's relation to the public through the
highly intricate conception of Moses in the wilderness to culmi-
nate in the somewhat revolting image of the dissected camel.
It is not so much the bad taste of this image as its utter artifi-
ciality that reveals the complete subjection of the man by the
poet. The sentimentality of the concept is more tolerable than
the nature-faking. For the camel is notorious among domestic
animals for never developing recognition of, much less love for,
its master. Even in this poem it is more true of Browning than
of Moses:

Never dares the man put off the prophet.

III

The paradoxical effect of this difference in temperament is
that, in these strictly personal letters, she who always spoke out,
spoke with wit and an enthusiasm often amounting to passion
of almost everything but herself; whereas he who always "wanted
to" spoke of little else, and of that little only as it touched him
personally. Mrs. Browning threw herself into, or rather gave
herself to, whatever she chose to write about, from Italian

politics to Robert and Pen. Robert is always the center of any subject about which he feels strongly enough to write.

It is natural, of course, that Robert should not write to George Barrett with the same vivacity and freedom of subject felt by Elizabeth. The bonds which united them were in their way as firm as those which bound brother and sister, but they had not been forged by nature and they were not so lightly borne. There is not the slightest reason to doubt the sincerity of Browning's affection so often asserted; yet about the expression there is always a formality, a conventionality of style which rather describes the heart than shows it. We cannot know the contents or the tone of "most" of Browning's letters to George which George says he burned (Letter 82, note 1), but there is no reason to believe that they were very different from those we have. The likeliest inference would seem to be that they dealt with greater iteration and more triviality of detail with precisely the same matter as those which George preserved. The men were in no sense associates. They seem sometimes to have met at the club (Letter 70); but Robert declined the only invitation to visit George, and there is no indication that George ever acceded to any of Robert's pressing requests to visit either himself or Pen. Here, again, it is necessary to emphasize that there was no coolness between them, only a distance which neither seems to have been able to bridge. It would, therefore, be unfair to infer too much from the total absence in these letters of any general comments or objective discussion of nonpersonal subjects. What the two men had in common were matters of business, Elizabeth, Pen, and only now and then literature, chiefly in reference to Mrs. Browning. It is impossible, however, to miss certain revelations of Browning's character in the tone and temper of what he writes.

When these letters are read, as properly they must be, along with the rest of Browning's published correspondence, they serve only to confirm the impression that he had no real interest in anything that went on in the world except as it touched Robert Browning. It is true that he considered himself a Liberal in politics, but the sonnet which explains his creed climaxes the assertion of his own freedom with another not to "discuss / A brother's right to freedom." Although in the latter part of his life he dealt often in his poetry with movements and ideas of the times, he did so always at a distance, as in *Parleyings*. There is more immediacy in "Cleon" than in "Dodington" or "Bartoli." In 1845 he professed himself ready "to die this moment in taking His part against any piece of injustice or oppression," and, no doubt, he meant it, at least in principle. But there is no indication that he was ever much moved by injustice and oppression except when they touched him personally. In such instances he rushed into the lists, at least verbally, hurling epithets with the joy of a knight-errant delivering blows. Of course, there is the well-known episode in which he was with difficulty restrained from throwing a decanter at Forster across the table, but generally his injured honor was salved by hard words written with obvious satisfaction to other people. He cannot mention the Boddingtons (Letter 66) without scorn, and he shared with Matthew Arnold the power of somehow expressing contempt by the mere mention of a name. With characteristic preference for action, his indignation generally took the form of threatening to kick, desiring to kick, or with difficulty restraining himself from kicking the offender. When he rejected spitting in FitzGerald's face as too hallowing a punishment, Browning distinctly set him apart from those for whom he apparently considered the gesture fitting. It is a favorite one with him on paper. One need not come to the defense of Alfred Austin to feel revulsion at Browning's gloating attack upon his physical deformity. Letter 76 establishes that Browning had thought of the apparently spontaneous jibe in *Pacchiarotto* a whole year before it was published.

The obvious delight which Browning took in abuse suggests forcibly the frustration of a man who all his life admired and praised action, and all his life did nothing except put words on paper. If, as the commentators are fond of pointing out, Browning saw in Caponsacchi, himself rescuing Elizabeth Barrett from the prison of Wimpole Street, he certainly failed to see that all the real courage, physical as well as spiritual, was hers. Yet

Browning was no hypocrite. He genuinely admired courage.
The nobility of his character, as Elizabeth well knew, was
real. She also knew that even love in him had a way of
expressing itself in anger. Writing to Isa Blagden in January,
1861, on the subject of the subscription for Mrs. Jameson's
sisters in which Browning refused to join, she said: "Robert
. . you know him . . he is like a rock. He is wrong, I think,
we see differently. He looks at the claims of the sisters — while
I look entirely to the memory of my dear friend Mrs. Jameson. It
would be a token of love to her . . . Robert thinks the sisters
weighed her down while she lived — therefore his regard expresses itself in a sort of indignation. Which is a natural mode
of love with him – I am sorry."[4] Caponsacchi, himself, is most
eloquent in expressing his love for Pompilia when he is venting
his wrath upon Guido. Browning seems to have found in verbal
violence a substitute for valor for which he had no occasion
except anger, and even to have cultivated indignation as an
opportunity for displaying his sense of honor whose only sword
was words. That sword, at least, was often drawn, and the occasion was always personal.

It must be admitted that these letters to George display fewer
instances of this violence than the bulk of Browning's correspondence, also that when they do not, they are less interesting in style
and content; yet there are other aspects which give the impression of a self-consciously reasonable man harassed by shysters,
hacks, and ingrates. Most of the references to Mrs. Browning
have to do with his efforts to keep from the public any information about her or with his irritation at the errors in such
accounts as were smuggled past his guard. The people who
sought this information were generally set down as hacks condemned by lack of talent to seek ignobly a precarious penny.
The public for which the information was designed is "gossip-
loving" (Letter 83), "careless and spiteful" (Letter 79), and
afflicted with an "unscrupulous hunger for old scandals" (Letter

    [4] Edward C. McAleer: "New Letters of Mrs. Browning to Isa Blagden,"
PMLA, LXVI (September, 1951), 611.

78). The long neglect of Browning by the "public" was not calculated to endear it to him, but the neglect had been sufficiently complete to preclude even gossip, and all these comments were made after the "British public, who may like me yet" had taken him to its heart. His anger at Julia Ward Howe's inexcusable attack on Mrs. Browning for her use of opium was thoroughly justified, but his generalized comment indicates a confidence founded on fear: "I find out people soon enough & know just what they will do one day to us, if they have the chance."[5] By way of contrast Mrs. Browning expressed only "pity for her . . . that she should have felt vexed *through me.*"[6] The better one becomes acquainted with Robert Browning the man, the more clearly the morbid dependence of the young author of *Pauline* shows through the confidence of the mature poet. That confidence was a faith deliberately maintained, and the persistent dramatization as well as much of the verbosity and involution of Browning's style are the measure of the effort required to keep it upright on so unsteady a foundation.

The confidence trembles visibly in the two most poignant situations treated in these letters. When Mrs. Browning died, Browning wrote first to his sister Sarianna. The letter (62) which he wrote two days later to George is less detailed than the former, but consistent with it in all respects. Yet there is a difference. Writing to George, Browning feels under a peculiar and torturing responsibility — a responsibility to defend himself before the Barretts against the charge, self-conceived, of having left disregarded signs of "obviously impending calamity." "You must not hate me," he begins, "for giving you pain anybody else might have spared you — though I am too stupid to tell how. She was never ill." Throughout this letter, which is written in an unusually large and unsteady hand, he is fighting the tragic realization that he has been guilty, not of neglect, but of not seeing what he did not want to see, what his desperately maintained confidence would not let him see. There is less room in this letter for

[5] McAleer: *Dearest Isa,* p. 25.
[6] McAleer: *Dearest Isa,* p. 30, n. 36.

dramatic details, for it is his own state of mind which concerns him, not selfishly or egotistically, but because inexorable circumstance has ultimately taken complete and invincible command. He had no justifiable reason to blame himself except the realization that he had not permitted himself to see what was plain even to him.

In the episode of Pen's failure Browning attaches no blame to himself, nor, it must be added, does he take any credit for the success which satisfied all his desires, but the letters which deal with both phases demonstrate both Browning's subjectivity and his enormous capacity for self-deception. His plan for Pen's education, though conceived in the comforting assurance that he knew exactly what Ba wanted and the pious resolution to carry out her wishes, was entirely his own creation. The boy was no more consulted than Ba's wishes were remembered. Yet there was nothing dictatorial about Browning's methods or objectives. It was simply a case of an unconsciously self-centered father assuming not only that he knows best but that the boy knows he knows best. Perhaps if Pen had been less amiable, he might have awakened his father to reality, but in all likelihood he would only have created trouble. Browning's pathetic despair at the hopeless collapse of his plans (Letters 72, 73, 74) is tragic not so much from his disappointment as from his total unawareness of his own blindness. This condition would be less notable, as one almost endemic in fathers, were it not for Browning's persistent confidence in his power to analyze souls, especially damaged ones. "There is something infinitely pitiable," he writes to George, "in this butterfly-nature with no fault in it but what is practically the worst of all faults,— weakness: a restive horse may be broken of his vice and made win a race against his will, — but how can you make a butterfly cross the room to his life, much less yours?" (Letter 73).

The butterfly did flutter brightly into his father's life, if not his own, but Browning's satisfaction was no more perceptive than had been his previous disappointment. It was as easy now to see what he wanted to see as it had been to see what he feared, and quite as impossible to see anything else. The simple fact is that

Pen preferred painting to studying Greek. He had amiably studied Greek, sporadically, but without interest in the matter or the goal. He painted diligently, and, so long as his father lived, gave him the satisfaction of seeing his son a success. Then he stopped. He clearly had neither the ambition nor the egotism which dedication to art demands — only the kindness to exercise his talent so long as it gave his father pleasure.

Pen Browning really has no claim on our attention here and, one is sure, would be happy to be ignored; but he will not relinquish it. He was the son of two great poets and the issue of the most romantic marriage in our literature. Measured by normal standards, he was possessed of no inconsiderable talent, but the distinction of his parents has belittled his small achievement to the point where it might have been better if he had shown none. Even the failure of his marriage has been magnified out of all proportion by the perfection of that of his parents. Indeed, without disregarding Pen's shortcomings, it seems likely that his parents' romance was an important element in the complex of forces which wrecked his own. Fannie Coddington married the son of Elizabeth Barrett Browning. Robert recognized this fact (Letter 85), but he does not seem to have realized that, however flattering to the mother, it was a poor augury for the success of the son's marriage. Fannie had never known her idealized mother-in-law in the flesh. Also, she belonged to a society which in its idealizing sought to ignore the flesh. Also, Mrs. Browning's physical fragility had etherealized her in the popular imagination to a degree which practically reduced Pen himself to a miracle. Granted that Pen's wife would have needed more than ordinary forbearance, whatever that is, she might have benefited if she could have heard her mother-in-law say, as she wrote to Isa Blagden: "I am afraid you don't sufficiently realize to yourself the physical tendencies of the sexes. Oh — you may laugh. But I do verily believe that you who are not spiritualist by profession are too spiritual in your way of apprehending the economy of sexual love."[7]

[7] McAleer: *PMLA,* LXVI (September, 1951), 611.

IV

Pen affords a convenient and appropriate bridge by which to pass from a consideration of his father's personality to that of his mother. There is hardly a letter in the last forty years covered by this correspondence in which he is not mentioned, though only in those of his father does he ever become the subject of the letter. Moreover, Pen resembled both of his parents more than the public realized, and so becomes a concentrated reflection of its misconceptions of each. The public was unreasonably surprised and disappointed that he did not inherit his parents' genius; it was deceived in its estimation of the one thing he could have been expected to inherit — the characteristics of their personalities. The public, as usual, accepted the man Robert Browning as identical with the poet, the robust apostle of vigorous, confident, buoyant vitality. It could not know what the poet so carefully concealed from himself: that the "weakness," "practically the worst of faults," which he deplored in Pen was a pretty accurate reflection of his own nature. Robert Browning, Senior, could never endure the discipline or risk the competition of the schoolroom. He learned a lot, it is true, but only what he liked, and he learned very little exactly. One cannot help wondering what crisis would have occurred had he found himself at twenty confronted with one of Jowett's examinations. He could reply to Isa Blagden: "I am quite of your mind about college acquirements and fame and how little they prove the owner a person of soul's quality," but he could report to George (Letter 72) with incredulous scorn that Pen had said "that he considered getting a first class no brilliant thing at all." Of course Robert had added to Isa, "but a race is a race, and whoever tries ought to win." He could not realize that Pen had never tried; his father had entered him in the race which he himself would never have dreamed of running. As a matter of fact Pen did enter races and win. They were mostly boat races and billiard tournaments, but there was also the recognition of the Paris

Salon. There was nothing contradictory about Pen except in the imagination of the public, and that recalls his mother.

Mrs. Browning, whose poetry during her lifetime was so much more important than her husband's, lives today as the fragile invalid rescued from death and the domestic jail of Wimpole Street by the impetuous love of a great and chivalrous poet. The *Sonnets from the Portuguese,* which relate so literally and so passionately the wonder and ecstacy of her love, have fixed in the public imagination her features as she drew them in her humility before the miracle. To say that the portrait is a partial one is not at all to disparage its validity; rather it is to admit that neither the decadent sentiment of the late nineteenth century nor the cynical naturalism which has succeeded it is capable of seeing in all its inclusiveness the face of love as perfect as human beings can find, of seeing that wit and anger, laughter, contentment, and irritation are at home in it as in the earth are the lakes and caverns, the glistening peaks and the level plains. Anyone would know that a portrait of Dante trembling in tears at the sight of Beatrice would be a partial one; yet even his hates — perhaps his hates especially — were rendered incandescent by the experience. Mrs. Browning was no Dante, but she too wrote her *Vita Nuova,* and the world has chosen to forget everything else.

This is a surprising result in view of the fact that the volume of her published letters exceeds that of her poems. The fact is that the letters arrived too late. By the time they appeared Elizabeth Barrett had been reduced to the status of Robert Browning's wife, which, in the light of the fame he then enjoyed, would seem eminence enough for any woman. Certainly, it would have delighted her. However, it was a status which focused interest on her weakness of body rather than her strength of mind and, in the aura of her husband's adoration, spiritualized the woman into an almost disembodied inspiration. It is likely that even the famous love letters, when they were published in 1899, were read generally with an eye to Robert and with little recognition that hers are the brighter letters and hers is the more vivid personality. The sudden decay of interest in Mrs. Browning as a poet was due to a number of causes, chief perhaps

among them her artistic lapses, but the prodigious rise in estimation of her husband's work had a great deal to do with it.
Now that both have faded it may be time for her shade to emerge
from behind Robert's, which hides her even in limbo.

The fifty-eight letters included here tell us little that we did
not know, or, at least, could not know from the great number of
her letters already published. The first thirty-eight, however, do
give us a more intimate picture of the Barrett family than we
have yet had. Of these, thirteen were written from Torquay
during the "exile" (1838-41) which began as a struggle for life
and ended in a far more vigorous battle to return to London.
Many of these letters are written in a hand so uncertain and
lines of such capricious slant as to suggest that the writer was
operating at an elevation something less than the forty-five
degrees in which she sometimes exults. Naturally these letters
contain many references to the state of her health, doctors'
opinions, conferences, etc. These are generally humorous in tone,
never complaining, and usually express confidence in improvement. Only in the summer of 1841, when she is confronted with
the probability of being removed from Torquay on the condition
of her once more being separated from her family — only then
does she become passionately concerned about herself. She becomes a ball of fire, albeit a fire which hopes not to have to
consume what stands in her way. We are confronted here with
the woman who could reiterate so often to her younger brother
her faith in the power of the will and at the same time realize
that it is not all powerful or "the earth would be one or two
shades brighter." She had her way; the family stayed in London;
she was reunited with it; and she kept her promise to George;
"When I reach you I will not talk so of myself. I shall subside in
content" (Letter 12).

As in most human affairs, the details are trivial. The tension
is everything. Torquay had become impossible. The very sound
of the sea, at all hours in her ears, recalled Edward and her
insistence on his staying — to drown. Yet to leave Torquay for
another place of exile was to live a little while detached from
all that made living worth the trouble. This was no ordinary

nostalgia. She felt no attachment to 50 Wimpole Street, and there never was a time when there were not brothers or sisters or aunts or even Papa — sometimes all at once — staying with her in Torquay. It was the necessity of not being a transient in the world, the necessity of *belonging,* which she could feel only when living with the children she had seen born and the father whose sorrows she knew but whom she could not, for his pride and her humility, pity. It is this feeling which makes the pathos of Letter 39. Papa is not an ogre to be feared. He is a proud man who needs protection, and the time has come when she can no longer say, he must not "be displeased," must not be "annoyed," "do not mention this when you write." Because she knows how he will feel, that letter is as tragic as it is ecstatic. She is as ready as Juliet to say: "And I'll no longer be a Capulet," but, unlike Juliet, she knows that, for all that, she is a Capulet, and that it is not the name which matters, but those who bear it. Compared with hers, Browning's part in the "elopement" was a lark. He could make quite a point of the impropriety of not telling his parents about the project although he knew that they would approve of anything he did, and his abstract honor would not permit him to call at Wimpole Street for a week after the wedding because he would have had to ask for Mrs. Browning as Miss Barrett. These were his troubles. She quite deliberately, but not lightly, laid conventional honesty and courtesy on the altar beside her father and her family and her home.

> If I leave all for thee, wilt thou exchange
> And be all to me? Shall I never miss
> Home-talk and blessings and the common kiss
> That comes to each in turn, nor count it strange,
> When I look up, to drop on a new range
> Of walls and floors . . . another home than this?

It is not the least of Robert Browning's claims to fame that for him Elizabeth Barrett forsook all others and clove to him only so long as she lived.

In a sense, the woman in Mrs. Browning's letters fares no better than the poet in Robert's, but for a different reason. In his letters the reticence and the disparity between character and conviction cast a veil over the poet, so that if we had only the letters, it would be difficult to discern the poet at all. Her letters tend, by their very mass, to shroud the remarkable personality they present, so that one's perception of the individual tends to be dulled by the accumulation of the ordinary. If no man is a hero to his valet, it is chiefly because valets are not notably perceptive. Even a hero is mostly a man, and most of what he does is very commonplace indeed. But the commonplace does not destroy the hero; it only shrouds him from view.

In the first place there are so many of Mrs. Browning's letters. The circumstances of her life, at least between Torquay and Italy (1838-46), made correspondence a necessity unless she was willing to live within herself. This it was not in her nature to do, and her conscious principles as well as her instinct rejected it. Much has been made of her reluctance, which intensified even to fear, of receiving or seeing strangers, especially during the five years in Wimpole Street. The feeling is several times expressed in these letters. Nevertheless, it is clear that she realized that it was at bottom morbid, that she disapproved of it instead of cherishing it, and that, all things considered, she received quite a lot of company. Her strength was limited and the demands of her art were pressing, so that there could be little of strength or time left after the intimate associations of the large Moulton-Barrett family and the Hedleys and sundry Graham-Clarkes and old friends from Hereford and Miss Mitford and Mr. Kenyon — until the advent of Mr. Browning. The wonder is that with her poetry and her intimates she could keep up such a voluminous correspondence with others whom she had never seen, like Horne and Haydon, and some whom she no longer saw, like Mr. Boyd. Her mind never willingly turned in upon itself even when she seemed to be shut in forever from the world outside. "A self-conscious heart," she wrote of Mr. Hunter, "is a ruin" (Letter 16), and in one of her last letters to Mrs. Martin, April, 1861, she concludes a comment on her weakness and fatigue two months before her death with: "Not that I haven't taken to work again, and to my old interests in politics. One doesn't quite rot in one's selfishness, after all."[8] It is remarks such as these which show the personality through the mass of intimate detail which fills her letters. But the fact remains that the great body of her correspondence was carried on with intimates and relatives with whom it would have been presumptuous and unnatural to write in any way but intimately of little things.

Later, when Robert had taken her to Italy, the struggle for Italian freedom and unity afforded a field in which, in her newfound freedom, she could exercise her interest in social and political affairs. At the same time, however, her correspondence became even more intimate, being limited now almost entirely to family and old friends like the Martins. It is here that the letters to George take on their special significance, for to her lawyer brother, although she always wrote as a sister, she wrote, with more argument and more sharpness of phrase than she used to others, of the political circumstances which called forth the poems of her Italian period.

It is not necessary here to enlarge upon Mrs. Browning's attitude toward Italy, Napoleon III, and England's part in European diplomacy during the eighteen-fifties. There is nothing in these letters that contradicts or significantly adds to what we already knew from the letters already published and the poems. One may be forgiven, however, for reminding a forgetful public, which no longer reads *Casa Guidi Windows* or *Poems before Congress,* that, on the evidence, Elizabeth Barrett Browning's poetical support of the Italian struggle is more than the emotional outpouring of a warmhearted but sheltered sentimentalist. "I don't dream and make a poem of it," she wrote to Chorley apropos of *Poems before Congress.* "I have tried to stand on the facts of things before I could feel 'dithyrambically'! Thought out coldly, then felt upon warmly."[9]

Now there are few things which offer to the human mind more opportunity to deceive itself than the attempt to read the temperature of its thought. However, the recognition of the

[8] Kenyon, II, p. 439.
[9] Kenyon, II, p. 383.

difference between the basic facts and the emotional expression indicates a detachment of mind which is borne out by the letters. After all, Napoleon did make Italy possible. "Observe, I may be wrong or right about Napoleon. He may be snake, scoundrel, devil in his motives. But the thing he did was done before the eyes of all."[10] Magenta and Solferino were real, and they were cause for rejoicing. Villafranca was a hard pill to swallow, but Napoleon, she recognized, was first of all Emperor of the French, and Prussia was threatening. It must be admitted that in "Napoleon III in Italy" Mrs. Browning was overly successful in feeling "dithyrambically" and that the unfortunate and irrelevant refrain, "Emperor / Evermore!", makes slush of whatever cold thought underlay it; but the thought was there. It was evidenced, as thought usually is, by the power to compromise hopes with circumstances, to absorb the cruel disappointment of Villafranca without pretending to like it or denying the nourishment of half a loaf. Both she and Robert had undertaken to write poems on the Italian question. He assured her that she "was gentle to England in comparison to what he had been." But Robert destroyed what he had written "after Villafranca (the Palmerston ministry having come in)." The humorous understanding of the punctuation is hers. It goes along with her remark (Letter 41) that Robert's "Britishness" stiffens in proportion to the distance he is removed from the island. Her poem was completed and published because "the poetical devil in me burnt on for an utterance."[11]

The "poetical devil" naturally burns lower in the letters so that it is easier to see the fuel which the mind provided. The letters reveal the same woman as wrote the poems, only they reveal her more clearly. Whatever Mrs. Browning believed or desired, she desired and believed passionately, but she did not permit her passion or her enthusiasm to cloud her realization that abstract principles are seldom completely applicable to the "incident that actually occurred," that idealists, if not ideals,

[10] Kenyon, II, p. 381.
[11] Kenyon, II, pp. 368-69.

are often funny, and that humor does not destroy nobility nor an intransigeant circumstance invalidate the compromised principle. One is reminded over and over again of the exchange of letters between her and Robert just before their marriage, on the subject of ransoming Flush from his kidnappers.[12] Robert would not pay "five shillings." He would say to the dog-snatchers "I will spend my whole life in putting you down . . . and by every imaginable means I will be the death of you and as many of your accomplices as I can discover. . . . You [Elizabeth] think I should receive Flush's head? Perhaps — so God allows matters to happen! on purpose, it may be, that I should vindicate him by the punishment I would exact." He allows that Ba, being herself, cannot do this. To which she replies: *"You* say that *I* cannot, . . . but that *you would*. You would — Ah dearest — most pattern of citizens, but you *would not* – I know you better. Your theory is far too good not to fall to pieces in practice."

In fact the most persistent aspect of Mrs. Browning's personality as revealed in her letters — these as well as others — is her humor. Not that she makes us laugh — she does sometimes — but that she lets us see that she is smiling even when she is most serious. Whether she is writing of people or ideas — about her health or her poetry, about Italy or the spirits or Napoleon, about Robert or Pen or those whom she dislikes as well as those she loves — her comments are illumined by a twinkle which shows that sense does not abdicate when the heart is moved and that the ultimate irony of all is the necessity of the human mind to rationalize what the heart knows. It is precisely this quality that makes so notable even in her uneven style what Chesterton characterized as "strength of phrase." "She excelled in her sex," he continues, "in epigram, almost as much as Voltaire in his."[13] This surprising juxtaposition of the French wit and the English wife becomes less absurd when one remembers that they both loved liberty and that the epigrams of each were more often warm with zeal than chilled with cynicism.

[12] *Letters of R. B. and E. B. B.*, II, pp. 502-29.
[13] G. K. Chesterton: *The Victorian Age in Literature*, London, 1913, pp. 177-78.

It cannot be claimed that her letters sparkle with epigrams. Epigrams are not at home in letters as intimate and unstudied as those of Mrs. Browning. But the stuff of the epigram is there — the quick perception of incongruity, the joy on recognizing the distortion worked by fervor and egotism and even love upon the face of truth and, above all, the capacity to unveil truth gaily by a neatly turned phrase, a pungent word, or even a device of punctuation. Letter 45, to cite a single example, is a long and chatty letter about the accommodations in Bagni di Lucca and the last days and evenings in Florence where the Brownings and their friends "commune about books, men & spirits till past midnight." It deals with almost everything which she took seriously — Robert, Pen, her family, Italian politics, and the spirits — and always with a humor which brightens without belittling the subject. "If Robert does not make good use of that cheerful little blue room with two windows, I shall give him up, I say." *Christmas-Eve* was already three years behind him and *Men and Women* two years off, and if the great poet was not being nagged by his adoring wife, he was surely being lovingly nudged. The anecdotes of Pen are those of a doting mother, but the amusement is as genuine as the affection. She "thinks by nature" of Arabella, but the fleas are a potent reminder to wonder whether Arabella would "submit to shake her petticoats and be happy in Italy." To admit that "the souls of the people are the state" is a "supernatural sentiment for a king," especially for one of "not much intellect." Mrs. Kinney is "not especially refined for an ambassador's wife, but natural, & apparently warmhearted to the point of taking you by storm." Even her defense of "the spirits," which she took very seriously indeed, is delivered to her skeptical brother in phrases which convey her confidence with humor. She does not even smile at the apparition of Calhoun or the ethereal music from the untouched guitar, but she can smile as well at her own gullibility and Robert's doubts.

It is this characteristic, much more than emotion or piety or religious fervor with which she is so often credited, that dominates Mrs. Browning's personality and informs her neglected masterpiece, *Aurora Leigh*. Her admirers surround this poem, as they did her, with a pink mist of sentiment and moral enthusiasm. Her contemporary detractors were horrified by its offenses against "delicacy." Neither really read the poem, and, as usual the defense did it more harm than the attack. When, half a century ago, the writer was being set by his teachers to learn many "vallooable thoughts" in verse, among them was:

> It takes a soul
> To move the body; it takes a high-souled man
> To move the masses

Only after many years did he discover Mrs. Browning's conclusion to that third line: ", even to a cleaner sty." The heroine of the romance of Wimpole Street and the object of Paracelsus' adoration was not supposed to know of sties, much less to be ironic. Unnoted went such things as her catalogue, both passionate and witty, of the harm that good men do, which ends with the prayer:

> Now may the good God pardon all good men.

Mrs. Browning's later apologists have done even worse. There is before me a book written by professors for students which calls *Aurora Leigh* "a sympathetic treatment of such forms of socialist communities as those advocated by Fourier in France." Which is precisely what the poem is not. Her letters state her position more briefly but no more emphatically than the poem. "I love liberty so intensely," she wrote in 1850, "that I hate socialism." I hold it to be the most desecrating and dishonoring to humanity of all creeds. I would rather (for *me*) live under the absolutism of Nicholas of Russia than in a Fourier machine, with my individuality sucked out of me by a social air pump.[14]

It is clear from Mrs. Browning's letters, all of them including these, that to a remarkable degree the woman and the poet were one. It is for this reason that all the characters in *Aurora Leigh* — even Lady Waldemar — speak the thoughts of the author. By far the weakest passage in the long poem is that in the sixth

[14] Kenyon, I, p. 452.

book in which the exigencies of the mechanical plot force Aurora, for a little while, to speak to Marion of her illegitimate child in terms of a social morality with which Mrs. Browning did not hold and within which neither she nor Aurora could say anything well. One would expect that this book "into which my highest convictions upon Life and Art have entered" would be shot through with spiritualism. One would expect it, that is, if one had read only the content of her letters without perceiving the personality of the writer, the enthusiasm of the believer, without her mind. As a matter of fact, the poem contains only one reference to "spirits." In the fifth book Aurora says:

> I've seen some men, veracious, nowise mad,
> Who have thought or dreamed, declared and testified,
> They heard the Dead a-ticking like a clock
> Which strikes the hours of the eternities,
> Beside them, with their natural ears,— and known
> That human spirits feel the human way
> And hate the unreasoning awe which waves them off
> From possible communion. It may be so.

It is true that the last phrase expresses more reserve than do the letters, but the attitude is the same: a passionate repudiation of submission to old habits of thought. Whatever one may think of the quality or the permanent value of Mrs. Browning's poetry, reading it in the light of her letters confirms what she wrote to Robert in 1846: "When I said, or when others said for me, that my poetry was the flower of me, was it praise, did you think, or blame? might it not stand for sarcasm? It might,— if it were not true, miserably true after a fashion."[15]

The same process applied to Robert furnishes equally strong confirmation for the sentence which immediately precedes the above: "Yet I am not likely to mistake your poetry for the flower of your nature, knowing what that flower is, knowing something of what that flower is without a name, and feeling something of the mystical perfume of it."[16] That flower is still without a name and the mystical perfume of it was a far more

---

[15] *Letters of R. B. and E. B. B.,* II, p. 181.
[16] *Letters of R. B. and E. B. B.,* II, p. 181.

personal possession of hers than the other face of her moon ever
was of his.

V

The personality which Browning was at such pains to conceal
in his writing as well as in his dealings with public curiosity
remains unrevealed in his letters. If one seeks to construct it
from the letters in this volume he finds nothing with which to
draw a clear outline and little to color what he draws. The outline is without distinguishing features. Neither in style nor in
content is there anything to distinguish the author from any
affectionate brother-in-law, bereft of his wife whom he adored,
concerned for his son, hopeful, discouraged, and finally delighted
in him. There is, of course, much talk about books, but it is all
talk about publication, neither aesthetic nor philosophical. There
are some sharp things said of certain people, but nothing is
sharply said about people or places or books. The man who
emerges from these letters is commonplace to the point of bore-
dom, and yet he is the man who wrote the poems and plays of
Robert Browning and in his nature Elizabeth Barrett "felt a
mystical perfume."

Other letters of Browning are more revealing, but not much.
The "love letters" reflect his enormous esoteric learning, the
startling shifts of subject and association, the involution and
obliqueness of thought. The lover is ardent and intense, but
Elizabeth, even while she cherishes every word of the letters,
says time and again in many ways: "This is not you"; "You
don't think like this"; "I know you." She did know him — so
well that she knew that the letters did not express him. She was
probably the only person who ever knew him, for she recognized
early and never lost faith in his genius. She saw in him the husband she described in Letter 39, and yet, without harm to either
vision, she could write to him between their marriage and flight:

"In your ways towards me, you have acted throughout too
much 'the woman's part,' as that is considered. You loved me

because I was lower than others, that you might be generous and raise me up: — very characteristic for a woman (in her ideal standard) but quite wrong for a man, as again and again I use to signify to you, Robert — but you went on and did it all the same. And now, you still go on — you persist — you will be the woman of the play, to the last; let the prompter prompt ever so against you."[17] This it must be to see with the eyes of love, which, far from being blinded to reality, see it clearly and are not troubled.

For the rest of us the problem of integrating the man, the husband, and the poet remains and grows. The first effect of reading Browning's letters can hardly be other than the conviction that he was right as a poet in discouraging all inquiry into his personality. He was right, too, in hoping that *Pauline* had been buried forever. In it, after much tortured confession, he had written:

> And thus it is that I supply the chasm
> 'Twixt what I am and all I fain would be.

But, as Mill pointed out, the chasm had not been bridged except by assertion, and, in fact, it never was. The boy of twenty wrote:

> E'en in my brightest time, a lurking fear
> Possessed me: I well knew my weak resolves,
> I felt the witchery that makes mind sleep
> Over its treasure, as one half afraid
> To make his riches definite.

The lover of thirty, reluctant to show the poem to that *"real Pauline"* who Mill had hoped might cure him, wrote to her: "it is altogether foolish and *not* boylike."[18] Half true, at least. Many years later and almost on his deathbed he took another fleeting glance into the chasm. He had been reading from *Asolando* to Pen and Fannie. As he finished the third stanza he closed the book and said: "It almost sounds like bragging to say this, and as if I ought to cancel it; but it's the simple truth; and as it's true,

[17] *Letters of R. B. and E. B. B.*, ii, p. 548.
[18] *Letters of R. B. and E. B. B.*, i, p. 400.

it shall stand."[19] Of course it was "bragging," and he knew it —
he who in *Pauline* had been glad

> To cast away restraint, lest a worse thing
> Wait for us in the dark.

But it was also "true," because he had been fighting for sixty
years to make it true. In all the gallery of his creations the most
complete and the hardest to achieve was Robert Browning,
which was why he never wrote "what I hope I was born to
begin and end — 'R. B. a poem.' "[20]

Yet the search for that unwritten poem may yet provide the
most persistent interest for the poems which he wrote. It must be
constructed out of the poems and the letters, read not in opposition to each other, as is the temptation; nor the one in explanation of the other, as is the usual reading of letters; but as
complementary elements in the version of life presented by
Robert Browning. The poet himself would have resented this
idea with a violence terrible to contemplate. He meant his poetry
to stand on its own feet, and he dared not realize that, for all his
effort, the only feet it had to stand on were his.

Browning's habit of dramatic composition has long been
recognized as a device, deliberately cultivated, to conceal the
man behind the poet. The letters should reveal that man, and
Browning feared they would. But they do so no more completely
than the "scrutinizing hat" revealed the poet of Valladolid.
Neither in social intercourse did the young dandy or the elderly
diner-out reveal the man. These show only *a* man who could
not possibly have written the poetry. It would be easy — too easy
— to draw from the letters a man the complete antithesis of the
voice in the poems: a man who glorified action, but who never
did anything; a man who violated willfully all artistic conventions and advocated the violation of moral conventions, and who
was yet in his person notably conventional in a conventional
society; a man who glorified fighting, but who only became

---

[19] W. C. DeVane: *A Browning Handbook,* 2nd ed., New York, 1955, p. 553.

[20] *Letters of R. B. and E. B. B.,* I, p. 17.

futilely angry; a man who could claim to "greet the unseen with a cheer," but who dared not inquire into his son's election to a club for fear of the imagined malice of a few "disgruntled academicians" who failed to materialize. But when we have drawn this picture, we know

> We were in error, that was not the man.

For whatever the name of that "flower without a name" of which Mrs. Browning felt "something of the mystical perfume," it was not hypocrisy. It was not even honesty.

When one reads Browning's letters and his poems together, one realizes, as the poet hoped he never would, what dedicated effort was required to maintain the faith which with such vigor and subtlety the poetry expressed. Life in Browning's version was a constant struggle because, being the person he was, it had to be. It was a struggle against himself, or, more accurately, against those aspects of his nature which operated to destroy his faith in all that he *knew* to be true and beautiful and good and noble — against the self of "weak resolves," "half afraid to make his riches definite."

"'No dream's worth waking' — Browning says," but no dreamer was ever more alertly awake than he. Although he was heir to the romantics, he was a child of his time; and on him their confidence in life and the destiny of man descended as a duty. It was not an easy duty for him, but he assumed it because he believed in the cause. But the strain told, and the twentieth century, weary of struggle and disillusioned about man, hears in Browning's call to cheerful struggle only the echo of an older, happier time, naïve or hypocritical or both. We are only now beginning to realize that what we used to scorn as the hypocrisy of the Victorians was more often the heroism of beleaguered men.

Browning has not yet shared in this new understanding of his contemporaries. Not many are left, and they well declined in years, who draw from him the courage to "greet the unseen with a cheer." The latest "portrait" of him presents a weak, inconstant, querulous man who "died, as he had lived, under the symbol of a divided nature."²¹ All the world — even those who have never read a line — remembers him as the hero of a romantic love-story. Yet the truth is that these three were one, and that, as with all human entities, the whole is greater than the sum of its parts. It was not Browning's nature that was divided. The division lay between nature and ideals, as it always must when ideals are there. The higher the ideals or the weaker the nature, the stronger the character which holds them together. There is no greater courage than the courage of a fearful and self-conscious man.

Childe Roland has at last come to the dark tower, indeed, long after he sank happily to rest in the Rezzonico Palace, and if he sees the faces "ranged along the hillsides" to view the last of him, be sure he knows them all, for they are not so much his peers as all the Robert Brownings he fought through a long life. And he may well blow dauntlessly, even if the note sound now a little thin, for he beat them all as nearly as a man can beat the men he was born, but will not be.

P. L.

Urbana, April 25, 1956

²¹ Miller: *Browning,* p. 282.

BIBLIOGRAPHICAL NOTE

A full bibliography of works concerning the Brownings is not included in this collection of letters. The complete references can be readily found in such sources as *Robert Browning: A Bibliography, 1830-1950* of the Cornell University Studies in English, 1953. Nor has the editor included in the notes references to obvious source books — *Dictionary of National Biography, Cambridge Bibliography of English Literature, Encyclopaedia Britannica,* and so forth. Rather, for the convenience of the reader, the frequently mentioned collections of letters, biographies, and studies have been abbreviated to a cue-title or author reference. The full reference to books cited only once will be found in the appropriate note; works used more than once are cited in the following list.

Letters

DeVane and Knickerbocker	W. C. DeVane and K. L. Knickerbocker, eds.: *New Letters of Robert Browning,* New Haven, Conn., 1950.
Hood	Thurman L. Hood, ed.: *Letters of Robert Browning Collected by Thomas J. Wise,* New Haven, Conn., 1933.

Huxley	Leonard Huxley, ed.: *Elizabeth Barrett Browning: Letters to Her Sisters, 1846-1859,* London, 1929.
Kenyon	Frederic G. Kenyon, ed.: *The Letters of Elizabeth Barrett Browning,* 2 vols., London, 1897.
Letters of R. B. and E. B. B.	*Letters of Robert Browning and Elizabeth Barrett Barrett, 1845-46,* 2 vols., New York and London, 1899.
Letters to Horne	S. R. Townshend Mayer, ed.: *Letters of Elizabeth Barrett Browning Addressed to Richard Hengist Horne,* 2 vols., London, 1877.
McAleer	Edward C. McAleer, ed.: *Dearest Isa: Robert Browning's Letters to Isabella Blagden,* Austin, Texas, 1951.
Miller: *E. B. to M. M.*	Betty Miller, ed.: *Elizabeth Barrett to Miss Mitford,* London, 1954.
Orr	Mrs. Sutherland Orr: *Life and Letters of Robert Browning,* London, 1891.
Twenty-two Letters	*Twenty-two Unpublished Letters of Elizabeth Barrett Browning and Robert Browning to Henrietta and Arabella Moulton-Barrett,* New York, 1935.

Biographies and Critical Studies

Griffin and Minchin	W. H. Griffin and H. C. Minchin: *The Life of Robert Browning,* New York, 1910.
Hewlett	Dorothy Hewlett: *Elizabeth Barrett Browning,* New York, 1952.
Marks	Jeanette Marks: *The Family of the Barrett,* New York, 1938.
Miller: *Browning*	Betty Miller: *Robert Browning, a Portrait,* London, 1952.
Reese	Gertrude Reese: "Robert Browning and His Son," *PMLA,* LXI (September, 1946), 784-803.

letter 1   [Torquay, 1838-1839][1]

Own Dearest Georgie,

My gratitude has been *rankling sore* within me for very very long – And I am sure that your anxiety for my morals demonstrated by the advice accompanying your present, must have been rankling within *you* — & that my silence has been suggesting to you the probability of this want of thankfulness being a symptom of a more general corruption of the moral sense. Acquit yourselves dearest Georgie & Beaumont & Fletcher. You are yet innocent of corrupting me & I am innocent of being ungrateful to any one of you – And though upon the appearance of the great poets I did feel properly indignant with the great lawyer for his breach of all consistency (except the consistency of his own dear always remembered kindness to me) yet the "flashing apparitions" of my wrath owed most of their colour to a very glowing affection & gratitude which have not left me at this present writing. But really Georgie, I did think that you considered it very improper to give anything away,— *I* at least, if I had done such a thing, sh[d] never have heard the last of it.

You are obeyed to the letter. I jump over all the puddles — & when I stand upon the dry ground & look round, the scenery is exquisite – Whatever light falls upon my poetry from Fletcher's — & some *must* — I shall remember that it came thro' *you* — *you* are the conveyancer — & my thankfulness holds the fee —

Dearest Georgie, do you know it is very impertinent of you to write anything in Arabel's[2] letters to me, not addressed to me. I really cant allow such a thing any more. Why wont you write yourself to me? – You promised & vowed to me that you would. Do you think nothing of perjury?

The manner of your introduction to Mr. Wightman[3] *made* me pleased in spite of all prejudices poetical. And after all, there *is* a nobleness in the act of concentrating the mind, whatever the object upon which it is concentrated, may be. The law is a low object (suffer a poet to assume so much) but mind contemplating Law is sublime in itself, & in the energy of contemplation. At any rate (I wont puzzle about the reason) I am proud of your energy & steadfastness of purpose Georgie — & if I live to witness your success in your profession I shall be very proud. The most consistent of us — even YOU — & far less *I* — grow inconsistent sometimes.

May God bless you my dearest Georgie —

Your attached Ba.

¹ The second sheet was folded to make an envelope, sealed and addressed: George Goodin Barrett, Esq. It was not posted. The envelope bears pencil markings: 1838,/38,/35-42, in three different hands. These, doubtless, refer to attempts at dating the letter, which must be done entirely from internal evidence. The same is true of Letter 2, following. The remark in Letter 2, "to behave so again and again," definitely places this one earlier and seems to indicate that the letters, like the gifts, came rather close together. Both letters must have been written from Torquay since before Elizabeth's "exile" there in September, 1838, there was no reason for correspondence between brothers and sisters. It seems that both letters were written after George had been admitted as barrister-at-law of the Inner Temple, November, 1838 (cf. Kenyon, I, p. 78). This letter, nevertheless, may be somewhat earlier. In a letter to Miss Mitford, dated February 17, 1837, Elizabeth wrote: "I have been reading your Faithful Shepherdess . . . how prodigal it is in exquisite poetry; and in those sweet lapses and undulations of sound coming and going without a reason — such as are not dreamt of in the iron philosophy of our days" (Miller: *E. B. to M. M.,* p. 12). George entered the Inner Temple as a barrister student in January, 1836, and so may be spoken of as a lawyer. However, he remained at home, so that there was no occasion for correspondence between him and Elizabeth (Kenyon, I, p. 35).

² Arabella Barrett (1813-68), the younger of Elizabeth's two sisters.

³ There is no direct evidence, but this was probably Sir William Wightman (1794-1863), eminent British jurist who transferred to the Inner Temple in 1830 and joined the northern circuit. A member of the commission of 1830 on the practice of the common-law courts, and of 1833 on the proposal for a criminal law digest, he became a judge of the Queen's Bench in 1841.

letter 2   [Torquay]
                                                [November-December, 1839][1]

My own dearest Georgie,

I entreat your forgiveness for the inscrutable & mystical wrong
I have done you, together with your acceptance of some expression of my gratitude for Ben Jonson whom I accepted before
as your gift upon Sette's[2] affidavit. Considering everything you
certainly are excusable in being so ashamed of sending such a
gift, as to disavow the doing so – A pretty person you are to
preach against extravagances — & then to behave so — Nay, to
behave so again & again & again!! If you had been Socrates you
w^d have sacrificed a pair of doves to Venus (doves) as well as
the cock to Æsculapius — you are inconsistent enough, qualified
enough for two sides of every question, to be fit already for the
heights of your profession. Seriously Georgie, were you Attorney
General, I sh^d say 'I am obliged to you,'— were you on the
Woolsack, I sh^d say "thank you"— but in the present state of
things, you are one of the very most incorrigible abominable
people I ever knew.

So I *wont* thank you. I read Ben Jonson & think of you
dearest Georgie instead.

In a letter from Miss Mitford,[3] dated not very long ago, she
says,—"I hate the law & *all its professors* – Dont *you? –*" Why
of course I do –

You are none of you to abuse me for writing — I have done
it day by day. I dare'nt write to Stormie,[4] unless my courage
revives.

                                        Your attached Ba –

[1] Sheet folded, sealed, and addressed: George Goodin Barrett,
Esq. Not posted. Bears pencil date 1839 in another hand.

[2] The family name for Septimus Barrett (1822-70), Elizabeth's
next to youngest brother. He died in Jamaica. It was chiefly due
to his mismanagement that the Barrett estates there had to be
liquidated by Charles (Storm) who took over after his death.

[3] Mary Russell Mitford (1787-1855). She is best remembered

now as the author of *Our Village,* but she was a versatile writer of many varieties of literature and in her day very popular. She and Elizabeth met about 1836 during the first period of the latter's residence in London, and they remained intimate friends and correspondents until Miss Mitford's death. It was Miss Mitford who presented Elizabeth with her famous dog Flush. For further reference see the following, all of which contain material concerning the long friendship between Mrs. Browning and Miss Mitford.

Mary Russell Mitford: *Recollections of a Literary Life,* London, 1859.

Henry Chorley: *Letters of Mary Russell Mitford,* 2 vols., London, 1872 (includes no actual letters of or to Mrs. Browning, but reference to her in others).

A. G. L'Estrange: *Life of Mary Russell Mitford,* 3 vols., London, 1870.

Friendships of Mary Russell Mitford, 2 vols., London, 1882.

Betty Miller, ed.: *Elizabeth Barrett to Miss Mitford,* London, 1954.

[4] Charles John Barrett (1814-1905), Elizabeth's brother, called in the family Storm or Stormie, apparently from his having been born during a violent thunderstorm. There are frequent references in these letters to his timidity and unwillingness to talk. He stuttered so badly that he refused to take his examinations at Glasgow for which he came up at the same time as George (Kenyon, I, p. 29). He was the last of the family to reside on the Barrett estates in Jamaica and died on the island. Elizabeth's need for courage probably arose from her having disobeyed Storm's injunction not to waste her strength in writing letters.

letter 3   [Torquay]
                                                    Jan. 4th, 1840.[1]

My dearest dearest Georgie,

Arabel[2] says you w^d much rather not hear from me & I dont contradict her — only you having just proved to me how pleasant it is to be pleased, I must be pleased again this morning by writing to you. The serpent tempted me & I did eat, & now I take another apple. I do thank you for all the pleasure you have given me. It was so very very particularly kind of you to write, with your thoughts occupied as they must have been with novel & grave matters. It was more than I expected although you know I did pretend to expect it, & should have been rather furious if you had not done it. All *that* is excellent logic — & the end of it is my gratitude to you – Thank you dear dear George –

As to the rest I am astounded at the majesty of your first steps. Papa will be more so still — for he told me that he did not think it at all likely you w^d have anything to do very soon. How pleased he will be! How I sh^d like to be first to tell him!! –

Wasn't it a breach of discipline to go by the mail to Ludlow? How did you shake the straw at the bottom from the feet of your nascent chancellorship, & preserve your noli me tangere from the attornies [*sic*]? There are many questions I would ask. And Bro^3 wants to know whether the prisoners whom you turned loose upon a grateful world, notwithstanding their crime & their character, were guilty of murder? – Certainly it w^d be as well to learn something of the particulars, before we raise your philanthropy to the rank of your legality. Of your consummate impudence there cant be a question. Oh Georgie! — how c^d you do so — even under cover of the wig helmet — unprepared & at a moment's notice!! That was the very sublime of impudence, & makes my head turn round to think of it!

Just as I had finished y^r letter in came Dr. Scully^4 — & I began to tell him what was the truth, that I had felt a little languor in the course of the morning. He felt the pulse & said — "Well, Miss Barrett — I sh^d not have detected the languor in the pulse." "Oh no — because I have just had a letter from my brother Georgie, & it has answered the exact purpose of a cordial"– Upon which he began to laugh & to congratulate me — & then we diverged into law subjects (not into any particulars about you — dont be frightened!) & he told me how if his own brother had lived he w^d have been at this moment most assuredly the master of the rolls in Ireland — & a great deal besides, not admissible into so small a sheet as this. Arabel says I must not have another, but I must & shall — quod ita probatum est. When you go to London you will hear the particulars of Dr. Scully's having afflicted me with the presence of Dr. Millar from Exeter for a consultation. You may suppose how much oratory went to accomplish that. Yourself did not do more when you persuaded your gentlemen of the jury to honorably acquit your assassins – I have not been *worse* at all – Dont fancy *that* – But a great deal was insisted upon the advantage of dyocephalus monsters, & upon the opportunity of Dr. M's being in the town. *My* verdict (I mean their verdict upon me) was tolerably satisfactory upon the whole.[5] They agreed exactly as to the case — & thought that with care I sh^d bustle thro' the winter & be better afterwards. But the way pointed out of "bustling through" is to keep on lying in bed — out of harm's way and air's way – I only hope & trust to be able & quietly allowed to get back to London early in the summer.— Otherwise there will be a rebellion, & the Chartists' nothing to it! –

God's pleasure sh^d be mine, without any "hopes & trustings" except in *Him*. Surely I have had reason for knowing that His pleasure is His tender mercy — but how far I am from being reasonable! –

Dear Mr. Hunter & May[6] have left Axminster finally — & I had a joint letter from the two this morning from Exeter which place they past thro' yesterday on their way to Kingsbridge. He has an engagement at Kingsbridge for a few months — & after that comes a blank. He speaks of having written to his friend the independent minister at Gloucester to bestir himself & procure for you whatsoever business is going on amongst the Dissenters there. It was kindly done –

Going on as usual at Torquay. Occasional quarrellings to clear the air & to keep up our respective characters. Bro was at Capt. & Mrs. Foleys yesterday — last night. Great favorites of his — members of the Herefordshire Foley family — & come to live at the Knoll. Bummy[7] & Henrietta[8] went off in another direction to Mrs. Inglises[9] — & Arabel and I talked wonderful sense tête à tête.

You are to restrain your wrath toward Arabel & Henrietta, & expand it upon your return to Wimpole St. Not a word did they remember to tell us about your last orders.

God bless & keep you dearest Georgie! —
I need not tell you how high & deep you are in my esteem &
love — and now that you have not forgotten me on the reception of y^r first briefs, I rejoice in feeling sure that you wont cut
me when you are chancellor.

Your truly affec^{te} Ba.

[1] No envelope has been preserved.

[2] During her stay in Torquay, Arabel was Elizabeth's almost constant companion.

[3] Edward Barrett (1807-40), Elizabeth's oldest and favorite
brother. They had grown up together as children at Hope End.
With him and his tutor she had studied her beloved Greek and
he had accompanied her in her illness to Torquay. When her
father decided that it was time for Edward to return to London,
Elizabeth begged so violently that he be permitted to stay that for
once Mr. Barrett allowed his decision to be changed by the wish
of another. Not long afterward Edward went sailing with two
friends and was drowned in Babbacome Bay, July 11, 1840. His
death was the great and unconsolable grief of his sister's life, tortured as she was by her realization that had she not prevailed
selfishly against her father's wishes, Edward would not have died.
Her reaction was confessedly morbid; she could never endure the
mention of his name, and her one reference to the incident occurs
in *Letters of R. B. and E. B. B.*, i, pp. 175 ff.

[4] The senior physician of Torquay who had served on the special
board of health for the cholera epidemic of 1832 (Marks, pp.
475-76).

[5] The report of an early consultation of doctors on Elizabeth's
health reveals that she showed the symptoms of "general tuberculosis" as early as 1821. See Appendix II, p. 341.

[6] The Reverend Mr. George Barrett Hunter and his daughter
Mary (May). He was pastor of Marsh Independent Chapel in
London where the Barretts worshipped. Elizabeth had become
acquainted with them in 1832 in Sidmouth. Mr. Hunter seems to
have loved Elizabeth with a passion which developed into a
troublesome and even alarming intensity. (See Miller: *Browning*,
pp. 99-100; see also Betty Miller: "Miss Barrett and Mr. Hunter,"
Cornhill Magazine, Vol. 165 [Spring, 1951], 83-97.)

[7] Elizabeth's maternal aunt Arabella Graham-Clarke, generally referred to as Bummy. She was the oldest of Mrs. Barrett's sisters, never married, and was a great favorite with the family.

[8] Henrietta Barrett (1809-60), the older of Elizabeth's sisters. In 1850 she married William Surtees Cook and suffered the same paternal ostracism as Elizabeth. Her painful illness and her death in 1860 were a terrible strain on Elizabeth's failing health.

[9] Not identified further.

letter 4   [Torquay]
                                                [May 14, 1840][1]

My own dearest Georgie,

Your two letters — or are there more which your kindness sent to me? — must not be unanswered any longer — altho' I know you w^d tell me not to write if I c^d hear your voice. But indeed it can do no harm to any part of me, This relief of heart in writing — & I want to tell you dearest Georgie & all of you how I love you & think of you & how grateful I am for every thought of yours – Of the past there is no news to speak. What is done, is done — & we knowing that God did it,[2] know in that knowledge the extremity of love & mercy involved in the doing. Oh may the great Doer teach us to bow low in unmitigated apprehension of Him as the Supreme in will — and in mercy also. Dearest Georgie, we do not know the meaning of the things we suffer more than of the things we see; but we "shall know hereafter"– In the meantime let it be enough that God does it all.

May He bless and keep you every one. Be sure that I am a great deal better — rather weak still certainly — but shaking off more & more of the weakness – It is my earnest wish to get home, & if I cannot do that, to *get nearer* – Dearest Minny[3] cant wish it half as much as *I*, tell her. Yet I am afraid they wont let me even try to get home. The "getting nearer" I shall insist upon in all events. Even you cant blame me for that obstinacy — but as they all say, there will be a more becoming time for such speculations when I am out of bed — & I hope to be on the sofa soon again. My dear dear Papa's being here is an inexpressible comfort — & he never seems to DREAM OF GOING AWAY, they say – We lost Jane & Uncle Hedley[4] this morning — regarding their past visit as indeed every detail of their conduct to us with grateful affection. If you go on any of you to Richmond, DO take care, & take the waterman.

Now mind you believe me to be a GREAT DEAL better. I am REALLY SO. And if the writing goes up & down, that is nothing but *want* of use. Bro is sailing with Mr. Vaneck[5] at this moment & Henrietta and Arabel walking out in the sun — & Papa reading on the other side of the green door.

Now I love you all! May God in Christ Jesus bless you. Give my affectionate love to dearest Trippy[6] — & ever to you love

Your Ba

Thursday.[7]

Torquay

[1] Envelope postmarked, Torquay May 15, 1840; stamp "prepaid 16 May, 1840." Pencil note, May 15, 1840, in another hand. Address: George Goodin Barrett, 50 Wimpole Street, London. Mourning paper.

[2] Death of Samuel Barrett (1812-40) of yellow fever, February 17, at Cinnamon Hill, Jamaica. He was Elizabeth's next to oldest brother.

[3] Mrs. Robinson, housekeeper at Hope End. She remained with the family and died in old age at Arabella Barrett's, 7 Delamere Terrace, London (Huxley, p. 3).

[4] Jane Graham-Clarke, Elizabeth's maternal aunt, married to John Hedley. It was probably to this aunt that Elizabeth was sent to stay in Torquay in the early fall of 1838 (Marks, p. 475).

[5] Mr. Vaneck, a Torquay friend, was one of the two drowned with Edward Barrett.

[6] Mary Trepsack (1768?-1857), a remarkable member of the Barrett household, whose life spanned five generations and linked the early Jamaica years with the later English life. In 1773 she had been left to Samuel Barrett of Cambridge, Jamaica, by his "friend and planter, William Trepsack." When Samuel died in

1782, she was taken to Cinnamon Hill by Edward Barrett, Elizabeth's great grandfather. His daughter Elizabeth Barrett Moulton (Elizabeth's grandmother) took her to England and "Trippy" lived as her companion until Mrs. Moulton's death in 1831. After that she made her home with Edward Barrett Moulton-Barrett (Elizabeth's father) until her death, "a few weeks" before his in 1857 (Marks, p. 601).

⁷ May 14, 1840, was a Thursday.

letter 5

Torquay
Wednesday
[June 17, 1840]¹

My own dearest Georgie,

When you are measuring the length and breadth of my ingratitude do make allowances for the time during which 'Glencoe'² lingered upon the seas. It never reached me until last week — & every day since has found me on the edge of a letter to you — Thank you my dearest Georgie – If you think as steadfastly of the rights of your clients as of my pleasures you will be *sacked* in no time. It was, as you well knew it wᵈ be, a great pleasure to me to look into Glencoe — and yet the play is to my mind a failure, even without thinking of Ion.³ The newspapers seemed however to speak well of its reception — the consequence perhaps of some melodramatic capability. Otherwise the febleness [*sic*] & want of concentrative power wᵈ be as obvious, I shᵈ suppose, upon the stage as elsewhere. High and tender thoughts there are, gracefully and harmoniously expressed — which is not *being tragic*. Thank you my dearest Georgie. Your part is more perfect than the Sergeant's.⁴

Thank you too for two notes — are there not two? — & for the *advices* in both. Bro is of opinion that I "move my legs & arms" (which was in yʳ prescription) "quite enough for anything" — and in regard to the movements, be patient & you shall hear of them. In the meantime deduct from your fancies about me that I am lying in bed, from fear of the exertion of getting up. When a medical man stands by saying —"Dont do it — you will throw yourself back again — it always does you harm –" it is rather difficult to take the other side of the question. Nevertheless, Papa being evidently anxious about it, I urged a repetition of the experiment upon Dr. Scully yesterday, — & he agrees to its being made tomorrow or next day, when the wind subsides. At the same time his reluctance was tolerably evident, & his words to Crow[5] when he left the house were —"If Miss Barrett does'nt take care, she will make herself ill again." When I was up last, there was not merely *fainting* — the consequences were agitation of the pulse for some days, & tendency to fever. Dr. Scully says "I am as anxious as anybody can be for you to be *able* to move — but I do wish you to gain a little strength (which you are doing slowly) before too much is attempted. The case is of such a nature, that it is far easier to make you much worse than at all better."– So now pray acquit *me*. I am afraid of nothing except of not seeing you this summer — & it isn't altogether as agreeable to lie here half in the dark as you might possibly fancy. The real truth is that the fever in April induced a degree of weakness from which it is only surprising, considering my previous debility, that I sh^d have rallied so far. I never was so ill or weak at any time in my life, to my own remembrance — & now all is past, by divine mercy, I may tell you that I myself did not suppose it *humanly possible* for me to be better anymore. Indeed Dr. Scully told me at the time, that if I were an older person he sh^d despond, but that he trusted to the elasticity remaining in the constitution. This accounts for my not reviving as quickly with the present summer as with the former one, — & since the strength is really & gradually though slowly coming, it sh^d do so *satisfactorily* to all of you — even to you my dearest learnedest George with your latent genius for MD = city.

You have heard of Arabel's and Brosie's separate romances.[6] The latter has discarded his green blind, and indeed ventures to show his whole face out of doors by twilight instead of waiting for the very pitch dark. As to Arabel, wasn't it an adventure? Poor dearest Bella. With the scolding after the perils! & after that ideal drowning and assassination, the real thorough fatigue of half running nearly eight miles! But two days *stiffness* was all the harm done.– She & the Mackintoshes[7] continue great friends, & I encourage her being with them as much as possible because their happy spirits & love of fresh air and country excursions are both exhilarating and advantageous to her — forming breaks upon the monotony & gloom which her kindness to me necessarily produces. She was so kind when I was so ill. It was all Dr. Scully c^d do to keep her from sitting up night after night — which w^d never have done. They were all of them very very kind.

I wish we c^d hear more of what you all do. Has Henry[8] made up his mind to some occupation which is not insurmountably objectionable to Papa? I am sure he is too kind, & I hope he is too wise, to cleave any longer to military or naval fancies, the fulfilment of which w^d entail such anxiety & pain upon many of us – And to anything else, there is a plain way. Why does'nt he think *hard* about it? – Affec^te love to him. Dearest Joc's[9] first vol. of Napoleon[10] shall go back in a better state than it came here. I like it very much. You know Mr. Horne[11] is editor. He sent me a ballad yesterday — & we continue fast-sworn friends. Did you see any extracts from Gregory?[12] I have the tragedy. Very fine — but not as overwhelming as the Cosmo.[13] Set writes nothing but happiness. My best love to dearest Trippy who ought to write to me. Make her stay [*continued on flap of envelope*] for a good deal. Bummy writes very seldom. Always talks of coming when she does but *she wont come*. Poor little May[14] has terrible sick headaches — but the rest of us are well enough to administer the emetics. Her father left Cork yesterday for Dublin & Liverpool whence he goes to Leicester on his way homewards. It seems almost certain that he will enter with a temporary engagement with the Kingsbridge people. God bless you all. I long to see you beyond all things — feeling it hard to be patient. God bless you my beloved George. Your own Ba. Love to dearest Minny whose kind letter I shall soon reply to.

[*Continued across top of first page*]
I am ordered to be raised to an angle of 45° today with pillows.

Will *that* please you? My thoughts day and night wander round about you – Oh you *dont* know how I love you all.

Ever fondest best love.

¹ Postmark, June 18, 1840. Address: George Goodin Barrett Esq., 50 Wimpole Street, London. June 17, 1840, fell on Wednesday.

² *Glencoe,* or *The Fate of the Macdonalds,* a tragedy by Sir Thomas Noon Talfourd, 2nd ed., 1840.

³ *Ion,* a tragedy by Talfourd, privately printed in 1835, produced in 1836. It was at a dinner after a performance of *Ion* in celebration of Talfourd's birthday, May 26, 1836, that Talfourd toasted Browning as "among the poets of England."

⁴ Thomas Noon Talfourd (1795-1854) is often referred to in these letters and generally as Sergeant because of his position as sergeant-at-law. Besides the plays mentioned here he wrote several others, but only *Ion* had a conspicuous success. He was well known in literary circles; both *Pickwick Papers* and *Pippa Passes* were dedicated to him. Later letters in this collection express Elizabeth's exasperation with him, especially on the subject of Miss Mitford and of the Haydon papers. A later ruction with Browning occurred in 1851 (DeVane and Knickerbocker, p. 50).

⁵ Elizabeth's maid.

⁶ Perhaps these and the following fragment of adventure were among those in Elizabeth's mind when she wrote apropos of Barrett romances: "I could tell you some dreary chronicles made for laughing and crying over," and continued in explanation of her father's attitude: "and then, the one person, by a curious anomaly, *never* draws an inference of this order, until the bare blade of it is thrust palpably into his hand, point outwards. So it has been in other cases than ours — and so it is, at this moment in the house, with others than ourselves" (*Letters of R. B. and E. B. B.,* I, pp. 328-29). Certainly, it was at this time that, because "Bro" was in love, Elizabeth tried unsuccessfully to make over her property to him (op. cit., pp. 329-30).

⁷ The Mackintoshes, several times mentioned as associating intimately with the Barretts, remain otherwise unidentified.

⁸ Henry Barrett (1818[?]-96), brother of Elizabeth.

⁹ Octavius Barrett (1824-1910), Elizabeth's youngest brother, generally called Ocy, Occy, Joc, or Joccy.

[10] *History of Napoleon,* 2 vols., 1840, "compiled" or edited by Richard H. Horne with the assistance of Mary Gillies, known as "Harriet Myrtle."

[11] Richard Henry (Hengist) Horne (1803-84). He adopted the name Hengist during his stay in Australia (1852-69). His correspondence with Elizabeth began in 1838 and continued voluminous until her marriage. They never met until afterwards. Their chief literary association occurred in the preparation of *A New Spirit of the Age* (London, 1844) and *Poems of Geoffrey Chaucer Modernized* (London, 1841). He later published Elizabeth's letters to him during these early years. (See S. R. Townshend Mayer, ed.: *Letters of Elizabeth Barrett Browning Addressed to Richard Hengist Horne,* 2 vols., London, 1877. A number of Horne's unpublished manuscript letters to Elizabeth are in the University of Illinois collection.)

[12] *Gregory VII,* a tragedy by R. H. Horne, published in 1840.

[13] *Cosmo De Medici,* a tragedy by R. H. Horne, produced in 1837.

[14] Mary Hunter.

The long break in the correspondence at this point (June 17, 1840 – February 15, 1841) is due chiefly to Elizabeth's complete prostration after the drowning of Edward (Bro), July 11, 1840.

letter 6

[Torquay]
Monday
[February 15, 1841][1]

At last my ever dearest George — I give some sign of being sensible to your kindness upon kindness in the shape of letters. I write to you at last. You know you frightened me away from doing so before with your solemn obtestations & protestations — and even now, Stormie has just said . . "Oh pray dont write to George, for he was very angry when you wrote to me." But the 'lex talionis' not being the law of the land I am clear of intruding any offence between the wind & your legality, in whatever other direction I may do so.

Here is my beloved Papa's letter too — drawing an answer out of my thoughts, with a golden cord.

Dearest Georgie, I do think of you so much, & hope for you so much & so strongly — with a hope partaking far more of expectation than of anxiety after all. Sooner or later, if God continues life & health, you will succeed. That I never in the least doubt about — because I am, as you probably know, a great believer in the "unconquerable will" as to intellectual successes. It is the beat of the drum to the soldier's march. A man with a mind may *will* himself into anything — & a wool-sack may be set down as a 'thing' in moderation — by no means the most glittering toy in the toyshop, or hung most out of reach. — You cant think how many engravings my thoughts & fancies have made (working together) from the picture you sent me of your retirement in Paper Buildings.[2] God bless you in all ways, dearest dearest George out of Zion *first*, & then from the other high places of the earth – Mind be careful of yourself — & dont be wet & cold — nor walk out your heart with rapidity, *tuo more*, for my sake, Georgie.

I was glad that you — and my dearest Papa speaks appro-bation too — liked my profile of the Man with a Soul. Only Georgie, it is'nt German & never was. Since you thrust the dis-honor of that suspicion on me, Mr. Horne said something which made me smile a little in relation to it. He said "Let us by no means have German names. People will call it instantly German mysticism, instead of what it is, a mystery of universal nature." No beginning has yet been made. He is so hard to please about names. What do you think of for a title, "Psyche Apocalyptic" or "Psyche Apocalypte?"[3] Oh — Papa is quite right – We are sure not to get anybody to read it except himself & you – But it is our business, you know, to make it *worth* reading & not to mind the rest — to work as the caterpillars do, without thinking of who is looking. Authors have low mercantile ways, sometimes, of con-sidering things — whereas they have no business with results. If God has given them any power (though but of a fibre's strength) they sh^d work by it, & if He has revealed any truth, according to it without taking into account the bookseller's pay in pence, or the public's in popularity.

Stormie's cold is quite vanished, I am very glad to say. And Jocky's[4] knees & ancles [sic] which suffered the pains & penalties of growing too fast, are quite strong again,— to give credit to his own testimony & that of his fellow walkers. They take very long walks on every possible day — and I heard Stormie remonstrating with Arabel for maintaining that "four miles were quite long enough for a walk"— Arabel's answer being, "Yes,— four miles there & four miles back." She and Ocky are opposed on this point to Stormie Henrietta & May — the two latter being considered decidedly 'lazy' & Stormie too practical. I never remember (or at least have not for years) to have seen Arabel so excursive and capable of exercise. And she has not had one cold this winter. It is a great mercy & comfort to me.

For my own part I think myself better, dearest Georgie. I do *think* so. I am low and fit for nothing in the morning — but that is the consequence in great measure, I am persuaded, by being over-excited the rest of the day by the brandy & opium. The three oclock fever is less than it was. Indeed today, my face was not flushed at all, & the palpitation was slight. It was nothing but the severe weather. Now we are as hot as we were cold — no — not quite!

Flush[5] amuses me sometimes when I am inclined to be amused by nothing else. There is no resisting his praying to be patted, — & he has some striking peculiarities — [*continued on envelope*] wont eat anything unless he is pressed — & then scarcely, unless he sees you do the same. We must make him friends with Myrtle –[6] Write some of you — will you? Do.– I did not mean to write so much after what my own dearest Papa said — but it is hard to begin & end — & all this was not written at once. Is dear Treppy with you? Affectionate love to her and the rest. God love & bless you George. Love to my dear Minny. I unalterably love you – No — *more than ever.* Ba

[*At top of first page*] Tell Papa and yourself, I did not write this all at once; so it will do no harm.

[1] Postmark: Torquay, Feb. 16, 1841. Address: G. G. Barrett, Esq., 50 Wimpole Street, London. February 15, 1841, fell on Monday. Mourning paper.

[2] Paper Buildings, Temple, were first built in 1609. They were destroyed in the great fire, and the buildings erected in their place in 1685 were also burned in 1838.

[3] *Psyche Apocalypte,* a projected poem to be written in collaboration by Elizabeth and R. H. Horne. A beginning was made and some fragments remain. Happily, to judge from these, the project was dropped.

[4] One of the several names for Octavius, youngest of the Barretts.

[5] Elizabeth's now famous cocker spaniel was given to her by Miss Mitford in 1840 and is thoroughly described as to appearance and temperament in the poem *To Flush, My Dog.* He accompanied his mistress when she left England in 1846 and survived into canine old-age to be buried under Casa Guidi in Florence.

[6] Myrtle, while not so well known as Flush, is also enshrined in verse in the following lines from Elizabeth's *Epistle to a Canary,*

> There is a little dog whose name is Myrtle! . . .
> A worthy dog in his totality, –
> Though wanting tact and ideality.

(*Hitherto Unpublished Poems and Stories with an Inedited Autobiography,* printed exclusively for members of the Bibliophile Society, Boston, 1914.) There are several references to Myrtle, none of them complimentary, in Miller: *E. B. to M. M.;* e.g., "My little brother's dog, Myrtle (a very brown ugly Myrtle, looking as if it had fallen into the sere and yellow leaf)" (p. 12), and "our brown and yellow terrier called Myrtle, whose noblest qualities lie in his mind" (p. 19).

letter 7   [Torquay]
                                        March 27, 1841[1]

My dearest dearest Georgie,

It is surely in equity & law, my turn now to write to you . . & just as surely my wish to do the same thing. I want to write to you. I want to thank you too, for your kindness in thinking of me more than you need have done, as proved by letters two or three. Thank you dearest George — *dearest.*

But still being human I am discontented — & being desirous of hearing something of your degree of legal success, you never say a word upon the subject – We saw your name in the paper *quoad* one trial — so that you cant be altogether briefless — which information was'nt enough to satisfy among us. You are turning your face to London by this time — are you not? You go, I think, from Monmouth to London? Would that I were you. And do you know, dear George, I am really going to London in *May,* or very early in the next month — & that Dr. Scully considers me "QUITE RIGHT" in meaning to do so. He has said moreover that I may pass the *winters* in London — & that I may do so with perfect impunity if with care. He thinks in fact that I must be shut up in one room during the winter *anywhere,* & that under such circumstances, I might as well be in London — to say nothing of the advantageous adjacency of medical advice better there than in other places – So if it sh^d please the Infinite Goodness to withdraw His hand from striking, we shall be at home late in May, or very early in June. Remember that. And dearest George, I beseech you, never to say a word or offer a gesture against it. All that remains to me of earthly happiness seems to me dependent upon my return to Wimpole Street. Dr. Scully's *honest* opinion is in its favor. I want to be with you *all* — none away, but those whom God has taken. And as to this air, however I may eat & drink or even speak & smile in it, it is & always must be to me by day & night like the air of a thunderstorm.

There was a letter from dear Set yesterday — no — from Set the day before, & from Henry yesterday. The only news is that Papa has dined twice with Mr. Kenyon,[2] and met Joanna Baillie[3] the poet Milnes,[4] Mrs. Coleridge,[5] & Babbage.[6] That sounds brilliant — doesn't it? Mr. Milnes professes Puseyism.[7]

I had a letter from Wolverhampton and Mr. Horne this morning. He still has "millions of pots and pans for a background" but has been able at last to enclose to me the skeleton-process of the first act of our Drama. You w^d like to look at it I know, but

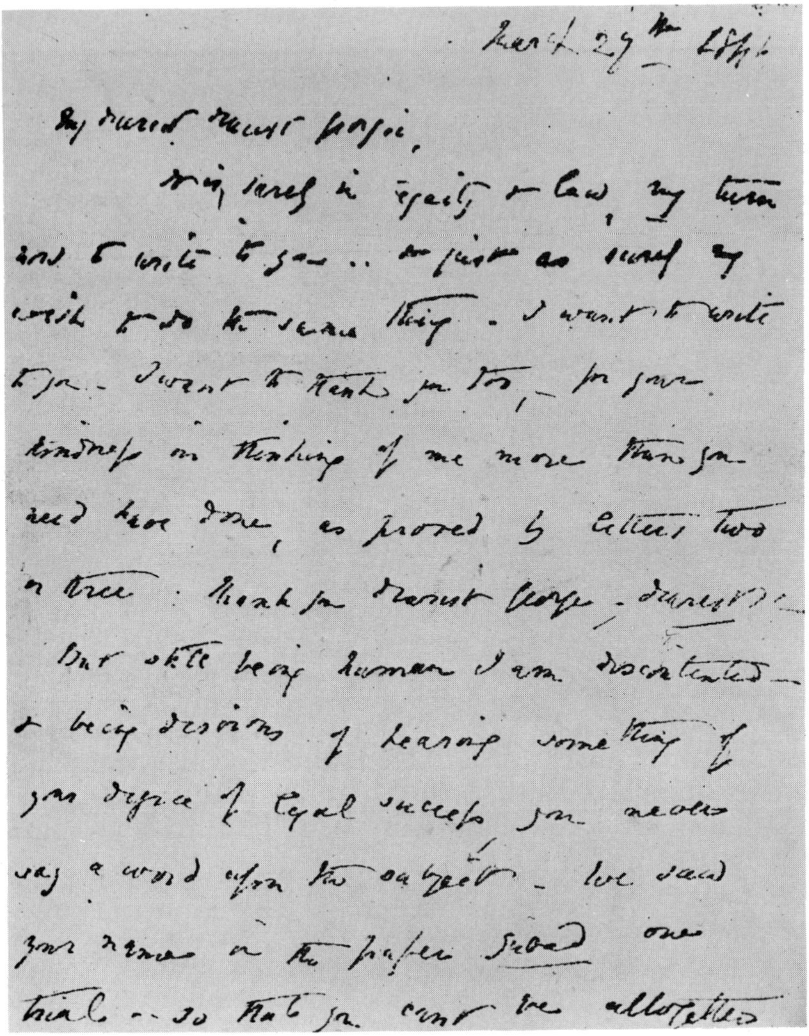

March 27th 1841

My dearest dearest George,

Being surely in equity or law, my turn now to write to you .. as just as surely my wish to do the same thing - I want to write to you - I want to thank you too, - for your kindness in thinking of me more than you need have done, as proved by letters two or three. Thank you dearest George - dearest!! -

But still being human I am discontented - & being desirous of hearing something of your degree of legal success you never say a word upon the subject - We saw your name in the paper [illegible] one trial -- so that you cannot be altogether

Plate I. Letter 7, March 27, 1841 (Elizabeth to George).

Plate II. ". . . a likeness of the white shadow of this face" (p. 57)
Miniature of Elizabeth made at Torquay, 1841. (Photograph from
Goewey Collection of Browning Pictures in the Mills College Library.)

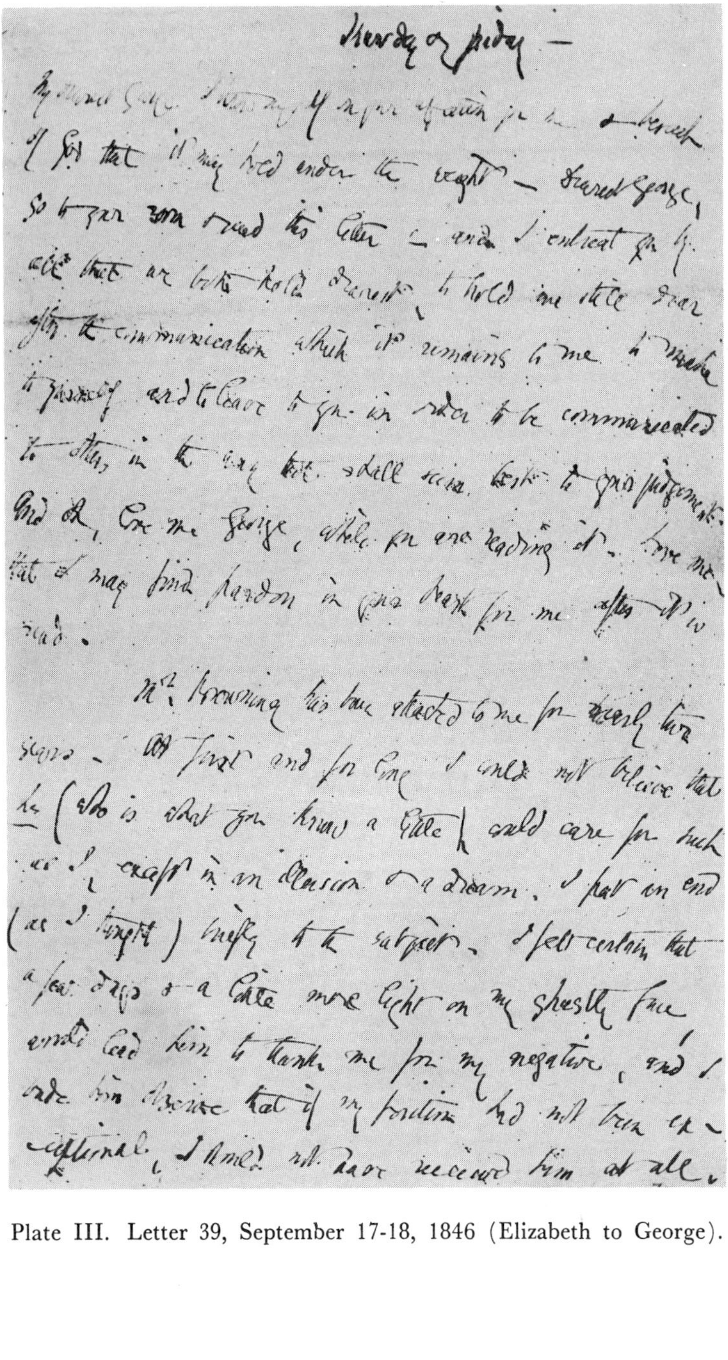
Thursday or Friday —

My dearest George. I throw myself on your affection for me & beseech of God that it may hold under the weight — Dearest George, go to your room & read this letter — and I entreat you by all that we are both held dearest, to hold me still dear after the communication which it remains to me to make to yourself and to leave to you in order to be communicated to others in the way that shall seem best to your judgment. And oh, love me George, while you are reading it. Love me, that I may find pardon in your heart for me after it is read.

Mr Browning has been attached to me for nearly two years — At first and for long I could not believe that he (who is what you know a little) could care for such as I, except in an illusion or a dream. I put an end (as I thought) briefly to the subject. I felt certain that a few days & a little more light on my ghastly face would lead him to thank me for my negative, and I told him likewise that if my position had not been exceptional, I should not have received him at all.

Plate III. Letter 39, September 17-18, 1846 (Elizabeth to George).

Plate IV. ". . . how the sun has succeeded in glorifying me"
(p. 222)

Photograph of Mrs. Browning made at Le Havre, September, 1858.
(Photograph, courtesy of Violet Altham, and of Dorothy Hewlett from
her book, *Elizabeth Barrett Browning,* New York: Knopf, 1952.)

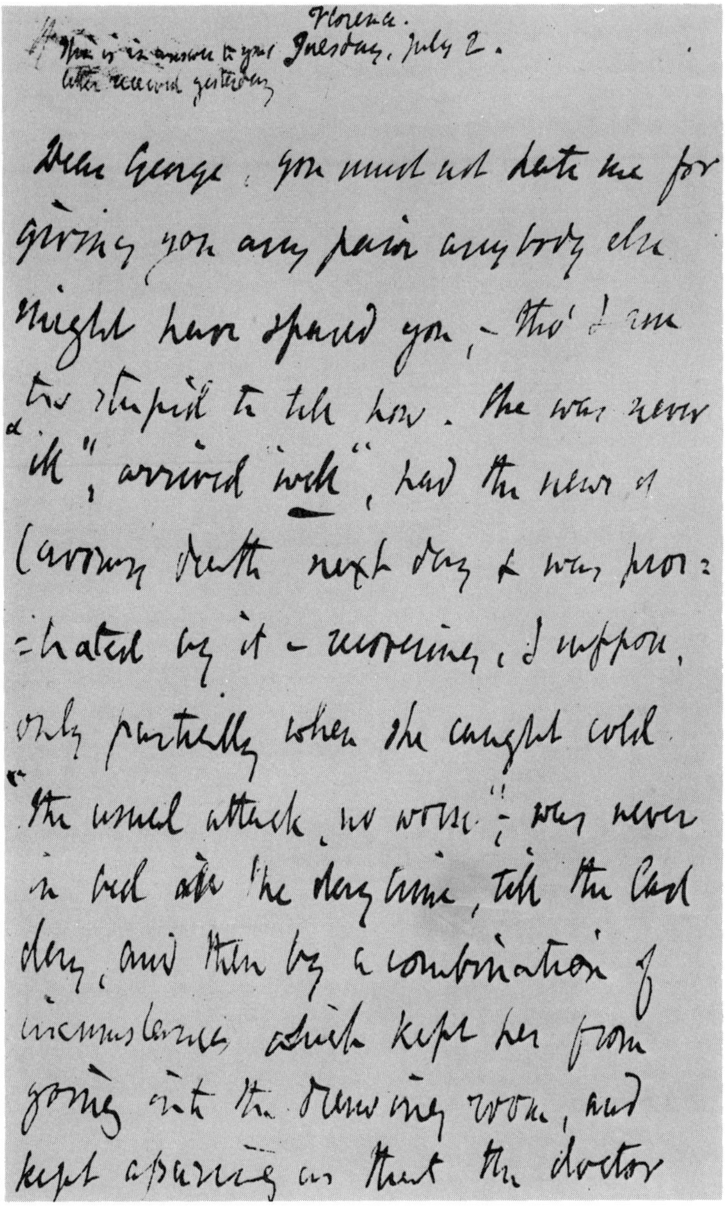

Florence.
Tuesday, July 2.

This is in answer to your letter received yesterday

Dear George, you must not hate me for giving you any pain anybody else might have spared you, — tho' I am too stupid to tell how. She was never "ill", arrived "well", had the news of Cavour's death next day & was prostrated by it — recovering, I suppose, only partially when she caught cold. "the usual attack, no worse"; was never in bed all the day time, till the last day, and then by a combination of circumstances which kept her from going into the drawing room, and kept assuring us that the doctor

Plate V. Letter 62, July 2, 1861 (Robert to George).

Plate VI. ". . . by the photographs I judge that Leighton's work is adequately rendered"   (pp. 284-85)

Mrs. Browning's monument in the English Cemetery, Florence. (Photograph by Ronald E. Freeman, May, 1955.)

Plate VII. ". . . something must be decided on at once for a
young man in his twenty-second year" (p. 293)

Robert and Pen Browning, 1870. (Photograph, courtesy of
Frances Winwar.)

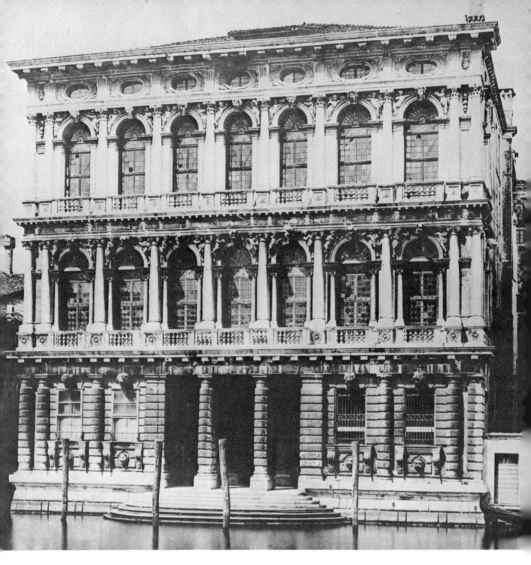

Plate VIII. ". . . a magnificent property worth more than
double what was paid for it"   (p. 317)

Rezzonico Palace, Venice, which Pen bought and in which Robert
died, December 12, 1889. (Photograph, courtesy of Wellesley
College Library.)

have'nt time to copy it out — more especially as Dr. Scully has come while I was on the verge of post-time, to push me down the precipice. And so much as I had to say to you! Mr. Horne desires me not to write a line of the Drama till the whole skeleton is completed. Did you hear of his sending me his picture "showing" how he looks when freshblack from the pits? — What a national dishonor it is, that high spirits sh[d] be thrust upon such work! Two thousand a year & a title for man-slaying, & for man-helping & glorifying, naught –[8]

My writing improves — doesn't it – And indeed *I* am improving, as a whole. I think so at least.

[*On flap of envelope*] Stormie wont go out now I am sorry to say — but take no notice. Ocy & Arabel & May walk every day & Henrietta *visits*. The visiting-love is stronger than I had ever supposed.— God ever ever bless you. My own dearest Georgie's Ba

[1] Postmark: Torquay, Mar. 27, 1841. Address: George Goodin Barrett, Esq., On the Circuit, Monmouth. Mourning paper.

[2] John Kenyon (1784-1856). He was born in Jamaica, was a second cousin of Elizabeth, and had been a schoolmate of Robert Browning, Senior. He first met Robert Browning, the poet, in 1836 and was thereafter a warm friend and appreciator. He watched lovingly over Elizabeth's literary career, and was the friend who brought Browning to write to Miss Barrett. When their son was born, he settled £100 annually upon them, and when he died he left them £11,000. He was a wealthy, cultivated gentleman, something of a poet, and magnificently generous.

[3] Joanna Baillie (1762-1851), well-known dramatist and poet, at this time past the high point of her fame.

[4] Richard Monckton Milnes (1809-85), poet, prose writer, and politician with a wide circle of friends of literary, political, and social prominence. He became 1st Lord Houghton in 1863.

[5] Sara Coleridge (1802-52), daughter of Samuel Taylor Coleridge, married in 1828 to her cousin Henry Nelson Coleridge.

[6] Probably Charles Babbage (1792-1871), mathematician and mechanician, Lucasian Professor of Mathematics at Cambridge. He spent many years and large amounts of money in an unsuccess-

ful attempt to produce a mechanical computer, and is credited
with having been a pioneer of many apparently modern industrial
ideas such as mass production and assembly line methods.

[7] The name currently used to signify the Oxford Movement,
derived from Edward Bouverie Pusey (1800-82), leader of the
High Church party and during mid-century the most influential
member of the Anglican church.

[8] Horne was at the time employed as commissioner to report on
the employment of children and young persons in mines and
factories. It was from him that Elizabeth learned of the conditions
which called forth her "Cry of the Children."

letter 8   [Torquay]
                                                       Thursday[1]
                                                       [April 15, 1841]

My dearest George

It is a pleasure to open one's heart — and for no other reason
do I write my first minutes thoughts of your kindest letter to
Paper Buildings where the freedom may lie between you & myself — & nobody else. The truth is, I am more troubled about this
Black Mountain[2] scheme than lately I have fancied it possible
for me to be about any temporal circumstance of that kind —
and join with you in devoutly wishing that the illusion may be
dispelled by the sight. Suppose the contrary to be the case —
what will happen then? – Why that the only comfort I have
dared to hope for must come to an end, & WE be no longer together – You are bound to London by your profession and unless
our brothers quench the energies of their lives in hunting and
fishing, they must necessarily be away too — while I leave you to
judge what possible human chance there can be for *me* to bear
rough roads & the distance from medical advice — look as far as
you can into the future. If our home sh^d be fixed there, it is the
knell of my perpetual exile — seems so at least — & I must be
anxious until the risk of the stroke be past.

I am sure my dearest Papa w^d be far happier in the end, by
disposing of whatever money he has to spend, in the purchase for

his sons, of shares or partnerships of whatever business may be suited to their inclination & capacity. Of course no one w^d suggest it to him — but he w^d, I am persuaded, be happier in witnessing their establishment, than in reigning alone at the top of a mountain where their society can neither cheer *him*, nor his hand help *them*.

Dont fancy that I am worrying myself — Oh no! – But I have been baffled and uneasy in a measure about this business for some time — long before your letter came — from hints in Sette's. By the way, is not Sette *advising* in this matter? I wish Papa w^d ask me. No — I dont –

I am not up yet George. Dr. Scully does not permit it until the sun shall seem inclined to tarry & in the meanwhile I am going to *lie for my picture*. Indeed it's true. You know I always meant to do it,— to *undergo* it,— in the case of any lady painter visiting the place — & the circumstance occurring, she is to be admitted to my bedside tomorrow. Four interviews will suffice — & four headaches will be well endured, sh^d the result be anything which my own dear Papa can have pleasure in looking at. Of course it is for *him* — a reflection of the kindness he spent upon me last year.[3]

It is so long since I saw a stranger that I shrink at the thought of the woman's coming tomorrow — even apart from her errand. And a beautiful picture will conclude all! — at least, if she succeed in making a likeness of the white shadow of this face.

Now keep my secret, George. My plan is, to send the picture to London by the post — *as a surprise* — supposing Papa to be there then. A miniature-painting, it will be.

Oh may we be free soon from this night-mare of Black Mountains. *Tell me* — [*on envelope*] *all you hear.* The removal of our home from London w^d be lamentable to me under any local advantage — but these Black mountains are black indeed. God bless you ever & ever, my dearest dearest George – I loved you always — but since your last visit here I have loved you *most* – You will easily gather *how* the love deepened – Your Ba.

[*Written across first sheet*]
Henrietta had a luncheon party here today. She goes out a good

deal. I wonder she can *bear it,* much less like it — but one heart can't judge for another — say nothing of this — nor indeed of anything else spoken by me today. God bless you George dearest. I am so glad you liked the chain.

¹ Postmark: Torquay, Apr. 16, 1841. Address: George Goodin Barrett, Esq., 3 Paper Buildings, Temple, London. April 15, 1841, fell on Thursday. Mourning paper.

² A location in Herefordshire on the border of Brecknockshire, elevation 2,000 feet. Mr. Barrett, to the understandable terror of Elizabeth, was thinking of establishing the family residence there. Miss Hewlett seems to have mistaken the Black Mountains for the Black Forest in Germany when she says that Mr. Barrett contemplated moving his family to the latter location (Hewlett, p. 82).

³ The picture was meant to atone for one of 1835 by Mrs. Carter, which Mr. Barrett did not like. In a letter to R. H. Horne, June 12, 1841, Elizabeth wrote: "How you would smile sarcasms and epigrams out of the 'hood' if you could see from it what I have been doing, or rather suffering, lately! Having my picture taken by a miniature-painter who wandered here to put an old view (Sidmouth, Devonshire, 1835) of mine to — proof. For it wasn't the ruling passion 'strong in death!' 'though by your smiling may seem to say so', but a sacrifice to papa" (*Letters to Horne,* I, p. 26).

The miniature, described on pp. 8-9 of the *Descriptive Catalogue of the Goewey Collection of Browning Pictures Owned by Mrs. James M. Goewey,* 1927, is reproduced on Plate II, following p. 54. Most of the collection is now at Mills College, Oakland, California.

letter 9   [Torquay]
                                              May 26, 1841¹

Although I have written to Papa and sent you almost message enough in reply to your letter, I must attempt I find, before I can be satisfied, some reply to its philosophy. Thank you first for its kindness. Ah — but you know I did in my heart, however lightly I might speak of anything besides. Yet *not* lightly — gravely & seriously, my beloved Georgie, I do assure you that

there is no "fever," no "excitement" in the thoughts you refer to
— on the contrary common sense and a rational deference to a
"MEDICAL OPINION." I know myself that I sh^d be better anywhere
than here — and Dr. Scully says — not to *me* (to please me) but
to others — "She will be as well in London as anywhere." Now
do, George, consider these things — and refrain from starting
again, when I speak of setting out in a few weeks – Why sh^d I
not move when it is possible? Why sh^d I not be better when I
can? Instead of starting, suggest to Papa the advisableness of
sending a carriage for me when the time arrives for its use,—
and enquire as to the *easiest springs*. Not that I am afraid. Not
the least fear is in me. I am in a different state altogether from
what you saw me in, and cannot be liable to the danger apprehended then. If there *were danger,* I w^d go — I dont deny *that.*
But there is none — and I shall act this time by what you call
with dignity "the advice of my medical attendant." And mind
George — mind this truth — *if God has an earthly blessing for
me He will take me home.* I do not limit His power or His mercy
— but I have no hope or capacity of joy, except for being once
more, not indeed as we were,² but as we can be, together in
Wimpole street.

In regard to that detestable Michael Church,³ what you say in
this note, disquiets me again *rather.* Papa's answer was obviously
"a pertinent one to an impertinent question," the *evasion of an
intrusion* — and even implies the possibility of his family being
settled there as a residence — which idea from what you told me
before about the "mere investment" and the decision against
parting with his London house, appears a new evil. My wonder
is great that under any circumstances he sh^d think of Herefordshire — thickly sown as it is with pain for all of us.⁴ I w^d rather
live in a wilderness, than there — how far rather – Matters of
feeling are not however subjects of argument –

Henrietta, it appears, very improperly (but you need not mention it in writing or otherwise) told the Holders⁵ that Papa was
"thinking of purchasing an estate —" mentioning the name of
this – Well! – They knew all about it. A cousin of their own was
a resident in it – And their report went on to describe it as "a

miserable place & quite unimprovable"— wretched house impossible roads — fine mountainous scenery, but not a tree."

Not that I care a feather, if it be *this or Eden*. My objections
are of another sort,— quite unremoved by your philosophy,
George — & unremoveable by any other. We are however here
to suffer — and I have little heart or strength left to struggle out
towards the light – It will be as God wills.

I was wrong in my last letter (long ago) to dwell at all upon
SELFISH objections. *I* ought not to be thought of, and certainly
w^d not *consciously* say that I wish to be thought of unduly.– *You*
were wrong too in interpreting words of mine into an opinion
that I sh^d w^d or might have constant medical attendance after
leaving this place. *I do not think of that.* Indeed I determine just
the contrary. When I go to London, I will see nobody unless it
sh^d be necessary. Only you see, Georgie, when certain attacks
come on — these hemorrhages for instances — it is necessary to
see somebody instantly or to take the bad consequence. Well —
but this is nonsense — I am not thinking of it, however I may
talk. Dearest Stormie, I grieve to say, never *goes out at all.* He is
just as he used to be — only he talks *quite enough,* if I may judge
through the walls. Henrietta does just the contrary — I dont
mean about the talking, or the walking, but the going out in
another sense. Only the place is thin just now of visitors. But
there is Lady Bolingbroke[6] still – Arabel paints resolutely – Dont
let Papa fancy that Ocky wishes to be idle — because indeed he
does'nt, dear boy –

You have my condolences about Mrs. Grant[7]— and poor
Papa seems to groan as deeply as any of you. He never hints to
me of Michael Church — merely of his prospect of having us
back in Wimpole street. God bless you all there, and us in our
return.

I am much much better — and sh^d not have been ill at all, but
for the mistake.[8] Certainly this last hemorrhage which was very
bad for some days, proves the weak state of the pulmonary ves-
sels — but still, there is the sunshine which I can feel, *though not
look at while I remain here,* and a whole summer, for gaining

strength and being reunited to *you*. So no word more against the moving, dearest Georgie – I do love you – I have written till I am tired.

Your most affectionate

Ba –

¹ Postmark: Torquay, May 27, 1841. Address: George Goodin Barrett, Esq., 3 Paper Buildings, Temple.

² Because of the deaths of Edward and Samuel Barrett, which occurred during Elizabeth's stay in Torquay, the family could never be complete again.

³ A parish in Herefordshire, five miles west of Ross.

⁴ Hope End, Elizabeth's childhood home, was located in Herefordshire, and in spite of happy memories, reflected in the descriptions in *Aurora Leigh* and other poems, she steadfastly refused to return there. "I never *could* go into that neighborhood," she wrote, "except to die" (Kenyon, II, p. 206). Her mother had died there and most of her memories of Edward were associated with the spot.

⁵ Unidentified friends of the Barrett family, possibly from Hope End days.

⁶ The second wife of George Richard St. John, Viscount Bolingbroke (1761-1824), to whom she was married in 1804. She had been Baroness Hompesch and had gone through a form of marriage ceremony with Viscount Bolingbroke in Austria before the death in 1803 of his first wife from whom he had been separated. She is described as "anything but handsome; a square little German with broken teeth, but they say very amiable." She died in 1848 at Torquay. (The Hon. Vicary Gibbs, ed.: *The Complete Peerage,* London, 1912, II, p. 208.) She is mentioned familiarly several times in these letters and also turns up in Elizabeth's letters to her sisters, generally in connection with helping to find a post for Surtees Cook, Henrietta's husband (see Huxley; also *Twenty-two Letters,* p. 24).

⁷ Unidentified.

⁸ Later, during her residence in Italy, Elizabeth speaks of a "mistake" in the strength of the morphine given her by a chemist which caused a severe relapse. This "mistake" may have been something of the same sort.

letter 10   [Torquay]
                                                    [June 21, 1841][1]

Ever dearest Georgie, I write on the only fragment of paper
within reach,— my strength being another fragment — for I
have been up today & tired by my letter to Papa besides. "Conspiracy!" Yes — conspiracy – That is the word. I beseech you,
George, not to acquiesce in it quietly, but to speak for me if you
have not spoken & help to avert the evil I have no courage to
face of remaining another year in this miserable place — another
year — involving perhaps the rest of my life.

The sending for Ocky c^d mean only one thing — that SOME
WEEKS (AT LEAST) delay in the removal was contemplated. I
must judge of things as I see them — & this is obvious. You say
"Dont come to London because we want country air"— & im-
mediately you send for Joc to London – What am I to infer? –
Are you *not* conspirators?

Now Georgie, my dearest kindest Georgie do try to produce
a decision, and let some sort of carriage be sent to me at once.
Why not Harman's? Twenty guineas — what is it, as a consideration?

Dr. Scully is nervous about the journey, & will say so. But it is
about the journey, about *any* journey & *at any time* — and his
opinion is that if I have resolved to do it (AND I HAVE) it had
better be done without loitering. He said himself —"Well —
Harman's carriage is the best means I can recommend," and he
hoped some decision might reach us by Tuesday. And now it
seems as far off as ever.

As to Clifton[2] . . "if I dislike it –" IF, George – There is no
if. Why you — everyone must know perfectly that there is no
hypothesis in the matter. Clifton w^d be better than Torquay because any place w^d be better — but almost any *other* place, Salisbury Plain for instance, w^d be better than Clifton. My object is
to be within reach of London — choose the place & I will thank
you all. But then Papa – He must not be displeased — he must
be pleased. He must, Georgie, to please me. But why sh^d he care
for that horrible Clifton? As to the railroad Dr. Scully bids me

beware of it. He [*on envelope*] wont hear of my trying it. And ask Joc what he said about "three days." I cant help being anxious — & the sort of twilight I am kept in is not likely to do me or anybody good. Oh Georgie — if I were well it w^d be different – But as it is if the thing be not done now, I may be forced into quiescence in this place. And I say solemnly that, in such a case *not one of my family shall remain with me* –[3] God bless you dear kind George. I really love you all every [*torn*] This [*torn*] y^r private hand[4]

Ba

[1] The letter is undated. Postmark: Torquay, June 21, 1841. Address: George Goodin Barrett, 3 Paper Buildings, Temple, London.

[2] Near Bristol.

[3] On January 27, 1846, in the course of explaining to Browning her love for her father, Elizabeth wrote: "I proved a little my affection for him, by coming to London at the risk of my life rather than diminish the comfort of his home by keeping a part of my family away from him" (*Letters of R. B. and E. B. B.,* I, p. 435). The importance of this motive is confirmed by her underlining of her resolution to remain alone, if at all. Most of the letters from Torquay maintain that her removal will entail no risk to her life, or, if a little, that that circumstance is unimportant.

[4] The tip of the flap of the envelope is torn so that a few words are indecipherable.

letter 11   [Torquay]
July 20, 1841[1]

Dearest dearest[2] Georgie,

I dont promise faithfully to fill you this goblet[3] up to the brim — but my own little half pint sheets have all, I find, been put into the post at different times & nothing is left to me but to "speak small" on a large surface. Dearest George, I meant & meant again to write to you before. Two or three letters of yours have witnessed to your thoughts of me, while mine of you said nothing. Mine of you, *were* nevertheless. I have been whetting my patience upon silence — or rather muffling my *im*patience in my silence — for that is the right metaphor after all. And then I felt smitten in conscience about having vexed Papa —, & made a deep vow at the moment, not to say a word more directly or indirectly — not even if it became clear, as I half feared it might do, that I was'nt to go at all. I w^d rather stay, than really vex him — and particularly if, as depended more on my own resolve, I got everybody away, except myself & Crow.

But however Papa said something yesterday about the present June weather being open to experiment — & that sounds as if he had not given me up. George, you are a very violent tempestuous person! – First, you look fierce at me for my impatience, — & then at others for their dilatoriness – No – No – Georgie – There is no unkindness *ever,* & least, now – It w^d have been better for me (that is my immoveable impression) to have performed this journey some weeks ago — better in several ways — but others did not account it so, or I sh^d have gone. And then — delay — delay — delay – The sum about the snail is the "full sum of us" – [4] We cant go on at all without stopping short – Our lagging is a part of our progression. And nobody knows *quite* (not even you, George –) the degree & detail of the repulsion with which this place acts upon me, whenever my mind is left, as all minds, however their will-organs may sternly turn them into abstracting occupations, must be sometimes, to the full influence of the locality.

Well — but never mind – It will end, I dare say now, in our going. Papa's expression in last Sunday's letter certainly seems, as if even he thought the time for action had arrived — or was near — although, by the way, he says not a syllable of decision on the point of our destination. May God bless you all, & grant the blessing to me of seeing you well, when I do see you, — well, and open to the pleasantnesses of life. Now I sh^d like to know (but without hoping that you will tell me!) if you meet gracious attorneys & take from their smiles any business at all. My fear is, that you look out over the hills, up to the present moment, for prosperity. But I dont fear what is behind the hills – No — not in any measure. A strong will, such as yours, will carry a city. You know my doxy – And Miss Mitford by letter I had from her some days ago, extend it into a paradoxy — holding that *strong wishes fulfil themselves.* Oh, *that* is not true or the earth w^d be one or two shades lighter. But if it sh^d be true Georgie, why you have only to "put to" my strong wishes for you to your strong will for yourself, and the two teams will take you up a mountain as steep as the Jungfrau. I do love you my dear dear George –

I dont deny my "hankering for Wimpole street." If I did 'Thou liest, thou liest, thou little foot-page,"[5] might be said to this page. But honestly, sincerely, I am ready with a full heart of content, for any place *very near London.* I sh^d be quite content with Reading — Reading being only half an hour off Marylebone. Or I sh^d like Twickenham or Windsor. The choice however, is very properly & very *pleasantly* (for I dont want to choose) out of my own hands.

Dear Miss Mitford is very anxious for Reading[6]— and then I c^d write an "and" and then a "but." The truth is, I shrink from the thought of looking upon anybody except yourselves — even upon such as I love. Well — no more of the going away.

Arabel gave a rural entertainment yesterday to the school — in a meadow at Upton — Henrietta very wonderfully wroth about it, I cannot make out why. Tea & cake & a run in the grass — were the head & front of the offending. She w^{d}nt go — or —. I was vexed a little I confess — but say nothing of this. A person may be as High Church as one steeple upon another, & yet care for the innocent enjoyment of poor children. Which is my end of controversy?

July 20, 1841[7]

Do you hear of the business in London at Moxon's –[8] How Miss Sedgewick[9] who was here you remember, two years ago, & received with open arms & kisses on each cheek by all the literate, (they never once suspecting "the deil, amang them taking notes,") put everything down about their eyes & noses & other humanities & sent it to the printer's — and how Mr. Kenyon surprised these interesting proof sheets at Moxon's half an hour previous to the publication, & after reading therein what a delightful person he was in particular, presumed upon the fair author's good opinion of himself to become her corrector of the press, & positively & then and there *cancelled* the things which appeared to him objectionable. He said he had "a moral right" to do it, and wrote this distinct opinion to America, to Miss Sedgewick. What is your thought? Is the moral right the legal? Was he justified *either* way? I doubt stedfastly [*sic*]. I am very sorry for the "altogether" about it. Miss Mitford wrote me a letter full of just indignation, at the wrongs perpetrated against her by the authoress — whom she had received as her friend, & who took advantage of opportunities so derived, to ask questions & take answers from the maid-servant where with to illuminate the new world. With all my love for literary gossipping, this is too much. It is a littleness — if not a baseness — a treachery, *in small.*

But, on the other hand, I am astonished at Mr. Kenyon's dagger scene at Moxon's. Think of the consequence, if everyone who pleased, walked into a publisher's shop, and cut down every writer's proof sheets to the measure of his own opinions! It w^{d}nt do — w^d it? Tell me –

Oh such a hurry, no time to read over – God bless you ever

Your ever & ever attached

Ba

[1] Postmark: Torquay [July?] 20, 1841. Address: G. G. Barrett, Esq., On The Circuit, Stafford. Pencil note on back "July /41."

[2] Throughout the letter penstrokes, certainly not Elizabeth's, have been drawn through *dearest,* once through *George,* through the signature *Ba,* and through two sections of the letter: (1) "And then I felt . . . tempestuous person."; (2) the last line before the interpolated date (*see below*).

[3] The letter is written on very large sheets.

[4] The quotation seems to be an adaptation of Portia's words:

> But the full sum of me
> Is sum of — something, which, to term in gross,
> Is an unlesson'd girl, unschool'd, unpractis'd;
> *Merchant of Venice,* III.ii.159-61

The "sum about the snail" may be a reference to the Fool's riddles in *King Lear*, I.v.26-34:

> Fool: Canst tell how an oyster makes his shell?
> Lear: No.
> Fool: Nor I neither: but I can tell why a snail has a house.
> Lear: Why?
> Fool: Why, to put's head in;

It may, however, refer to some commonly known riddle concerning the snail's always being at home no matter where it goes, as in

> And seeing the snaile, which every where doth rome,
> Carrying his owne house still, still is at home,
>
> Donne: *To Sir Henry Wotton*, ll. 50-51

This, however, seems hardly to conform to Elizabeth's state of mind — she certainly was not "at home" in any sense.

[5] See *The Romaunt of the Page*, stanza xlii for a "lying page."

[6] Miss Mitford's home.

[7] "July 20, 1841" is here inserted in another hand. The letter itself is, however, dated clearly, July 20, 1841, but the month of the postmark on the envelope is illegible. The reference in paragraph 2 to "the present June weather" and "yesterday" indicates June rather than July for the date of the letter. If this is a case of Elizabeth's characteristic carelessness in dating, it is possible that the envelope with the previous letter, June 21, 1841, would better fit this letter according to this internal evidence, disregarding the actual dating.

[8] After 1842, Elizabeth's publisher, Edward Moxon (1801-58). He was started in business in 1830 by Samuel Rogers. On his list of authors were Barry Cornwall, Lord Lytton, Tennyson, and Robert Browning.

[9] Catharine Maria Sedgwick (1789-1867), an American novelist and writer, of a distinguished Massachusetts family. After visiting Europe she published in 1841 *Letters from Abroad to Kindred at Home*.

letter 12   [Torquay]
                                                     [July 24, 1841][1]

My ever dearest Georgie

Not to be over maniacal I propose myself to you as a person ready to believe for the best, that all anxieties and tribulations in relation to the journeying subject will end in a bona fide removal & not merely in one bona spe. You will admit however that apart from your interpretation, Joc's² recall wore a strange aspect. You will admit that without any "maniacal" tendency, it was enough, when, taken in conjunction with the delays & the discussions & the contradictions and the universal tendency towards treating me as a baby — to excite the most unexcitable —'Forgive me (then) this mania.'–

Dr. Scully himself has been vibrating in a manner provoking to me. I dare say you put down as sure that all his sayings in relation to "the beginning of the argument," such as "she is quite right," "it is very natural," "it is very reasonable", "it is very possible," were misrepresented or at least warmly coloured by me. Nothing of the kind — it was all clear approbation at first – But when he saw that I was actually *in earnest,* he fell straightway into a tremblement – Then came, a list of the risks & the dangers & of all the things which would could or might peradventure befall me. He sate by this bedside & tried hard to frighten me — not as to *the time,* mind, my dear George, but as to the movement essentially. He sate at this bedside, & endeavoured to persuade me to go into another house & to another part of Torquay.– You may suppose how I answered — admitting that he had done right in telling me all, but resolute as to the act. Indeed he cᵈ not deny, when I put the question to him, that *if he were I, he wᵈ go.*

Well — we must allow for the unpleasant feeling of responsibility. I do not blame him — although all this prudential counsel, not being confined to my ear as I begged it might be, makes everybody cry out in different voices & keys, so as to consummate the discord of indecision. Now I AM GOING — THAT IS SETTLED. And I leave it (no! I dont *leave* it) I *put* it to the wisest amongst you, whether, granting there is a risk, it be not increased by delaying & discussing one week after another.

Dr. Scully calls me "excited." Now the two last conversations on the subject began with himself — & all the impatience about getting me away, was expressed BY himself. Two days ago, he came with earnest anxious looks – "Had I heard?" "Was the

house taken?" "What! not yet?" "Oh — it w^d be far far better
for you to go at once. You are excited, naturally, & must remain
so until the journey is over — and there is no use in doctoring the
body while the mind is restless. In your case, this is eminently
true. IT IS THE LEAST OF TWO EVILS THAT YOU GO AT ONCE."

Then he went on to tell me how he got up at four in the
morning to make notes about me, & to examine a map of London & the situation of Wimpole street. He approved of the latter,
and after enquiring about the aspect of my bedroom, expressed
his opinion for the twentieth time that I sh^d be *as well there as
here in the winter.* The thing necessary for me, he said, was an
airy room which c^d be warmed, with a south or western aspect, —
and the neighbourhood of good advice. His own leaning evidently is to send me *direct to London.* He thinks it w^d be better
for me, and that the journey being begun had better be ended
at once. That was his opinion as he rendered it to me, two days
ago — Crow being witness – But of course I explained to him
that Papa's plans for my brothers did not allow of this direct
passage to Wimpole street. Oh no — I w^d not break upon *them.*
At the same time it does appear to me hard, rather hard, that the
Clifton question sh^d be carried against me, when I am the only
person affected either for good or evil by that particular locality,
& when the evil threatened to me by it, is all unmingled evil.
Dearest George, do say a word, when the opportunity occurs.
You must see how it is, as plainly as I do. I shall have no rest
of spirit at Clifton – I shall have encountered this "risk" which
is talked of, without an equivalent object. Certainly I shall have
left Torquay — but a removal to the first stage from Torquay
to Chudleigh[3] w^d accomplish *that,* without a step beyond. All
the effort, all the expense, will be made & paid for next to in
vain. It will be a sovereign in change for sixpence. Not that
I forget the blessing of being free from this place — but all
besides, — and I have lived upon the blessed hope of being
settled at home with you all — will be *lost!* – Do you not see?
— Do you not feel how it is? – Dr. Scully himself says "I understand *You object reasonably."* As to Reading, I do not say Reading more than Twickenham or any other place of the vicinity.

I dont want to have my own way about it — indeed I have no "own way" to carry – I want you all to choose – I want Papa to choose. Only, if he persists in this Clifton plan, I shall scarcely, I feel, have spirits to travel away from all my hopes, to another place of exile & scene of separation — yes, & of more than separation, George, OF ISOLATION — such as Clifton SHOULD be to me if I went to it – Why I might quite as well remain at Chudleigh — quite as well. There w^d be an escape from the pressure of actual associations[4]— and nothing more. But nothing more can be said of Clifton.

I leave these things with your 'professional' judgment to turn over & discern. Remember — I am forbidden, in any case, to attempt the railroad. That is that. And I ask you to task your fancy, as happily you cannot your experience, & try to image what peace & rest & *safety of heart* there w^d be for me in the feeling of being at home or close to home. After this present sense of banishment & seperation [*sic*].

Oh dearest dearest George! It is all very selfish! – How selfishly I have written! – Only INDEED I w^d not that one of you sh^d sacrifice a good or a pleasure for *me* – I have no good or pleasure but yours — except *you* – It is the living apart from any of you which drives me to say so much or to say anything — & I cant bring myself to think that living apart from you can be the cause to you of good or pleasure. Hemel Hempstead, or Twickenham, or Reading, or Tunbridge or Walthamstow[5]— all places where we can be together & whence we can remove together, are equal to me. Would it not be hard — no! — not hard perhaps — , but unhappy, if the only place where I cannot rest, sh^d be fixed upon for me to travel to.

My mind turns round & round in wondering about Papa's fancy for Clifton that hot, white, dusty, vapory place, & scarcely an 'inland place too'– And then sometimes I grow dizzy & fearful that he looks to Michael Church! – Oh but I WONT fear it. I wont fear anything. I will hope a little, while there is room. So you are going next week

My dear dear George. I will write to you on your way. *I* will

be the "kind heart," George, & write — that is if they dont wear
me out with these "rubs" backwards & forwards. The "conspiracy" is discredited upon your assurance. One word more.
Dr. Scully did not like the idea of a carriage from Bristol &
seemed to think too much depended upon the *best,* not to have
it from Harman himself —

[*on envelope partially torn*] or Willoughby without considering
the expense [&] the safe[ty] He says besides that — [*top of first
sheet*] *Twenty guineas* is no extortion — that on the contrary a
patient of his who removed from hence to Brighton in a conveyance of the kind, paid more. But I think I shall say this to Papa,
or have it said. God bless you. When I reach you I will not talk
so of myself. I shall subside in content Your ever attached Ba

[*Across first sheet*] I dont want Papa to come! Is there any use?
He will be over anxious & nervous & uncomfortable. Tell him not
to come. Do you know Dr. Scully wants you? He distrusts dear
Storm's firmness, it appears   *But say nothing.* Oh, of course you
would not! Storm w^d do everything very well — & I am fearless.

¹ Postmark: Torquay, July 24, 1841. Address: George Goodin
Barrett, Esq., 3 Paper Buildings, Temple, London. Mourning paper.
    ² Octavius Barrett.
    ³ A town in southeast Devon about ten miles southwest of Exeter.
    ⁴ One of the associations she was most anxious to be rid of was
the sea.
    ⁵ All inland locations within a short distance of London.

letter 13   [Torquay]
                                          July 25, 1841¹

Ever dearest George,
    I squeeze myself in, you see, out of my turn, & intent to write
to you again. The usual letter came yesterday (my first thought
must be my first word) but with no decision in it – Indeed Papa

says justly that the weather was miserable all last week — only taking no note of the brightness of the Saturday on which he wrote — that is, if the Saturdays here & there wear the same aspect. Here, we have had one two & three days full of sunshine & warmth – Something must surely be decided soon – The weather refuses to hold up the train of a delay, an hour longer —

Dearest Georgie, why dont we hear from you. It seems almost strange that we dont. I begin sometimes to think about the railroad. Write, dearest George, — if but a line with a pencil under the bower of your wig —

They are well in Wimpole street — and here we are well too– For myself I gather strength, — get daily to the sofa, & *sit up on it*. Dr. Scully has not seen me these three days. But what's the use of it, if I stay on, wait on, in this dreary way? Well — there is not a remedy – I cant vex Papa again, or have him vexed – He will decide presently – I hope still –

From what he says, there has just arrived a bad, or worse than bad, account of the West Indian crops, — very bad indeed it seems to be. He hopes to pay the expenses of cultivation — but fears for his Statira[2] who cannot be properly laden – Altogether he felt too annoyed, he said, to go on writing.

Did anybody tell you (while we are on commercial matters) that the Newton bank had broken, & that poor Dr. Scully among others yet poorer, was a sufferer by six hundred & fifty pounds?

Stormie, kind fellow, gave me Blanchard's Life of L E L,[3] the other day, which though a wrong thing to do, was a thing I c^d not choose but suffer gratefully. It is a dreary melancholy book — by no means satisfactory, in touching either upon her life or death. I sh^d like to hear you talk legally upon the evidence & the witnesses connected with the latter's dark mystery,[4] and leap at some conclusion for me. And then the biographer is parsimonious of her letters, — which always tell a story of life better than the best abstract of it, elaborated by the cold hands of another –

I shall like to introduce Flush to you, Georgie, when we see each other — Mr. Flush as they sometimes call him. He is such a companion to me all day long — lying close beside me & when I move to the sofa, leaping there, beside me still, and always marking his sense of the change of place, by kissing me in a dogs way, most expressively – If Crow tells him to "go to Miss Barrett" in any part of the house — indeed she tried it this morning from the outside of the house — up he comes leaping & dancing & shaking the handle of my door. A sort of dog, George, to whom you could'nt reasonably refuse the franchise, in the case of any liberal extension of it. He understands almost every word you say! I like him to be beside me. It does'nt do anybody any harm.

Arabel's rural entertainment to the schoolchildren answered very well — so everybody said — and they made delightful tea in kettles, upon a foundation of sugar & cream – or milk I think it was. Crow went — and I had my tea at four o'clock instead of six on purpose not to cross their purposes.

Henrietta goes out indefatigably — quite wonderfully to me — day after day, week after week — the consequence of course being, that when she falls back upon *only us,* we are found hard & dry. Stormie stands on the remote pole — refusing to leave the house, even for the purpose of worship. He is just as he was, dearest George, — just — altho' I had hoped differently — *just,* — except in a greater freedom & tendency towards conversation. With us, he talks continually & very cheerfully — I hear him talking for hours together through the wall. But I do wish the other wall of insuperable shyness c^d be thrown down [*on envelope*] or blown down — or at the very least w^d admit a window.

God bless you — ever & ever

Your most attached
Ba

---

[1] Post mark: Torquay, July 26, 1841. Address: George Goodin Barrett, Esq., On the Circuit, Hereford. Mourning paper.

[2] The name of a ship belonging to Mr. Barrett.

[3] Laman B. Blanchard: *Life and Literary Remains of Letitia Elizabeth Landon,* 2 vols., London, 1841.

[4] Letitia Elizabeth Landon (1802-38), better known as L. E. L., was a popular poet and a novelist of considerable contemporary vogue. An engagement to John Forster was broken, and she later

married George Maclean, Governor of the Gold Coast. After a few
months of very unhappy married life she died in Cape Coast,
Africa, from an overdose of prussic acid, presumed to have been
taken by mistake. (Cf. Elizabeth's poem, *L. E. L.'s Last Question.*)

letter 14   [50 Wimpole Street]
                                                Thursday
                                                [October 21, 1841][1]

Thank you my dearest George for your obolus – I wont reproach
you for not being generous, over-generous I mean, when all I
begged you to attain to was the first element of charity. Thank
you for the note & the line   I jumped as high as I could for it.

Arabel wrote to you yesterday. I meant to write to you first,
although not yesterday — if it were only to prove what 'a lion'
or a 'mouse' I could be in gratitude. That I write to you for
pleasure's sake besides, ceases to be fabulous.

Dearest George, I am trying to be as glad as possible at your
being away — particularly since people say that the result of the
absence must be your increase round the waist by an inch. I try
to be glad by the ell. And if it were not for the wild horses &
the guns, I sh[d] wish you to go to Kinnersly[2] & Frocester,[3] &
stretch your stay (not stays) & waist together. Oh, you are sure
I think, to go to Frocester. I make myself sure of *that.* Give my
love with everybody's to dear Bummy[4] & Arlette[5] & Cissy[6] — &
dont forget to say how remorseful I was about remembering
them all too late.

Now let me see what there can be to tell you – That Trippy
is in your place, Arabel has told you of course. Mrs. Orme[7] dined
here yesterday & thought me or flattered me "looking better."
Henrietta dined with Lady Bolingbroke on Saturday, on Monday, & went with her on Wednesday (with her & Daisy[8]) to
Exeter Hall to hear Spohr's Judgment.[9] On Monday she dined
in company with Mrs. Whithead[10] — & yesterday I heard such
things of the latter, of her reputation or the lack of it, that I
mean to use your authority in putting an absolute end to the

acquaintance – Under Henrietta's circumstances — unmarried & without a chaperone — it is incumbent that she sh^d be particular in regard to her associates. I am more annoyed about this business that [sic] I can tell you here, but not more than I will tell you – I am above, (or below — which you please — the suspicion of prudery or particularity or I-would-not-do-such-a-thing-ness, but *some thing* must be done under certain circumstances, the present being those. Well, the scandal will do for some day after tea.

I sent back the third skeleton act of the Psyche, revised & emended, yesterday — & perhaps we may begin to build in the course of another ten days. My hand shakes before it takes up the trowel. The poem looks so well in my head that I am afraid of disappointing myself. But I will try — that is sure – And do you know, George, my plan is, to bind the book (when it's done) in a bright, perhaps a rare fashion, so that it may outwit the annuals — and to have the back overspread with mystical figures — perhaps a great rampant lambent silver serpent lifting its solemn crest & uplifting from the earth in the dreadful pressure of its folds, a man — to typify how, according to our subject, the humanity agonizes within the sense of Psyche's eternal. Well, then — we need only have some black-&-white spiritual-pictures, by Martin,[11] to put in between the leaves — and the book will "have a run." That's my plan, Georgie! I have Capt. Maryatt's America from the library — & Pepys.

The gossip down stairs is, that Papa is going to have a stove put into the back drawingroom instead of the fire-place. The bookbinder was here this morning & waited for orders about binding the work-table (yes — binding the top of it) but Papa w^d give no orders because "Sette was'nt at home." How could he, they said, when the master of the house was'nt at home? – Sette is studying at the London university, Logic, Metaphysics, ancient & modern history, the English language & literature, to say nothing of debating & gymnastics. I think it must be a little overwhelming. But he is resolved on being a special pleader & wants to be historical & logical [*on envelope*] & oratorical all at once. Sundry "dreadful notes of preparation" appear to him necessary.

God bless you dearest dearest George. I am very tolerably well — my voice continuing to make inharmonious progress towards audibility — the sense of fitness & comfort in being *here,* increasing day by day. God be thanked. He is tenderer to me than I deserve – Oh how far! He might well have denied to me this *remaining blessing* – May you have business — but dont be discouraged if you have'nt –

Ever your Ba.

[*Across top of first sheet*] Flush's love. His present taste is for ratafies[12] but his affections he says are unchangeable.

[1] Postmark: Gloucester, Oc. 21, 1841. Address: George Goodin Barrett, Esq., Mrs. Palmers, Westgate Street, Gloucester. October 21, 1841, fell on Thursday. Elizabeth had returned to Wimpole Street in September, 1841. Since George also lived there, letters are written only when he is away "on the circuit."

[2] John Altham Graham-Clarke, Elizabeth's maternal uncle, married the daughter of Leonard Parkinson of Kinnersley Castle, where they resided.

[3] Frocester is a parish and village ten miles southwest of Gloucester, evidently the home of the R. P. Butlers.

[4] Elizabeth's maternal aunt Arabella Graham-Clarke.

[5] Charlotte Butler, Elizabeth's cousin, daughter of Charlotte Graham-Clarke and the Rev. R. P. Butler.

[6] Cissy Butler, sister of Charlotte.

[7] Mrs. Orme had been Elizabeth's governess at Hope End.

[8] Family nickname for Elizabeth's brother, Alfred Barrett (1820-1904).

[9] *Die Letzte Dinge* by Louis Spohr, German violinist and composer (1784-1859); composed in 1825; English version by Professor Edward Taylor.

[10] Unfortunately Mrs. Whithead's "reputation" has not survived. Its nature may be surmised. She seems to have had little influence on Henrietta.

[11] John Martin (1789-1854), painter of large canvases on Bibli-

cal subjects, highly esteemed at the time. He illustrated *Paradise Lost*.

[12] A small sweet biscuit flavored with almond paste. Flush's fondness for macaroons was notorious.

letter 15   [50 Wimpole Street]
                                                 March 2, 1842[1]

My ever dearest Georgie,

I said to Papa last night, "We *may* hear from George tomorrow"— *that* was an ebullition of good opinion of you! But "oh no"— he said — nothing can be more unlikely. If he writes at all, he wont write tomorrow.

Thank you my dearest dearest George for the letter which came after all. If you knew how I cared to have it you w^d 'do so again' very soon. You have only to breathe once or twice over the paper & let your hand move at the same time, & the work is done. –

I feel quite triumphant about the six cases, & we are all as pleased as possible. Fortune will come if you wait long enough where the three roads meet & restrain your natural discontent at the dust.

I am a chronicler with nothing to chronicle, having heard nothing, out of my own heart-beating & head-working, & that not worth repeating, since you went away. Mr. Soper does not dine here today, & Papa was scarcely pleased at his being asked —"Why did George ask him when he was not here to entertain him? Certainly you could'nt have waited dinner for *me*. *I* shall not be back perhaps until half past eight." So spake he yesterday, & Henrietta being abashed never explained how Mr. Bell and Mr. Somebody else were coming — so there will be a delightful surprise for him at half past eight. Henry met Arabella Soper yesterday — of course she inquired after "dearest Ba" but notwithstanding the dearestness leaves town today without coming to Wimpole street.[2] I had Mr. Townsend's poem of 'New Zealand'[3] yesterday too, with a request that I w^d dispose of a few copies, as assistant to Seely[4] in his heavy publishing labors, & in help to the charity. Not knowing nor having access to many buyers of poems (unfortunately for myself) I shall decline the proffered occupation. I shall say "I am still busy with the Seraphim! & have'nt sold it yet by — how many copies – ?

I have no doubt that your Scotchman, your accidental Scotchman, admired you quite as much as he admired me. "Very like a whale" & Carlyle indeed! – I suppose Carlyle stands for an author in the far north — & that there's an inversion in those parts of the old phrase — ex Hercule pedem.[5] Mr. Boyd[6] approves of my first part[7] but objects to the injustice of including Gregory[8] & Synesius[9] in the canaille of poets, & using one grand swoop of a *they* to all. "My third" inclines to end itself – Sh^{dnt} you like to see the ghostly grin of enforced courtesy, with which Mr. Dilke[10] will [*on envelope*] receive the intimation of a fourth's being necessary? I think I must propose *un*paying back — i.e. the taking off of a half guinea for every supernumerary column. Everybody's love. God bless you my own dear Georgie –

Ever your Ba

Do write.

[1] Postmark: Gloucester, Mar. 3, 1842. Address: George Goodin Barrett, Esq., Mrs. Palmer's, Westgate, Gloucester.

[2] Clearly friends of the family but otherwise unidentified. Mr. Bell could be the same who in 1847 "gives up his heiress then, and is not thinner for it, I dare say" (*Twenty-two Letters*, p. 23).

[3] The poem was written in 1842, published by Seeley, and sold for 2s/6d. No further information concerning it has come to hand. It dealt, doubtless, with the matter which fills a vehement paragraph in Elizabeth's letter of March 24, 1832, to Miss Mitford (Miller: *E. B. to M. M.*, p. 112). "I like the waste of the public money upon bishops of New Zealand!! and of Jerusalem!! as little as you do, and have ventured to be open with Mr. Townsend and tell him as much. . . . A bishop of New Zealand! No . . . The bishops are impotent, and have been found to be impotent, in all situations of the kind – " The author was R. E. Austin Townsend, who contributed a poem entitled *Elizabeth* to *Finden's Tableaux*

for 1838 and another entitled *Home* for 1841. Miss Mitford was the editor of the publication or at least solicited contributions at £5 from 1836 or 1837 to 1842 or later. The *Tableaux* consisted of drawings by the brothers William and Edward Francis Finden. Prose and poems were used to accompany the pictures. Elizabeth contributed *A Romance of the Ganges* to the number for 1838, *Romaunt of the Page* for 1839, *Lay of the Brown Rosary* and *The Dream* for 1840.

4 Robert Benton Seeley (1798-1886), publisher; noted for the publication of books of evangelical opinion.

5 The usual form is *ex pede Hercules,* signifying the recognition of Hercules from his feet, or, generally, the whole from a part. Elizabeth's "inversion" is in keeping with her comment on what George had written, which, unfortunately, cannot be restored from the fragments here preserved.

6 Hugh Stuart Boyd, blind poet and classicist, Elizabeth's old friend from Hope End days with whom she kept up an extended correspondence, much of which was published by Kenyon. He had himself published some translations of Greek Christian poets. He died in 1848. Elizabeth's letters to Boyd can be found in Barbara McCarthy: *Elizabeth Barrett to Mr. Boyd,* New Haven, Conn., 1955.

7 Elizabeth's essay *The Greek Christian Poets* was published in four parts in the *Athenaeum* during February and March, 1842.

8 Gregory Nazianzen, St. Gregory of Nazianzus (c. 329-389), one of the fathers of the Eastern Church. His poetry, which, alone of his works, is treated in the essay, seems to have been a pastime of his later life, though he is said to have written 30,000 verses.

9 Synesius of Cyrene (c. 373-c. 414). Elizabeth calls him "the chief, for true and natural gifts, of all our Greek Christian poets."

10 Charles Wentworth Dilke (1789-1864), proprietor and editor of the *Athenaeum.*

letter 16   [50 Wimpole Street]
                                               March 30th, 1842[1]

My ever dearest George,

I marvel at myself for not having answered your letter with the first breath I drew after receiving it — but I knew that you had letters if not mine — & the last paper[2] tired me so utterly & I had such a heap of letters to answer after the accomplishment of the Athenaeum business, & you yourself besides offered me such a pattern of intersectory spaces between writing & writing, — that I being tempted sinned in my silentness. Forgive it — write directly — I beseech you, George, write!

You have heard of the measles & our dear Set together. This morning he has gone to the baths for purification, & therefore you may be well assured there is nothing more to be uncomfortable about. I have not seen him yet — because — I dont know why!! for he has been down stairs to breakfast & dinner & might with equal impunity come into my room. Occy complains of nothing up to this now. I hope he may escape it after all.

My dearest George I w^d give a whole penny piece to amuse you for one half hour — not knowing however where the amusement is to come from. You have heard, I suppose, all the vibratory movements here upon mirrors, & pictures, & a house in Harley Street (contemplated for purchase!!!) & how "the income tax will prevent many persons from keeping their carriages who had thought of doing it –" & of the proposal & election by persons unknown of Papa to the Reform Club – The vibratory movements of the house[3] are not much more than such – For the rest there is dining as usual — & breakfasting with the Fortescues[4]— & drinking tea with Trippy. There is nought to tell you that is either 'curious or improving.'

Uncle James[5] heard you speak — & Bummy gives me the echo of his commendation of the speaking. *I* will hear you speak too, George, some day, — if I ever have life long enough & strong enough to suit the purpose. In the meantime or otherwise, I fancy the speaking to myself — & clap you with the (wings?) hands of my imagination.–

Papa is pleased I think — indeed I am sure — with his election to the Reform Club — inclusive of the privilege of paying forty five guineas entrance fee,— ten annually. He wishes that it had been always so with him since his settlement in London but the rein upon his neck was a most transcendental fear of being blackballed. Therefore he w^{dnt} be proposed, and was startled by the notice of his election one morning at breakfast, from the propriety of the eating of muffins, into an honor uncourted, unsought, unexpected. *I* am quite glad too!

Miss Mitford writes to me every two days just as she used. I am not sure that I c^d do without it now — not without the missing as of a morning star in any case. I love her better & better certainly — & she does not seem to love me much less — which is more wonderful. Her father[6] seems to have lost both health & hope — the natural result of a strong man *in the body only,* losing the strength of the body — , mere animal spirits departing with the animal health, & the soul bending like a reed. Nothing keeps him up, she says, but reading one newspaper after another all through — & she, poor thing, just reversing his condition, she, strengthening her feebler frame by her strong heart, is reading, reading from morning to night — reading her very breath away! It is most lamentable to think of — thinking too what *she* is – Some of her friends cry aloud, Mr. Kenyon tells me, "I wish he was dead!" — but that is a want of faith in the love which is in her! – She w^d droop lower beneath that stroke than beneath any burden –

Mr. Kenyon has multiplied kindnesses lately in coming to see me — three times last week — & promised for today or tomorrow – He brought me the last time my series of papers as marked & remarked upon by Burgess the Grecian[7] & Browning[8] the poet — & Mr. Burgess sent me, *gave* me, a lost scene of the *Bacchae* of Euripides, restored by himself & imitated long ago (according to his view) by my Simeon Metaphrastes. He is going to send me moreover a concatenation of his remarks on the *Christus Patiens* — & rather wished to bring me himself, until that was explained to be out of the question. Mr. Kenyon proposed also to introduce to my sofa-side — Mr. Browning the poet — who was so honor-giving as to wish something of the sort. I was pleased at the thought of his wishing it — for the rest, *no!* – You are aware how I estimate — admire (what is the sufficient word?) that true poet — however he may prophecy darkly. Mr. Kenyon says that he is a little discouraged by his reception with the public — the populace — he sh^d have said. "Poor Browning," said Mr. Kenyon. "And why poor Browning?"—"Because nobody reads him,"– "Rather then, poor readers!" Mr. Carlyle is his friend — a good substitute for a crowd's shouting!

I have been reading Emerson. He does away with individuality & personality in a most extraordinary manner — teaching that what Caesar did, we did — (*we = everyman*) & (which is scarcely so "pretty to observe") what Caesar's bondslave did, we did — & that every man's being is a kind of Portico to the God Over-soul — with Deity for background – This malformation of philosophy does not, you may be sure, admit other than a malformation of theology in this side — there are heresies thick as blackberries. Still the occasional beauty of thought & expression, & the noble exactness of the thinking faculty gave me "wherewithal to glory."

Mr. Kenyon brought me the book of Mr. Crabbe Robinson's lending –'Holla' – quoth Robinson the next morning —"*You* have lent *Emerson* to Miss Barrett!! You have done very wrong indeed." To which Mr. Kenyon responded that Miss Barrett read "an infinite deal of *everything* & had a healthy digestion." "A healthy digestion perhaps — but you sh^d not on that account overtry it to the extent of distension & —"

It was a pretty simile but not over delicate — & so I will stop there. Mr. Kenyon on the other hand without stopping at all set off to me, hoping that he had committed no offensive solecism in lending me a book which he had'nt read — that "the book in question was in fact 'too strong' for Crabbe Robinson himself who leant towards heresy, & might haply prove so to *me!*" Upon which I begged to keep it one day longer than I sh^d have done otherwise. And there is a story & a moral for you, both together — I hope they may be profitable.

Dear Mr. Hunter[9] was here yesterday for an hour or two — & although it is not certain that he is now on his road to Brighton, it is left to us as a probability. He speaks at once sadly & bitterly of his position at Brighton & altogether appeared to be in spirits most oppressed & oppressive. He wants abstracting by the exertion of an outward-working energy. The very owl leaves its ruin sometimes or would hoot out its own knell — & a self-conscious heart is a ruin, if old enough.[10] May[11] is quite well, I am glad to say besides. She evidently does not like my papers — "they are written, not gravely enough, & with an obvious effort which is fatiguing to the reader." Otherwise — I mean by other people, they seem favorably received.

Arabel has just come in, having dined with the Bazulgettes.[12] She was at the Suffolk street exhibition, with Occy, two days ago, & very much pleased. In association with which subject — Mr. Haydon[13] has stabbed his foot with a javelin.

[*On envelope*] My dearest George, what shall you do about Frocester. If Miss Hayward[14] or any other person there continues to have the typhus fever *I entreat you not to go.* That is my entreating and beseeching to you. Otherwise you will do right to refresh yourself with a little ease, to the uttermost. The weather is delightful & ^{ng} fire[15] extinguished. I am very tolerably well — & also (tolerably I hope) —

Your ever & ever attached Ba

[1] Postmark: vs. Mar. 29, 1842. Address: Goodin M. Barrett Esq, Barrister at Law, Oxford Circuit. Pen-lines have been drawn through paragraphs 2, 3, 4, and the two last.

[2] *The Greek Christian Poets.*

[3] Elizabeth had not yet taken up spiritualism.

[4] Unidentified friends.

[5] Uncle James Butler was the younger brother of Sir Thomas and the Rev. Richard Butler, husbands of Elizabeth's maternal aunts. James was a sort of uncle-in-law (Huxley, p. 67n.).

[6] Miss Mitford's father, Dr. George Mitford, was a spendthrift, supported and cared for by his daughter whom he kept poor. He died in 1842.

[7] George Burgess (1786?-1864), classicist and poet of sorts. A "lost scene" from the *Bacchae* appeared in the *Gentleman's Magazine* in 1832. It was written by Burgess on the basis of a parallel in *Christus Patiens. Christus Patiens* has often been printed in the works of Gregory Nazianzen, but is certainly not by him. Elizabeth, in her essay, attributes it to Apolinarius and points out how closely in it he has adapted the phraseology of *Medea.* Simeon Metaphrastes is treated in the fourth part of her essay.

[8] The first reference to Browning in these letters. She had mentioned him often in 1841 to Miss Mitford, but this seems to be the first suggestion of a meeting.

[9] Pen-marks through *Hunter*. The Rev. George Barrett Hunter. See *Letter 3, note 6,* p. 43. Miss Betty Miller (*Browning,* p. 99) says: ". . . this man was in love with Elizabeth Barrett" (see also Appendix III).

[10] This striking phrase was an afterthought inserted with a caret.

[11] Mary Hunter.

[12] Unidentified.

[13] Benjamin Robert Haydon (1786-1846). Elizabeth never met this distinguished and controversial artist, but they did carry on a correspondence "which lasted through several months and was very pleasant while it lasted" (Kenyon, I, p. 278). For her part of this correspondence see *Letters from Elizabeth Barrett to B. R. Haydon,* edited by Martha Hale Shackford, London, 1939.

[14] Unidentified.

[15] *ng.* refers to morning fires.

letter 17   [50 Wimpole Street]
                                                   [September 11, 1842][1]

My ever dearest George,

Having recovered from my surprise at the readiness (only a fortnight after you went away) with which you wrote to me, I proceed first to thank you for the letter, & next to propose "a case" to your consideration.

A asks *B* to go to *H* for him – *B* goes. *A* asks *B* to go to *W* for him – *B* goes. *B* will go to *L* for a word from *A* — but when *A* asks *B* to go simply to *C* for him, *B* wont do it for all the eloquence in the alphabet – Now going to *W* and going to *L* include going to *C* — involve at least the labor of going to *C* — and why is it that *B* sh[d] object to *C?* Pray send me 'an opinion' on my case.

You will apply it in a moment. You have gone for me to twenty shops in a day — & besides other less analogical kindnesses, have written two law letters in defence of my "rights" to

Mr. March² of Hanover street. Why then refuse the three lines
I supplicated for myself, which wᵈ have cost you just one penny
and two minutes of time inclusive of the sealing? Why force me,
through the lack of it, into the dungeons of a chateau d'Espagne,
when I *might* be easy about you? I appeal to the logical part of
your nature, Georgie! – Only one reason occurs to me for the
fortnight's silence — that perhaps you fancy me not in earnest
— that perhaps you think my prayer to write, only a fashion of
words & no sign of real uneasiness to come – Be sure for the
future, it is not so — and do try, were it only for law's sake, to
be more given to reasoning consequently & writing accordingly.
All *my* reasoning, you will discern, hangs upon the fact of your
being one of the very kindest in the world to me, in general.
That is my 'philosophia prima'— and you wont say that the
circumstance shows my gratitude to advantage.

The Hereford newspapers spoke of you, they tell me — for I
did not manage to catch a sight of them — and we may congratulate you through the cloud of your silence upon the five or
six cases — How many at Gloucester & elsewhere? Last week
you were at Frocester (what an entertaining letter I am writing!) & now we are wondering whether you are turning your
face to Colwall. If so, give my kind love to dear Mrs. Martin &
to Mr. Martin³ besides, & tell me how they look.

Well, my dearest George — we are missing you very much
as we always do — and I am subject still to vibratory turnings
towards the door, at the hour for your coming from chambers.
We are preparing too for your return — the whole of the window
in your room having left its charge to a tarpaulin, while itself is
given to renovation. All new wood — & then all new paint, as a
corollary — and you will be twice as comfortable dear George,
in winter-times & draught-times.

Thank you for your *cordial* judgment of my last paper⁴— only
of course, in the greater part of your criticisms, I am right &
you are wrong. Seriously, it pleases me much that what I have
written shᵈ in any way have pleased *you* — & perhaps I think,
myself, that dramatic paper the best of the series. Mr. Dilke
sent me proofs of the *last* a few days since, with a command that

I sh^d let him have them tomorrow or the next day — so that I suppose the intention to be to make room for me in some chasm of British association reports, next Saturday. But oh the length, George — the length — I mean, of my last paper. It is the longest of any ever perpetrated by me — eight columns! And yet I did it all in as little room as I could breathe in — & was short-breathed too.

Mr. Boyd wrote to me to say in the midst of great approbation, that of the whole passage about Shakespeare, nobody can find the least sign of its being written "by a female." It is impossible to help exulting in the compliment.

And my dearest George, three or four days ago, I had a letter from Mr. Kenyon *who writes to me in his flight* — containing several little branches & buds out of Wordsworth's garden, sent to me by Wordsworth himself with kind regards, & affectionate enquiries & all sorts of things. I asked Mr. Kenyon to send me a little slip of green which he was to supplicate *for himself*[5] — but "how c^d you expect" said Mr. Kenyon "that I sh^d bear the ignominy of such fantastic sentimentality?" So he mentioned my name — & certainly I do not care for the ignominy while I get what I wanted. Set has planted them — & prophecies are ominous — but I do trust that the Muses will interpose with all manner of invisible dews & secure the sprouting – Ora pro nobis.

The large table for the drawing room has re-appeared today in a satisfactory state, they say. We are low on news. Mr. Folkes *another friend of Henry's,* dined here last week — son of Sir William Folkes — just called to the bar. He is six feet four & a half — & broad to match — and Papa must have thought him a compendium of all possible dinner-company when expecting to see one or two ordinary persons, he met him at the drawing-room door.

I haven't heard from dear Miss Mitford for several days — she called for "dear Mr. George Barrett" when she wrote last, & was thankful for the second accosting of Mr. March. Dearest Georgie, may God bless you in all things.

[*Across top of first sheet*] I am wonderfully well — & you may think of me as up at twelve oclock every day – The walking too goes on improvingly. & I have stood up *quite alone,* altho with a tendency to falling backwards or forwards, & Crow close by to catch me. But I STOOD. Will you write? Write   You love your own Ba?

¹ Postmark: Sept. 11, 1842. Address: G. G. M. Barrett, Esqr. Colwall, near Ledbury. There are ink scratches drawn through the first four pages of the script to the end of paragraph 5, also through the last paragraph.

² In a letter to Mrs. Acton Tindal, June 1, 1842, Miss Mitford mentions that she reserved the copyright of the letter-press to *Finden's Tableaux,* of which she was the editor. The material was published in monthly parts without her consent. "On stating the story to a most kind friend, at the Chancery bar [probably George], he took the case to another friend, an eminent Queen's counsel, who agreed to do what they could to redress the flagrant wrong; and they have agreed that if my kind contributors will write as follows to Mr. Marsh, 4 Hanover Street, Hanover Square, the presumed clerk of some person, house unknown, to whom Messrs. Finden have assigned the property, it will afford the best chance of inducing such a compromise as may be better for all parties, and less unjust towards myself." (Henry F. Chorley: *Letters of Mary Russell Mitford,* 2nd Series, London, 1872, II, pp. 294-95.) Mrs. Tindal, then Miss Harrison, and Elizabeth Barrett were both contributors. They were to say that they had not parted with the copyright even to Miss Mitford, "informing Marsh that, in default of knowledge of the person calling himself proprietor of this publication, you shall hold him — Marsh — legally responsible, as publisher, for the infringement of your rights" (ibid.).

³ The Martins were an old banking family living at Colwall, Herefordshire, near Hope End. There are many references to them in these letters, and Kenyon includes many letters from Elizabeth to Mrs. Martin.

⁴ *Book of the Poets* by Elizabeth Barrett was published in four papers in the *Athenaeum,* June-August, 1842.

⁵ The letter in which this request was made is published in Kenyon, I, p. 59. It is there dated "1838?", which, in view of the certain date of this letter, must be an error.

letter 18   [50 Wimpole Street]
                                               March 13, 1843
                                               Monday[1]

My ever dearest George   I mean to write to you a little sheet
today notwithstanding all my wrongs suffered in your silence.
I mean to write to suggest what people who have consciences
usually do with their pens when they dont see each others' faces.

The note to Set goes for nothing with me I must explain, because I have never seen it. And yet it is better than nothing,
dear George — my second thoughts confess it is so.

I saw Stormie this morning for the first time these three or
four days, & found him looking both thinner & paler for his cold
& cough which he called influenza & refused to carry within my
reach until it became better. So, that I saw him today, is a proof
to you of his being better, dear fellow, & shall be a pleasure both
to you & me. As to Arabel, she walked to Hampstead today with
Occy & one or two Macintoshes — make your best inferences!

A melancholy story of the poor Theodore Monros[2] has quite
haunted me since I heard it. A week ago a child was born as
you know, and child & mother are both passably well. But Theodore who has struggled on with illness for a long while, was
sent suddenly away three days after the child's birth to Cheltenham, the medical men here having detected disease on the lungs
— and now, since his arrival there, an attack has supervened
which has caused Dr. Baron to pronounce that he has lost one
lung & is in actual extremity. In the meantime poor Emma knows
nothing, fears nothing, beyond a little natural anxiety about a
supposed cold. Before she can stand on her feet with her baby
in her arms, she will probably be a widow — and, so, will
terminate, in a climax of misery, this miserable marriage. You
will feel for her I am sure. *I* did, through & through my dreams
last night.

But I am writing a lively letter, & you wont pay it the compliment I paid yours, of being better than nothing. My chief
gaieties come from Flush — & he is at Hampstead[3]— so I shall
be obliged to talk of Tennyson instead. Think of Mr. Tennyson

saying to Mr. Moxon who said it again to Mr. Kenyon —
"There is only one female poet whom I wish to see — & that is
Miss Barrett." Think of his saying so — *if* he said so! – But he
has not written.

Another prosperity too I must tell you. Mr. Cross[4] the insect
maker wrote to take Mr. Kenyon's opinion (now remember, this
is in strict confidence to *you,* George!) upon publishing a volume
of poems with a pecuniary result. Mr. Kenyon wrote to explain
to him the desperate case of all poetical matters — how money
was to be lost, not won, in the printing of poems — and, afterwards in conversation with Moxon, told him cursorily of the
application & the reply, — *as* conversation simply, & not as feeling his way through Moxon's charities, "which (said Mr. Kenyon
to me) I have vowed never to do for any friend with any bookseller." Moxon assented of course abundantly to the 'sentiment'
of poetry not selling – Whereupon Mr. Kenyon said, "Why, did
you not once refuse a volume of Miss Barrett's poems?" Moxon
answered pathetically in the affirmative — & went on to affirm
that he had never had a night's sound sleep since, for the aching
of his bibliopolic heart, that he was suffering agonies of remorse
— wore sackcloth under his linen & ashes in the crown of his
hat — after which general confession, the particular terms of
which are indifferent, he went on to ask Mr. Kenyon to take a
message from him to me, offering to ruin himself for me, & me
alone, by accepting any MS. I might please to send him. He
said besides, to add to the heroism of the proposal, that the
poets had been the death of him, — that for three years he had
made nothing in the world — and that when the commissioners
came to torture him with the Income tax, he gave in as his
annual proceeds an hundred & fifty pounds, through the mere
shame of giving in nothing. Well — you are surprised at the
message — and so indeed was *I* – But I am not the least more
inclined to print my book, for the pleasure of ruining Mr.
Moxon. Besides the fancy has passed with me — for the season.
Say nothing about it in your letters.

Miss Mitford's subscription[5] amounts, as far as she can guess,
to some thirteen hundred pounds. Queen Adelaide[6] gave twenty

pounds, with the remark that she was one of her favorite writers. Victoria gave twentyfive *as a secret* — so mind you dont tell it! – Yes — and Miss Mitford's letter to Miss Shennet[7] she snatched out of the latter's hands & read from the beginning to the end – Luckily there was nothing in it unfit for Royal eyes –

I had a letter from my tender friend Mr. Cornelius Mathews[8] of New York this morning, who begs me to send directly for ten pounds if I have *resolved* to write for Graham's Miscellany. They seem to be good paymasters in America — and certainly, not many resolutions are worth ten pounds.

Mr. Kenyon went to Brighton on Saturday & returns today– I saw him during the early part of last week.

I am better my dearest George. My heart beats very respectably under the change of wind — and (Oh! what a lovely day this is! –) I am tolerably respectable altogether, I think.

I meant to write one little sheet — & this is my third! Write to *me* George! And be open-hearted as I am to you & tell me how you go on legally — whether the briefs are more frequent & the near prospects brighter. May God bless you better even than I love you –

                                                        Your Ba.

Uncle James has been here this morning, & is likely to come back again & dine.

Not a word from Tennyson. Is that worth hearing twice?

[1] Postmark: O. C. S. Mar. 13, 1843. Address: G. G. M. Barrett, Esq., Mrs. Dillon's, Bye Street, Hereford.

[2] There are in these letters numerous references to these close but unidentified friends, usually on the subject of ill health.

[3] Flush was visiting with Miss Mitford (see Kenyon, I, p. 131).

[4] Andrew Crosse (1784-1855), a student of electric phenomena. In 1837, in the course of experiments on electric crystallization, he observed the appearance of insect life in immediate connection with his voltaic arrangements. These insects were proved to belong to the genus *Acarus* and were observed in metallic solutions supposed to be destructive of organic life. Crosse published his discovery, and, as he says, "met with so much virulence and abuse

. . . in consequence of these experiments that it seems as if it were a crime to have made them. . . . I have never ventured an opinion on the cause of their birth, and for a very good reason: I was inable to form one" (*DNB*). He is mentioned again with the derogatory title in Kenyon, I, p. 72.

⁵ When Miss Mitford's father died, a subscription was taken among her friends and readers for the purpose of paying his debts. It produced a surplus for the daughter, who had been receiving a civil-list pension since 1837.

⁶ Widow of William IV.

⁷ Probably a lady in the Queen's service.

⁸ The letter from Mathews which, though dated January 21, 1843, arrived London, March 13, appears in Appendix V. The previous letter referred to in the text is also printed, as it has much to say about publication in America and refers to Elizabeth's praise of Browning. Cornelius Mathews (1817-89) was a versatile writer of poetry, drama, and sketches. As his letters indicate, he was much interested in the production of an independent American literature and a vigorous advocate of international copyright. In addition to "the unfinished poem 'Wakondah'," he published in 1839 *Behemoth, a Legend of the Mound-Builders,* and in 1841 a political satire entitled *Career of Puffer Hopkins. Graham's Magazine* was established in Philadelphia in 1841 and was for some years very successful. Poe was for a time an associate editor and Longfellow, Lowell, and Hawthorne were contributors.

letter 19   [50 Wimpole Street]
                                                   March 31, 1843¹

My ever dearest Georgie, it is your turn to reproach, you think,— and indeed I am by no means sure that I am not ashamed of myself – The fact is, that I have been busy with all sorts of persecutions on the part of the east wind & Pan,²— the former exhorting me to be still in an apathy, & the latter insisting 'on the part of' Mr. Kenyon, that I should correct all his corrigible faults & improve him by new stanzas & write him out fair. You understand the Pan I mean — not your Pan of the rural districts & flocks & herd, but mine of the lyrical poem which you did so much honor to one evening in this room by your euphonic delivery — the Pan who "is dead." It happened after this fashion. One day Mr. Kenyon asked me to send him one or two of my MS poems — so I sent him 'Pan' & some sonnets &c. He was delighted with Pan & 'jealous' he said of his prosperity — & to prove the jealousy he made various criticisms & threw me into a maze of difficulties from the necessity of altering passages with unique rhymes at the end of them.[3] At last I have come to a prosperous conclusion,— to dear Mr. Kenyon's satisfaction & to my own — & Pan is much the better for his various chastisements, & I am at liberty to write to you without sending to you unaware news from the gods. Mr. Kenyon says "You will never write anything better than *that*." We shall see.

My dearest George you were twice mentioned in the Hereford paper, & that's all we know of your prosperity. You speak of it very vaguely — most briefly of your briefs. We may go to hear of them to the Eleusinian mysteries — & come back again without information.

The Martins are in London — & I saw Mr. Martin on Saturday & Mrs. Martin on Sunday, & have seen neither of them since. You understand about the 'great pump case' at Ledbury,[4] as they w^d say at Little Peddlington — & how it unfortunately happened to come to a compromise before it came into court. Otherwise you w^d have had the business — for Mr. Martin recommended you graciously to the prosecutors.

We are all very well — & I am pretty well. The east wind made me uncomfortable, but I have hopes that it is gone, or about to go. As an amends, Mr. Tennyson *did* write to me – "He had reason to be obliged to the reviewer — but far more was he gratified by the good opinion of a British poetess – " It was a very kind note — & ended "Yours very truly"– Mind, George, if you see Mr. Venables,[5] to make him comprehend that I am sensible of the honor of being written to by Mr. Tennyson, & that I am ready to kiss his shoetyes any day. This is not in joke — it is grave, solemn earnest.

Moreover Mr. Wordsworth had the great kindness to send me a little printed, not published, poem, of some four pages, called 'Grace Darling,'⁶ with his 'very kind regards'– and I should have written to him today if I were not bound irresistably [*sic*] to you. Moreover, Mr. Moxon — calling upon Mr. Kenyon yesterday morning, Mr. Kenyon repeated one of my sonnets to him,— whereupon Mr. Moxon cried out —"I do hope you delivered *that* message to Miss Barrett – I do hope she understands that whenever she is inclined to publish, I shall be most happy to undertake the business."

Nevertheless, George, I *am* — sulky, or something as incapacitating — only dont say so *loud out* again, in your next letter. My inclination for publishing this year has in fact passed away — Next year it may be different –

Poor Southey has passed through many forms of death to his repose⁷ — having a few weeks ago an attack of apoplexy, & dying at last with typhus fever. He recovered no light of intellect — & went without transition from the darkness & blank & silence to which he had been reduced, without transition, without dawn, full into the perpetual glory & resounding Hallelujah – Who can weep for him? Not his tenderest friend. Least of all, his tenderest friend.

Can you believe it possible, that *that* woman, his new-made wife, would only permit his daughter to see him for *one hour during the week!* — She now says bitterly *"I have got my father back again."* Is there not a thrilling truth in those words?

Poor Emma Monro! I suppose you have heard that she is at Charlton with her husband, & that his case is represented to be "perfectly hopeless, altho' he may survive one or two months."

I will write to you soon again my dearest George! – May God bless you. I think of you & long to have you at home — so please the briefs. Miss Mitford has £1500 –⁸

Write to me George.

                                        Your attached Ba –

¹ Postmark: O. C. S. Mar. 31, 1843. Address: G. G. M. Barrett, Esq., Oxford Circuit; redirected, Hereford, Mrs. Dillon, Bye Street; redirected, Gloucester, Oxford Circuit. The envelope contains additional postmarks: Monmouth, Apr. 3; Hereford, Apr. 4,

5; Gloucester, Apr. 5. It appears that the service was better than Elizabeth thought.

[2] *The Dead Pan.*

[3] See Kenyon, I, pp. 127-31. In a letter dated "about March, 1843," Elizabeth answers Mr. Kenyon's criticisms: "I *will not* either alter it or print it." If the date is accurate, the difficulties were rapidly resolved.

[4] This must, it is feared, be filed with the unreported cases of Sherlock Holmes.

[5] George Stovin Venables (1810-88), a frequently anonymous journalist and friend of many writers. *The Princess* is dedicated to him. He was admitted to the Inner Temple in 1836, and, like George, practiced on the Oxford Circuit.

[6] Probably as bad a choice as Wordsworth could have made. The story of men saved from shipwreck by a lighthouse-keeper's daughter inevitably reminded Elizabeth of the death of her brother Edward. See Kenyon, I, p. 142 where she speaks of this poem as causing her "so much pain from the nature of the subject."

[7] Southey died on March 21, 1843. "*That* woman" refers to Caroline Anne Southey, née Bowles, whom the poet married in 1839. His memory was already failing, and his mental state became hopeless soon after the marriage.

[8] From the subscription mentioned above.

letter 20   [50 Wimpole Street]
                                                    April 4, 1843[1]

My dearest George,

I wrote to you some two or three days ago, but as I was judicious enough to direct my letters to you — Barrister at Law, Oxford — without a word of 'circuit'— it is likely to go for nothing in a very literal sense. Therefore, & also because you have had the kindness to write to me again, you shall hear from me tomorrow & enjoy the collateral privilege of being tolerably well scolded for some of the wisdom in your last letter – Really George, it was too bad of you to write as you did. Had you no *instincts?* Could you not understand without an explanation, that it might'nt be agreeable to me to be *exposed* as the patroness of organists to the whole of this house? –[2] Could you not have deferred the delivery of certain messages quoad bishops & deans, until you & I stood face to face, & my door was shut? In your first letter you kept your duty of silence about Moxon very sorrily — by a mysteriousness of expression which excited more questions than the truth without the mystification need have done! – And now — here you are with sin the second. If Stormie had not taken away your letter & lost it by accident, I sh[d] have been perplexed in the extreme. As it is, I am satisfied with sending you this humble remonstrance.

You are far more like a vulture George, than a dove; & all your pretensions to the romantic might be covered by the second volume of Blackstone. To be sure you do write to us every day — there is no denying *that*. Suppose you leave out the last syllables of your applicatory Latin — Nulla dies sine li —. The application is undeniable so.

I have written, but very briefly this time, to Wordsworth, and in the meantime Mr. Kenyon has sent him a sonnet of mine & some of the stanzas of 'Pan' — in hopes that he will ask for the rest. Mr. Kenyon talked also of sending the whole to Mr. Landor — & to Mr. Browning — and to several other of the demigods – I put in a new stanza about Bacchus who had been left out before –

It is whispered that the poor Laureate told Moxon a few years ago, of his intention to leave a posthumous poem which w[d] bring as much money as Lallah Rookh did.[3] Moxon said so the other day to Moore who smiled scornfully[4] at the thought — poets' profits being so merely mystic nowadays.

Dear Miss Mitford's subscription has past the *sixteenth* hundred, — & nothing is yet received from America, upon which I "calculate." She is going almost immediately into Devonshire, via Bath where she will stay a week — & has resolved, I am happy to know, to settle finally in her old residence at Three Mile Cross, the landlady having lowered the rent by five pounds in the year. The Theodore Monros are expected in London this evening, in passing through to Brighton where the medical men have sent him — 'to die easily' I suppose — for there remains no

ground for hope whatever. Mr. Mackintosh is dying. But poor
Emma! I return to *her!*

I would give my kingdom for some news to tell you — but I
say so as vainly as Richard did when he had lost his. Be informed,
however, that Mr. and Mrs. Martin are travelling towards you
while I write, & that if you are inclined to visit them at Colwall,
they will be at home, & probably very glad to see you.- They
had wished to remain here longer — but Mrs. Hanford's[5] ill
health & anxiety to be at home forced them away as her companions — and I c^d not remonstrate or grumble much, — altho'
I was disappointed at this cutting short of pleasure in my own
selfish consciousness. Mrs. Martin said to me (now dont talk
openly of this — pray do be discreet, George, for once in your
life!) that they sh^d probably resolve on spending some months
of every year in London — as Mr. Martin enjoyed exceedingly
being at the root of the world & seeing it grow — & as this great
city presents the only equivalent for continental variety, — and
as, besides, nearly all their friends are here, & very few of them
in Herefordshire. I am afraid also, that poor Mrs. Hanford is
in a precarious state — & that that last tie may break too soon.

You go away from Hereford — *where* do you go? That's what
you dont say. I eagerly came to the conclusion that you w^d be
at home on Wednesday — & you wont I suppose. Papa was
scarcely pleased at their not employing you in the Ledbury
murder case – Have you flourished generally in murders? Are
burglaries *up?* If you go to Gloucester, as certain of us suppose,
you will see Bummy again (dear Bummy!) & be enticed into the
Cheltenham soirees – Henrietta & one or two of them dine at
the Biddulphs[6] today.

My heart has acknowledged a moderator in the late & present
soft winds — that is in the winds of the last three days. I have
no fire — not even a comet — for you see what the learned
called a comet, has turned into a zodiacal light.

May God bless you my dearest dearest George. I love you
more than I could say if I tried.

Ever & ever your attached

Ba –

I had a whole sheet full in a letter from Mr. Haydon last Monday — ditto last Tuesday — & all about the Duke of Wellington & Napoleon! –

[1] Postmark: I, Ap. 5, 1843. Address: G. G. M. Barrett, Esq., Oxford Circuit, Gloucester. In another hand over stamp, "too late."

[2] The reference here is obscure, but the context along with other injunctions to silence and remonstrances to George's lack of tact indicate at once the intimacy of the Barrett household and the secrecy engendered by restraint.

[3] The contract price for *Lalla Rookh* was 3,000 guineas and it was an immediate success. By this time the profits which have accrued to publishers, editors, and scholars from *The Prelude* must bear out Wordsworth's estimate.

[4] Moore's scorn may have resulted from the financial straits in which he had lived since shortly after the publication of his so remunerative poem. It was not a usual reaction for this genial poet.

[5] Mrs. Hanford's health must have improved, because she and her husband witnessed the marriage settlement of the Brownings in Florence on May 21, 1847 (Huxley, p. 31).

[6] Mr. and Mrs. Ormus Biddulph. No more is known of them than that they were also friends and, perhaps, neighbors of the Martins and the Hanfords in Herefordshire (Kenyon, I, pp. 34-35).

letter 21   [50 Wimpole Street]
                                        June 27, 1843[1]

My ever dearest George   You are the most beneficent of barristers, not "ever" indeed, but at times. Arabel came up stairs herself with your note, knowing what gold it was to me – Thank you dearest dearest Georgie –

Inside you will find Mr. Horne's letter to me yesterday, which came embedded in hay which did in its turn embed a posy of hedge-rosebuds, looking as if they considered themselves still on their hedge at dew-time. I have put them near *your* roses,— & I took the opportunity of entreating the last to hold their breath & live until you come back again – You will see from the note that Mr. Horne suspects me before he has evidence against me — & that he is not a little pleased to find his Dragon of the Athenaeum turned into such an innoxious sucking dove by supernatural agency —[2]

Uncle Hedley dined here yesterday — & Mr. Bell of course — & one or two other Mr[s] besides. whom I am persuaded he w[d] have preferred the absence of. Robin[3] comes this morning to say that he (Robin) is likely to go to Dresden with a travelling tutor who is 'going that way,' because somebody has been preaching "nonsense" to his father about the impropriety of his remaining idle until October. The Dresden plan appears to be anything but agreeable to the principal — but he will go I dare say! –

Hear all you can of Tenysoniana [sic], & prepare to be amusing when you come back —. And I suggest that you write down such facts as are the hardest to recollect, in a pocket book,— not to beguile me as you did before. Now I am going down stairs. Perhaps I might have gone out — but the wind which was for half an hour in the west, returned to the east, & disappointed or relieved me . . as you think sounds wisest or most natural. I leave my character to you.[4]

May God bless you my dear dear George!

Your own attached Ba.

[1] Postmark: U, Ju. 27, 1843. Address: G. G. M. Barrett, Esq., Miss Graham-Clarke, Oriel Lodge, 9 Lansdowne Place, Cheltenham. If not there to be forwarded.

[2] Elizabeth reviewed Horne's *Orion* in the *Athenaeum,* June 24, 1843.

[3] Robin Hedley, Elizabeth's cousin.

[4] George clearly persists in suggesting that Elizabeth is malingering.

letter 22   [50 Wimpole Street]
                                                  July 8, 1843[1]

My dearest George: If you did not receive my letter addressed to you at Cheltenham, you must think me unworthy of all yours,— to say nothing of the want of gratitude for all yours, which will be equally obvious to you. So I hope you received it. Afterwards I go on to applaud your resolution of taking the rural holiday while you had the opportunity of it, although my own private disappointment upon this occasion c^d not be repressed by my consciousness of its utter selfishness & foolishness – To see you again on Saturday was a fixed idea with me — & it was hard to put six weeks more between me & you. There! *that* is as much groaning as is necessary — & particularly when I recognize the immorality of any groaning at all – Haec hactenus.

Miss Tennyson[2] is a very radically prosaic sister for the great poet,— does her best to take away the cadence & rhymes of the sentiment of life. What a disgrace to womanhood! The whole is a climax of *badness* — ! to marry at all — bad! — to keep the annuity, having married — worse! to conglomerate & perpetuate the infidelity & indelicacy, by giving the sacred name to the off- spring of the "lubberly lieutenant"—— worst of all!! That last was a desperate grasp at "a sentiment"— & missed.– I am sorry for Tennyson's sake, & also for Mr. Hallam's, who behaved nobly both in conferring the annuity & in suffering her to retain it under those changed & grievous circumstances. There w^d have been a deficiency in tender consideration for his son's memory, had he resumed the money — as if he had given it as a special retainer of her fidelity. No — it was right to let her keep it. How she *could keep* it, is the wonder — & how the lieutenant, lubberly or not, could accept a wife & three hundred a year with an incumbrance of such recollections & a willingness to compound with them by giving the name of her first lover to his own first child, is a wonder scarcely of the second class – "Can such things be"? Not without disgusting us, *I hope.*

Mr. Horne has written to Miss Mitford that as she wants him to stay at Three Mile Cross for several days instead of for one, which was the limit he set in his first imagination on the visit, he must delay the period of it until from the second to the fifth of August, when he w^d go down to her, prepared to work in her garden, drive her out in Tom Thumb's chaise, & play for her, if she likes music, on some kind of portable instrument. She has

acceded to the whole arrangement & is charmed by the manner
of it. Orion is shining expansively, and the poet has offered to let
me see the various critical letters he has received on the subject
of his work. Of course I said 'yes'. It was the very thing you
know, likely to please me. Mr. Kenyon praised the poem warmly
when he came to see me two days ago & found me prostrate on
the floor in Papa's room — he praised it warmly, & accused me
of the paper in the Athenaeum³ as a matter of course. I struggled
vainly for a denial, & he laughed me to scorn. Somebody had
observed to him, he told me, in relation to it, that "Miss Barrett's
power & perversity were equally visible in the paper" — a sort of
topsy-turvy compliment of which I cannot see the precise application. Mr. Kenyon's brother has not arrived yet — but he is
almost ready for him & has received & unpacked & paid the
duty & carriage of from abroad to the amount of one hundred &
seventy pounds, books & packages belonging to the travellers.
This fact delights Mr. Kenyon, because it proves that his brother
is about earnestly to settle for life in Harley Place.⁴

He told me that an American called upon Carlyle the other
day & begged to see him. The philosopher declined the honor
upon the plea of being at dinner. The republican walked away
to the nearest public-house, called for ink & paper, & addressed
to Mr. Carlyle the most insolent letter possible, desiring him to
consider what wᵈ be his own reflections if upon penetrating to
the backermost Back settlements of America & calling upon *him,*
the American, he had received for answer that he (the American) wᵈ not see him, being at dinner!! I dare say the writer
flattered himself that he was writing with a dagger — but the
analogy between Back settlements & the metropolis of England
was scarcely made out clearly. Mr. Kenyon, by the way, has
himself had an irruption of fourteen new Americans in one week;
& finding it what he calls "a social impossibility" to entertain
them he has begged Miss Sedgewick not to send him any more –
Fancy fourteen Americans coming, each with a letter of introduction in his hand & a modest request to be granted an immediate access to all the "most distinguished persons of Great

Britain"! – That was the manner of the irruption — & I dont wonder, nor will *you,* that Mr. Kenyon fled before the face of the irruptors.

Ah — dear Cissy![5] I fear she is very ill — & your account is not reassuring. And yet that she sh^d remain for so long a time in a state of suspension of the more dangerous symptoms, helps one to hope for her — & I hope & fear by turns. Uncle Hedley who was vexed to see you only for half an hour, does not confirm your good report about her spirits. On the contrary he seems to think that she is too languid and oppressed, poor thing, to care to say or do anything — but a good appetite & an inclination as well as power of being wheeled about in her chair, she certainly has — & these things are good as far as they go. The medical man told him, that when he was first called in, he found her in a very *dangerous state,* & that now she was in a *critical state,* however decidedly better. The distinction seems more nice than satisfying. 'It was impossible to say' (he also observed to Uncle Hedley) 'how it w^d end.' I am afraid. Dearest Georgie when you have an opportunity of seeing her again & poor Bummy, you will not neglect it I am sure.

Dear Mrs. Martin tells me that you go to her on Tuesday,— & she speaks murmuringly of your giving them only one week instead of two weeks. I told you so! —

The Hedley boys[6] go to the north on Wednesday; Uncle Hedley probably not until the week after next; Robin, not at all, as he prefers spending his *English time* in London to all your northern ruralities –

I am in a poetical fit just now, which is attended with ominous symptoms of having been beaten all over my body.[7] My ivy is growing triumphantly, & a little sparrow sate & chirped in it "this morning very early." All this being as dull as possible, you will be not sorry to be rid of me. Dearest Georgie, I love & think of you continually –

Ever your attached Ba.

Give my love dutifully at Kinnersley. I hope that Leonard's[8] spirits are putting out new shoots –

[1] Postmark: July 10, 1843. Address: G. G. M. Barrett, Esq., Kinnersley Castle near Hereford.

[2] Emily Tennyson, sister of the poet, who was betrothed to Arthur Hallam at the time of his sudden death in Vienna, 1833. She later became Mrs. Richard Jesse.

[3] Elizabeth reviewed *Orion* in the *Athenaeum,* June 24, 1843, pp. 583-84. She does not consider it a true epic, but still a true poem. "To thoughtful minds the poem will be welcome for its original cast and elevated cheerful teaching; and by poetical minds it will be received cordially as a poet's gift."

[4] John Kenyon's house which he turned over to his brother (see Kenyon, I, p. 166).

[5] Cissy Butler (*Letter 14, note 6,* pp. 74, 76). On May 13, 1843, Elizabeth wrote to Miss Mitford: "Today we received a sad account of our poor cousin, little Cissy Butler, to whom with her sister, my aunt Miss Graham Clarke [Arabella] has been a mother since they lost their own; and who has been pronounced consumptive by the medical men at Cheltenham" (Miller: *E. B. to M. M.,* p. 180).

[6] The Hedley boys were named George, Robin, and John.

[7] Elizabeth frequently complained of physical discomfort attendant upon composition. However, in this case see letter to Mrs. Martin (same date): "I have been writing to George and am the less prone to activities from having caught cold in an inscrutable manner, and being stiff and sore from head to foot and inclined to be a little feverish and irritable of nerves" (Kenyon, I, p. 147). She seemed to identify discomfort with the "poetical fit."

[8] Son of Elizabeth's maternal uncle, John Altham Graham-Clarke of Kinnersley Castle, who was married to the daughter of Leonard Parkinson of the same place. Leonard's spirits were low because in May he had been left, practically at the altar, by his cousin Isabel Butler, daughter of Sir Thomas Butler and Elizabeth's Aunt Frances. By October Isabel relented and the wedding took place November first. Elizabeth's comment was: "Leonard is generous and a lover — and Isabel is, to my mind either capricious and silly, or weak and a victim — for I cannot help fancying that she has been persuaded or scolded into the palinodia." (Miller: *E. B. to M. M.,* p. 203. For an account of her last illness, see *Letter 38,* p. 148, and Huxley, p. 8.)

letter 23   [50 Wimpole Street]
                                        July 13, 1843[1]

My dearest dearest George — Tomorrow is your birthday,[2] &
I consent to run all risks of the post in my run after you, to wish
you all possible human joy, not so much OF it as *on* it. Perhaps
you may have my letter before you leave Colwall, otherwise it
will be sent in your track — & you will become aware, either
way, of my good intentions. May God bless you my dear dear
Georgie! As long as I live I must love you tenderly as one of the
very dearest things left to me on earth to love — and afterwards,
may you have children & grandchildren to call this day their
holiday & love it for your sake. Before we get to the grandchildren
(whom you may think premature) I hope it may be celebrated
by a host of clients in a shower to briefs meeting you at Worcester
tomorrow evening. You w^d rather be the "honored instrument"
of hanging your complement in this generation, than of multi-
plying the generation after next — you translate the "vita brevis"
by life's a brief — and your prospective talk of grey hairs is all
metonymy for a chancellor's wig – Therefore I violently put
down my disposition towards pathos & sentiment, & wont commit to your scorn one section of the thoughts I shall have of you
tomorrow or of the prayers which I shall make for you. Dear
dear Georgie! — There now! – I have done –
    Arabel who wrote to you yesterday probably told you of the
bad account from Cheltenham. I do hope Bummy will think of
writing again in a day or two as I have entreated, & that the
next letter may be modified for the better in its statements – But
it's a bad case I much fear. *That* Dr. Shaw sh^d not have gone
away, leaving his patient with a man who cannot act upon his
own responsibility. The heat, Bummy suggests, may make her
more languid — but oh — I fear, I do fear – I am very anxious
about it.[3]
    Dearest George, you must forgive me, & Miss M Bulman[4]
must forgive me — but notwithstanding your 'noble expectations' from my vanity, I never did think, from the moment of
reading your first letter to the moment of reading your second,

about the autograph. It went out of my head in a flash of darkness. Here however it is enclosed — and inasmuch, George, as I can by no means consent according to your suggestion to enclose it myself to your fair friend, with a — "Miss Barrett does Miss Bulman the honor of presenting her with the treasure of her autograph," I must leave it to you to arrange the transmission – *Deus in machina.*

Mr. Horne has been kind enough to let me see some of the letters which he has received on the subject of Orion — from Browning, Goethe – Lewis[5] (Meaning that Lewis wrote on Goethe), Powell,[6] Tomlins[7] of the Synthetic society,[8] Douglas Jerrold,[9] Leigh Hunt, L[d] Lyndhurst[10] & Reade[11] who w[d] be greater than all the rest. You who know my tendencies toward divination from handwriting & familiar phrases, will understand how well I have been amused. Browning sends a drawing of a spider's web growing from a skull in his writing-room — something like this — [drawing][12]

"A picturesque bit of ghostliness — in this little writing-room of mine are two skulls, each on its bracket by the window. Few brooms trouble walls & ceiling, you may be sure — so here has a huge field-spider woven his platform-web from the underjaw of one of these sculls [sic] to the window-sill."

Mr. Kenyon came to see me yesterday for a moment, & sate for an hour in his wet things — but might well be kept from catching cold by the glow of happiness in which he talked of the return & settlement in England of his brother & new sister. They arrived suddenly on Saturday, & she is *"too well* pleased" he says with everything, too joyous in the first dawn and forms of England, & repeating, when people wish she may be happy here, — "Happy! I could be happy in Africa with HIM". She speaks good English, & combines in good German, simple active household habits with refined & intelligent tastes. *My* Mr. Kenyon is delighted with her, & with the sight of his brother — & I could understand his joy so well that it quite moved me to sadness.

My poetical fit continues, but the muses have done beating me — and my 'aches' have gone away. If the "softness" you suppose in me were rightly supposed, & the soreness & stiffness I moaned about, proceeded from actual blows, I sh^d be nothing more nor less than batter pudding by this time — or peradventure, reduced to the melancholy liquidity of a custard. But as it happened I was *not* soft, Mr. George, & retain my 'face divine' accordingly. I am writing such poems — allegorical — philosophical — poetical — ethical — synthetically arranged! I am in a fit of writing — could write all day & night.— & long to live by myself for three months in a forest of chestnuts & cedars, in an hourly succession of poetical paragraphs & morphine draughts. Not that I do such a thing! —'The flesh is weak,' And —— nota bene, you are not to say a word of morphine when you write next, or something worse may happen than your being sent to school to learn to write!

Papa says that he is going to the city to get your money, & that it shall be sent tomorrow. How is Mr. Venables, & what does he say of Tennyson?

Tell us too about your business, & whether you do by any means flourish in the strict legal sense.

My ivy is fit for Bacchus, or the Isthmian games. I shall live in a bower at last.[13]

That is all I shall say today. Collin Mackintosh is to marry on Tuesday week, & Arabel is bridesmaid – All our loves to you & God's blessing!

Your most attached   Ba

(Did I remember to tell you that you are the kindest of kind people for writing — or rather *in* writing.

[*On envelope*] Kind love to dear Mrs. Martin, & *Mr. Martin* if you please, & have not lost the opportunity of giving it.

I have sent a *sonnet,* as being the shortest. Brevis laboro esse – The rest is inapplicable OF COURSE![14]

---

[1] Postmark: O. Jy 14, 1843. Address: G. Goodin M. Barrett, Esq., Colwall near Ledbury, Herefordshire.

[2] This, as well as others of George's birthday letters, indicates that we must not take too seriously Elizabeth's laxity in matters of time. See Miller: *Browning,* p. 79: "At Hope End . . . she had

greeted every birthday with its mock-heroic ode: now, (1844) she confessed, 'I could not tell you the age of one of my brothers or sisters.'" Of course, she may not have known George's age — her own was for a long time shortened by three years — but she did remember his birthday.

[3] Refers to Cissy's illness.

[4] Not identified further.

[5] George Henry Lewes (1817-78), English critic and biographer of Goethe, who later entered into a liaison with George Eliot.

[6] Thomas Powell (1809-87), poet, critic, biographer, worked with Horne on *A New Spirit of the Age* and collaborated with Leigh Hunt. His rascality seems to have followed Browning most of his life and became the object of some of the poet's bitterest invective (see Hood, *passim*).

[7] Frederick Guest Tomlins (1804-62), journalist, critic, publisher, worked on *Poorman's Guardian* and *Weekly Times,* signing articles, Littlejohn. He founded the Shakespeare Society in 1840.

[8] Perhaps the Shakespeare Society is meant; otherwise unidentified.

[9] Douglas Jerrold (1803-57), long-time contributor to *Punch* and editor of *Lloyd's Weekly Newspaper.*

[10] John Singleton Copley, Lord Lyndhurst (1772-1863), born in Massachusetts and taken to England by his father, the famous painter. He was Lord Chancellor in Sir Robert Peel's cabinet 1841-46.

[11] John Edmund Reade (1805-70), English poet and novelist.

[12] Here appears a drawing which, except for the verbal context, would hardly be intelligible.

[13] It would seem from this and the "chestnuts and cedars" above that Elizabeth's wish to have the ivy completely cover her windows sprang from a mood more romantic than morbid (see Miller: *Browning*, p. 78).

[14] Horace: *Ars Poetica*, 1. 25. Horace's order is: *Brevis esse laboro.* "The rest" may refer to the following six lines which explain how the attempt to avoid faults leads to defect if the poet lacks art. However, the words immediately following: *Obscurus fio,* express the charge most frequently brought by critics against Elizabeth's poetry.

letter 24   [50 Wimpole Street]
                                                  Monday
                                                  August 1, 1843[1]

My dearest George, your letter is thrice welcome though nine times long in coming – The amusing part of the thing was, that you gave yourself northeasterly airs about not hearing from *me* — quite wondered, Bummy said, at my silence! – Indeed! – But I pause in the midst of what I could say on that subject, since you have written at last & set all right by writing! A long letter too.– I thank you again & again for it, my dear kind George — late most lazy! –

Dearest George, your account of poor Sissy is bad indeed, yet scarcely worse than I expected to receive from you, as Bummy had evidently become aware of a sudden change for the worse, by her letters of the time. Since then, they have tried a new medicine — & she seemed to rally a little — but the symptoms, if they relent momentarily, are gravely decided in their character,— and I do fear that, without almost a miracle, it is a lost case. May God support our poor Bummy. That she is prepared, I am glad to ascertain, however mournful the preparation may be. I suggested to her, as she has probably told you, that if she wished for either Henrietta or Arabel, she shᵈ write to Papa, & I cannot doubt that he wᵈ send either of them willingly. By her silence on this point it is evident (just as I supposed it would be) that she prefers being without them. Now, George, mind you do not hazard allusions to this suggestion of mine when you write *towards us*. Every post hour makes me nervous & fearful of the next news from Cheltenham, for I cannot hope upon such material as has reached me lately, & must fear. It was kind & right of you to go so often to Cheltenham when you had it in your power – Bummy thought it very kind, & dear little Sissy had pleasure in seeing & hearing you.

Your Serjeant[2] has stirred me up into a fiery wrath against him. Let the subscription be needed or not, or deserved or not, *his remarks upon it* were in either case most unnecessary & unjustifiable. Is this the "right use" of friendship & long confidence

& association — to be nearest with the spurning heel? I suppose so – This at least is the fine moral apprehension of it attained & displayed by the author of Ion. I am very angry. He has justified now to me with an emphatic justification, all Miss Mitford's misgivings of his truth, &, what I have sometimes called, prejudices in his disfavor.

As to the subscription, *I* wish too that the memory of it was blotted out from the account books of the money-givers! It is true, I admit, that the world is not so delicate & noble, as that we can stoop to pick up its halfcrowns with impunity — and in such a case, it is better to work for halfpence, though we work hard. I wish with all my soul that my poor friend had worked hard for her halfpence — & that Mr. Sergt Talfourd had kept his ten pound notes. As it is, I detest the very thought of the subscription as much as he can do — if not for precisely the same reasons.

From the advertisement I perceive the 'Cry of the Children' in the coming Blackwood,[3] & am quite frightened to look at the print of it, through the excess of my anticipation of printers' faults. So stupid as it was in me, not to beg from the first moment, for a proof sheet! – So hurriedly as the MS. copy was transcribed! So rapidly looked over! I shall be sure to be made misunderstandable in spite of myself.

I have been writing, writing, writing, since you went, & have almost finished a long poem, 'A vision of poets,' in some six hundred lines[4]— besides 'sundries.' Moreover, I have been out in the chair — went out last Saturday, stayed out ten minutes, & except from a falling off in sleep the night after, by no means suffered from it. I shall persevere & go again in a day or two. To go back to the poetry, I mean to ask your advice some day soon, as to whether I had better knock again at Blackwood's door, or turn my face to a distinct & absorbing purpose of separate publication. The new long poem — I do not know what to say about. There may be good points in it,— but I tremble to "give an opinion." Only one thing is quite clear — that it cannot be popular; and *that,* from its allegorical character.

Where do you think Henry is? You may guess three times &

all wrong, & at last I cannot tell you, not knowing myself. The history of it is, that, from birthday luck, he *has money* — of that he paid his fare down to Dover yesterday, & in the evening told Papa that he thought of paying a visit to Mrs. Minto.[5] "To Mrs. Minto! — What nonsense! What can you want to do at Dover?" No answer – Conversation changed, & taken up on both sides cordially. This morning before breakfast, Henry vanishes with his carpet-bag — explaining to nobody where he is going — only leaving behind an undefined impression of his meaning to stay away some five days. At breakfast people waited in awe for the enquiry "Where is Henry"? — but Henry was supposed to be in bed, or not supposed at all, for no enquiry came — and now I should be worse fidgetted than I am if it were not for a secret hope I entertain, of his not going farther than Canterbury, & returning before an actual explosion. He has left behind him the key of his carpet-bag, or rather of Mr. Chapman's carpet-bag — which will not encourage him in an onward course — & then Papa's voice "What nonsense" may follow close on him, in reverberative echoes! Oh, I do wish he were back again – Not that his passion for pilgrimages does not seem to me the most innocent & even deserving of passions! I should like myself to be on the Hartz mountains, looking down on the black-bearded pinewoods even while I write.[6]

You know that Mary Hunter is staying with Trippy? She is spending the day here, & so is Cecilia Bazulgette,[7] & Arabel chaperones them. Emma Monro was in London yesterday & took leave of her previous to her return to Charlton – "In better spirits" Arabel calls her.

Dearest George, you dont say a word of your legal successes –

  'Why so still & mute young lawyer
  'Why so still & mute'?

And this reminds me of your question about Prior's poem of Henry & Emma. I am ruffled to *think* of the thing called "Prior's poem of Henry & Emma" — & if I do not write quite calmly of it you will not wonder. — No, you need not wonder indeed – For, one of the most beautiful & true of our Ballad-poems, is the

antique original of the 'Notte browne Mayde'— its author unknown, & written (I think it is supposed) in the fifteenth or early
in the sixteenth century, probably in Henry the seventh's time,
most touching in its sentiment, most lovely even in the tune of its
versification,— & most vilely prophaned & desecrated by the
modernizing hand (with a ring on it) [3] of Matt Prior in his wig!

Your tenderly attached Ba

[1] Postmark: O. C. S. July 31, 1843. These slight discrepancies
in date are not unusual in Elizabeth's letters. Often she avoids them
by giving only the day of the week. Address: George Goodin
Moulton Barrett, Esq., Oxford Circuit.

[2] Sergeant Talfourd.

[3] Appeared in *Blackwood's*, August, 1843. In a letter to H. S.
Boyd, September 8, 1843, Elizabeth comments on this poem: "It
wants melody. The versification is eccentric to the ear, and the
subject (the factory miseries) is scarcely an agreeable one to the
fancy" (Kenyon, I, p. 153).

[4] The poem was not so nearly finished as she thought. By September 19 she is writing to H. S. Boyd: "I have just finished a
poem of some eight hundred lines, called 'A Vision of Poets',
philosophical, allegorical — anything but popular" (Kenyon, I, p.
157). The completed poem contains something over one thousand
lines.

[5] There is a Mary Minto, scarcely more identifiable than this
Mrs. Minto, who turns up with some definite ideas about men and
marriage and is answered by Mrs. Browning through Henrietta on
January 4, 5, 6, 1848 (Huxley, pp. 70-71). In view of Papa's exclamation, Mary might be the unmarried daughter of Mrs. Minto.
If so, the "explosion" may well have been anticipated since
Elizabeth described her at the time of this letter as thinking "of
nothing but Mesmer" (Miller: *E. B. to M. M.*, p. 191), and a
few months later as having several times thrown Henrietta into
a trance, and as begging for a lock of Elizabeth's hair to send "to a
chief Rabbi of the Magnetisers in Paris" (ibid., pp. 205-206).
Mary fades tantalizingly from the picture in 1853 with: "I wonder
if anybody has heard of Mary Minto — once so called — I forget
her present name at this moment" (Huxley, p. 180). For a further
reference to Mary and her parents, see *Letter 28*, p. 124.

⁶ This intimate picture of the Barrett household emphasizes the well-known subservience of the children to their father. Henry was at the time twenty-five years old. It also indicates that Elizabeth, in spite of her timidity before strangers, thought longingly of the world beyond her room.

⁷ Unidentified. The name also appears in *Letter 16*, p. 83.

⁸ If this refers, as seems likely, to Prior's *Hans Carvel*, it throws some light upon the freedom of reading and talk in the Barrett family.

letter 25   [50 Wimpole Street]
                                              Dec. 21, 1843¹

My dearest George   You speak the words of foolishness — but as that is only to be expected from your sex, I will not wonder or dwell upon it. In the first place however, I have not had "a cold for some weeks." Some weeks ago I had a sore throat; which is no argument for or against my having a cough now,— I appeal to the gentlemen of the jury – In the second place, being considerably better, it has not become necessary for me to call a consultation of physicians – I will put *that* off, so please you, until I am quite well — when, upon the showing of your own peculiar system of logic, the reasons will be stronger for it than even now they are.

And then, again, I am angry with Henrietta, Arabel, & you, for saying, repeating, & believing that I have taken Miss Martineau's dedication to myself,²— and I do beseech you, George, not to say in an aside to Mr. Vennables or any other learned brother, that a sister of yours had any such atrocious vanity. Between you and me — in entire confidence — the idea did occur to me of the dedication being to me — & less because I considered it applicable, than because it breathed the same spirit which moved me to so much gratitude in Miss Martineau's MS letters to me. But a passage in the body of the book, where specific areas in politics are attributed to the "fellow-sufferer," which are neither mine nor cᵈ be imagined into being mine,— quite fixed me in the conviction of my former mistake & of the

book being *by no means dedicated to me.* I am certain it is NOT
— absolutely certain that it is NOT. Mr. Kenyon came a few
days ago & agreed with me that it was NOT — "but" he added,
"*that* only proves how you & I are the most sensible people in
the world — because everybody else in the world has determined
on giving you the honor. Moxon when he sent me the book
observed that *he was not in the secret of the dedication but believed it to be addressed to a relative of mine — Miss Barrett –*
Other persons (whose names he mentioned) 'could not doubt'
about it — it is to Miss Barrett. And Mrs. Reid's[3] last words to
me just now, after a long discussion on the subject were —'*As
sure as I sit on this chair, it is to Miss Barrett.*'" So far, Mr.
Kenyon. So take notice, George, that if for half a moment, my
vanity grew dizzy & doubted, the rest of the world did not
doubt merely, but speak determinately to the same end. You
mistook about Moxon's relative (you see) 'claiming it'— it was
Moxon who attributed it to 'Mr. Kenyon's relative.' Mrs. Reid
too is Miss Martineau's most intimate friend & has lately been
spending some time with her. Only she (Mrs. R) acknowledged
that she was not in the secret — she *knew* nothing — Miss
Martineau had mentioned the book to her & only to her of all
her friends — but there had been no specific mention of the
dedication. Still I do not, any more, from the multiplication of
these opinions, take the dedication to myself — the internal evidence being to me stronger *against,* than the testimony of any
mere opinion can be *for* the attribution. What makes people
think of *me,* is the circumstance of the person, dedicated to,
being an invalid of a longer date than the dedicator, & being
a sort of friend of hers & some hundred miles away from her — &
unseen, unheard, in face & voice. But still, all this may apply to
some other person — and MUST I think — MUST, I am very
sure. As to your fancy about its being applicable & intended to
apply to M or N,— to anybody or everybody, you will not think
so upon consideration — there is too much truth & individuality
& living heart-feeling through every line. It is a beautiful book
— & full of exaltation. The very passing idea of my having any
connection with it, affected me much — almost too much — pass

the honor I would rather, I think, be *unconnected* with it —
there are circumstances which are not painful,— which are even
pleasurable, & yet which oppress like pain.

Well — and Mr. Kenyon asked a good deal about the new
book (my own) & approved of the ultimatum about Moxon's
having it — & felt sure, he said, that I sh^d not lose even money
by it. In the meantime I get on with Eve,[4] nearly to the end, &
past the thousandth line. But if, when it is written out, I dont
like it,—perish Eve — I wont make use of her, & am able to do
without her. Tell me if you see Tennyson by a bird's eye view —
& *that* an owl's. And know, my learned brother, that albeit I
did unaware mention Tennyson next to a poem of mine, I put
my head into the dust on recognition of that associative accident.

The Barretts are still uncertain as to the day of departure, &
it seems more & more doubtful — from the fact of wolves &
bears from Cumberland, howling up & down the streets, whether
he will be able to go openly at all. I hear that he does not dare
to move from his own door today & has sent for Papa to go to
him. Messers Bodington etc. have, on the other hand, rejected
his propositions, & given him "till Saturday" to reconsider theirs.
It is a bad business — and if your advice had been taken at once,
to propitiate the Bodingtons & consent to economize on the continent, the wisdom of the step w^d be as apparent now as is the
foolishness of the step away from it.[5]

I heard from Mr. Hunter this morning — & he is about to
remove with his pupil, on the suggestion of the pupil's father,
into London lodgings, & to endeavour to secure other pupils upon
like terms. The prospect is gloomy — but the only thing to be
seen, &, if one's window looked into a back yard, *that wd^{nt}* be a
good reason for shutting the shutters.

This letter goes to prove to you that I am not in articulo mortis
— & not much besides.

May God bless you my dearest George –

Your attached Ba.

Give my love to all your hostesses at Barton Court –[6] I heard
from Mrs. Martin that she w^d like to see you — the other day —

& if she does see you, give her my love & my promise to write
soon. Of these long silences, assure her that I do not consider
myself guilty.

Write to me, George – A hundred briefs be with you!

¹ Postmark: Dec. 22, 1843. Address: George Goodin Moulton
Barrett, Esq. Barton Court near Ledbury, Herefordshire.

² *Life in a Sick-Room: Essays by an Invalid* by Harriet Martineau, published November, 1843. Miss Martineau's health had
broken down in 1839; she remained an invalid until 1844 when it
was almost miraculously restored apparently through mesmerism.
Since she had been for some years one of Elizabeth's most cherished correspondents and since much of the Dedication seems to
apply directly to Elizabeth's condition, it would appear that in
spite of her disclaimers she was the one addressed. It must, however, be admitted that the details of time and space are contrary
to this assumption. The Dedication, after veiling the name with
quotations from Shakespeare (*Richard II,* II.i.8; also *Julius Caesar,*
III.i.283-85 and *King Lear,* III.vi.109-14) continues, in part, as
follows:

I have felt that if I spoke of these things at all, it must be to some fellow-
sufferer — to someone who had attained these experiences before me or with
me; and, having you for my companion throughout (however unconsciously
to yourself), I have uttered many things that I could hardly otherwise have
spoken: for one may speak far more freely with a friend, though in the
hearing of others, than when singly addressing a number. . . . It matters
little in this view that we have never met. . . . While I was as busy as
anyone on the sunny plain of life, I heard of you laid aside in the shadowy
recess where our sunshine of hope and joy could never penetrate to you.
. . . As the evils of protracted unhealthiness came upon me, one after
another, I knew they had all visited you long ago; and I felt as if they
brought me a greeting from you. . . . Here I end my greeting. . . . I
shall not direct it to your hands, but trust to . . . human sympathy to
bring these words to your eye. If they should have the virtue to summon
thoughts which may, for a single hour, soften your couch, shame and banish
your depression and pain, and set your chamber in holy order and something of cheerful adornment, I may have the honour of being your nurse,
though I am myself laid low,— though hundreds of miles are between us,
and though we may never know another's face or voice. (2nd. ed., Moxon,
1844)

Miss Martineau's knowledge of Elizabeth Barrett was derived
entirely from her letters, and these, even at the lowest point of
their author's health never presented the desolate picture of her

spirits or her life implied in the last sentence of the dedication. The two were, of course, much less than one hundred miles apart.

[3] "There were country houses where I went every week or two, to meet pleasant little dinner parties, and to sleep, for the enjoyment of country air and quiet. Such of these were . . . and my old friend Mrs. Reid's, in Regent Park." (M. W. Chapman, ed.: *Harriet Martineau's Autobiography*, 2 vols., Boston, 1877, I, p. 283.)

[4] In *A Drama of Exile*.

[5] The over-all situation presented in this paragraph is clear enough, but the identity of the main actors remains in doubt. One unit of the large Barrett family, related to, but distinct from, that to which Elizabeth and George belong, has become involved in financial difficulties with creditors from Cumberland, and the head of this unit finds it convenient to remain within the protective shelter of his own house. These "Barretts" are probably the same who are mentioned in a letter to Henrietta of January 7, 1847: "Tell me of the Barretts – I heard that Maria had a sixth child – Poor children, poor mother! He ought to get something to do on the foreign railroads, which should not be difficult" (*Twenty-two Letters*, p. 23). Messrs. Boddington are solicitors who appear again in *Letters 65, 66* (pp. 278-82), relative to the sale of shares in the *David Lyon*.

[6] The home of the Peytons, which adjoined Hope End.

letter 26   [50 Wimpole Street]
                                           Monday
                                           [? about March, 1844][1]

My dearest George   It seems to me that the prudent way is not to write to you at all. It brings one the most letters. Certes I have behaved abominably to you, never written once — & you, returning my evil with good, much more like a Christian than a lawyer, write twice to *me!* Thank you my dearest George. The fact is, I have been so busy day after day, that the sun set before I could turn my head towards you. I have been so busy, so vexed — so anxious — so absorbed in all manner of ways except thinking of you —— There now! That will do! I had better not say any more lest I should spoil it!

To begin my biography since you & I parted, day after day I fell lower & lower in my thoughts of my poem,[2] & my hopes from its publication; and at last I came to the last step & the resolution to publish it by no means. I determined to make one or two extracts from Lucifer's speeches & mix them up into a monodram which I might call "Lucifer," & publish that alone with the rest of my Miscellanies.[3] This was my ultimate resolution — or final despair — call it which you please. Mr. Horne failed me. He was ill with the effects of his first edition, — & preparing for a second. I could not press my poem on him, & have his murder on my soul. So I adopted that final resolution instead. In the midst of it, came Mr. Kenyon, — kindest of friends. I never sh^d have spoken — I was DOWN — ! but *he* spoke, & enquired what I was about with my poem. I said, it was all over — I had given it up — and taking it up in my left hand, added in a voice of elegy that I had done my best for it, but had failed signally & for evermore. He took it from me, & looked at a passage or two by flashes-of-lightning-looks, & was very exclamatory & interrogative — and then, — without my asking him — for indeed I never sh^d have had courage to ask him, — proposed of his own accord, & with a kindness which between this & the day of my death I never shall forget, to read it through himself. "He w^d tell me his precise impression. His prejudice was against poems of religious subjects — but then his prejudice was in favor of *me;* & the two feelings being mutually neutralizing would leave him a just judge."[4]

The next day, he sent the MS back to me — & I was so prepared for a "Dont publish it" that the circumstance of his sending it so soon, only made me a little surer of his negative. On the contrary!! He wrote me a letter, a long letter, to *enjoin* the publication; & assured me both there & since, that I never wrote anything equal to the poem before, as to sustained power. I shall enclose this letter to you I think, — & you can bring it back. Never mind sending it. He has spoken more in detail to me, since, in conversation; and I must tell you that the *zodiac* in particular struck him as being forcible & expressive, & carefully worked out. You saw nothing but a fragment, & were not in a position to judge of the whole, from the partial view you had – Therefore I do not consider this a differing judgement from yours, the least in the world. I hope you will not like the zodiac least, when you see it in its full effects.

And now you see, that Mr. Kenyon's *imprimatur* is, from various & obvious reasons, a stronger thing to me than Mr. Horne's w^d have been — on account of these very oppositions of his against sacred subjects & mystical tendencies. If I had been in good spirits about the poem myself, Mr. Horne's veto to the publication w^d have been more final & satisfactory,— but as I said *veto* to myself, under the actual circumstances, Mr. Kenyon's least '*nay*' w^d have been quite final enough. As it was, I was raised, astonished, electrified — encouraged wonderfully. And it is settled that Moxon will do it; & that it will be done in four or five weeks,[5]— & that I am to come out *in two volumes,*— which will be rather sublime, I think. Moxon advises the two volumes. Also my American friends have commanded an edition, which is to come out in numbers, with *half-profits* for the author — and a separate preface to the American edition being also commanded, I am going to set about it instantly.

This is an example-letter for you — *you* who never say a word about yourself — not one word.!

Crow causes me to break off suddenly though,— when much remains to tell. A long letter for instance from Miss Martineau! May God bless you my dearest George.

Ever your most attached
Ba.

And Mr. Mathews asks about my relationship to Mr. Tennyson!

---

[1] No envelope accompanies this letter. Internal evidence as shown by the notes below locates the letter in the early spring of 1844.

[2] *A Drama of Exile.*

[3] For this decision see letter to John Kenyon (Kenyon, i, p. 168).

This letter, also undated, is placed by the editor "about March 1844."

[4] These comments by Kenyon were reported to Hugh S. Boyd on March 22, 1844 (Kenyon, I, p. 172).

[5] There ensued a long delay in publication. The letter to Boyd referred to above also mentions the "two volumes" and the American "command."

letter 27   [50 Wimpole Street]
                                                Wednesday[1]

My dearest George   You are justified in your complaints, as I am in my silence. Which is not after all a paradox. You had a right to expect to hear — and I have been by turns so busy & tired, that to put off the performance of a duty, seemed to me the most moral, & was the most natural thing in the world.

To reply — The 'Spirit of the Age'[2] speaks very kindly of me — & analyzes me into the extreme of Greek, Latin, Hebrew & Chaldaic. Shows me shut up in a dark room — & frightens people away from me, with very beneficent intentions, — as a sort of dictionary-monster, past bearing. Then, at the conclusion, my poetry is spoken of, with excellent kindness still, but by no means critically or with any philosophy. The article suggests the idea of the writer being in an agony to build up (with cards) a monument to the memory of a personal friend — & I have been expecting, — in a little counter-agony of my own, — the good-natured critics to insinuate so. I am grateful to Mr. Horne, & thoroughly aware of the full kindness of his intentions — but (in the strictest confidence between you & me) I sh^d have much preferred his giving a calm & honest estimate of my poetry, in some half page of simple writing, with whatever severity of accompanying stricture. It w^d have been more really flattering to me as a writer —. You know I am the last to pique myself upon dictionary-pedantries — & have a sort of scorn & disparaging judgement of such acquirements, — which are possible to the lowest intellects (with a little patience & memory) and often injurious to the highest. Also, it strikes me that whether I live in the dark or not, or write "charming notes" or not, is of small importance to the public. Therefore, you see, I am both satisfied & discontented with the notice. What is amusing, is the courtesy of the Athenaeum, who starts up, crying — that this, & this, & this, is not said of Miss Barrett,[3]— & puts a note of depreciative astonishment at the 'grand-junction' with Mrs. Norton[4]— tearing the book, otherwise, all to rags. Well — you will see what you will think! Mr. Horne's *kindness* is the only certain & most prominent thing to me in the whole.

The Weekly Chronicle, in a very clever article,— written, he c^{d} not tell by whom,— finds fault with the want of unity & consistent philosophy, (quite a true objection — only the fault of the publishers!) & observes that, in the utilitarian & transcendental parties, now striving, Hariet [*sic*] Martineau & Elizabeth Barrett are forward combatants — referring also to "the powerful poem of the factory children in Blackwood."[5] The Morning Chronicle is very severe against the book,— from personal reasons, I suspect,— but nothing unkind has been said or implied against me. Generally, the criticisms are very favorable.

Do you hear in Herefordshire whether Mrs. Archer Clive[6] has published lately a prose romance in one volume, called *Agathonia?*[7] I have just received a copy "from the author," & the book being anonymous, I guess at the origin, simply from the unusual circumstance of the title page motto, quoted from *V,* being advertised with the title. It makes me think that V is in the authorship of the whole.

And then, I have had two proofs — which look tolerably well. And Mr. Merivale has sent me his translations of Schiller's lyrics[8] — and Mr. Lowell of America (Boston) the new edition of his poems.[9] You who expect to hear everything & never tell anything, must be satisfied now.

Bells and Mintos are coming here today, either to dinner or to tea — and Henrietta & Henry dined with the Chapmans yesterday — and I was in Papa's room for several hours yesterday — and I have my window open today — and Mrs. Smith (Dr. Adam Clarke's daughter) has desired Mr. Boyd to tell me that if I w^{d} write to her occasionally *to describe the course of my "physical improvement & brilliant literary successes,"* she w[d] have no objection in the world to answer my letters; & wd probably be "improved in her tastes" by the correspondence, as well as receiving a great deal of personal satisfaction. This last is the most curious piece of news I can find for you. Without assuming too much, it w[d] not be difficult to 'improve the taste' of the author of the proposition contained in it — do you think so? –

One thing more there is — but I have not courage or heart to write about the approaching parting with my dear Crow — so inexpressibly painful to me. It is well for me that I have more to do than is comfortable just now — for the sake of *excluding* as far as may be, thoughts more painful than fatigue. How I shall ever bear to have a stranger — with my morbid feelings about strangers — I cannot guess.[10] A necessity however is a necessity. Only it is not a necessity to talk of it. You will be sorry for me, I am sure.

May God bless you, my dear dear George. Give my love to Aunt Clarke & every one at Kinnersly.   Ever your most attached Ba

[At top of first sheet] Occy likes Mr. Barry & architecture *so far.*

[1] No envelope preserved. Internal evidence places this letter in the spring of 1844.

[2] *A New Spirit of the Age* by R. H. Horne, 1844. Elizabeth had collaborated by correspondence in the preparation of this book. In her letters to Robert Browning she several times expresses the same disdain of "dictionary pedantries."

[3] The *Athenaeum,* to which Elizabeth had been a frequent contributor, said: "No writer on Miss Barrett's genius should have failed to award high honor to the 'Romaunt of Margaret' or done such scanty justice to the rare lyrical sweetness of some of her measures, as 'The Deserted Garden'. Her deep and quaint learning, her tendency and taste for mystical contemplation, are obvious beyond mistake; but of her merits as an artist, the public has not yet a sufficient relish" (March 30, 1844, pp. 291-92).

[4] The article quoted above speaks of the chapter "strangely uniting Mrs. Norton and Miss Barrett." Caroline Elizabeth Sarah Sheridan (1808-77) was the granddaughter of Richard Brinsley

Sheridan. In 1827 she married the Hon. George Chapple Norton, brother of Fletcher Norton, 3rd Duke of Grantley. The marriage was unhappy, and the trial incident to their separation, June 23, 1836, was a sensation. Her poems, *A Voice from the Factories* (1836) and *The Child of the Islands* (1845), express her intense interest in improving social conditions. She also wrote several novels. In the last year of her life she married Sir W. Stirling-Maxwell, historian and writer on art.

⁵ *The Cry of the Children* appeared in *Blackwood's*, August, 1843, vol. 54, pp. 260-62.

⁶ Mrs. Archer Clive (1801-73) published *IX Poems by V*, 1840, second edition with nine additional poems, 1841. Her best known novel was *Paul Ferroll*, 1855. She did not write the novel in question.

⁷ *Agathonia, a romance* by Mrs. Catherine G. Gore, London, 1844.

⁸ John Herman Merivale (1779-1844), author of *The Minor Poems of Schiller of the Second and Third Periods*, London, 1844. His translations had appeared in *The New Monthly Magazine* in 1840.

⁹ *Poems*, Cambridge, 1844.

¹⁰ Her distress was probably due, her affection for Crow apart, to the difficulty of achieving with a stranger the intimacy which her health required, particularly in the matter of her morphine doses. A letter to John Kenyon dated March 21, 1844, mentions the imminence of Crow's departure and adds: "the idea of a stranger is scarcely tolerable to me under my actual circumstances" (Kenyon, I, p. 170). The date of this letter to George must be somewhere near that of the Kenyon letter.

letter 28   [50 Wimpole Street]
                                                  August 4, 1844¹

My ever dearest George,   What evil are you thinking of me? for evil it must be! Come, let us shake hands & be friends – And that I may not appear over-arrogant in expecting such a reconciliation after such an offence on my side, let me explain how it happened that my silence has grown to the said height or depth.

I fancied I had done with my poems,— that I had sent away

my last proof, & might like a gentlewoman of England sit down at ease, & economize my new idleness. On a sudden came a ukase from Mr. Moxon, who having weighed the two volumes & found the second heavier by seventy pages than the first, insisted that it sh^d be denuded of half of the seventy, & the other invested with them. Think of such a thing! That my 'Dead Pan,' whom as a flourish of trumpets & to please Mr. Kenyon, I had kept for *the last,* sh^d be rent away by violent hands & thrown back down the staircase. Papa said, 'If I were you, I never w^d consent to such a thing.' And what was I to do? I wrote & proposed to transplant one or two of the shorter poems, instead; & to see in the meantime if I c^d finish another poem I had in hand. Mr. Moxon was particularly anxious (said the reply!) to bring the work out instantly,— in fact, w^d not wait a moment. So I took up the ballad-poem[2] you know I had begun, & of which half was done,— & wrote the other half,— that is, wrote *nineteen of the printed pages, on one day* — feeling that if I c^d finish it then, well — & that if not, I must give it up! I finished it on one day, feeling just as if I were in a dream from morning to night,— transcribed the whole, the day after, & satisfied everybody,— the first volume having now a continuation of forty pages in the shape of a ballad-poem called "Lady Geraldine's Courtship, a Romance of the Age." But all this, & various troubles it brought with it, & the dreadful haste I have been in to get the whole of the remaining proofs, Geraldine & all, ready for the American mail yesterday, present my excuse to you for a silence inexcusable under less stringent circumstances. Do I stand excused? Answer benignantly.

I[3] had great interest in writing it. Yesterday I received from Mr. Langley,[4] my New York publisher, the Democratic Review with half the Drama of Exile in it, & a few words of introduction mentioning the opinion "by a competent judge" that "it is the finest poem since Manfred"— also an extract of all Mr. Horne says of the author in the "New Spirits of the Age." In another part of the Review however is a critical essay on the said 'New Spirits" very depreciatory of it, (Mr. H'S book) — & letting down English poetry of the present day humiliatingly low – The writer being of opinion that in a strict high [sense?][5] there is no true poet in England alive *except Wordsworth* — although "Leigh Hunt, Barry Cornwall, Tennyson & Elizabeth Barrett were so, in a lower sense" — While in a "still lower deep came Elliot the corn law rhymer,[6] Milnes, & Mrs. Norton" — Of course, I individually feel myself *praised* by a depreciation which leaves my name in the same clause with Tennyson's — but still, on the other hand, the praise of a judgement which c^d deny true poetical genius in the highest & strictest sense, to Tennyson & Leigh Hunt, is scarcely worth the having.

All this is egotistical to the quintessence of *ego* — only I know that *tu* will like to hear it.

Poor dearest Henrietta's mumps are almost gone, but she wont come near me for fear of dispensing some "sweet influences" from them. It is great nonsense — & moreover I say that it shows a wonderful deficiency, in her, of general benevolence in contrast to a redundancy of family love; inasmuch as she goes to church with the said mumps, & visits about with them. Now if there is really a risk of *dispensing mumps* I hold that she sh^d shut herself up & see nobody — if there is *not,* she sh^d see *me*! Two horns of a dilemma as equal, as my two volumes by Mr. Moxon's metronomy — or more equal, certes. I shall be delighted to see her — and to see *you* also, my very dearest Georgie. *Do* write in the meantime. I thank you much for the letter you have already written to me, — but was sorry to find from it that Mr. Martin's cough had not entirely left him. I wonder they do not travel — and I do NOT wonder that dear Mrs. Martin sh^d be very uneasy at the least & slightest sign common to a disorder which has been so fatal in his family. If I were she, I sh^d certainly persuade him to travel. The change, & the rescue from the vicissitudes of our climate, w^d be two points gained — and then, the safe passage through the shooting season without its pains & penalties of walking through wet grass & staying out (in the nympholepsy of hare or pheasant) under the dew of the evening is a third! Dieppe did him no good, but harm! And why? –

Because he was up to his knees fishing, a great part of the time. I w^d go to Rome for the winter, if I were she. Why not suggest it to her? I am afraid of writing on the subject, or I would, but she has warned me not to write much or gravely about Mr. Martin's health, because it makes him nervous & uncomfortable. But when you see her alone, tell her what I say. Now, mind you do – It w^d do him good in every way, nerves, spirits & all — & if there is any susceptibility on the chest an English winter is a hazardous future for it, unless the subject turns into a patient in the most literal meaning, & shuts himself up between four walls. Also it is easier to get into such a prison than to get out of it — as in my own case.

Tell me if you see Mr. Venables, how Mr. Tennyson is — now do tell me everything about him. You know what my interest is. Tell me also [?]⁷ if you want your five pound note.

Dear Occy has a very bad cold — so bad that he has not been to Mr. Barry's⁸ these two days — but he is something better, I understand, this morning. We are all very well otherwise — *I,* not tired to death. Mr. Minto has sailed for the West Indies,— & Mary & her mother for Germany. Other news I have none. Oh, did you know that I had a letter from Miss Martineau? Was that last letter *before* or *after* you went away? I cant remember. She wrote to ask me to send her my book by somebody, last Saturday week.

Arabel is *not* going to stay with Emma Monro — which I think very stupid — as she wished it much, & Papa told her she might do as she liked — *only he did not look so.* I certainly think she might have gone, & without displeasing him. She has nearly finished her wedding gift for Emily Mackintosh, all in a broidery of fruit & flowers & watered white silk. A writing case fit for Titania to write love-letters withal,— but rather too large. Henrietta is embroidering a basket quite as pretty in its way, for Louisa Tulk⁹ & is thinking — intending seriously, I believe — to carry it herself on the wedding day to Tothridge Park. Somebody else (Daisy¹⁰ I fancy) is invited instead of *you.*

Well! — there is no more to say! May God bless you my dearest dearest George! I love you dearly & always. We have seen your name in the papers — & look for it. Tell me how you *do,* in matter of business — & all the rest.

With everybody's love I am

Your most attached

Ba.

[1] Postmark: August 6, 1844. Address: G. G. M. Barrett, Esq. Oxford Circuit.

[2] *Lady Geraldine's Courtship,* which contains the well-known reference to Browning.

[3] This paragraph is written on a single sheet with a corner cut out.

[4] Henry G. Langley published *The Democratic Review* with his brother until January 1, 1844, at which time he bought out his brother's interest. It was published in New York as *The Democratic Review and United States Magazine.* The review appeared July, 1844, vol. 15 N.S., pp. 72-73.

[5] The word has been cut out, but was probably *sense.*

[6] Ebenezer Elliott (1781-1849). In *Corn-Law Rhymes,* 1831, he bitterly assailed the "bread-tax" to which he attributed his own financial losses and all national misfortunes.

[7] A mark resembling y+ appears here, meaning unknown.

[8] Where Occy was pursuing the study of architecture.

[9] Probably younger sister of Sophia Tulk, who later married Count Cottrell. "A whole colony of married Tulks, including the father" had settled in Florence by 1848 (McAleer, p. 202).

[10] "Daisy" was the family nickname for Alfred Barrett (1820-1904). He was the only one of Elizabeth's brothers who married before their father's death, and he suffered the same punishment as the girls. For an earlier association of Daisy with Lady Bolingbroke, see *Letter 14,* p. 74.

letter 29   [50 Wimpole Street]
Saturday
[August 10, 1844][1]

My ever dearest George

I have, two hours ago, sent you off my book, committing it to your tender mercies as barrister at law & critic by grace. Perhaps

I sh^d not be writing to you immediately after,— but Papa came in & said "I wish you had told George that I received his letter," so I took it into my head to write. By the way, George, I wish you w^d not write to Papa such nonsense about "estates" &c &c. He brought me your letter yesterday,— & I in vexation of soul cried out "What *is* this about? I dont understand" – To which he replied —"Oh — only some nonsense — (I think he said nonsense, George — I think he did – It was a synonyme [*sic*] in any case!) "about some immense estate." And his manner of making the remark, set me at ease.[2] Take no notice of this when you write here, to me or anyone else,— mind – Not a word in remark upon either my report or my observations on it – *Not a word — mind –*

I sent the books down stairs to Papa, with the page of the dedication[3] cut, & when he came up stairs at one oclock, he seemed pleased & touched by it — only the satisfaction to myself in expressing my natural feeling, is deeper (must be) certainly, than any which his tenderness c^d receive. There is an advertisement of the book in the Athenaeum today — as conspicuous as possible.

I wrote to Mr. Moxon to desire him to accept whatever copies he cared to have, & he wrote to tell me that he w^d take one for himself, a second for Miss Martineau, & a third for Tennyson "who is now in town." To which I retorted that he must change the destination from Miss Martineau, as she had promised to accept one from *me* — but that with regard to Tennyson, I had so much wished to give him one, yet so much feared to seem forward past bearing, that I was delighted to accede to a mediate arrangement. Tennyson, they say, professed to be quite well on his arrival in London, cured by hydropathy, but has since relapsed, & been very unwell indeed. If you hear about him, tell me.[4]

Today I had a letter from Miss Martineau — kind but not long. Mrs. Reid who comes from her, assures Mr. Kenyon that she is in no respect worse, & gives no sign of increase of disease, or loss of strength.

Miss Mitford does not go to France after all. In fact she says that she will put it off to next year, & take me with her.

Mr. Kenyon is to send a copy (*will*, he swears to me in the face of remonstrance) to Mr. Eagles,[5]— & he has in the meantime been praising the 'Drama of Exile' most extravagantly. *I* say, "most extravagantly"— It grows upon him, he asserts — and he re-iterates, that although he had not thought weakly of me, he had believed me incapable of so much "sustained power."

If I repeat such things to you I hope you comprehend that I do it less for vanity than to keep up my hopes in the book. I am very nervous & restless indeed — & feel inclined to cry in a parenthesis, every now & then.

Are you " 'ware", as we say in the ballads, that Johnnie Hedley has been here & is gone? George is kept at Paris, by a happy stroke of the measles. I heard from Jane[6] from Ems today,— & she leaves a possibility open, of her coming to England before she returns to France.

In haste — one word running over another —

Your own affectionate
Ba –

---

[1] Postmark: August 12, 1844. Address: G. G. M. Barrett, Esq., Oxford Circuit, Monmouth (this last in another hand). August 10, 1844, fell on Saturday.

[2] It seems that the fear of being removed from London was always close to the surface.

[3] The *Poems* (1844) were dedicated TO MY FATHER, and the first paragraph especially of the Dedication is eloquent of the emotional tensions which bound father and daughter:

When your eyes fall upon this page of dedication, and you start to see to whom it is inscribed, your first thought will be of the time far off when I was a child and wrote verses, and when I dedicated them to you who were my public and my critic. Of all that such recollection implies of saddest and sweetest to both of us, it would become neither of us to speak before the world; nor would it be possible for us to speak of it to one another, with voices that did not falter.

[4] See Hallam Tennyson: *Alfred, Lord Tennyson: A Memoir,* 2 vols., New York, 1897, I, p. 221.

[5] Rev. John Eagles (1784-1855), a frequent contributor to *Blackwood's,* also an artist. A volume of these contributions, *The*

Sketcher, was published in 1856. He was curate at Kinnersley in the 1830's to 1841.

⁶ Aunt Jane Hedley, mother of the Hedley boys mentioned.

letter 30   [50 Wimpole Street]¹

Dearest George,

The publication does not take place until Tuesday — so make the most of your privilege in having the books a few days before.

Be very gently critical, I beseech you! –

Your attached

Ba –

Saturday

¹ An afterthought to the preceding written the same day. No envelope. (See following letter, *note 1.*)

letter 31   [50 Wimpole Street]
                                                     Monday [?]¹

My dearest George

You must write a line to your Hereford lodgings where my books, (by a mistake which I give you leave to call foolish as it is not mine,) are lying in the desert air.

Ever your affectionate

Ba.

I have sent no copies to anybody in Herefordshire — for fear of giving offence by not giving to all — & therefore perhaps you had better not talk among our friends if you see them, of my sending the book to *you.* If Mrs. Martin were here, I sh⁴ like to give her one, — but think what scrapes I sh⁴ get into by sending to her only, — or to her & the Commelines² & Lady Margaret Cocks³ only, as I thought once! And I shall have to give some thirty copies as it is. But advise me.

Perhaps Mrs. Martin may be coming soon to London, — that

is, if she acts on the continental plan,— & then she can have a copy from me, should she care for it.

---

[1] Postmark: Gloucester Station, August 11, 1844. Address: George G. Moulton Barrett, Esq., Oxford Circuit. (Since August 11 fell on Sunday, this may be the envelope to the preceding note.)

[2] The Commelines were friends of the Barretts at Hope End. Kenyon includes several letters to Miss Commeline, the last in the spring of 1845 (Kenyon, I, p. 240). From these it appears that, though the friendship was vivid, the correspondence was desultory on both sides.

[3] Lady Margaret Cocks was another friend from the vicinity of Hope End. Along with a Lady Caroline Cocks she is mentioned as being in Florence in October, 1847 (Huxley, p. 57). A vivid description of Lady Margaret occurs in *Letters of R. B. and E. B. B.*, II, pp. 126-27, which, after many kind remarks, concludes: "she does not love me after all, nor guess at my heart, and *I* do not love her, I feel. Woe to us! for there are good and unlovable people in the world, and we cannot help it for our lives" (cf. Browning's *Time's Revenges*).

letter 32   [50 Wimpole Street]
                                                Saturday
                                                March 9, 1845[1]

My dearest Georgie,

Thanks upon thanks to you for letting me know so soon of your vision in the fender of Alfred Tennyson. I envied you notwithstanding the tobacco smoke. Such things may be, overcoming as with a summer-cloud,— while the *recollection* would remain as an essential good — and that, I envy you. Still, you might have been more particular in your chronicle & told me a little of what he said. That he sh^d say nothing of *me*, I do assure you neither surprised nor vexed me — though if he *had* said anything of me, I sh^d have been surprised and pleased. It was more natural that he sh^d say nothing of me — and I have sense enough to think so. But was a word said of poetry at all? of his own? Do answer this question.

I waive the dirty shirt. It was by way of lyrical transition into the society of lawyers with dirty consciences. Dont imagine that in *my* idea of him, he wears a dirty shirt. It is just the contrary.

Henrietta & three of our males dined with the Peytons yesterday, & found them beginning a sigh for Barton Court — & this really does *not* appear to me according to the instinct of an intelligent animal. At their ages too,— with life just beginning — & shutting down all the doors & windows to the entrance of new ideas & images!! It may be innocence — but it is not wisdom.[2] For the rest, they talk of returning this day week, next Saturday.

Have Mr. and Mrs. Martin gone? Probably they have — for I have heard nothing of them since you went.

Dearest George, I think of you much, & wish earnestly that you were back again with a heavy purse, & a sprig of laurel jutting past the left ear. If you are magnanimous you will write to me again soon. Mr. Kenyon wrote to Mr. Browning to enquire respecting the authorship of the review in the Metropolitan,[3] & received of course an assurance that it was not by his hand. It is wonderful to me how anybody could fancy such a thing in the course of a flash of lightning. And then Mrs. Coleridge (Sara, the poet's daughter) has written to Mr. Kenyon a letter he sent me — & among other things in it, she says that people who do not like *Barrettisms,* prefer the dialogue part between Adam & Eve in the Drama of Exile, and the *sonnets,* to anything else in my two volumes. Which I can believe,— & partially see the reasons of. Not that they are the best, because the preferred.

You shall hear from me soon again. It is much warmer today — much.

May God bless you, dearest George!

Your ever attached
Ba –

Papa's love with the enclosures – After you have acknowledged (n.b) these halves, you are to have the others. So be a good boy & write.

¹ Postmark: March 8, 1845. Address: George Goodin Moulton-Barrett, Esq., Oxford Circuit. March 9, 1845, fell on Sunday. Elizabeth knew she was writing on Saturday, but mistook the date. She was habitually inaccurate in such matters.

² Such a comment as this indicates more restiveness than resignation in her own seclusion. See Miller: *Browning,* p. 78, for an opposing interpretation.

³ The review in *The Metropolitan* for March, 1845, was extremely laudatory. Its authorship is the subject of several letters in Kenyon (ɪ, pp. 243, 245, 248). The last states that it "was written, I hear, by Mr. Charles Grant, a voluminous writer, but no poet."

letter 33

[50 Wimpole Street]
[Wednesday]
March 13, 1845¹

My dearest Georgie

I send you the 'restored fragments' of the poetry of the world,² & hope you may be able to translate them into all manner of pleasure & prosperity. In the meantime you grow misanthropical, — more than becomes a chancellor *picturus in rus,* — & do moralize a most superfluous quantity of melancholy, methinks, on the 'moral disabilities' of the legal brotherhood. Why, what is the matter, George? Is it possible that the abuse of a friend is immelodious to your ear? already? –

After all, when we come to analyze matters & motives, there is a very near turn, that, round the corner, of "generous emulation", — and the scraping against 'malice, envy & all uncharitableness' is the probable accident. Ambition is a selfish passion – "*Alone, I did it.*" The essence of the *ego,* makes the spirit of it. And yet — I have always believed & shall believe, that true greatness rather climbs than jostles, — & that the greatest do not soil their coats & shoes in climbing. This, certainly in literature – In law, you must allow me to say that there is more room for dirt – It is more practical business — and the necessary condition of the successful candidate is not pure genius, but power of a more complex character – Hinc illae iræ –

Here is a letter from Brighton, which belongs to you according to its address. Today there has been a falling down of the wall of the drawingroom, & the revelation of a comfortable hole which permitted the approximation of deal boards & flue soot, & leaves all the world marvelling how it happens that we are not in cinders as a matter of course – The 'smoke' is more perfectly accountable.

Which reminds me of Alfred Tennyson & that I agree to defer the disclosure, till it may be made with shut doors. Why you wish to undeify him to my imagination! That is wrong. Browning sent me another letter this morning.[3]

On Thursday Trippy is 'at home' to a large concourse of fashionable company, inclusive of Peytons Nugents[4] Barretts & the like,— & in order to be so, goes home to make lollepops [sic] on Wednesday evening — today. You are aware that she is in your *habitat,* 'at these presents'. The Martins returned to Colwall yesterday,— Mrs. M – not at all well, from a cold. The Peytons have not decided, it appears, on leaving London on Saturday.

Shall you go to see Emma Munro again? Why not? She will be vexed to lose your visit.

All this, in great haste. It is my third letter — & Mr. Kenyon is coming, & I must keep a little breath besides what is spent. Did Venables write the first Westminster article?[5] or who?

May God bless you ever & ever –

Your most attached

Ba –

[1] No envelope has been preserved for this letter. The date is slightly confused. March 13, 1845, fell on Thursday, but in the body of the letter Elizabeth writes "Wednesday evening — today."

[2] The reference here is obscure. It may be to the same poems which Elizabeth sent to John Kenyon with a letter dated "Saturday" and placed by the editor "beginning of April 1845." They included her verse adaptations of Apuleius (Kenyon, I, p. 249).

[3] The correspondence with Browning began January 10, 1845.

His sixth letter is dated "Tuesday Morning" and postmarked, March 12, 1845 (*Letters of R. B. and E. B. B.,* I, p. 37).

⁴ Unidentified, except by associations.

⁵ The meaning here is unclear. If Elizabeth is referring to the first article in the current issue of the *Westminster Review,* March, 1845, it is clearly initialed "J. G. P." and is on the French Economists. The previous issue for December, 1844, contained a fairly laudatory review of *Poems,* initialed "S. F. A." Perhaps this question is part of a comment occurring in George's letter to her, lost to us, of course.

letter 34   [50 Wimpole Street]
                                                [July 14, 1845]¹

Ever dearest George

Two letters in debt to you, the first one shᵈ certainly blush not to feel more golden corn in its pocket for the purposes of re-payment – Still perhaps it will be able to "echo you, as if it had a devil" (instead of a ducat) "in its thought,"² & send you back a little reverberation of mourning upon the dulness of times & persons, . . . I myself being at the dullest "at this writing". Not that I have to tell you of swearing against Flush as 'a pend-ant' to your canine commination service. Flush being more likely to turn the tables & swear against *me* who have turned the chairs,— or rather replaced my sofa by a loan-chair of dear kind Mr. Kenyon's . . to the obvious inconvenience & dejection of my poor companion for whom there's no room close to me –³ Well — pass to things more material — I congratulate ourselves in you upon your success at Usk. May it be the first of a series of prosperities! — which is an appropriate wish for the day — in-asmuch as my dear dearest Georgie, my letter will reach you on your birthday,— & affectionate thoughts, past expression in this place, will be crowding round you while you read it. May God bless you — in things of more consequence than even worldly prosperities, & make you happy in the fullest meaning of happi-ness. How dearly I love *you,* there is no need of saying.

Trippy has been beguiled by a Round Robin (commonly so

spelt, I hope) into the heirship of your bedroom — she *stayed* on Monday night — & is staying on. The next great news — going backwards — is the "great fact" of my having gone out in a brougham last Monday, & of my getting as far as Devonshire gate.[4] I tried hard to reach Mr. Kenyon's — but, that first time, the ambition was beyond my strength. – What I *may* do, is a different thing. If the rain keeps off I repeat my daring today — but the carriage shook beyond any imagination of my heart or power of my body. Still my strength is returning so fast that I dream dreams of reaching the botanical gardens perhaps, or rounding the circle, before the winter comes — the fatal hour of the undoing of my Penelope's web. As it is, I walk as well as most children of two years old!

Mr. Kenyon went away for ten days today — & the grand pic nic[5] of this whole house, consummated apart from the knowledge of the head of it, took place near Reading — at Miss Mitford's cottage last Wednesday.[6] I was walking on hot coals, all day with terror, lest there sh[d] be a discovery — but it *past* — & such a pic nic, they all say, never was before. Miss Mitford gave strawberries & cream in her summerhouse — There is no room to enter into details, & your other correspondents are better [*top of first sheet*] informed than I am, besides. Uncle Hedley & Arabella came from Brighton today to go with Jane to the Duchess of Northumberland's fete at Lion House tomorrow — & on Wednesday, they all return to Brighton & Ibbet's eyes lighted anew. –[7] May God bless you – Mind you write, but avoid pic nics as a subject.

Your Ba.

[1] Postmark: July 14, 1845. Address: G. G. Barrett, Esq., Kinnersley Rectory, Kinnersley, W. Hereford.

[2] *Othello*, III.iii.106-107. Quoting from memory, Elizabeth writes *devil* for *monster*.

[3] The furnishings of her room had been rearranged, doubtless, for the accommodation of "Mr. Browning," whose visits had begun on the afternoon of May 20, 1845. On the Monday on which this letter was written she was looking forward to a visit on Wednesday

(see *Letters of R. B. and E. B. B.*, I, p. 127). For Flush's discomfiture, see Virginia Woolf: *Flush, a Biography*, London, 1933.

⁴ For this trip see *Letters of R. B. and E. B. B.*, I, p. 119.

⁵ *Picnic* is habitually written as two words.

⁶ In discussing this "adventure" to Miss Mitford's with the hostess, Elizabeth expresses a not uncharacteristic attitude toward the head of the house. ". . . did you understand that the escapade yesterday was unknown to the High priest here? – to Papa, I mean? Very wrong! Yes — *that* is true. *You must not mention it!* A little over-strictness sometimes *drives* into temptation" (Miller: *E. B. to M. M.*, pp. 251-52).

⁷ Daughter of Uncle John Hedley and Aunt Jane.

letter 35   [50 Wimpole Street]
                                                 Wednesday
                                                 [September 3, 1845]¹

My dearest George,   You will wonder at my silence perhaps,— & if you called me ungrateful "at the top of wonder," I shall not be surprised at all. Still, I have been so tossed & ruffled in every direction — I have had such an equinox of mind,— with a 'yes' & 'no' pushing and pulling at one another, & no peace for me with either, . . that to write on the subject² seemed only a worse manner of thinking of it. In the meantime I have been much obliged to you for your note ever since I received it, & heartily thank both you & the other dear adviser in chief, for sending me so strong & full & early an opinion. I admit too that your note has had its right weight with me, & that since receiving it I have turned my face steadily towards the south, & kept the agitation within me rather in my heart than in my mind. Still it is hard to think of going out of this room to the south of Europe under such circumstances. Growing gravity in Papa's eyes, & perhaps displeasure deeper within him — If he *should* be displeased — But his *manner* is most affectionate to me — affectionate in a marked manner & measure — which indeed was needed to stroke down & smooth a little, my poor ruffled feathers, after that hard cold letter of his – Perhaps he has relented in his

thoughts of me — or perhaps, George (which I conjecture sometimes) perhaps he takes for granted that I have given up my
scheme, & his good nature is meant for my compensation –
However this may be, I am making every preparation — & as
an opening step, saw Chambers[3] on Saturday. And now guess
what he said — He said, after using the stethoscope, that a very
slight affection of the left lung was observed but which threatened no serious result whatever, if I did but take precautions —
that I was comparatively well . . the harm being so slight —
& that the long struggle of the morbid part of the constitution to
set up an incurable form of consumption was coming to an end,
& leaving the life to triumph, if these precautions were used . .
The pulse he thought somewhat fast — & the nervous system
much shaken, & the muscles covering the lungs receiving strength
— and he not merely *advised* but ENJOINED the trial of a warm
climate . . *naming Pisa.* It is the very best thing I could do,
he said — & everything in the way of restoration was to be expected from it. He dwelt a good deal on the *weakness,* which
he seemed to consider the chief malady now — but still, he reminded me that in a case like mine, the bad symptoms might
be soon beckoned back & that I should take very great care. He
forbade wine & malt liquors, & did not say much for animal
food. Milk & vegetables are to be my chief diet. Which shows
that he is not free from apprehension on certain obvious points
— however satisfactory his opinion might be. For the sea-voyage,
it is to do me every sort of good he says, & no sort of harm – If
I am sick, there is no injury likely to occur. All is sheer gain, &
not a risk to be considered – He rather wished me to go at once,
& see Nice on the road – Not that Nice was a place for me to
winter at,— ("By no means," he said —) but that as early as
September I might be there with advantage – Well for Dr.
Chambers to say, but impossible for *me* to do — for I have
barely heart & courage enough to get away by October in one
grand 'swoop' of heroism! – Well — what do you say? Write &
tell me – What does Bummy say? – And how does she look —,
which is still more important, I have the modesty to add. Now
write, George, & tell us your Parisian impressions, . . which,

reproduced on legal vellum, must be so effective – Our news here in London is low. Mr. Kenyon is still at Dover. I have written this like a racehorse . . pawing the air with haste. May God bless you always – Everything is passing, of course, in the most solemn silence — that is, I am having a new gown made & saying not a word about it. I have written too to Mr. Andrews of the steamers — & the next day of steaming to Leghorn is not fixed. It is likely to be on the third of October, which will suit me.

I have had a proposal from the New York booksellers, to publish a volume of my 'prose-works', consisting of the Athenaeum papers, & other things . . criticisms on American literature. But they want to do it directly, & I cannot, you see, with the steamer waiting — and the papers in question require new-writing. Ah — I write as if my heart were at ease — & *it is'nt* —

But ever your affectionate Ba.

[1] The envelope preserved with this letter bears no address or postmark. It is quaintly directed: á Monsieur (in upper left) Monsieur Barrett (in middle). On the inside is written: "Set and Occy are gone to Wales." In a letter to Browning, postmarked September 8, 1845, Elizabeth wrote: "It appears that the direct Leghorn steamer will not sail on the third . . . One of my brothers has been to Mr. Andrews of St. Mary Axe and heard as much as this." Her remarks about the sailing in this letter date it not later than Wednesday, September 3, and it is hardly likely to have been written more than one or two weeks earlier (*Letters of R. B. and E. B. B.,* I, p. 189).

[2] The letters which passed between Elizabeth and Robert at this time and, doubtless, their conversations when they met, were filled with discussions of this projected winter trip to Italy. It was Mr. Barrett's attitude towards the plan, which seemed to Elizabeth to be for her a matter of life and death, that finally broke the back of her loyalty to her father and prepared her to be willing later to incur his wrath. George supported her plea to be allowed to go, without success.

[3] Dr. William Frederick Chambers, her physician. He was one of the most distinguished physicians in England, physician in ordi-

nary to Queen Adelaide, William IV, and Victoria (Marks, p. 474).

letter 36   [50 Wimpole Street]
                                                 Wednesday
                                                 [April 1, 1846][1]

Dearest George, You are good & I am bad, & there's an end ——
I hope, not of both of us. Every day I have meant to write to
you,— but once when I was really inspired to do it, Henry
bought a horse which he had to talk to you about, & I retired
before the cavalry.

By the way you see what we have been doing in India —
winning a victory at the cost of blood & tears[2]— the world
should be too wise by this time to pay so much too much for its
whistle. Some of these days our "great Indian Empire" will
stand upon its own legs, & make use of our own rope to scourge
us to a distance.[3] What right has England to an Indian empire?
No more than the Duke of Sutherland to his broad estates.[4]
Wait a little, & we shall see it all arranged according to a better
justice, on the small scale & the large.

Yesterday Arabel had a message from a Mrs. Munro in
Harley street who wanted to see her immediately. She went,
expecting to see Jane — and there was Emma instead. She has
come to stay throughout the summer — in town & at Bushey[5] &
of course Arabel is delighted.

And you have been making yourself as agreeable as a lawyer
could, I understand, at the Bartons – Nora wrote exstatically of
a walk with you to the Herefordshire beacon, & of losing herself
in a wood with you — best of all.[6]

A few days ago I had Mrs. Jameson[7] here — she came one
day & the next, & she gave me a beautiful etching of St. Cecelia
lying dead — just as she lies in marble at Rome before a high
altar.[8] The lifelessness is exquisite in the arms & hands . . .
Then — let me see for other news — I am going to receive for
half an hour a Mrs. Paine who comes from Farnham[9] for that

purpose, & has been so affectionate in her letters that I cant say no to her when she entreats to see me. Living at a distance I shall not be interfered with much, it will be half an hour on Friday — & there, an end. Then I have been translating the parting of Hector & Andromache from the Iliad —"with my usual modesty," as Mr. Kenyon says severely. Pope & Cowper are both as bad as can be,— & old Homer laughs us all three to scorn, I know very well. Still being asked to attempt it, I attempted it.

Today I shall go down to the drawingroom. The weather has been just cold enough to prevent my doing this for a week past,— but not cold enough to hurt anyone in the world — even me. My dearest George, how do you get on? You know I do not praise you for writing voluminous letters or very communicative ones. Only you have been better than I. Dear George, I have a true affection & confident esteem for you in all your acts & thoughts, and I desire you always to bear this in your mind — always & under all circumstances.[10] Is it overgrave of me to say it so suddenly in the midst of apparent light speaking? Perhaps — yet I spoke suddenly, because suddenly my heart made me. May God bless you, dearest George

Love your ever affectionate
Ba

Oh — we have heard through the Bells, of Paris. It was before Robin arrived. Uncle Hedley saw in the paper how his regiment was sent to India, but as Jane & they all were about to go to a ball, he deferred communicating the bad news. In the middle of the ball, up came an ingenious gentleman (very much at a loss for a subject) with a face of polite condolence.– "I am very sorry to hear, Mrs. Hedley, that your son's regiment must go to India"— down she fell in a fainting fit — Poor Jane –

[1] Postmark: C. T. April 1, 1846. Address: George G. M. Barrett, Esq., Barrister at Law, Oxford Circuit.

[2] The great battle of Sobraon, February 10, 1846. On February 20 Sir Hugh Gough occupied the citadel of Lahore, ending the First Sikh War.

[3] Another century proved her right.

[4] The reference is to George Granville Leveson-Gower, 2nd Duke of Sutherland who succeeded to the title and estates in 1833. His father, bearing the same names, originally held a barony as Baron Gower of Sittenham, Yorkshire. He obtained possession of the greater part of Sutherlandshire through his wife, Countess of Sutherland in her own right, in 1785. He inherited the Bridgewater estates through the death of an uncle who had been Duke thereof and the Seltenham estates from his father. He was created Duke of Sutherland in 1833. For Elizabeth's views on property, titles, and hereditary distinction, compare the following from a letter to Henrietta, April 1, 1848. The occasion here is the confiscation of Royal Estates in France.

Whatever, for instance, touches upon property is wrong, and whatever tends to the production of social equality is absurd and iniquitous, and oppressive in its ultimate ends. Every man should have the right of climbing — but to say that every man should equally climb (because the right is equal) is a wrong against the strong and industrious; and there has been wrong enough in God's world as He knows, without introducing a new kind of wrong. Confiscating the royal property seemed to me, too, unhappy and unworthy: and why destroy titles? Why not retain an inexpensive mode of recognizing public services — so much better than any money way, and as good as the inch of colored ribbon in the button hole? *Hereditary* distinction, is a different question. Let the notion of privileged orders perish as it ought. Robert and I agree nearly on all these points, but here and there we have plenty of room for battles. (Huxley, p. 81)

[5] Bushey is in Hertfordshire, sixteen miles northwest of London.

[6] George is, as usually on the circuit, visiting the friends in Herefordshire. Elizabeth seems to welcome any suggestion of romance in the lives of her sisters and brothers. Her hope that George might marry was doomed to disappointment.

[7] Mrs. Anna Brownell Jameson (1794-1860) wrote successfully on many different subjects. Her best known works are *Characteristics of Shakespeare's Women*, London, 1832, and *Sacred and Legendary Art*, including *Legends of the Saints*, 1848; *Legends of the Monasteries*, 1850; and *Legends of the Madonna*, 1852. A final volume, *History of Our Lord*, was completed, after her death, by Lady Eastlake. Mrs. Jameson first visited Elizabeth in November, 1844 (Kenyon, I, p. 217). She at once "ran into . . . 'one of my sudden intimacies'" and remained a close friend throughout her life. By a fortunate accident she met the eloping couple in Paris and was of inestimable service to them on their flight to Italy. The letters of both Elizabeth and Robert contain frequent

references both to her and to her niece, Geraldine Bate, later Mrs. Macpherson.

[8] In the church of St. Cecilia in Trastevere.

[9] Mrs. Paine's errand must stand sufficient to identify her. Which Farnham she came from cannot be determined.

[10] The projected marriage and consequent flight from Wimpole Street were already in her mind.

letter 37   [50 Wimpole Street]
                                             Friday
                                             [July 10, 1846][1]

My dearest George,

I have some things 'on my mind' & they must be off it for the first relief, before I begin to talk of other things. Very much I have been pained & perplexed & surprised lately, & you shall hear how.

It appears that poor Mr. Haydon[2] has left a paper declaratory of his last wishes, now in the hands of Mr. Sergeant Talfourd, in which to my infinite astonishment, he makes a bequest of his memoirs & other papers to *me* desiring that I should edit & place them for publication in Longman's hands. Mr. Forster[3] called on Mr. Kenyon to apprise him of this, & Mr. Kenyon came to tell me of it at once.[4]

I was amazed – The memoirs of which you may remember that I was shown a part, about a year & a half ago, though curious & interesting, are perfectly unfit for publication without large modification — as I told Mr. Haydon at the time. There are said to be twenty six volumes of them — & you may imagine that if a blind man would be an unqualified president of the Royal Academy, *I* must be quite as unqualified for an editorship of such a description — *I,* without the experience of art & of the world — who belong to a later generation & know nothing of the persons mentioned or the events referred to — that you must see at a glance. Also it is scarcely work for a *woman* –

Now then — Mr. Kenyon advised me to write to Mr. Sergeant Talfourd, to desire information respecting this paper — I waited however for a day or two. I felt unwilling to write to Mr. Talfourd.

In the meanwhile, Mr. Browning dined in Russell Square last tuesday — (he was of course aware of all these circumstances).[5] Scarcely had the men entered on their wine after dinner, when Mr. Serjeant Talfourd took up the subject of poor Haydon & of the bequest he had made to me — & read a letter of Miss Mitford's & two letters of mine — or parts of them — (which either in copy or in the original, she had taken the great liberty of sending straight to him, after having called him "the falsest of men" two days before in my room!) an absurd letter of Miss Mitford's, to compliment Talfourd on the occasion of poor Haydon's carrying out the principle of '*Ion*'— (conceive *that!*) & to communicate the contents of my letters, in which, with natural expressions of feeling, (how can I remember what I said in a moment of emotion, to a friend like Miss Mitford?) I spoke of the boxes & pictures which I had. – "*And so speaks our great poetess,*" ended she ecstatically. Which Talfourd commented on by supposing drily that when Miss B wrote of Miss M; it was — "And so speaks our great dramatist." You know he hates her — & none of the ridicule of what appears to have been a most ridiculous letter, was let fall to the ground.

So somebody said one thing, & another; another somebody said that Miss Barrett was plainly a *very* particular friend of Haydon's — & somebody said that her house appeared to be the receptacle for his goods against his creditors — till at last Mr. Browning, no longer able to contain his indignation, (observe that Edwin Landseer,[6] Babbage,[7] Forster & more were present!) took it upon himself to answer for it of his own knowledge, that I had never seen Haydon in my life, & had received the things he sent, just as anyone would, who had too much heart to throw them out into the street. Afterwards he took Talfourd aside, & told him that he had been long in correspondence with me & *knew* the circumstances in question — & Talfourd agreed with him that I had been selected for the editorship precisely *because* of my inexperience & isolation from the world, & in the hope that I would print *everything* & spare nobody. 'But,' said Talfourd, 'she must beware of printing anything at this time — & beware also of its being known that she has in her possession any deposit from Haydon — otherwise she will subject herself to a legal prosecution' So spoke the great man of law.

Mr. Browning thought it advisable that I should write at once to Talfourd, therefore, stating fully yet briefly the facts — that Mr. Haydon had written to me — which led first into our correspondence of some months — that I had not heard from him above a year, till the week preceding his death — that I had received a deposit from his hands no more than twice — *once* before the last fatal time! & that what I received, had no pecuniary value as he represented it, consisting of private papers & a few sketches, & his oil — that I never saw him in my life, & was astonished & perplexed at being named for an office for which I considered myself unqualified – All this, I wrote to Mr. Talfourd, ending by begging to know what I could do, not to do wrong — & he had my letter, I suppose, before he left town for circuit yesterday morning. I have yet had no reply.

Now, George, he probably will speak to you on the subject — he probably will. Therefore remember & take heed to your speech. I am very desirous of paying every respect to poor Mr. Haydon's memory — everything that I could do, I would do. At the same time let Mr. Talfourd understand the simple facts, & that this house was not used as a receptacle for the purpose of defrauding his creditors, & also that I never saw him in my life —, People were 'astonished how Miss B came to know' &c —— Poor Haydon did not lead the most prudent of lives, it appears. See what a scrape I am in —— Mr. Kenyon might well say as he did —'You, of all in the world, I should have thought, would have been safe from the danger of such a position.'

I took the precaution of saying to Mr. Talfourd, in my letter to him, that in agreeing to receive those things, it would have [*been*] better if I had first consulted my father & brothers, but that I could not hesitate so long as to admit of it – Which I said lest you might be blamed more gravely than *I* could be for an act of pitifulness! — Besides it was only *just*. It was my own

deed. If I had asked Papa he w^d not have let me, you know —
& I did not ask him.

You will observe too that Mr. Browning's account to me of
what passed at Mr. Serjt. Talfourd's table, is not to be referred
to or repeated, anywise or anywhere — nor Miss Mitford's
name, mentioned. I have no claim on *him,* Talfourd — he is not
my friend — he judged of things as he saw them at the first
glance. As to Miss Mitford — she was foolish & thoughtless —
but meant no harm, though I am very angry in the shadow
of my soul. But I heard all this from Mr. Browning, & you must
not on any account let it be breathed upon by other breath
than our own. I never saw him so angry since our acquaintance
began. Worse things were said or implied I do not doubt, than
what he told me, he was *so* angry.

If his name should be mentioned *at all* between Talfourd &
you — that is, if Talfourd sh^d mention it to you . . — remember
that he only knows of our *correspondence* & not of our personal
acquaintance. – Mr. Browning's & mine – So be on your guard.[8]

Papa knows nothing of this turmoil, except generally of the
bequest.

Have I made it clear to you, George? I have been vexed, perplexed, more than you will fancy perhaps — yet I am sure you
will see that it is an unpleasant position. Write your thoughts
to me & advise.

Poor, poor Haydon — What are *we* — to complain of the
dust upon his grave? Poor Haydon! –

To shift this subject to another, — I was very sorry, my
dearest George, not to see you the day I might have seen you!
Bummy & Arlette[9] complain loudly of your absence. The former
looks far better than I expected to see her — & Arlette is pretty
& pleasing, to my fancy, with a more *steadfast* countenance than
Arabella's though with less general grace & brilliancy. Uncle
Hedley arrived in town yesterday — & the bridal people[10] are
to come today. Bummy whispers to me *privately* that Mr. Bevan
has only five or six hundred a year, & that it is a "very *bad
match* for Arabella." When Aunt Jane is called *worldly* — observe (which I have always seen) she is infinitely less so than

some of the callers. Dear Bummy has very low spirits — to oppression, it seems to *me* – Arlette thinks it better for her not to
return to Paris –

So much more I had to say, but must end here –

> May God bless you, dearest & ever dear George
> I am your affectionate Ba –

Our love to everybody. Bummy will stay here, I think, until
after the marriage. I have just now a letter from Miss Mitford,
unconscious as she is that I know of her freedom with my letters.
And she has heard from Mr. Serjt. Talfourd, she says, who
writes of *"Our great poetess, as you very properly call her &c"*
&c Oh Mr. Serjeant Talfourd! – Oh — Oh, the *flummery* of
Sergeants at Law! May it not well make one sick! – Sweet
indeed in the mouth, & bitter in the digestion, is the parlance
of this world! –

He said to Mr. Browning — "If she will put me in possession
of the facts, I can arrange everything with her brother, when I
meet him on circuit – I know him — he is a VERY PROMISING
YOUTH! – " Which was *sincere,* at least — I suppose, for he need
not have said it to *RB.*

---

[1] Postmark: P. D. July 11, 1846. Address: George Goodin Barrett, Esq., Kinnersley Castle, near Hereford. The penciled note on
the envelope, "Apr. 10, 1846," either does not refer to the date of
the letter or is in error by three months. Both dates fell on Friday.

[2] Haydon shot himself June 22, 1846.

[3] John Forster (1812-76), best remembered today as Dickens'
biographer. He knew intimately most of the literary figures of his
time and was one of the earliest admirers of Browning. He reviewed *Paracelsus* in the *Examiner,* September 6, 1835, and remained a powerful though somewhat exacting friend of the poet
through most of his life. In the 1863 edition of his collected works,
Browning wrote: "I dedicate these Volumes to my Old Friend
John Forster, glad and grateful that he who, from the first publication of the various poems they include, has been their promptest
and staunchest helper, should seem even nearer to me now than
thirty years ago." A few years later the two old friends quarreled
bitterly.

[4] For the story of Mr. Kenyon's announcement see Elizabeth's letter of July 6, 1846 (*Letters of R. B. and E. B. B.*, II, p. 302).

[5] For Browning's account of this dinner see his letter of July 8, 1846 (*Letters of R. B. and E. B. B.*, II, p. 314).

[6] Sir Edwin Henry Landseer (1802-73), English artist, best known for his paintings of animals.

[7] Charles Babbage. See *Letter 7, note 6,* p. 55.

[8] Cf. Browning's letter cited above, p. 317.

[9] Arlette is Charlotte Butler, later Mrs. C. W. Reynolds.

[10] Arabella Hedley and Mr. J. J. Bevan, who were married the next year (Huxley, p. 3).

letter 38   [50 Wimpole Street]
                                                         Wednesday
                                                         July 15 [1846][1]

My dearest George

The first word must be a congratulation to yourself & to us on the meaning of this day, your birthday, & earnest wishes from my heart, that you may have as many reasons, through much happiness hereafter, for loving life, as *we* have for loving *you;* dearest George — for holding you in all love & esteem –

Your letter I have, & thank you for — but you will know by this time, by the letter of Talfourds I enclosed to you, that the whole trouble was built upon the clouds, & his negligence — very pardonable, for the rest, under the peculiar circumstances, as he properly says, of 'hurry & horror'; though before he allowed Forster to apprize me through Mr. Kenyon he should have been more accurate – For the rest, my dearest George, any *jealousy* was out of the question, be sure — just as it would have been for me to retire from a duty of that sort on the plea of ill health, my health being good enough now to be no source of excuses that way –[2] It was only the *impossibility,* as I saw it, which hindered me — not to say that in my secret soul I was unwilling to assume such a responsibility – Oh — if you thought it covetable by Talfourd or another, you were three times wrong – But enough of this.

Mr. Browning only told me enough to make me full & direct in my explanation to Talfourd, to make me explain that what I took in was of no *pecuniary value.* You see how Talfourd answers on that point – So it is all right. Mr. Browning said not a word that he was not obliged, through his feeling for me, to say — & it was just that reserve, perhaps, which made me exaggerate to myself what might have been said. For certainly he was very angry with Miss Mitford, & with poor Haydon even himself — but now an end to all this — George, do not say a word to Talfourd on the subject — and if he mentions it to you, which he will not perhaps, be brief, & let it pass. There is nothing to be vexed about now – And I am quite well.

The Hedleys dined here on Monday with Mr. Bevan & the latter did not hazard his reputation of a sensible man by saying twenty words. For the rest, he sang — he does not understand music but he has a good voice, they say — & he is estimated too to be gentlemanly – Arabella is in the highest possible spirits. *Do not mention this* — but the income is said to be only five or six hundred a year, so you see that no worldly motives are in case. For my part, I think the better, for it, both of Arabella & her mother – Do not mention this, now – They go into Switzerland after the marriage, then return to England, then go to Paris for the present. & to *live,* I dare say. The day is not fixed yet — but about a fortnight may see the end of it.

Since the last sentence was written, I have seen Mr. Bevan. A sensible face, a facile expression in conversation, a gentlemanly manner. Above six feet of a man, well-attested, therefore.— I like him, I think. I heard before seeing him, that *his peculiar subject* was ecclesiastical architecture, which, being by no means *my* subject, nor one to which I had affinities in the way of feeling,— I resolved to keep clear of it, & began to talk a thousand miles off it, about French society. In a minute it was observed that he never could find a frenchman [*sic*] capable of entering with proper reverence into the subject of —— *ecclesiastical architecture!* So there was no help — I was enfoncée – He is a Puseyite to the heights of possible Puseyism — has studied the question, has formed his opinions — can talk them out well — &

I like him, I assure you, notwithstanding all. Yet to hear a man say that it was awful audacity to think for oneself on church subjects — it seemed to me strangely foolish. The people I talk to, are so much in a higher purer atmosphere, that I quite started to hear such a thing from a man with a sensible face. It seemed fabulous that such a thing should be held in earnest, by that man with the sensible face! A man superior to the masses, of course, too — though I am a little spoilt for ordinary men, through having listened to the gods here.

But I like Mr. Bevan. I really do. How sorry I am to hear of Isabel's[3] illness! Did *you* hear of its being desperate, from good authority? My love to them all. May God bless you, dearest George

Ever I am your attached Ba

[1] The envelope to this letter is lacking. Like the preceding letter, this one bears a confusing pencil note, "Apr. 15, 1846." George's birthday was July 15.

[2] As is well known, Elizabeth's health improved surprisingly during the winter of 1845-46. The winter is generally reported to have been mild, but the open admission of her love and the prospect of marriage and freedom were probably the strongest contributory factors in her improvement.

[3] Wife of Leonard Altham Graham-Clarke, son of Elizabeth's Uncle John (p. 76) of Kinnersley Castle. She is also Elizabeth's cousin, being the daughter of Sir Thomas Butler and Aunt Frances. (For an account of the courtship and marriage of the pair, see *Letter 22, note 8,* p. 102. For news of her death, see Huxley, p. 8.)

letter 39   [50 Wimpole Street]
                                 Thursday & Friday
                                 [September 17-18, 1846][1]

My dearest George I throw myself on your affection for me & beseech of God that it may hold under the weight — dearest George, Go to your room & read this letter — and I entreat you by all that we both hold dearest, to hold me still dear after the

communication which it remains to me to make to yourself and
to leave to you in order to be communicated to others in the way
that shall seem best to your judgement. And Oh, love me George,
while you are reading it. Love me — that I may find pardon in
your heart for me after it is read.

Mr. Browning has been attached to me for nearly two years –
At first and for long I could not believe that *he* (who is what
you know a little) could care for such as I, except in an illusion
& a dream. I put an end (as I thought) briefly to the subject.
I felt certain that a few days & a little more light on my ghastly
face, would lead him to thank me for my negative, and I bade
him observe that if my position had not been exceptional, I
should not have received him at all. With a protest, he sub-
mitted, and months passed on so. Still he came continually &
wrote, & made me feel (though observing my conditions in the
form) made me feel with every breath I drew in his presence,
that he loved me with no ordinary affection. But I believed that
it would be a wrong to such a man, to cast on him the burden
of my sickly life, & to ruin him by his own generosity – He was
too good for me, I knew, but I tried to be as generous. I showed
him that I was altogether bruised & broken — that setting aside
my health which, however improved, was liable to fail with
every withdrawing of the sun,— that the common advantages
of youth & good spirits had gone from me & that I was an
undone creature for the pleasures of life, as for its social duties.

His answer was — not the common gallantries which come so
easily to the lips of men — but simply that *he loved me* — he
met argument with fact. He told me — that with himself also,
the early freshness of youth had gone by, & that throughout it
he had not been able to love any woman — that he loved now
for the first time & the last. That, as to the question of my
health, he had been under the impression when he first declared
his attachment to me, that I was suffering from an incurable
injury on the spine, which would prevent my ever standing up
before his eyes. If *that* had been true — he bade me tell me how
it should have operated in suppressing any pure attachment of a
soul to a soul. For his part, he had desired under those circum-

stances, to attain to the right of sitting by my sofa just two hours in the day as one of my brothers might — and he preferred, of deliberate choice, the realization of such a dream, to the highest, which should exclude me, in the world. - But he would not, he said, torment me - He would wait, if I pleased, twenty years, till we both should grow old, & then at the latest,— too late,— I should understand him as he understood himself now — & should know that he loved me with an ineffaceable love.[2] In the meanwhile, what he asked I had it in my power to give. He did not ask me to dance or to sing,—but to help him to work and to live — to live a useful life & to die a happy death — *that* was in my power.

And this was the attachment, George, I have had to do with, & this the man - Such a man.- Noble he is — his intellect the least of his gifts! His love showed itself to me like a vocation. And I a mere woman, feeling as a woman must, & in circumstances which made every proof of devotion sink down to the deepest of my heart where the deep sorrow was before. Did he not come in my adversity? When I had done with life, did he not come to me. Call to mind the sorrow & the solitude, & how, in these long years, the feeling of personal vanity had died out of me, till I was grateful to all those who a little could bear with me personally. And *he,* such a man! Why men have talked to me before of what they called love,[3]—but never for *any one,* could I *think* even, of relinquishing the single life with which I was contented. I never believed that a man whom *I* could love (I having a need to look up high in order to love) . . could be satisfied with the loving *me.* And yet *he did* — does. Then we have one mind on all subjects — & the solemner they are, the nearer we seem to approach. If poets, we are together, still more we are Christians. For these nearly two years we have known each other's opinions & thoughts & feelings, weakness & strength, as few persons in the like position have had equal opportunities of doing. And knowing me perfectly he has entirely loved me — : At last, I only could say —"Wait till the winter - You will see that I shall be ill again - If not, I will leave it to you".

I believed I should be ill again certainly. But the winter came, mild & wonderful – I did not fail in health — nor to *him*.

I beseech you, George, to judge me gently, looking to the peculiar circumstances,— & above all, to *acquit him wholly*. I claim the whole responsibility of his omission of the usual application to my father & friends — for he was about to do it — anxious to do it — & I stopped him. That blame therefore belongs to me. But I knew, & *you know,* what the consequence of that application would have been — we should have been separated from that moment. He is not rich[4]—which w^d have been an obstacle — At any rate, I could not *physically bear* to encounter agitating opposition from those I tenderly loved — & to act openly in defiance of Papa's will, would have been more impossible for me than to use the right which *I believe to be mine,* of taking a step so strictly personal, on my own responsibility. We both of us comprehend life in a simpler way than generally is done, and to live happily according to our conscience, we do not need to be richer than we are. I do beseech you, George, to look to the circumstances & judge me gently, & see that, having resolved to give my life to one who is in my eyes the noblest of all men & who loves me as such a man can love,— there was no way possible to my weakness but the way adopted with this pain. The motives are altogether different from any supposable want of respect & affection where I owe them most tenderly. I beseech you to understand this — I beseech you to lay it before my dearest Papa, that it is so – Also, to have *consulted any one of you,* would have been ungenerous & have involved you in my blame I have therefore consulted not one of you. I here declare that everyone in the house is absolutely ignorant & innocent of all participation in this act of my own. I love you too dearly, too tenderly, to have done you such injustice. Forgive me all of you for the act itself, for the sake of the love which came before it — & follows after it — for never (whether you pardon or reproach me) will an hour pass during my absence from you, in which I shall not think of you with tenderest thoughts.

It appears right to say of dear Mr. Kenyon — to whom I ever shall be grateful, that he has *not any knowledge of these circumstances* – It appears right to say it, since Mr. Browning is his friend.

And I think it due to myself, to observe, that I have seen Mr. Browning only in this house & openly — except the day of our meeting in the church of this parish in order to becoming [*sic*] his wife in the presence of the two necessary witnesses. We go across France, down the Seine & Rhone to Pisa for the winter, in submission to the conditions considered necessary for the re-establishment of my health, & shall return in the next summer. As soon as he became aware that I had the little money which is mine, he wished much that I would leave it with my sisters, & go to him penniless – But this, which I would have acceded to under ordinary circumstances, I resisted on the ground of my health — the uncertainty of which seemed to make it a duty to me to keep from being a burden to him — at least in a pecuniary respect.

George, dear George, read the enclosed letter for my dearest Papa, & then — breaking gently the news of it — give it to him to read. Also if he would deign to read this letter addressed to you — I should be grateful – I wish him in justice, & beseech him in affection, to understand the whole bearings of this case. George, believe of me, that I have endeavoured in all this matter to do right according to my own view of rights & righteousness – If it is not your view, bear with me & pardon me. Do you all pardon me, my beloved ones, & believe that if I could have benefitted any of you by staying here, I would have stayed. Have I not done for you what I could, always? *When* I could – Now I am weak. And if in this crisis I were to do otherwise than what I am about to do, there would be a victim without an expiation, & a sacrifice without an object. My spirits would have festered on in this enforced prison, & none of you all would have been the happier for what would have [been] bitter to *me*. Also, I should have wronged *another*. I cannot do it.

If you have any affection for me, George, dearest George, let

me hear a word — at Orleans[5]— let me hear. I will write —
I bless you, I love you –

I am

Your Ba –

This letter, like good wine, needs no bush. The wonder is that it
should have had so little effect. George, to Elizabeth's great sorrow
and surprise, sided with her father. In consequence there is a break
in this correspondence until the reconciliation between brother and
sister during the Brownings' first visit to London in 1851.

[1] Postmark: Sept. 19, 1846. Address: George Goodin Barrett
Esq[re·], 50 Wimpole Street. The wedding took place on September
12 in Marylebone Church. On September 19, in company with her
maid, Wilson, and Flush, Elizabeth left the house, met Robert, and
sailed for Le Havre.

[2] The determination here expressed inevitably brings to mind
The Statue and the Bust.

[3] That this reference to normal experience comes as a surprise is
due to the fact that the voluminous records of Elizabeth's life as
an invalid and later as Mrs. Browning dim one's imagination of
the bright, vivacious girl, only briefly and mildly ill, of earlier
days. She was now forty years old and had been a "prisoner" of
ill health for eight years. When the Barretts had left Hope End,
where they had many friends, Elizabeth was twenty-six. Then
came the generally happy years at Sidmouth, from which the
family moved to London in the summer of 1835. In January, 1836,
she wrote to Mrs. Martin: "You see we are in London after all,
and poor Sidmouth left afar . . . Half my soul . . . seems to
have stayed behind on the sea-shore, which I love more than ever
now that I cannot walk on it in the body" (Kenyon, I, p. 35). It
was not until early in 1838 that her serious illness began.

[4] Certainly an understatement.

[5] Letters reached Mrs. Browning at Orleans: "They were very
hard letters, those from dearest Papa and dearest George – To the
first I had to bow my head . . . But for George, I thought it hard,
I confess, that he should have written to me so with a sword . . .
Only he wrote in excitement and in ignorance." At the end of this

letter, written to her sisters from Roanne on October 2, 1846, she adds: "Ah — dear George would not have written so, if he had known my whole heart, yet he loved me while he wrote, as I felt with every pain the writing caused me" (*Twenty-two Letters*, pp. 1-11).

It is hard to understand how George, after reading his sister's letter, could have "written in ignorance," but, perhaps, the fact that, even in his anger, he preserved it testifies to the truth of her judgment of his feelings. No more letters to George, however — and there were more — have been preserved until 1851.

letter 40   [Paris]
                                 [138 Avenue des Champs Élysées]
                                 [December 4-5, 1851][1]

So it has come at last my dearest George — I dont mean my letter to you[2] but the coup d'etat. We all "felt in the air" as Robert said, that something was coming, but how & when, nobody guessed, except it might be poor little Thiers,[3] who *knew* it as the snails do rain, & is selfjustified at Havre now for being frightened out of his wits at Paris a week ago. Things could not go on as they were — the assembly fighting like rats, while the house was falling (which the real rats, by the way, wouldn't have done) - A most prodigious state of things it must be allowed to have been — yes, and to be.

We have had magnificent advantages of situation here, & I have scarcely left the window these two days, watching the pouring in of the troops, to music, trumpets & shouting, with splendid military maneuvres of every kind. The president himself rode immediately past our windows through the great thunder of a shout which reached from the Barriere de l'etoile to the Place du Carrousel — "vive Napoleon" - People tell us it was "Vive l'empereur", but I tell *you* what I heard myself. Very grand it was! I would not have missed it, — not for the sight of the Alps, scarcely –

He's a bold man, to say the least of him. He may be shot dead from a window at any moment. "A madman," some people call

him, but certainly a bold man. We hear of a league of young
men who have sworn to "shoot him like a dog" at the first
opportunity. There's a rumour too, which I cant believe in,
about a distribution of manuscript cards in the street, signed
Victor Hugo, declaring him "hors de la loi"— a mark for
assassination. A bold man, really! –

Bad, I do not say. I confess myself to be carried away into
sympathy by the bravery & promptitude of his last act. Call it
perjury, usurpation of rights, what you will — call it treason
against the constitution which it assuredly is, The fact is that out
of 85 'conseile generaux' 79 had declared in favor of a revision
of this said constitution, and that the assembly had rejected
their prayer. De facto, the assembly opposed the wishes of the
people instead of representing the people. Now the form of a
thing is not to be respected beyond the spirit of a thing — and
the question being only between divers parties, tearing the
country to pieces as to which should first dash out its claw into
the vital places,— why the lion is justified in coming to the
rescue on his own account though he shatter the barriers of the
law in coming – There's a higher right than legal right, we all
feel instinctively — the living people are above the paper constitution. Therefore if Napoleon is loyal & true in his appeal to
the will of the people & in his intention of abiding by the issue
of the approaching election, "je fais acte d'adhesion," I, for one,
& hold him justified to the full extent of his revolutionary act.
But I wait to see. One cant quite trust a man in his position, &
with the Napoleon blood in him, which he evidently has to the
ends of his finger-nails – My sympathy with his audacity &
dexterity, is rather artistical sympathy than anything else — just
as one cries 'Bravo' at a 'tour de force'. Who could "think the
young man had so much blood in him," when he was taken at
Boulogne with the live eagle?[4] The live people is worth more —
if indeed he holds it on his fist.[5]

Some fighting took place yesterday in the fighting quarters,
from the faubourg St. Antoine to the rue St. Denis, but nothing
persistent, & whatever was, was mostly in consequence of certain
excitements of exrepresentatives. Everything was quiet this

morning – Now they are again fighting — and as near as the
Rue de Richelieu, & Robert, at the end of our avenue, was
turned back by our landlord, who cried out "For God's sake,
dont go any farther – A ball whizzed by my head." So Robert
remembered his faithful promise to me not to go into danger, &
returned at once – I suspect, notwithstanding all, that the people
of Paris, as a mass, acquiesce in the position & admire the coup
d'etat. Accounts from the provinces were favorable this morning. And the authorities on the Bourse (always worth listening
to) are of opinion, or were this morning, that the movement
will succeed. Of course, nothing except popular sympathy, will
justify Napoleon. There is not the least cause for apprehension
about *us,* so none of you fancy it. Even Wilson, who was in a
panic, a fortnight ago, begins to think, now that the peril has
broken on us, that "we are as safe as in England."

As to Wiedeman[6] he is in ecstasies at the sight of the soldiers,
& the sound of the music. If you ask Wiedeman if he likes the
revolution, he says —*"Less-"* (yes!) "buono, buono!" Desiree,
our french servant, a small, headlong, vehemently joyous creature, an immense Napoleonist herself, teaches him to say "Vive
Napoleon"— to which, he adds out of his own head, "Bwavo,
bwavo!" (bravo). He has taken to be very noisy these two
days in his mimicry of the "revolution"— and out of doors he
shouts in the face of the soldiers, Wilson says, till they cant help
laughing. That he should go out at all, will prove to you that
we are safe in our part of the town. Still, Wilson was turned
back today, by a man as pale as death, who begged her to take
care of "le petit" and carry him home. The danger is, from the
sudden sweep of the cannons, from which there would be no
escape. While talking of Wiedeman, I must tell you one thing
of him. The other day Robin Hedley came to see us, & the child
was in the room. He ran directly out to Wilson & told her that
he had seen "Tio George"— & when she hesitated to understand
him, not believing that he could remember the little he had seen
of you, he took hold of his pelisse, the blue pelisse, & made signs
with voice & hand, that he meant the same 'Tio George' who
had given him that pelisse. He took Robin for you: not a very

accurate remembrance you will say, but still a remembrance in some sort or other.

Friday morning – I stopped in my letter yesterday, the accounts beginning to be very threatening. The cannons were taken past this house at full gallop as the trumpets gave signal from the place du Carrousel. There were dreadful rumours, & it turned me sick to hear the rounds of firing which reached us from the distant boulevards. Poor mad people! — poor Paris – The president went out himself, at great personal risk of course – He may be shot at any moment, & the consequence would be tremendous. There were dreadful rumours, as I say — and we heard within five minutes that the troops of the line had refused to act, — & that General Castellane[7] was marching against Paris from Lyons. Not true at all, as it proved afterwards. The army is devoted to the president, & Castellane has given in his adhesion. Our landlord, an Irishman, who has not distinguished himself by personal courage through the whole business, removed with his family, from the pavillion in our garden which he generally occupies, into the room at the top of our house — frightened out of all sense of comfort. The only possible danger is from pillage, &c, if the insurgents should triumph — such triumph being scarcely possible, I think, for it seems to be only the socialist party which has risen. On the other hand, if the people rose *en masse* (which would be the condition of any insurgent victory) there would be no pillage to dread. But I continue to think that as a majority the people uphold the president.

After all it was terrible last night. Robert had some writing to do, & I would not go to bed — so when I was undressed I put on my dressing gown & a shawl, & sate with him by the fireside till nearly one in the morning. Not from the least personal apprehension, observe, but simply that one shrank from going quietly to sleep while human beings were dying in heaps perhaps, within earshot. It was quiet however after eleven oclock as far as we could hear – Yet the fighting was not over till three in the morning, and I fear that much blood was shed, particularly in the great barricade of the porte St. Denis –

I shall send this letter today, lest you should be uneasy. I dont write to Arabel because I hear of her being expected in Wimpole street on Friday — today — so much the better. When she is in London, I shall feel nearer to her a great deal, & she may rely on having another account from me in another post or two, for I flatter myself we are in rather an interesting position just now upon the whole — & that she will care to know that we are neither carried to prisons of state nor "a la lanterne" —[8] All was quiet this morning, but they have recommenced fighting, it appears. Pure madness surely, when the resource of universal suffrage is open to everybody!

Lady Elgin is the widow of the marble man[9] — "fixed statue on the pedestal of shame" as Lord Byron called him without reason — & mother, of course, to the present Earl — She is a cultivated, sympathetical woman, having still fire enough under the snow of her white hair — Oh, and she is rather elderly than old, in spite of it. She has lived for years in Paris, occupying a noble apartment in the Faubourg St. Germain, & knowing the best of everybody, for the most part,— A great deal of attention she shows to us — and I *make* Robert go, though I cant, occasionally to her Mondays. Once she proposed coming here to have tea with us,— she & Madame Mohl[10] together — & we had such a pleasant evening talking of Shelley &c,— that they both mean to come again — & fixed on next Saturday – Only, in the present state of affairs, such engagements fall of course – People cant get at one & another in the evening without running risks. Last night we in vain expected the M. Milsand[11] who wrote the review on Robert in the Revue des deux Mondes of the 15th of August. (Did you see it?) He found us out & asked to be received,— & we were glad to make his acquaintance, & said so, & he was to come yesterday evening. I hope he wasn't shot on the road – There's a Miss Fitton,[12] unmarried, & rich, & by no means young, who has called on us — & there seems to be a good deal in her – She knows Mr. Kenyon, & has lived for years in Paris – And through her, we are to know Major & Mrs. Carmichael Smith (Thackeray's mother) as they are good enough to desire it particularly. Are these relations of Sir James Carmichael?[13] I think they must be. We mean to try to keep out

of uninteresting acquaintances, but really it will be difficult.
People are very kind & flattering in all sorts of ways to us. As
to the Ma^{dme} Mohl, you ask of, she is the wife of the oriental
professor at the Institute, & is a delightful person. I am inclined
to love her already – Full of cleverness & character, & interpene-
trated with womanly goodness. Paris is a very agreeable place,
I assure you, in spite of the cannonading – Poor Paris –

It has been cold — but the weather has been much milder for
the last week or more – They had a lovely soft air & glittering
moon last night for cutting one another's throats – Oh, that
moon was like a pathetic protest in Heaven, as it seemed
to me! –

In the worst cold though, I had a good deal of cough & un-
comfortableness. I was not as unwell as I was in England last
August – Also, the weather has been exceptional everywhere –
Even at Rome there was snow, and at Florence, fogs – Robert
thinks that by general accounts, we were better off here when at
worst, than people have been at most other places. Still, one
must wait deeper into the winter, to know about the climate.
We have very warm & comfortable rooms — and the air is
decidedly LIGHT, which is a great point with me. I write this in
answer to your kind solicitude.

I was delighted, dearest George, to have your letter & shall be
still more delighted if you will conquer your repugnance to writing, so as to let me hear from you sometimes. I meant to have
answered your letter instantly, but I waited, because Robert has
been saying ever since we were in the railroad carriage travelling
from London, "I shall write to George as soon as ever we are
settled", & I wanted to put our letters under the same envelope.
He has been absorbed between his father & sister (whom he had
to carry about Paris from morning till night when they were
here)¹⁴ & the Shelley edition,¹⁵— which is off his hands today,
But I wont wait another post for him, so as to lose this, – He
shall write by himself, & it will be better. His best love, however,
I will send you now.

Dearest George, it's a bad season to ask you to come to Paris
— but you are a bold man & might venture it,— & if you have

a holidaytime to spare about Christmas, besides, everything will probably be quiet by that time, & you can have a room in this house & be our visitor without expence to yourself, & to my great delight, & to Robert's true gratification. – Do turn it over in your mind. Paris is worth looking at just now, I assure you, & I think we might amuse you in various ways. Henry *promised me to come,*— &, whenever he is able, we are more than willing, let him also understand. Mr. Phillimore[16] used your name in introducing himself to me, & no worse thing – He spoke of you as highly & even as *affectionately,* as man could speak of man – It was a great success with me, of course –

How glad you will be to have Arabel back! – By the way, she is to send to Mrs. Thompson's for the Daguereotype of Wiedeman which is Sarianna Browning's gift to her – The picture is very like, but makes the child look much older than he is – Aunt Jane says it will be more like him in some four years, than now –

I am gabbling on with this letter, till the hour of the post strikes – My impression continues to be that the Napoleon movement will succeed – Probably it will secure to France as *much* of a republic, as she can bear, or aspires to –

God bless you – Love to everyone of you – Believe me ever
dearest George, your most affectionate Ba –

I cant read over what is written –[17]

[1] Postmark: Paris, Dec. 5, 1851. Address: George M. Barrett Esq. 50 Wimpole Street, London, Angleterre.

[2] See Huxley, p. 147 ff. In her letter to Henrietta, dated December 13-14 and written from the address above, Mrs. Browning mentions having written all the particulars to George. It appears that George did not show this letter to Henrietta.

[3] Louis Adolphe Thiers (1797-1877), French historian and statesman. He defended the constitution of the Second Republic, was arrested in the *coup d'état* and escorted out of France. He returned the next summer but did not re-enter politics until 1863, as an anti-imperialist. He negotiated the peace of 1871 and became the first president of the Third Republic.

[4] In July 1840, Louis Napoleon made an *opéra bouffe* attack on

Boulogne. The "eagle" appears to have been a vulture brought on board the *Edinburgh Castle* as a mascot by Colonel Parquin. After the fiasco "Colonel Parquin's vulture, which had remained disconsolately on board during the expedition, was consigned to the town slaughter-house; but being a bird of spirit, it escaped and ended its days in a more honourable captivity with a coal-merchant at Arras, after providing the humourists of a continent with a succession of jokes of which they never wearied on the subject of the new Emperor and his eagle" (Philip Guedalla: *The Second Empire,* New York, 1923, p. 121).

[5] Mrs. Browning's admiration for Napoleon III is well known. It began with some reservations but seems to have grown with the necessity of her defending it. The Brownings differed on this subject from the beginning. "Robert and I have had some domestic *émeutes,* because he hates some imperial names; yet he confessed to me last night that the excessive and contradictory nonsense he had heard among Legitimists, Orleanists, and *English,* against the movement inclined him almost to a revulsion of feeling" (Letter to Mrs. Martin, December 11, 1851, Kenyon, II, p. 37).

[6] Robert Wiedemann Barrett Browning (otherwise Pen, Peni, Pennini), born March 9, 1849.

[7] Esprit Victor Élizabeth Boniface Castellane, Count (1788-1862). He served with distinction in the Russian campaign (1812) and continued in the French army, becoming a Lieutenant General in 1833, a peer in 1837, and Marshal of France in 1852. In the war with Austria in 1859 he was named commander of the army of Lyons.

[8] Lynched.

[9] Thomas Bruce, 7th earl of Elgin (1766-1841), so-called because while envoy to the Porte he arranged for the transference to England of the "Elgin marbles" including the frieze of the Parthenon.

[10] Madame Marie Mohl (1793-1883), born Mary Clarke, married Julius Mohl, Oriental Professor at the Institute, 1847. "Madame Mohl was a most extraordinary-looking person, like a poodle, with frizzled hair hanging down over her face and very short skirts. Her salon was at that time (1857) quite one of the social features of Paris" (Augustus J. C. Hare: *The Years With Mother,* ed. Malcolm Barnes, London, 1952, p. 133).

[11] The article referred to was the second of a series entitled *Le*

Poésie anglaise depuis Byron. The first had dealt with Tennyson. Mrs. Browning shared the third with John Edmund Reade and Henry Taylor. At the time she was generally rated second to Tennyson. The review dealt with all Browning's poems but especially with *Christmas-Eve and Easter-Day.* Joseph Milsand (1817-86) became and remained until his death one of Browning's most cherished friends. The 1863 reprint of *Sordello* was dedicated to him.

[12] Since, in spite of this sharp characterization, Miss Fitton's identity remains obscure, it may be worth while to quote the following from a letter to Miss Mitford, dated Christmas Eve, 1851: "Our child is invited to a Christmas tree and party. . . . The lady of the house, Miss Fitton, an English resident in Paris, an elderly woman, shrewd and kind, said to Robert that she had a great mind to have Eugène Sue, only he was so scampish" (Kenyon, II, pp. 40-41).

[13] Thackeray's stepfather was the uncle of Sir James Carmichael.

[14] According to Miss Miller, Mr. Browning, Sr., was in France more or less to escape complications with a certain Mrs. Von Müller, who later successfully sued him for breach of promise (Miller: *Browning,* p. 161).

[15] Browning's "Essay on Shelley" was meant to be included in a volume of Shelley's letters which were proved to be forgeries and were withdrawn from publication.

[16] One of a well-known family of jurists. Either Sir Robert Joseph (1810-85) or John George (1808-65).

[17] This is one of the most plainly written of all the letters. Mrs. Browning's health was good, and she was thoroughly interested in her subject matter.

letter 41   138 Avenue des Ch. Élysées
                                       Feb. 2 [1852][1]

My dearest George,

I was delighted to have your letter & grateful to you for writing to me without regard to old debts – Thank you, dearest George — of course Miss Mitford's affair[2] quite upset me at the time, & threw me out of the habitual ruts of letter-writing – I

felt inclined to go off to Egypt & burrow in the sand somewhere – She might as well have cut off my fingers as a proof
of friendship – Also, that you & Arabel should have taken just
our view of it, confirms me in the belief that it is'nt all disease
on my part, as I might fancy, to listen to Aunt Jane, who "sees
nothing offensive or wrong any way" in what has been said. On
the other hand Robert says that it strikes many people as a glaring indelicacy & want of feeling. Well — I was in a fever of
anxiety to read the whole passage — but when the Athenæum
came within reach, I couldn't take courage to glance at it — I
couldn't make up my mind to that,— & Robert took the thing
away & shut it up, & cut it out of another newspaper which was
sent here by an accident – At the same time, he insisted on
reading the part which was not painful — he said — "out of
justice I ought to hear it" — so I heard it – . Very kind & foolish,
certainly — only people must cry out as to how dreadfully I
must be altered since I had those "large eyes"! — !!! To tell
you the truth, Robert was rather pleased however, upon the
whole, at the account of me. For my part, I never was in greater
difficulty how to act, how to speak to a person, who undeniably
intended by these coarse means to give me pleasure, & as assuredly gave me more pain than I have felt for a long time. "If
an enemy had done it" one would know how to deal with it —
as it was, I was in great difficulty – At last I wrote to her[3]— a
very affectionate letter; — recognizing her affectionate & generous intentions everywhere, but not attempting to conceal that
she had occasioned me extreme pain – There is no answer yet,—
and I shall be most sorry if I have offended her in return for
intended kindness – What can one do? The truth is, that one
ought to be let alone while one's alive – The vultures SHOULD
wait a little till the carrion is ready, & not pluck out the living
eyes – There's a time for all things, says Solomon — and so do I,
who am not Solomon by any means – Apart from painful subjects; — to be dragged into the light & examined as to the
colour of your hair & the number of your teeth, is a hideous
ceremony, & you have a right to protest against it while you live
& feel & blush.

George Sand is in Paris again. Whether we shall get at her this time remains uncertain — for it appears that she has a wholesome horror of lion-hunters & book-makers. Oh, I dont wonder indeed. And then from the notoriety of her private[4] as well as literary distinction — from the fact of her manner of life (her loves as well as her books;) enemies come to stare, & go away to write fierce accounts of a "shameless woman"– The Germans especially have done this. Still, I hope we shall succeed this time – My heart is set on it. She has only just arrived — her "arrest" in the country being one of the innumerable lies which (reversing the idea of the Biblical lion) run to and fro, seeking who shall devour them –

No, George — I am not an apostate. It is on the pure demo-cratical ground that I set my foot, when I cry aloud for respect to the opinion of a great people . . let it be a mistaken opinion or not. Respect for the people — and two other virtues—*justice, & patience,* are considerably in arrear, it seems to me, with the mass of thinkers (especially in England) upon this particular subject. Certainly the people may be mistaken — but they wait to see, and we all must wait – So far, it is only a provisional government. The persons sent to Cayenne & Algiers[5] were all subjected to precisely the kind of judicial commissions, used by the republic under Cavaignac.[6] The severities employed are not comparable to what were called into use then — the number of persons affected is insignificant in comparison. No revolution ever took place in France without six or seven times more blood-shed than we have had this time. The expulsion from France of distinguished men implicated in various parties, was probably the mildest way found possible, of maintaining the peace of the country. They will be recalled in a short time, I do not at all doubt – At the best, however, I am no Buonapartist — I dont accept his constitution as a model one — & it will be modified by degrees — that's the intention. Also, there can be no *"des-potism"* while the people hold the taxes in their hands, & we must not call names without reason. What I consider the worst thing yet done, is the decree against the Orleans property, which admits of no apology,[7] though it is popular I understand among the poorer classes – My hope is that the protestations by the lawyers will be efficient in causing it to be revoked – Most of the lawyers in Paris have protested — & M. Dupin's[8] letter appeared to me very dignified – Observe, people have the power & will to protest, when they discern a wrong — do, observe *that* –

Robert & I have fought considerably upon all these points – I always think that England influences him just in proportion to his removal from England. Patriotism gets the upper hand of judgment, & he drops into a vortex of national sympathy. As for me, I'm a bad patriot, I believe – I care more for the world & humanity every year, & less for local & national interests. The English journals seem to me just as mad & bad with regard to French affairs, as they seemed to me last winter about the ecclesiastical titles[9] — much good, all that fury did them, & much good, will this! – For the invasion — the "pope" was coming before — & now come the "wooden shoes" & Louis Napoleon – The danger & likelihood are about equal perhaps – Well — Arm, arm! See to your rifles! – sharpen your swords – They will distract your thoughts from the "combined workmen"[10] at least, & keep you from the worse kind of melancholy.

Lady Elgin spent last Saturday evening, (no, the evening before) with us, and told us all sorts of supernaturalisms which charmed me. Just think of my ill-luck, George! That Mr. George Thompson[11] who sate by my side three quarters of an hour once, & conscientiously bored me with his American experiences of martyrdom for the slaves, knew all about the "Rappists", had heard the spirits "rap," knew how a spirit gave a kiss to one lady, and an autograph to another — was ready to swear to all these facts from personal knowledge, & I might have heard him swear, & didnt!! I call this the extremity of ill luck – Dont you?

The weather is almost too warm, and I am much better, & have recovered my voice within the last few days — just in time to speak to George Sand perhaps! It's rather hoarse still, but to speak at all is a decided gain. Also, Robert declares that I am looking very well — though I dont altogether agree with him — being thin & pale — with the cold & the shutting up together. After all, if the winter ends so — Wilson says "it's nothing of a winter" — but it has been something to *me,* though brief, if counted by the number of cold days. Little Wiedeman grows more & more a darling. He never ceases talking the most extraordinary mess of a language you can imagine! & is most amusing to us all. Tell Arabel that he has managed her name after a fashion at last & calls her "la zia *Jatella."* We dont teach him yet to say grace or even regular prayers. I am so afraid of tying up the pure free spirit in formalisms, before he can understand significances. But he understands perfectly that God is good & makes him good, & gives him gifts – And quite of his own accord, the other day, after breakfast, he said, turning his bright face up to the ceiling & lifting up his right hand, —"Thé buono — grazie a Dio". And now he does it constantly, quite out of his own head, I assure you.

We had a very satisfactory letter from Florence about our apartment there, and I am triumphant, because as our not giving it up was my fault, I should not have liked to have been proved very much in the wrong. It is let till the third of May, & was let from September. They dont pay enough for it, — but our expenses will be covered, with some five & twenty pounds, perhaps, as matter of profit – Not so bad. As to booksellers they dont condescend to send us an account, & they *must* have money in hand for us — that's certain. Robert has written, but no answer –[12] We must wait in patience – Probably there is a reason, and we dont like the idea of dunning them unnecessarily.

The review in the Athenæum was *not* by Mr. Chorley. The book[13] was dedicated to him, & could not therefore be reviewed by him, unhappily.

Do get the Revue des deux Mondes for the *15* of January — or get to see it somehow – I should like you to read the paper on me, because it pleased me (with some drawbacks) & because I have really a regard for the writer –[14] You will observe how he has cut out the 'sting' of Miss M's remarks — improving the likeness, by the way, by putting in "cheveux noirs"– ! But he was obliged to do something, poor man, on account of the wish of the proprietors –

When shall I hear from Arabel? I know it is my fault – I

knew it – Tell her how I love her dearly. God bless all of you –
I love you all. Is dear Trippy quite well, except that horrible
gout, of which I heard something? And was she frightened at the
fire in Welbeck street. Let somebody tell me. Dearest George,
write to me as often as you can, & love me as much!
I am your ever attached   Ba

[*Across top of first sheet*] I want to know how Papa is – You
did not mention him.

[1] Postmark: Paris, Feb. 4, 1852. Address: George Goodin
Moulton Barrett Esq. 50 Wimpole St., London, Angleterre.
[2] Miss Mitford's *Recollections of a Literary Life* (1852) contained a chapter on Mrs. Browning with an account of the drowning of her brother Edward. In the *Athenaeum* review (January 3,
1852, p. 110) the longest selection quoted from the book is that
dealing with Mrs. Browning. It graphically describes her prostration and feeling of guilt over the drowning of her brother, and
even mentions that Vaneck, who was drowned with him, was the
only son of a widow (see letter to Mrs. Martin, January 17, 1852,
Kenyon, II, p. 43).
[3] See letter to Miss Mitford, Kenyon, II, p. 45.
[4] *Private* has been written over *personal*. The meeting took place
February 12 and is described in a letter to John Kenyon (Kenyon,
II, p. 52 ff.).
[5] "There were no death sentences; but three hundred men were
transported to Cayenne . . . Less than two thousand were exiled,
and ten thousand more were sent to Algeria" (Guedalla, *The Second Empire,* p. 221).
[6] Louis Eugène Cavaignac (1802-57). He directed the troops of
the provisional government during the bloody street fighting in
Paris, June 23-26, 1848, and was defeated in the presidential election by Louis Napoleon.
[7] Mrs. Browning had a British sense of property rights. Compare
her remarks on the Duke of Sutherland's estates (*Letter 36,* p. 138
and *note 4,* p. 140).
[8] André Marie Jean Jacques Dupin (1783-1865). When Louis
Phillipe abdicated in 1848 in favor of the young count of Paris,
Dupin presented the latter to the chamber. In spite of the failure
of the move he remained *procureur-général* under the republic and

after the *coup d'état*. He resigned when the decrees confiscating the property of the house of Orleans were made effective.

⁹ Refers to the disturbances in England during 1850-51 in protest against the Papal bull creating "a hierarchy of bishops deriving their titles from their own sees, which we constitute by the present letter in the various apostolic districts," and the subsequent appointment of Cardinal Wiseman to be Archbishop of Westminster. The Ecclesiastical Titles Bill of 1851 was the subject of long and passionate debate in Parliament. The act, though passed, was never put in force and was quietly repealed in 1871.

¹⁰ Labor unions.

¹¹ George Thompson (1804-78). English abolitionist, associated with Garrison and Whittier in the antislavery movement in the United States. President Jackson denounced him and forced him to leave the country in 1835. Perhaps Mrs. Browning was bored; she was already a convinced abolitionist in spite of the enormous financial losses incurred by the Barrett family through the freeing of the slaves in Jamaica.

¹² See DeVane & Knickerbocker, p. 53.

¹³ The book in question was Miss Mitford's *Recollections* referred to above, which she dedicated to Chorley.

¹⁴ Joseph Milsand (see *Letter 40, note 11,* p. 161).

letter 41a   Avenue des Champs Élysées 138
                                   Feb. 4, '52¹

My dear George –

I consider that the very kind letter you wrote to Ba (too long ago!) was, after all, rather mine than hers — for besides my natural claim to the whole of it, there was so much addressed to me in particular that you have no right to complain of getting two answers — let this of mine thank you most heartily for all the pleasure you gave *her* — she will take the like care of me, I am certain. I daresay you fancy us in the middle of noise & bustle, as indeed we are — but our little nest hangs at the far-end of a twig in this wind-shaken tree of Paris, and the chirpings inside are louder to our ears than the bluster without. The weather has helped to shut us in — that is, to shut Ba in — she

suffered much more than I had expected, coughed far too often
& deeply, and for a long time lost her voice all but completely.
With better weather came better things — the cough may be
considered *gone,* except when changes from hot rooms to colder
provoke it — & the voice is restored. Let us but once get fresh
air & a little exercise and she will go well as ever, we may hope.
Our babe — boy, he is now indeed, is thriving & like to thrive.
Ba will tell you, however.

Is it not strange that Ba cannot take your view, not to say
mine & most people's, of the President's proceedings? I cannot
understand it — we differ in our appreciation of facts, too —
things that admit of proof. I suppose that the split happens in
something like this way. We are both found agreeing on the
difficulty of the position with the stupid, selfish & suicidal Assembly — when Louis Napoleon is found to cut the knot instead
of untying it – Ba approves – I demur. Still, one must not be
pedantic and overexacting, and if the end justifies the beginning,
the illegality of the step may be forgotten in the prompt restoration of the law — the man may stop the clock to set it right.
But his next procedure is to put all the wheelwork in his pocket,
and promise to cry the hour instead — which won't do at all.
Ba says, good arrangement or bad, the parishioners, seven millions strong, empowered him to get into the steeple & act as he
pleased — while I don't allow that they were in a condition to
judge of the case, at liberty to speak their judgment, or (in the
instance of the very few who may have been able to form & free
to speak it) of any authority whatever on the previous part of
the business — for I or you might join with the rest as to the
after-expediency of keeping a bad servant rather than going altogether without one — we might say, "Now that you have
stolen our clock, *do* stay & cry according to your promise — for
certainly nobody else will." And he does *not* keep his promise, as
you see by the decrees from first to last; on that point Ba agrees
with us again — but she will have it still that "they chose him"
— and you return to my answer above, that denies the facts.
And so end our debates, till the arrival of the next newspaper.
You are infinitely better able to see how affairs go, you in Eng-

land, than we here — for all our information is reflected from
your newspapers — every other voice is mute — & "voice"
means the speech of a man to his neighbour in the street, or of
a lady to her guest in the drawing-room. Just to instance the
oblique line by which opinion must travel to be harmless —
people are waiting curiously for the sort of reception Montalembert[2] will have to-morrow at the Institute, where he "reads
himself in" — those who, as liberals, hate him most (for his ultra-
montane bigotry, "legitimate" opinions & so forth) will see it
their duty to applaud him to the echo, on the ground of his
having broken with the government on its promulgation of the
spoliation measures — just as if he had not done his utmost to
help that government when it most needed help — and now
that, in consequence, it can act as it pleases, Montalembert cries
out on it & expects sympathy! None of mine shall he have when
I hear him tomorrow, as I hope to do.

Meantime one must make one's little, satisfying world out of
& inside the great one — & be happy *there*. Your sympathy, my
dear George, is a great element in the happiness of ours — & I
am grateful for such evidences of it as your letter. Will you
remember me with all cordiality & affection to your Brothers &
to Arabel? I don't consider that a visit to London is so chimerical
an adventure as she fancies — but we must wait & see. We have
heard great news from Florence — our rooms are let, and not so
badly — there being few visitors this season. At all events we
lose nothing by that speculation. There is just room to re-affirm
myself, my dear George, yours most faithfully ever,   RB

[1] This letter of Robert's seems to have been enclosed with the
preceding. Perhaps he felt it necessary as an antidote to Mrs.
Browning's defense of Napoleon III.

[2] Charles Forbes René de Montalembert (1810-70). His reception into the Académie francaise furnished the occasion for Browning's poem *Respectability* ("Guizot receives Montalembert!"). The
occasion was exciting because, although Guizot was a constitu-
tional-monarchist and Montalembert a vigorous liberal and anti-
imperialist, convention required that the former deliver the *dis-
cours de réception*.

letter 42   138 Avenue des Ch. Élysées
                                               Saturday
                                               [February 28, 1852][1]

Thank you, thank you my dearest George! You are too kind & generous — & really I could almost reproach you in right earnest for sending me Longfellow's poem.[2] As to the letter, *that* was acceptable without a drawback. You are dear & good, George – Robert's most affectionate regards & thanks for it –

The poem is, as you say, not very full of poetry though we both consider it by far the best production of its author up to this time. While there are beautiful conceptions & images — the language occasionally is very conventional & watery, & the scheme of the poem generally, is taken, I understand from a German work. Longfellow can do anything except be original – Much of the style he has adopted in some places, is imitated from Robert, (as indeed we heard from England it was) only, as might have been expected, the familiarity has not his keenness, nor the idiomatic simplicity his raciness. After all, however, it's an interesting poem, & more likely to be popular perhaps than if it were better –

Reynolds[3] was two days in Paris before giving us what he brought. We did not think him looking ill, but he declared he had had a weekly illness throughout the winter; & I set it down as very foolish, that he should have let slip the opportunity of spending the cold months in the south. He declared he could not before get his business done. I have had two notes lately from Mrs. Peyton & Bessy – Did I tell Arabel, I wonder?

Just now I received her darling letter – Yes, Wiedeman is better, I thank God. Dr. Macarthy did not think it necessary to repeat his second visit, & therefore he is of course sincere in making light of the affection — but the child is not altogether *well,* notwithstanding. He continues to have slight attacks every night — slighter & slighter — & we hope the thing is wearing itself out. I say "every night" but it is rather the morning now,— for the attack which came on as he went to sleep has now ceased, & he is only affected upon waking in the morning at five or six oclock. Also, for the last two nights there has been no laughing — only a convulsive thrill through the body, with a gasp of breath, & sometimes a striking together of the teeth. The most curious kind of siezure [*sic*] it is that ever was observed I should fancy in so young a child – He fixed his eyes this morning on the ceiling with a most seraphic expression, for a moment or two, as if looking at something intently & rapturously — & then came the usual spasmodic shudder — after which, without a moments pause, he began to beat time gently with his hands & sing to himself softly, in his usual way & with quite his usual calm. On asking him afterwards what he saw in the ceiling, he said that he saw an angel playing on a trumpet — "musica bella"– I observed perhaps it was a "captain"– 'No' he persisted . . 'no, mamma! no 'apitano . . . angiolino – " *not a captain, but a little angel.* Wilson is half inclined to think that the child has real visions. Its curious altogether. But plainly, (we all are of opinion) the affection is diminishing gradually, and, in the daytime, a more joyous, healthful little rosy creature you could not wish to see – Oh yes — tell Arabel we keep him as much back as we can, & as quiet, — but that is very difficult – He ran into me yesterday to make a grave complaint against Wilson – "Mamma, Lili no buona. Peninni 'viva Peone', e Lili cina Peninni – " Lili wasn't good. She was going to give him medicine because he cried *Viva Napoleone.* Certainly a hard case – A case indeed of decided political persecution, it seems to me.

I am afraid dear Minny is right in her conjecture about our having waited too long to give him medecine [*sic*]. That never shall happen again in any case. Also, when the two teeth are through, much of the irritation is likely to cease — by God's will.

My dearest George, I could say a great deal in answer to your letter to Robert – Certainly crimes are crimes — whether perpetrated by a people or an individual — but "crimes" must be proved if you please, as well as charged — though I know that is'nt the way of the Times, & some other newspapers. I believe, upon the whole, that no revolution ever took place in France with so little bloodshed & suffering, as the coup d'etat of the second of December — and that the exiling of the heads of

parties, was the most merciful alternative of civil war, possible
to the government – Even now, some of the men sent away, are
readmitted into France — and after a time, the others will be
received, I do not doubt. Here is Cavaignac standing for Paris
meanwhile – I hold fast to the hope that we may see our way
more clearly presently. It is right to observe, that, after all the
stringent laws on the press, & the particular article upon foreign
newspapers, we get our English journals (with their frantic
invectives & exaggerations) precisely as usual — Times, Examiner — Leadei, & the rest. (Punch, excluded by Louis
Phillippe, enters freely now.) This is curious at least. The president seems to choose to have all the reins in his hand, but to
pull them only when the necessity occurs. A bad system of government, you will say, & I agree with you entirely. Still, let us
distort & exaggerate nothing – The French are a most extraordinary people, & the present position of the country is not to be
siezed at a glance – A democracy with a responsible man at its
head, is no *despotism* whatever ugly despotic signs may be shown
by the actual executive. What vexes me extremely in the English
journals, is their denial of facts — the great fact for instance, of
the freedom of L N's election – Truth, truth — do let us have
truth – "C'est la verite – " said George Sand —"on ne peut pas
la nier."

I understand that Thackeray disapproves of the violence of
the Examiner. So much the better. It quite refreshes me to hear
a little sense (though the sixth of a grain) from an Englishman
talking on French affairs. As to our beloved friend Mr. Forster,
I would chain him up & gag him (if I had my own way) for the
next six months,— even if dear Mr. Kenyon's social dinners had
to suffer for it.

Lord Malmsbury, your new secretary for foreign affairs,[4] is
said here to be a personal friend of Louis Napoleon, & very
acceptable on that account,— but the government papers dont
like the change of ministry in the main – They are afraid of the
Tories who always have been unfavorable to France,— & there's
an idea (I hope unfounded) that the new ministry will be more
likely to encourage the war-cry than the Whigs were – Louis

Napoleon shows marked attention to the English – At the great ball at the Tuileries last Saturday, to which the Hedleys went, he walked through the rooms with the wife of the English ambassador on his arm – Aunt Jane almost fainted through the crowd & crush –

Yes, tell Arabel, I heard all about Anna Hedley,[5] & it was a dreadful case, as like insanity as a different thing could be – She looks better though pale — she never looked *ill* exactly. The intimidation used was, to apply hot irons to the soles of her feet — anything but a homeopathic remedy, I should fancy – Mrs. Stewart Mackenzie[6] called in a homeopathic man a month or two ago, & was much the worse for it — I *believe,* to a certain extent — but, in the case of rapid remedies being needed, my faith breaks in the middle.

We have not yet seen Lamartine (but shall) — nor have we seen George Sand yet for the third time – Tell Arabel she is far too severe on her indeed – There was not the least intention on her part of being otherwise than most cordial to us — & the confidence she showed us was fuller of compliment than any banality of mere manner could be – The effects were singular notwithstanding — you should have seen the disdain with which she looked at my respirator – I took it out of my muff to show it to her — because her chest is not strong, & though better since she came to Paris, she has had a great deal of cough & was bled for this the other day – "Oh"—said she —"life wouldn't be worth the trouble of such precautions"– And when somebody enquired how she was —"Je ne me porte pas bien," she answered —"but as to that, I never think of it except when I'm asked"— which perhaps was a way of saying "Dont ask." She nevertheless looked very well that day – Brilliant eyes, certainly, & a smile which outflashed them — only so rare a smile!

So Henrietta is to be in London on Wednesday – I envy *her* a little — and I envy *you.* Let Arabel write me a long descriptive letter, as she [*on envelope*] promises about Altham[7] & about Henrietta herself. I am going to write to *her* very soon, being deeply in her debt, dear thing! I mean Henrietta –

This envelope is scarcely an improvement on my last – It's

too thick now – But I will reform it all, tell Arabel – Give my love to Sam Barrett.[8] Best love to Trippy & all of you says dearest George's ever attached Ba.

[*Across top of first sheet*] Mention Papa whoever writes. And ask Arabel to say how Mrs. Orme[9] is. Ask her too, to find out for me whether *Mrs. Jones*[10] is quite well, as a friend of hers enquires.

[1] Postmark: Paris Feb. 2(8?) (The second digit is not quite legible); also B.I. Mar. 1, 1852. February 28, 1852, fell on Saturday.

[2] *The Golden Legend*, 1851. The German work, referred to below, on which it is based is *Der Arme Heinrich* by the twelfth-century poet Hartmann von Aue. Mrs. Browning's opinion, both praise and blame, is in substantial agreement with that of later critics, though the "imitation" of Robert may be exaggerated.

[3] Reynolds Peyton, eldest son of the Peytons of Barton Court.

[4] James Howard Harris Malmesbury, 3rd Earl (1807-89), foreign secretary in 1852 and again in 1858-59.

[5] The Hedley daughters were named Arabella, Ibbet, and Fanny. Anna could be a relative (sister?) of Uncle John.

[6] Mrs. Mackenzie is mentioned also in Erskine's *Anna Jameson* as having attended a party at which the Brownings were also present. There is no further identification (Mrs. Steuart Erskine: *Letters and Friendships of Anna Jameson*, New York, n.d., p. 265).

[7] Henrietta's eldest son. Henrietta married William Surtees Cook, a distant cousin, April 6, 1850.

[8] Probably Mrs. Browning's cousin, Samuel Goodin Barrett of Jamaica.

[9] Mrs. Browning's governess at Hope End.

[10] The name has provided the lady with an impenetrable mask.

letter 43   138 Avenue des Ch. Élysées
                                           May 13-14 [1852][1]

My dearest George,   Since I wrote last to Arabel we have all been ill. La grippe (commonly called influenza) griped Robert to begin with, and then Wiedeman, & then Wilson — and I think I have had a pinch from it myself, although the three dampish coldish days which occurred about a fortnight ago may be accountable chiefly in my case for having revived my cough in a vexatious way – I am getting better however in this magnificent weather, & the trace will soon be worn out – All the sooner that my darling Wiedeman has turned the corner of his attack, for I couldn't help being very sympathetical with him – For eight nights he had fever, with a state of oppression in the eyes & head which quenched all his spirits & unmade him from what he was – I never saw him half so unwell before. Now he has cough, but the fever has left him, & he has recovered his vivacity — though pale & thin, much pulled down in every respect – We called in no medical advice – I had cried "wolf" so often, that Robert was incredulous about the necessity for rifles — and I did not like to press it this time — certainly the treatment for common influenza is obvious enough –[2] Still Wilson & I are perfectly persuaded in our own minds that the child has the hooping cough – So much the better perhaps, now that the worst is over. He has hooped again & again, and the previous symptoms, the state of the eyes especially, & the obstinate feverishness were not characteristic of an ordinary attack of cold – Mrs. Ogilvy[3] who has just come from Florence, thinks the cough just like hooping cough & keeps away her children – Whatever it is, however, he is a great deal better, & my anxiety is almost at an end – Soon we shall take him to Fontainbleau for a day or two, which will set him up I hope before the time comes for London, as I should not like to take him into your thick atmosphere till he is strong – Then, the change will do good – So bright & rosy he was looking before this. The Ogilvys thought him greatly improved, & with much more appearance of strength than he had last year – Robert too has been extremely unwell & looking like a ghost — only not as unwell as Wiedeman nor in the same way, Wilson & I maintain obstinately — never mind. Both of them are convalescent now – Peninni is in ecstasies this morning over a kitten which he is nursing tenderly in his pinafore – Desirée offers to buy it – He refuses with decision – She says she will give him "quatre sous"– Oh no, Detitée –" "cinque sous"– "No –" "Dix sous"– 'no'– "Cent sous"– "No Detitée, puis pas." (meaning "Je ne puis pas". He understands French perfectly, and English, besides his Italian — and the other day when Wilson was complaining of not knowing the French for a donkey, he suggested "*ane, Lili,*" With all which his own manner of talking is most hard to make out — it's the most Babylonish of Baby-tongues –

I had a letter from Mrs. Martin this morning – The Martins are to be here on saturday if the rooms they have written for are attainable, but the difficulty of getting a closet even in Paris just now is great. The Selwyns[4] will tell you how they fared & paid – I was glad & surprised when they walked in to us the evening before last, having come from home in five days – We both liked him extremely — he seems to have both kindness, & cleverness & cultivation — & Bessy is radiant with happiness in spite of the dust of the journey.

Do you know, George, I went to the Champ de Mars & saw the military fête — the giving of eagles?[5] I had been anxious to go in proportion to the difficulty of getting tickets – Seven pounds were given for a ticket, & many persons failed in procuring them at whatever cost – We had tickets for an atelier from which you had a bird's eye view of the whole, but till the very morning there seemed no hope of admission to any tribune on the Champ de Mars — when at half past eight oclock Lady Easthope[6] had the great kindness to send us two tickets — one for Mrs. Jameson & one for me – It was courageous to go without a gentleman, but we none of us had the least idea of what the crowd would be, and Robert, after consigning us to a citadine went off to the Ogilvys with his atelier tickets without the least anxiety. You may imagine the crush when I tell you that on an ordinary day one might drive from this house to the Champs de Mars in ten minutes, & that we actually accomplished it in about three hours & a half. Mrs. Jameson was a little afraid because she "had promised Robert," as she said, to "bring me back safe," and was'nt sure how she should be able to accomplish it – She was loud in reprobation of the "want of

management," and of the "absence of police –"— which I told
her was the consequence of our excess of republican liberty – Not
a policeman anywhere scarcely, the people having it quite their
own way in the thoroughfares, & men in blouses assisting us to
our places in the tribune. For my part I was'nt at all afraid &
was extremely amused — only the fête itself disappointed me,
grand as it was, because our places were not good, & we could
not see the president nor hear the music satisfactorily, nor feel
the heart of the great show therefore. You see, the size of the
Champ de Mars is enormous — three miles round — & I should
not have been quite satisfied with anything less than the position
of the ambassadresses – Lady Augusta Bruce & her sister[7] wandered into the tribune of Louis Napoleon & were turned out
of course ignominiously – We have heard of all sorts of misfortunes on all sides – The heat was extreme, yet there was a
breath of breeze now & then to keep one alive, & the canvass tops
of the tribunes warded off the sun. Before the ceremony concluded Mrs. Jameson & I crept away with the hope of escaping
the crowd & getting a carriage – Not a carriage anywhere! –
One man was bribed to go & fetch one, but he came back with a
hopeless countenance —"Not for a thousand francs could we
get a carriage, if we went all over Paris for it –" Every likeness
of a vehicle was engaged – I said in despair — "My strength is
at an end –" (for we had been wandering about, observe) "It is
absolutely impossible for me to walk much farther – If we can
reach where the shops are, you shall go home & send me the first
carriage you can." Well — we got onto the Boulevard des In-
valides — but the whole place was crowded with tables & people
eating & drinking — & Mrs. Jameson cried, "I never *can* go
back to Browning & tell him I have left you among all these
men — we must sit here together & wait." A byestander observed
that in two or three hours perhaps we might attain to a carriage,
so it was rather hopeful altogether – But what a thing it is,
O Louis Napoleon, to have a glorious destiny! After ten minutes
up came a cocher —"he would desert two ladies for us, if we
would be quick & get into his carriage & give him three francs
for a 'pour boire' — the said ladies had left him for a moment,

& we might be off before they returned –" I am ashamed to confess our baseness – We concluded the compact & tumbled into the fiacre without a moment's hesitation – What two ladies could be as distressed as we? – Off we drove as if pursued by Conscience & a legion of devils – But at the bridge ("de la Concorde") there was a dead stop – The bridge was densely packed with the people — no possibility of passing – "Vous pouvez voir," said our coachman looking over his shoulder —"c'est tout a fait impossible – Donnez moi deux francs de plus et je vous prendrai par Chaillot –" So we agreed, & were driven the full circuit round by Chaillot, & arrived at home in a condition of thankfulness & exhaustion we shall not very soon forget, I think – But I am glad I went — though Robert w^d not have let me if he had had an idea of the state of things. It is considered miraculous that we fared as well as we did – Mrs. Streatfield,[8] for instance, paid fifteen francs for being conveyed to her tribune by a citadine, and had to walk the whole way home though extremely unwell & unfit for it.

And now do you look at one another & wonder whether I was bent (being of this adventurous metal just now) on getting a ticket for the President's ball? No, Arabel — dont open your eyes with horror at me! No, George — I eschewed the ball really,— balls are not at all in my way, except when I play at them with Peninni. You might observe that a review might seem as alien to me at the first glance — but it was'nt the review itself — it was the significance of the whole event that I cared to study & try to understand – And, after all, I saw nothing but the mere military pomp — which is nothing to me. I liked the crowded streets better.

But the fireworks — oh I would have certainly gone to see the fireworks if it had not been for this horrible cold & cough, which would not even let me go up to Mrs. Jameson's rooms, last night where she had assembled some friends for the purpose of seeing what was to be seen. Not much could be seen there — not much more than our own terrace commanded. I could see the rockets, & the tops of the fire-glories even from these windows, and I stood here watching them through the trees opposite – Most glorious – I could hardly help going to wake Peninni — though Wilson declared it would frighten him – Desirée was highly poetical in her enthusiasm – "Cela me fait un effit [*sic*] extraordinaire! C'est comme un coup d'estomac quand je vois cela –"

Paris is running over with population, & as tranquil as possible,— Louis Napoleon's government stronger than ever, & more likely to stand – We have a personal friend of his in this house, Admiral Askew,[9] with his wife & daughter — an English sailor of the antiquest type — who is a personal friend of Peninni's as well as the president's, & pays him the utmost attention — sending up strawberries to the child when he is unwell & doing all sorts of kind things. Peninni is very popular in general – Admiral Askew calls him "my boy," & gives him his cocked hat to set on his curls, & swears at him familiarly – "You are a little devil – Aren't you a little devil?" "No, Peninni no Debil. Peninni, Peninni –" Wilson says that he sits in an armchair opposite the admiral, & talks Italian to him in his way, most imperturbably –

Oh — dont let me forget to tell Arabel – We were out one evening — & at the soirée (where by the bye we heard Tellefsen[10] play Chopin's music beautifully) was Madame Hahnemann, the wife of the original homœopathist –[11] She is a most peculiar looking woman – The face is striking — and the hair, as white as snow, & perfectly uncovered, was dressed in a profusion of ringlets, with plaits behind – Altogether it looked like snowflakes — drawing one's attention very much, & forcing one to quite admire the peculiarity – She prescribed for Robert who was suffering from influenza at the time, & he took home with him globules & drops enough to complete his cure – She used to prescribe for her husband's patients during his life – Well — the effect was just nothing — that is, just what Robert expected. By the way there was a Polish princess who desired to be introduced to me that evening, & was full of M. Philarete Chasle's[12] lectures – She was intelligent & agreeable though, and talked well of literature. Of course I told her that there was scarcely a word of truth in what she had heard of me.

Now ask Arabel to skip this paragraph. Guess what enormity I have committed lately George! We went to see "La Dame aux Camelias," which you moral English are crying out against, & which we immoral French dont admit of "les demoiselles" going to see at all. I wont allow (I being neither French nor English but a mere citizeness of the world) I wont allow that it is immoral, or is in the least calculated to do harm by its influences – The acting was most exquisite — too exquisite — it really almost killed me out of my propriety – I sobbed so, I could scarcely keep my place — & had a splitting headache for four & twenty hours afterwards, the remembrance of which will avail to keep me away for the future from any like exhibites. The play is by Alexandre Dumas *fils* — & the success has been something prodigious – When people want their hearts broken, they have only to go & see – There is a caricature representing the whole pit with umbrellas up to defend themselves from the tears raining out of the boxes. It is too affecting — it passes the bounds of art — and that's the very worst of it to my mind. Mrs. Jameson wants me to go again with her — but I say —"Oh no thank you – Take Robert if you like — but for my part I have had too much of it already." Why, the tears ran down Robert's cheeks — he could not resist it himself –

We had Lady Elgin here last Saturday evening again, and the evening did not go off half as well as usual —, because of a decided dyspathy between her & Mrs. Jameson – Lady Elgin is a great spiritualist with a leaning to Irvingism[13] & a belief in every sort of incredible thing. While she talked of a communion of souls, Mrs. Jameson began to talk of private madhouses — in a way which made my blood run cold – I really thought there would have been an explosion between the two women, & that Robert & I, who agree so admirably with Lady Elgin,[14] (for whom I bear quite an affection) would never carry the evening to an end safely. Lady Elgin *did* say —"Perhaps you think me mad."

Now I must finish – Will you, whoever of you writes to dearest Storm, give him my best love?

I feel sure that Wiedeman has the hooping cough,— but the

worst seems to be over – Uncle Hedley goes to England, I hear, on Monday – What a scramble of a letter, George. I cant correct the press — there's no time for reading.

When is Arabel going to write to me? Did she get my sesquipedalia sort of letter – God bless you all – I love you dearly, dearly –

Thank you, dearest George, for letting me hear of you. Oh — I do trust we shall be more together this summer than we were last – Love to Trippy always –

And Robert's love to you –

I am your ever attached Ba.

[1] Postmark: Paris, May 15, 1852. Address: Angleterre, George G. M. Barrett, Esq. 50 Wimpole Street, London.

[2] Another Victorian confidence now lost.

[3] Mrs. David Ogilvy. She and her husband met the Brownings in Florence and became intimate friends. "She published some time since a volume of 'Scottish Minstrelsy', graceful and flowing, and aspires strenuously towards poetry" (Kenyon, I, p. 445). (Mrs. Ogilvy wrote a short memoir of Mrs. Browning prefixed to F. Warne and Co.'s edition of her *Poems, n.d.*)

[4] Probably the lately married Bessy Peyton and her husband.

[5] Among the many acts of Napoleon III calculated to revive in the French army the elegance of the First Empire was the restoration of the imperial eagles to the standards of France.

[6] Wife of Sir John Easthope (1784-1865), politician and journalist, M.P.; purchased the *Morning Chronicle* 1834; created baronet 1841.

[7] Daughters of Lord and Lady Elgin. Lady Augusta became the wife of Arthur Penrhyn Stanley, Dean of Westminster. Lady Charlotte, her sister, married Frederick Locker-Lampson, the poet.

[8] "Mrs. Streatfield was the widow of Major Sidney Robert Streatfield, 52nd Light Infantry, by whom she had four children. She married secondly on August 5th, 1852, Captain Henry Francis Cust, 8th Hussars, M.P. for Grantham, by whom she had six children. She died September 14th, 1867" (Huxley, p. 157). So full a life seems to warrant a full note.

[9] Unidentified. Since the name does not appear on any of the naval lists, the "Admiral" may have been a courtesy title.

[10] Thomas Dyke Acland Tellefsen (1823-74), Norwegian musician, pupil of Chopin with whom he visited England in 1848. He taught piano in Paris and was well known, chiefly through his intimacy with the master.

[11] Samuel Christian Friedrich Hahnemann (1755-1843) promulgated in 1796 his doctrine that diseases are cured by those drugs which produce symptoms similar to them in the healthy. Some years later he became convinced that drugs are effective in much smaller doses than are generally given. It is this aspect of the system which was responsible for the "globules and drops."

[12] Victor Euphémion Philarète Chasles (1798-1873), from 1841 professor of comparative literature at the Collège de France. He wrote some fifty volumes of literary history and criticism, and of social history. In 1852 he greatly disturbed Mrs. Browning by announcing, in a course of lectures on English literature, "an extended notice of E. B. B., 'the veil from whose private life had lately been raised by Miss Mitford' " (Kenyon, II, p. 43).

[13] A movement headed by Edward Irving (1792-1834), minister in the Church of Scotland and later founder of the Catholic Apostolic Church. He communed with the spirits of the prophets of old from whom he received guidance. He and his congregation believed that the apostolic succession had not been completed and that he was called to found this new church.

[14] It would seem from this that Robert had not yet displayed his complete antipathy to spirits.

letter 44   Florence, May 2 [1853][1]

My dearest George,

I thank you again & again for your very kind letter about Colombe,[2] & so does Robert. I insisted on going down with him yesterday morning early to get the letters & afterwards examine the newspapers at Vieussieux's[3] before anybody else arrived – So frightened I was. Robert was calling on me to admire this bright light across the mountains — that black shadow on an old wall — but I could'nt look at anything for my part – My heart beat so I could hear it with my ears. Well! on the whole, I am satisfied. Your letter was a great relief – Then, the 'Morning Post' was very satisfactory & flattering — we are only in advance of our age, thats' all – Daily News favorable too – Times illnatured in its usual snarling way, but admitting a success. Oh — as you think, there wont be a run probably — but it's a 'succes d'estime' & something more — & favorable to the position in literature, calculated to give a push to the poems –[4] In the meantime Chapman & Hall dont use the opportunity of advertising – They are worse than Moxon himself to my mind – For instance — how do you make out that from the sale of a large edition of my two volumes (above a thousand copies) at sixteen shillings, my share of the "half profits" should be only about a hundred pounds? Do you really imagine that booksellers pay themselves after the same fashion, & buy villas at Wimbledon out of such pay? I believe more easily in Rapping spirits.

Mr. & Mrs. Twistleton[5] have just come back from Rome, & are to spend this evening with us to meet Mr. Tennyson[6] & young Lytton –[7] He[8] is a brother of Lord Saye & Sele, & has married an American,—a rather pretty woman. An intelligent man, & said to be a scholar, besides modern accomplishment.

Mr. Lytton was here last night too. He came chiefly to announce that a table had been moved at Florence at the house of acquaintances of his – There was a great crackling, & then it spun round – They had tried before & failed — sitting in the circle for an hour & forty minutes. When they succeeded they were standing — the standing position being said to be most effective. In that case I give up the glory of helping to move a table. Standing for an hour & forty minutes would be of itself supernatural work with me, to be possible work. So Humbolt[9] speaks contemptuously of these things! So be it – Even Humbolt has not seen the end of all wisdom –

Have you heard a volume of poems by Dr. Arnold's son, ('by A')[10] spoken of in London? There is a great deal of thought in them & considerable beauty. Mr. Lytton lent them to us the other day.

Yesterday being the last day of the races Penini & Wilson went to see – He was enchanted, & told us all about it, & how the "green man" was "the prettiest," & "kept behind all the others" — which he seemed to consider an advantage – He liked it better on the whole, he thought, than the Boboli gardens, & in fact set it down as "velly funny indeed."

My dearest George, I heard of your being named in the House of Commons, & I do earnestly hope that after all this uphill work, this walking in bogs (called the law) you will get soon upon smoother ground – You have done well & uprightly in life, — which is certain good, let what will, come of it. Social life is difficult in our days, & the struggle is necessary to everybody, let us try for what we may — even poetical prizes! — Oh the poor — how sorry I am for them. What will be done with _____? _____[11] will be very much vexed of course.

We are still uncertain in our plans — have not made up our minds. Robert seems to think we are not qualified for Rome in the present state of our finances — & as Colombe is not likely to run into a gold mine,— why, I dont know what to say. It is not decided one way or another you are to understand.

Robert bids me say, with his love, that he thanks you deeply for your kindness about the play – Your letter was the first we opened, & there were few beside –

God bless you, dearest George! Do write to me sometimes, & love me always — as truly & most tenderly I love *you* –

Your Ba

[1] The envelope preserved with this letter is blank, except for George G. Moulton Barrett Esq. The long break between this letter and the preceding is partly accounted for by the fact that from June to November, 1852, the Brownings were in England with rooms at 58 Welbeck Street. Also, it is possible that some of the letters of this period may have been destroyed in accordance with Robert's desire to suppress as much as possible of the evidence of her enthusiasm for spiritualism. Later letters, however, show clearly that George did not destroy all — if, in fact, he destroyed any — of her disquisitions on this subject.

[2] Helen Faucit's production of *Colombe's Birthday* ran for seven performances in London in April, 1853.

[3] Gabinetto Vieusseux, a library and reading room still flourish-

ing in Florence in the Palazzo Strozzi. It was much used by the English colony in Florence during the nineteenth century, particularly for the periodicals and newspapers available there.

[4] Mrs. Browning was always much concerned over the popular failure of Robert's poems. Throughout her life she was the more successful poet.

[5] "Edward T. B. Twistleton . . . was a barrister and politician, who enjoyed the curious distinction of having 'probably served on more commissions than any other man of his time' " (Huxley, p. 288). His wife, Mrs. Ellen Dwight Twistleton (1829-62) of Boston, came to England as a bride in 1852. She met the Brownings through Carlyle (McAleer, p. 99).

[6] Frederick Tennyson (1807-98), elder brother of Lord Tennyson. The Brownings saw much of him during their years in Florence where he lived. He wrote poetry of some merit and was an ardent spiritualist. Hallam Tennyson records a visit in 1887 with his father to Frederick then living near St. Heliers on the island of Jersey. "My uncle," he says, "had grown more spiritualist than ever" (*Alfred, Lord Tennyson: A Memoir*, II, p. 342; see also Kenyon, II, p. 113).

[7] Edward Robert Bulwer-Lytton (1831-91), 1st Earl Lytton. He spent most of his life in the diplomatic service and was at the time second secretary at Florence, where he became an intimate friend of the Brownings. In spite of his distinguished diplomatic career he is perhaps better known by his pen-name, "Owen Meredith."

[8] The following comment refers to the Twistletons, *note 5*, above. It certainly does not fit Lytton, who was an only son and did not marry until 1864.

[9] Friedrich Heinrich Alexander Humboldt (1769-1859). The culmination of his extraordinary career as traveler and scientist was his *Kosmos* (5 vols., 1845-62), a description of the physical universe.

[10] Matthew Arnold. The reference is probably to *Empedocles on Etna, and Other Poems* by A., 1852.

[11] These words have been completely inked out.

letter 45   Casa dolomei — Alla Villa — Bagni di Lucca
          July 16-17-18 [1853][1]

My ever dearest George,   The first thing I do in our new nest is
to write to thank you for writing to me. Also I want you all to
know where I am to be written to for the next three months —
so it's a little for you, you see, & a great deal for me. We arrived
here yesterday – We did not mean to come to the Baths of Lucca
— still less to this part of it which I never shall like as well as I
did our hermitage at the top of the mountain where we lived
four years ago.[2] But hearing accidentally of this house, for which
we are to pay eleven pounds for a term of above thirteen weeks,
the cheapness & convenience — for the house is large — beguiled us, & here we came directly – We cant occupy all the
rooms — there's a separate sittingroom for Robert to write in —
& there's a spare bedroom where we may have a friend — &
there's a garden — and a beautiful view out through that row
of seven planetrees to the mountains beyond. The people are too
likely indeed to infest us, but we have made it public (by means
of our acquaintance Mr. Sunderland)[3] that we mean to be
private — it's impossible to submit to a flood of visitors in the
way of wateringplaces — & we are going to work hard, George
— if Robert does not make good use of that cheerful little blue
room with two windows, I shall give him up, I say. Peninni is
enchanted – "Oh how pety lese Bads of Lutta –" Ferdinando, it
seems, has bought a "real gun" — I hoped he was'nt going to
kill the birds. "Oh no! only mans!" Which made me open my
eyes, till it was further explained that the object was to make
men "hear the thunder of the gun, & not make them die." On
our arrival last night horribly tired, the child proposed to take a
walk directly to the top of the mountain. "I not a bit tired —
oh no –" Dont let me forget to tell you that when it was proposed for us to go into the mountains to live, though charmed
at the thought, he considered me directly. "But," said he to
Robert gravely, "I aflaid lose cold mountains & all y snow will
mate Mama not velly well." Nothing less than Mont Cenis was
in his fancy – We had to pluck him down from that sublime

height. But was'nt it dear of the child to think of me in the midst
of his joy? – By the way, the word "snow" was idealizing itself
into pleasure about the time we left Florence, the heat being
intense, suffocating – It was necessary to come away, I assure
you – The two last nights I couldn't sleep, & Peninni had grown
paler. We left Casa Guidi in the hands of Ma^{dme} Biondi's husband,[4] with the hope of its being let a part of the summer at
least – Well — I was sorry to leave Florence notwithstanding the
heat . . . & the fleas – If I did'nt think by nature of my dear
Arabel often & often, the fleas would remind me of her – Affecting & poetical association! – Seriously I do wonder whether
she could submit to shake her petticoats & be happy in Italy –
Even I, who am tolerant, have rushed about the house at
Florence this summer in a frenetic state, like Io from another
sort of fly. Then Mr. Tennyson would calmly observe in the
course of conversation —"Dont you find the fleas worse than
usual this year, Mrs. Browning?" "Yes indeed, Mr. Tennyson."
"By heaven he mocketh me,
    As if there were a monster in my thought."[5]
namely a centipede –

July 17. But I was sorry to come away – I am always sorry to
leave Florence, & this time we had been happier than usual — *I*
had, at least. Also, there was something painful in breaking the
thread & letting our pleasant friends roll off like lost beads – Mr.
Tennyson goes to England for three months – We quite love
him – He used to come to us every few days & take coffee &
smoke (I graciously permitted the smoking) & commune about
books, men & spirits till past midnight. (n.b. Wilson didn't like
him as well as we did.) He was with us the last night. So was
Count Cottrell[6] for half an hour, bringing Sophia's goodbye. So
was the American minister from the Court of Turin, Mr. Kinney
& his wife[7]— which made rather a press for our disconsolate
household, but we couldn't help it. The American Excellences
had arrived a few days before, & had given us one previous
evening; then hearing we were suddenly going away, they proposed to come again on that last night – What could we say?
Mr. Kinney pleased us much – He has a certain nobleness of

mind & opinion,— of general atmosphere — as well as considerable intelligence – He warmed our hearts with hopeful news of
Piedmont concerning the rapid progress of the people & the
honest intentions of the King[8]— who is not a man of much
intellect, but is capable of good fixed ideas — such as — "that
he is not the state, that his ministry is not the state, but that the
souls of the people are the state." A supernatural sentiment for a
King! – Mr. Kinney told me he had pointed out to the King
that passage in "Casa Guidi Windows" about his father Charles
Albert,[9] & that he was "much gratified." "If you were to go to
Turin" added Mr. Kinney, "he would give you a cordial reception." What pleased me more was another thing mentioned —
that Azeglio[10] when prime minister, quoted the poem in the
Piedmontese chamber – That, I liked to hear. Mrs. Kinney
dabbles in literature, wrote a review once upon Robert — & was
about to write two years ago to invite us to visit them at Turin
when she heard of our having just left Italy — which vexed her
so that she "cried"– So she swore — & I believe — I who am
credulous. She is a vivacious, demonstrative, rather pretty
woman, with what Alexander Smith[11] w^d call a cataract of
auburn ringlets — (no dishonor meant to Alexander Smith who
is a poet —) — not especially refined for an ambassador's wife,
but natural & apparently warmhearted to the point of taking
you by storm – They have come south for his health – As we
were going to the Baths of Lucca, "Oh certainly they would go
too, if it were only for a week." So the wife said, & the husband
assented. They inaugurated their arrival in Florence by being
cheated (through the ignorance of their maitre d'hotel) to the
extent of twelve pounds sterling in payment for luggage.

The evening before our last at Florence was spent more
pleasantly. That, I really enjoyed – I dont know when I have
enjoyed anything more – Mr. Lytton invited us to a bachelor's
party at his villa, to have tea on the terrace – Its a villa perched
high up at Bellosguardo, close to Galileo's, and the double view
from that terrace — on one side, Florence seething away in the
purple of the hills — on the opposite, wood & mountain pressing,
gaining on one another, into the far horizon-line still bloodied

from the sunset — is past describing – It was nearly nine when
we had tea – There was a sofa on the terrace, & chairs — & the
table spread with cakes & fruit,— and as we were all bachelors
I made tea like a bachelor — that is, as awkwardly as possible –
The teapot wasn't large enough, & the cups were too large —
but I managed it at last by giving everybody half a cup – Our
friends were there — Mr. Tennyson, Mr. Powers,[12] & Signor
Villeri,[13] a Sicilian, one of the most accomplished men in Florence – It was quite cool & enjoyable, & as we consumed floods
of strawberries & cream, & the stars pressed out over us to meet
the fireflies underneath, we were very sociable & had quantities
of interesting & harmonious talk. Nobody struck a discord – For
instance, we agreed that Faraday's[14] letter on the moving tables
was "insolent & arrogant" & Robert did not extenuate – Signor
Villeri suggested the desireableness of expounding the advent of
the spirits to the Italian mind in a book which he seems to contemplate writing. Such stories were told!! The old ghost-stories,
George, are effete, stale — they are nothing to the everyday
events of the present generation that eats strawberries & cream
in talking of them – We were a company of believers, except
Robert, who believes every other day, with intervals of profound
scepticism – He will make no profession of faith till he has the
testimony of his own senses, he declares — but in the meantime
being a reasonable man, he shakes a little – Really he is dying
hard – Nobody can set him down as too credulous – But he &
all of you must come into it — as surely, George, as I sit in this
chair & look out from it to that mountain! I tell you — I warn
you. Why wait to embrace a truth with the servants of the age,
the running footmen of the age — those who lag behind? – Mr.
Faraday will have to eat every indigestible word of that letter of
his – The letter does not meet the facts of the case — only the
imitations of the facts — only those amateur performances which
mimic the actual phenomena – I, for one, have always been
aware (I think I said so in a letter to Wimpole street) of the
fallacies which might & did conceal themselves in various of
those operations, & that a very slight & unconscious muscular
movement, on the part of several persons, would move a rather

heavy table – But — for instance — no muscular movement, conscious or unconscious, of fingers laid on the surface of a table, however light, would lift that table into the air — nor can Faraday's explanation affect the numerous cases where tables, sofas, lamps &c are moved & lifted without the touch of a finger or foot – An American gentleman, Mr. Coale,[15] spent two evenings with us in Florence before we left it – Mr. Powers brought him to us, & we had a great deal of talk on the subject – He is an underwriter to an Insurance Company in Boston — a man of considerable quickness & apparent conscientiousness – He told us that he had given to the subject a dispassionate examination — just as he would to any matter of business — & he had come to the conclusion that a communication between the natural & spiritual worlds was established beyond contesting – We were talking of Faraday's letter – "But" said he, "Faraday knows nothing of the facts. I have seen again & again tables moved & lifted without a touch. On one occasion, in a private house, I maintained that the table should *not* be moved. I held one leg of it with all my force, & my brother held another" – The medium was sitting several yards away — & no human being touched the table except the holders of the legs. Yet it was lifted violently, "wrenched" out of their hands — that was the expression. He has seen tables make a figure of S on the floor, as if a man skated it on ice — without a touch — simply at a desire. He has seen tables lifted on end — so[16] [*drawing*] — while pencils, lamps, books, which under ordinary circumstances would have slipped off, kept their places as if they were nailed to the surface, at an expressed desire – He has seen young children in private houses produce these effects – It is common for children to be mediums – A child of a friend of his in New York, whose name he told me, a child six years old who did not know how to form a letter, in the normal state, writes faster than people write a running hand, when the spiritual influence siezes [*sic*] her & numbs & impels the arm — writes rapidly & earnestly page after page things of which she is not conscious – The wonderful revelations he made to us exceed even these which I have told you here — but there is no room to enter into the heart of them. One can only say in reply, three things — "You lie" — or "You are mad" — or "there are great wonders on the earth." If the man were alone in his testimony it would be reasonable, I admit, to choose one of the *two first* conclusions, – But in the present case when I myself have received accumulated personal testimony of the same sort from men & women of good reputation & more than average intelligence, I conclude according to my reason, on the *third*. If I did not believe these things I should not believe in Augustus Caesar, or any person or fact of history –

You should hear Mr. Kinney talk on this subject — a grave, reasoning man, who has had to do with politicians all his life instead of mystics – He said to me these words as far as I can recollect — "I began of course by disbelieving — then I kept my "opinion long in suspense – Now, what am I to say? Baron "Humbolt has just observed to me in a letter treating of other "matters — '*there are epidemics of the mind as of the body* — "*& the actual mental epidemic relates to spiritual influences*' – "Well! — if indeed it be an epidemic, the malady is reaching its "crisis. Within these few days, & since I last saw you Mrs. "Browning, I have received accounts from America of the most "extraordinary character – The first men of the country, jurists, "statesmen, economists, men of the highest character in respect "to mind & conscience, — my own personal friends — have come "out frankly before the public — committed themselves entirely "with the public & risked their political deaths in doing so — testi-"fying to their own spiritual experiences & to their having re-"ceived communications specifically from the spirits of Calhoun, "Webster, & Clay – Now, I ask you – Am I to sit in this chair "& say of such men, whom I have been accustomed to hold in "reverence, & with some of whom I have been bound in intimacy "for fifteen years — these men are insane — & I, I who sit in this "chair & judge, I only am sane? I cannot indeed say it." He would have sent me the papers he had received on the subject but we were to leave Florence at seven the next morning — there was no time – One letter I saw from Mr. Tallmadge,[17] member of Congress, whom Mr. Kinney knows well,— a political econ-omist of high character. Mr. Tallmadge after frequent commu-

nications with Calhoun's spirit, desired a clearer proof of
identity, & was directed to place paper & pencil under the table
— he heard the sound of writing — then, said the raps "Look"–
On the paper was written —"I'm with you still – Calhoun."
The autograph was precise, Calhoun's son & various of his friends
testifying to the facsimile of it. Also, Mr. Tallmadge was desired
to place a guitar under the table, which was played upon by
invisible hands in the most exquisite manner – "I have heard fine
performers on the instrument," says Tallmadge, "but anything
equal to that spiritual music, I never heard." Is Tallmadge a liar
or a madman? Answer, George — Mr. Kinney calls him an able
& honest man, firstrate in his department, & as little likely to be
visionary as our economist of England, Macgregor –[18]

Mr. Coale is religious. He says there is a great admixture of
evil spirits, & a great amount of personation, & that persons in an
unspiritual state of mind are apt to abase these things to their
own undoing – At the same time good has been accomplished
by their means, & he knows one individual personally whose
whole course of life has been renovated & turned to God, besides
others who have been benefited in various ways. That the good
spirits come — he considers undeniable – A young lady, a friend
of his in Paris, is a medium, & receives constant communications
from the spirit of her mother – Once she asked —'If evil spirits
could have communication with her'– The answer was —'Not
only they can, but they have had it.' Since, she will never begin
any intercourse of the sort without using the test of the apostle
John 'Do you acknowledge that Jesus Christ is God in the flesh'?
It seems to be a mixed influx from the spiritual world.

And you will set me down as an unmixed idiot, George. Nevertheless, you will change your views & I shall not change mine.
Arabel likes me to tell her the things I hear, & perhaps you dont
— who knows, as Penini says – But what you cant read you can
throw over to Arabel – I must, while on the subject, write out a
few sentences from Sarianna's[19] last letter, because they are curious as coming from *her* —"I should like to see Miss Kemp[20]
again, for so little can be gained from one experiment, but I fear
she is leaving Paris – I have read Professor Faraday on the sub-

ject & must say it scarcely applies to what I saw. The wonder was not in first setting the table in motion,— a very, very slight pressure w^d have done that,— but in the odd turns it took when fairly roused to action, & its singular position. No involuntary pressure of the muscles could keep a table running on one leg in what the Americans call a 'slantingdicular'[21] direction. The rapping of course must have been made wilfully, not involuntarily, — yet I kept my eyes fastened on Miss Kemp & her fingers, touching them from time to time, without detecting how it could be done. Once, when the table answered wrongly, she gave it a slap & cried "Que tu es bête"— *It twisted itself up and down like a child in a passion.* Again I say I cannot presume to form an opinion from one imperfect experiment – Miss Kemp may be a clever manipulator, & I a poor detective,— it is quite possible,— but it is downright nonsense to call it an involuntary action of the fingers: it was a wilful deception, if one at all. Miss Kemp told me that the first time she tried it, was with a large party — they sate for an hour & a half without the slightest success & she thought it all nonsense. Some time afterwards she tried a hat, and to her surprise, moved it very quickly."

There is just one thing proved in Faraday's letter — that the simplest phenomena of moving tables are not to be accounted for by the *known* laws of nature – Yes, there is another thing proved – That the humility of Bacon & Newton does not distinguish the scientific men of this age, any more than their genius does –[22]

I dont instruct Penini in these things I assure you, but he hears people talking – He said to me the other day —"Dear Mama, you knocked at mine door?"— No —"Well"— turning round a face radiant with satisfaction —"then it *muss* be *pinnets.*" Not that he considers it to be the least wonderful or frightful or anything of the kind; — the supernatural & natural are on the same level to Penini just now. He gives me a great deal of trouble in walking about the house with him —"Tate me at Lily, dear Mama"— and I said foolishly the other day, 'that I was tired of it, & that if he didn't mean to go by himself, he ought to have an angel to carry him, who wouldn't be tired –'

On which, in a moment, he cried out aloud, looking upwards —
"Tome, angel"! The next moment the strange child was down
on his knees with his hands clasped, & face turned to the ceiling –
"What are you doing, Penini," said I, a little alarmed. (I fancied
he was praying to the angels which w^d have been *un peu fort.*)
"Mama Dont you memember lat pretty picture in the newspaper – All y angels toming down, & all y peoples waiting and
looking up – I put mine hands up just lite *lat.*" He was thinking
of a picture in an American spirit-publication called the "New
Era or Heaven opened",[23] of which Mr. Powers lent us a number. The illustrative engraving represented an angelical descent,
while men & women were on their knees with eager hands
stretched out. A most Yankee publication, by the way, it was,—
but Penini admired the picture excessively & had remembered it
for some weeks.

Robert rushes in from his blue room & asks for space just to
write in a few words to you –

. . . .

My dear George – I never read Ba's letters[24] — and she knows
so well what I feel & think, that no doubt she has told you, in her
perfect way, the little that I should try & put down, otherwise.
Besides, I bade her send you a message by Arabel — but no
messages, nor amount of putting down, can thank you enough
for your great kindness – The opinion[25] you gave set so many
fears,— indeed nearly all my fears — at rest, comparatively.
These horrible nightmares slip off one's breast at last, and become a laughing matter – While they hold us, they are formi-
dable enough. Well, we are again at this green, cool, bright,
quiet, noisy place — for it is all these in a piquant mixture, for is
it not white, in its houses — & green, in its sycamores, vines,
hempfields & chestnut-trees — cool, *for Italy* — & bright, at the
same time, as a great sun makes it by day, and an even greater
moon by night, lending *such* colours on the mountain-side & such
shadows in the valley! Then, we are quiet — for there's nothing
civilized beyond us, on *this* side, but a few charcoal-burners'
huts, the river & the woods — still, on the other side, it is too

true that there's the "Sovereign's" family ("our moderator," as
people say here, from pure contempt) and the late "sovereign"
(the Prince of Parma) coming, and an Empress hoped for – So
that this place is, as it were, an epitome or picture-in-little. (see
the rest, in any treatise on the variablness of mundane affairs)
Now, dear George, here we are — here we may not always be –
It is too foolish to *ask* you, to *invite* you — but, *if* your vacation
could coincide with the three months' stay we meditate, — think
what a truest delight you could give us! In any case, remember
me for yours, ever most affectionately,

RB.

[*Across top of first sheet*] It is deliciously cool here – Oh that
some of you w^d come to our spare room! Come, George, do!

[*On envelope*] I hope you dont, any of you, justify the Times
for the infamous part it is playing about Russia. As to Louis
Napoleon he acts well on this question – That seems incontest-
able even in England. The bishop of Maryland[26] came with Mr.
Kinney to our door, & sent his "love" to us both, with a message
to Robert that he had "read Christmas Eve through twice in
one night". There's a bishop for you! He didn't come in to see
us because of his ill health.– He was afraid of talking. Ask
Arabel to write & speak of herself especially – George, *do* manage to get her out of town this summer. It is *necessary* – You or
Henry ask Papa –

[1] Postmark: July 25, 1853. Address: George Goodin M. Barrett
Esq. Angleterre Via France, 50 Wimpole Street, London.

[2] Miss Miller (*Browning*, p. 151) paints a very gloomy picture of
the Brownings' earlier stay in Bagni di Lucca, darkened by Robert's
reaction to the death of his mother. Nevertheless, the period and
place seem to have lingered pleasantly in Mrs. Browning's memory.

[3] The only other reference to the Sunderlands seems to be: "We
have been to Mrs. Sisted's, and to Mrs. Sunderland's" (August 30,
1853. Huxley, p. 193).

[4] Both Madame Biondi and her husband have so far eluded us.
They may, of course, be the people from whom the Brownings
rented Casa Guidi.

[5] *Othello,* III.iii.107. "As if there were some monster in his thought."

[6] A young English artist, and member of the household of the last Duke of Lucca from whom he received his title. Sophia Augusta Cottrell (née Tulk) was his wife. Mrs. Browning's poem, *A Child's Grave in Florence,* was written on the occasion of the death of the Cottrells' infant daughter Alice Augusta, 1849. Cottrell was later in charge of seeing that the design for Mrs. Browning's monument in Florence was properly executed. See *Letters 68* and *75,* pp. 284, 298.

[7] William Burnet Kinney (1799-1880), journalist and diplomat; advisor to Harper and Brothers. President Tyler appointed him to be representative of the United States at the Court of Sardinia in Turin (1850-53). Cavour consulted him about the American system of government. At the expiration of his term he went to Florence, did research on the history of the Medicis, and became a great friend of the Brownings.

[8] Victor Emmanuel II of Sardinia and I of Italy (1820-78).

[9] Charles Albert (1798-1849), King of Sardinia. Although he distrusted liberalism, he risked everything to achieve liberty for Italy and brought upon himself the hatred of liberals and conservatives. He abdicated after the defeat at Novara (1848) and died in a monastery at Oporto. The "lines" referred to occur near the end of Mrs. Browning's poem and include:

Yea, verily, Charles Albert has died well;
And if he lived not all so, as one spoke,
The sin pass softly with the passing bell.
For he was shriven, I think, in cannon-smoke,
And, taking off his crown, made visible
A hero's forehead.

This estimate is at complete variance with that of Browning expressed in *The Italian in England* (1845). The first wish of the Italian is to throttle Metternich and the second:

Charles, perjured traitor, for his part
Should die slow of a broken heart
Under his new employers.

Elizabeth, when she read the poem in 1845, called it "serene" and "noble" (W. C. DeVane: *A Browning Handbook,* 2nd ed., New York, 1955, p. 157).

[10] Marchese Massio Taparelli d'Azeglio (1798-1866). He was a leader in the risorgimento, helping to foment the revolution of

1848 and secure reforms from Pius IX. He was premier of Sardinia 1849-52.

[11] Alexander Smith (1830-67), Scottish poet. His *A Life Drama and Other Poems* (1853) created something of a sensation. He is, perhaps, best remembered as the author of *Dreamthorp: Essays Written in the Country* (1863).

[12] Hiram Powers (1805-73), American sculptor. He settled in Florence in 1837 and remained there the rest of his life. Mrs. Browning wrote a sonnet upon his celebrated statue "Greek Slave" (1843). She wrote to Miss Mitford October 1, 1847: "Mr. Powers the sculptor is our chief friend and favorite, a most charming, simple, straightforward, genial American, as simple as the man of genius he has proved himself needs be" (Kenyon, I, p. 347).

[13] Pasquale Villari (1827-1917). Italian historian, statesman, and educator. He was for a time professor of history at Pisa and at Florence, and later became a senator of the kingdom. His wife was an English woman (née Linda White), widow of Vincenzo Mazzini. Villari's best known works are *Storia di Girolamo Savonarola e de' Suoi Tempi* (2 vols., 1859-61) and *I Prima Due Secoli della Storia di Firenze* (2 vols., 1894-95). Both Brownings consistently misspell his name.

[14] Michael Faraday (1791-1867). His essay on unconscious muscular action published in the *Athenaeum*, July 2, 1853, pointed out that the personality of the medium could be responsible for phenomena which were given spiritualistic explanation.

[15] Fortunately Mr. Coale has been pretty fully described. We have been unable to find out any more about him.

[16] A sketch of a tilted table is inserted here.

[17] Nathaniel Pitcher Tallmadge (1795-1864), United States senator from New York 1833-44. When President Tyler appointed him Governor of Wisconsin Territory, he resigned his seat. He was removed from office in 1845 and devoted his time to writing religious tracts. He became a convert to Spiritualism.

[18] John Macgregor (1797-1857), statistician. He was joint secretary of the Board of Trade in London, 1840, and in 1847 M.P. for Glasgow. He was a free-trader, extreme materialist, and utilitarian.

[19] Sarianna Browning, Robert's sister.

[20] Obviously a medium. Many of those practicing throughout Europe at this time were Americans.

[21] Meaning in a slanting direction. Listed by Thornton in his *An*

American Glossary (ii, p. 806) as first occurring in America in 1832 as *Slantindickelar.*

[22] This is obviously unfair to Faraday's character and reputation.

[23] The picture, not the publication.

[24] A fortunate habit for this letter. It is certainly one of those which Robert was so anxious to destroy.

[25] The "opinion" cannot be clearly identified. It might conceivably have dealt with some phase of the difficulty Robert Browning, Sr., was having with Mrs. Von Müller (*Letter 40, note 14,* p. 162). A letter of the poet's to John Kenyon, January 16, 1853, deals somewhat guardedly with the matter "which has grieved me as few things could" (Hood, pp. 38-39).

[26] This feat must distinguish him sufficiently; his name cannot be found.

letter 46   Lucca, October 7th [1853][1]

My ever dearest George. I must tell you at once how much I thank you for your letter particularly as I want to make known to all of you that you must write to Florence until you hear farther. We leave this place on Monday next, having seen the season to the end. There are five folding doors (only that) in the room where I write — not a carpet of course. Extremely pleasant for the summer, but by no means desireable for the sort of weather we are beginning to have now. Mountain-places catch winter by the forelock — it will be warm in Florence, and yet the Prato Fiorito where we penetrated some three weeks ago, is already covered with snow which chills the air of the vallies. I told you I think of our excursion there. The distance is six miles off, but the ground being absolutely perpendicular, the guides forced to walk at every animal's head to prevent a general precipitation, you can scarcely calculate the amount of necessary fatigue. Said I to Mr. Lytton as we approached home —"I am dying. How are you?" "A quarter of an hour ago" he answered, "I thought I should have to give it up altogether, but now I am rather better." Think what the fatigue must have been to bring such an answer from a young man one & twenty who had ridden the whole way. Certainly he is very delicate. For a week afterwards I could not stir from the house but I never suffer permanently when the weather is so exquisite as it was. Oh George! we have enjoyed our summer here very much! If you had come, how much better still. And Bradshaw beguiled you wrongly in his representation of the time necessary for the journey to Italy – A week would bring you here, even if you travelled quietly, in the case of your coming by Marseilles – Well — its over now — only remember another time. We have been very happy here & not idle either. Robert especially has done a great deal of work, & will have his volume[2] ready for the spring without failure he says. I have been more indolent — but my poem[3] is growing heavy on my hands — & will be considerably longer than the 'Princess' when finished. I mean it to be beyond all question my best work — only intention does not always act itself out into evidence, you know. For the sake of this poem I should prefer staying at Florence this winter where there would be more opportunity for quiet concentration — but we cant defer Rome any longer – To see Rome is a necessity, previous to our return northwards. Oh George — I wish I could drag you all over the Alps, & then I would give up my nationality with an excellent grace, really! We should have to go to England to see our books through the press of course — but after that, no more of England for me – I should be content with our Italy here for all the purposes of life.[4] As it is, we must try Paris. Doubtful it is to me whether the climate will be possible to me after one winter — but we must try. Paris is delightful for everything almost, except the climate — which is not Italian, at the best.

Why is it that Arabel does not write to me, when she has a letter of mine to answer? I want to know how she is, and you dont say a word, George – She is very naughty about writing.

The Storys[5] went away last Wednesday with the intention of spending two or three weeks at Florence on their way to Rome. The evening before their last at Lucca they spent with us here (indeed we used to meet almost every day at one anothers houses) and he tried the 'tables' for some twenty minutes –

Under such disadvantages though.— for Robert just laughs &
jokes — we had to turn him away after five minutes — there
was only Mr. Story, . . . his wife & I assisting . . . & I am
almost immediately stupified with the mesmeric effects. Mr.
Story would mesmerize me with looking at me almost, if I did
not get out of the way,— I object to subjecting myself to this
power of his – Also, the table, though it creaked sympathetically,
would have required a small host of spirits, to move it, the
Luccka [sic] tables being of most peculiar formation. We are to
try these things at Florence, it is agreed. Well — but Mr. Story
told us to put letters into his hands, which (without looking at
them of course), he received specific impressions from enabling
him to tell the characters of the writers. He had never tried it
before. He said he felt himself so charged with influences of some
kind, that he could do this – And certainly — as Robert said,
"his guesses were most happy". We gave him your letter — one
of Miss Wills-Sandford[6]— one of Henrietta's — one of Mrs.
Story's — some writing of Roberts, & some of mine — & most
curiously right the descriptions were. I cant help thinking that
he would make a good medium, if he would persist & believe –
As it is, though he has moved tables again & again, he has never
elicited the *intelligence* which is the common characteristic of the
phenomena. Oh, I must tell you, George, a piece of gossip which
we had from young Lytton. After we left Florence he was asked
by some people there to join a party who were going "to try at
the spirits." He, being a poetical & serious person, objected to
the levity of the terms & people, & wouldn't go – Well — he
heard afterwards that there was a great deal of success notwithstanding — and that upon one table in particular flying off
with great velocity towards the door, old Mrs. Trollope, being
one of the visitors, exclaimed in a state of extraordinary excitement — "*Damn it, let it go.*"!! "That was rather hard upon the
spirit concerned," observed Robert.[7]

My dearest George, you surely must see that an "a priori"
argument against these phenomena or any other is contrary to
all philosophy. Whether it is reasonable to believe a thing possible, cannot be argued in the face of a fact. You & other un-

believers are using just Strauss's argument against Christianity — the most unphilosophical of all arguments. Internal evidence is to be examined of course on other grounds — but what will you do with your internal evidence when the external evidence is established in opposition to it? When a thing *is,* the time is past for considering the probability of its being. For the rest, if the phenomena in question were confined to the practice of a few persons, I should be inclined altogether to agree with you in attributing them to trick & charlataning. But as it is, the denial of the facts on the ground that they are not probable, appears to me really absurd – You may as well deny that men saw a comet this summer or any other palpable experience of mankind. Of course I dont insist on your believing in the spirits. If you think that "the unconscious projection of a second personality attended by clairvoyance" is a more reasonable solution than the spiritual solution, accept it – I do not blame you though I could not myself come to such a conclusion – But a denial of the *facts* must really be classed with the shutting of one's eyes at mid-day and[8] the observation "it is dark."

For my part, I would not touch with the end of my finger an *a priori* argument with regard to anything in nature – Of the laws of nature, so called, we know so little, that we can feel forwards scarcely a step. Cause and effect, as a relation, is a mystery to us still, as you are well aware. *"The laws of nature"* is a mere phrase for our small experience.

Mr. Story had a letter the other day from an American friend in Florence, who said — "There are rumours that the spirits are beginning to *show themselves* in the western states." Take the "rumours" for what they are worth. If the visible form be assumed, you will be shaken it seems to me — & this has been expected for some time. Meanwhile Galignani[9] (who disdained to give us Robert Burn's communication) allows us to read that a machine has been constructed at Berlin to facilitate the phenomena, by offering a more delicate & susceptible instrument to the influences whatever those are. I have not had my letter yet from Mr. Westland Marston.[10] I do hope it's not lost on the road, for of course I attach a great deal of interest to such personal experiences as he has it in his power to give me.

Dearest George, you quote Alfred Tennyson's "honest doubt" – I wonder what Alfred Tennyson thinks of it all, at this hour of the day. We shall hear from his brother, who is incapable of "honest doubt" I really believe – I never saw so believing a man — never! Why, George, when he talks he makes me feel like an infidel – And I am generally supposed to have a good stock of credulity, too; am I not?

So you set up Alexander Smith against us – Well — may Sparta have him (& others) for worthier sons than we! – Only in order to that, your Alexander must work. His genius is undeniable, but quite *in ore*[11] at present. He is not the least of an artist, George. His imagery is, as the gods please — heavenly enough in the stuff of it, but dislocated by the fall from heaven into his earthly hands. Still, I have read him only in extracts you must consider, & my opinion can scarcely under these circumstances be worth having.

Tell Arabel, Miss Blagden[12] from Rome enquires much concerning her. Miss Blagden has been reading Swedenborg,[13] & is clearly "infected" tell Arabel. It is extraordinary how Swedenborg gains ground with the thinkers of the day. I understand that young men of a certain order in England are inclining much to him — but it is in America that he has his public *par excellence*.

Well, George — is it to be war, or not war? We are coming to a point, it seems to me, & must be prepared for all conclusions. Hating war as I do I have hated the Aberdeen procrastinations[14] still more. If the allies had acted with decision from the first, the Czar would probably have retreated by this time,— but now his pride & obstinacy are deeply engaged & retreat is more difficult. The Aberdeen-stone round the neck of Louis Napoleon, has been a desperate drawback – I am glad at any rate that it is'nt to the point of dishonour both to England & France. Robert & I have been writhing with rage & inquietude. It is curious, the state of things here – The poor Italians cry "war, war," as starving men would cry "bread, bread". Their hope is in a war

— & in Louis Napoleon. Admit, George, by the way, that he is doing pretty well even in English eyes, just now – Do you know, I heard Mr. Story say the other day — "Well! I began by loathing that man — but he certainly gains on me! I begin now to think there's good in him." Yes, and wait a little longer. 'You will see what you will see.'

That horrible cholera. My states of anxiety are coming back again in great spasms. Now if you dont write to me you unkind Arabel, it will be absolutely cruel. I do entreat you all to take care — to use every precaution of diet & medicine. It may not be bad in London perhaps — may God grant it, & preserve you all, most dear as you are! –

Yes — it was strange — that *misprint* of papa's![15] The habits of memory are stronger with some, than the habits of the affections.

Oh George, I can write no more.

They come for my letter. We are in great bustle this last day — for I kept it to another day to finish –

Your ever most attached Ba.

Send this to Trippy.

Roberts best love –

[1] Postmark: Bagni di Lucca, Oct. 9, 1853. Lymington, Oct. 15, 1853. Angleterre via France. Address: George Moulton Barrett Esq., Milford House, Lymington, Hants.

[2] *Men and Women.* It was not published until November, 1855.

[3] *Aurora Leigh.*

[4] Compare Browning's *"De Gustibus –"* for similar thoughts.

[5] William Wetmore Story (1819-95) lived in Rome from 1850 where his studio became a center for distinguished English and American artists and writers. The friendship between the Storys and the Brownings was particularly intimate and the letters of each family are studded with references to the other (see Henry James: *William Wetmore Story and his Friends,* 2 vols., London, 1903).

[6] Miss Jane Wills-Sandford. In a letter dated May 5, 1868, she mentioned not having seen Browning for years. In this and two succeeding letters she is solicitous about Pen and his education.

(*Intimate Glimpses from Browning's Letter File,* Waco, Texas, 1934, pp. 38 ff.)

[7] On the occasion of this incident, the editor may be permitted to admit an experience of his own. In the Pennsylvania village in which he grew up, the focus of social life for six or eight late teen-agers was "Aunt Molly," a widow of more than sixty. She was a large woman, elegant of manner, gay, and charmingly worldly, so stiffened with rheumatism that, though she could walk alone once under way, getting her up out of her chair required a community effort, generally accompanied by a series of groans expressive equally of her comic sense and of pain. This woman, without any shade of mysticism in her character, who would have laughed to scorn any suggestion that she was a "medium," possessed the power to move tables. Often, though always with considerable reluctance, she was persuaded by the young people to perform the trick for their entertainment. One evening the table to be moved was an old-fashioned oak extension table about four feet square standing on a carpeted floor in the dining room of the editor's home. After laboriously seating herself at one side, "Aunt Molly" laid her hands flat on the table-top about two inches in from the edge. Hers were the only hands on the table. The editor, still skeptical after many demonstrations, clasped his fingers lightly around her forearms so as to detect any muscular contraction incident to push-ing. There was none. Suddenly, with a futile attempt to rise from her chair, Aunt Molly cried: "Catch it! There it goes!" and there it went, violently, over the carpet to crash into the wall three feet ahead. No one, least of all the operator, pretended to explain the phenomenon, and no one gave "spirits" a thought; but the table did move swiftly, obviously, demonstrably — the dent in the plaster remained for years. The editor, himself, tried later to push the table with his palms from a sitting position and was unable even to budge it by muscular effort. "When a thing is true," as Hilaire Belloc observed, "one must believe it, no matter how im-possible it may seem."

[8] *and* written over *with*.

[9] Galignani owned a newspaper in Florence which bore his name.

[10] John Westland Marston (1819-90), dramatic poet who, after Bulwer-Lytton, maintained the poetic drama on the stage. Mrs. Browning's interest in him was doubtless due to his membership in the mystical society of John Pierrepont Greaves and to his editing of *Psyche,* a mystical periodical.

[11] In the mouth; i.e., much talked of.

[12] Isabella Blagden (1816?-75). Probably the best known and certainly the Brownings' most intimate friend in Florence. Her parentage and the place and date of her birth remain a mystery though there is a suggestion of India. She and the Brownings saw each other almost daily. She visited Mrs. Browning on the day of her death and during the dark days immediately following took charge of Robert and Pen. When Browning left Florence they made an arrangement to write to each other once a month, she on the twelfth, he on the nineteenth. (For these letters see *Dearest Isa: Robert Browning's Letters to Isabella Blagden,* edited with introduction by Edward C. McAleer, University of Texas Press, Austin, 1951.) Miss Blagden was the author of a book of poems introduced by, of all people, Alfred Austin, and of several novels among which are *Nora and Archibald Lee, The Crown of Life,* and *The Woman I Loved and the Woman Who Loved Me.* Her treatment by Chapman and Hall was a contributing cause to Browning's break with that publishing house (see DeVane and Knickerbocker, pp. 393 ff.).

[13] In a letter to Miss Blagden of about the same date as this one, Mrs. Browning writes of Swedenborg: "There are deep truths in him, I cannot doubt, though I can't receive *everything,* which may be my fault." Then, turning to her favorite subject of spirits, she continues: "If a spiritual influx, it is *mixed* — good and evil together. The fact of there being a mixture of evil justifies Swedenborg's philosophy (does it not?) without concluding against the movement generally" (Kenyon, II, pp. 145-46).

[14] Lord Aberdeen (1784-1860) had been foreign secretary in 1844 when Czar Nicholas, visiting England, first proposed the dismemberment of Turkey. As prime minister in 1853 he engaged in protracted negotiations with Russia, France, and Turkey, hoping at once to restrain Russia and avoid war.

[15] There is no indication as to what this statement refers to, but it is a fair conjecture that the "misprint" is in some way connected with Mr. Barrett's determination to treat his daughter as dead.

letter 47   43 Via Bocca di Lione
                                             Jan. 10 [1854][1]

My ever dearest George   I have your letter this moment & answer it directly. I shall be vexed indeed if Arabel has not received my long one long ago, since writing which I have written to Henrietta. Mind — Two letters have gone to Rome to Arabel, & one to Henrietta – I am afraid the posts are not regular. I should feel very guilty if I left you in anxiety willingly. Forgive me for involuntary sins – You make me sad about dearest Papa, though you call him better & though a return of cough & asthma was a natural thing under the circumstances of your severe English season – Do let Arabel write to me every detail, for I shall be very anxious, let me struggle ever so much against it –

My dearest George I am going to calm you down a little from your vexations about this wise man's preface to Robert Hall.[2] What we should chiefly be sorry for is that Robert Hall should have an editor with so little common sense — & for the rest, I really fail in getting up the steam to be sorry at all. When women go into a crowd they cant help being jostled a little by greasy coats — happy they, if nobody treads on their toes! Now I consider that the least of my toes is perfectly unaffected on this occasion. When you have a wife, George, keep her out of print, if you object to jostling, for she will avoid it on no other conditions — and even then, she may wear a gown too high or too low, or of the wrong colour or fashion, like Ma^{dme} Soulé's[3] & be called "Margaret of Burgundy"[4] by somebody, & you may have to fight a duel for her — "who knows?" as says Penini when he is speculative exceedingly –

Let us examine the charges against me.[5] *1st the tendency of my poetry,* (and of Robert's!!!) *is to Swedenborgianism.* Well — I have heard that before, & always consider it an immense compliment to my poetry. There's great truth in Swedenborg — and if I used it before I knew it, so much the better for me, I say – But secondly, I "was a liberal Unitarian" — When was I a unitarian, I wonder? When I wrote Swedenborgian poems? That was being round & square at the same moment, understand, — Swedenborgianism being the exact contradiction of Unitarianism whether liberal or unliberal. 3dly And *"now I am opposed to the whole Christian church."* If that means opposed to Church-domination, priestcraft & creeds over & above what is

written in God's Scriptures, yes, yes, it is true – (Also I think
that all the churches have something either over or under God's
Scriptures — tho' certainly I am far from pretending myself to
the infallibility which I can recognize no where else.) But you
will do me the justice to admit, George, that; however impo-
tently & inconsistently; I do hold in love Christ's universal
church — trying to "hold the Head", believing from my heart &
soul that in Him was the fulness of the Godhead bodily, & that
by His work we are saved – Why George — the common charge
against me has always been a too unscrupulous toleration — a
willingness to walk with all sorts of company as far as we could
be "agreed". A position of absolute schism my worst enemies &
critics never found for me before! – Well — now it would be
easy (supposing I had the address of editors &c) to contradict
what has been written of me. I might say — "The tendency of
"my works it belongs to my readers to decide upon,— but I take
"leave to say of myself personally that I never had any tendency
"to Unitarianism, liberal or otherwise, in any part of my life —
"& that, at present, if a union with the Christian church means a
"recognition of Jesus Christ as my Lord & my God, then is it a
"calumnious error to represent me as a schismatic from the
"church & an example of modern infidelity." Easily I may say
that — but is it worth while, do you think? Will Alfred Tennyson
condescend to send a commentary on his verses, do you think?
Is'nt it far better to let one's books & one's life speak for one?
After all its rather amusing to be set down among infidels by this
apprehensive person, while infidels are setting one down for a
fanatic — which I am sure several infidels have done by me,
though making generous admissions of my being tolerably good
tempered & gentle — "only so credulous" | — A lady at Florence,
literary & philosophical, said to Mr. Stuart[6] lately —"I cant understand how a woman of Mrs. Browning's genius can believe as
she does in the fictions of the Christian religion"– Dearest
George, I omitted to ask a question of Arabel which I hope she
will answer now I do ask it, in the letter she is to write to me
directly – You received your copy of the 3ᵈ edition — two were
sent (Hall[7] had directions to that effect) — and you must tell me

if any mistake occurred – Also the Hedleys had theirs? Arabel saw to that? Poor little Edith Story[8] has attack upon attack of Roman fever (fever & ague) every day or two, & is looking much reduced – They should take her away, I think, she will never shake it off while she stays here for all their quinine. She has been out in the carriage twice, Penini going with her – She is very fond of him & he of her. "I love Edith more of evellybody". "What! – more than Mama & Papa" – "Oh no — I not mean lat."— Also Thackeray has been ill for the second time, & talks of leaving Rome "which does'nt agree with him." That is, the combination of dining out & Rome doesn't agree with him — one at a time would answer perfectly – I propose that he should give up the dinners & remain at Rome — but it's impossible he declares. He cant live without dinners — he must have his dinner & two parties at nights, or in the mornings he finds it impossible to set to work at Vanity Fairs or Newcomes. The inspiration dries without port. By the way, let me tell you — Two nights ago we were at Mrs. Sartoris's at a musical soirée, listening to magnificent music from herself (you know she was Adelaide Kemble) & other professional friends male & female. A great many people were there — & the excessive mildness of the night admitted of my going too – (We have a general invitation to her musical fridays) Mr. & Mrs. Archer Clive[9] being present, I went up to say a word to her & interrupted some talk with a pallid gentleman at her left, who looked; hair, complexion, even eyes; to have been snowed upon for a certain number of centuries till he was assimilated to snow both in colour & cold – "Mr. Lockhart"[10] said Mrs. Clive – He was properly introduced to Mrs. Browning – "Well'— said he to me — with his lean frozen voice —'I am sorry to hear that Mr. Thackeray is ill.' I said what I have been saying to you – "Dining out at Rome" he exclaimed — if a staccato effort of the voice may be called an exclamation —"Why who *can* dine out at Rome? *I* have never dined at all since I came – I have seen nothing I could eat – And for the wine — nobody touches it unless in search of poison – No – I will tell you what hurts Thackeray – Those girls hurt him – Those girls annoy him & teaze [sic] him. If he wants to be well, he should get a governess, or an aunt, & dispose of the girls." I ventured a few words in extenuation of the girls, who are nice & frank affectionate & intelligent — (& turn tables without touching, moreover) but Mr. Lockhart was in his snow — and after all, Thackeray does complain that "domestic life is heavy on him –" *that*, there's no denying — & Lockhart understands why better than I pretend to do – From Mrs. Sartoris's we came home to a quadrille-party in the apartment below us, at Mr. Page's.[11] He is an immense favorite with us both, & his wife had begged us so to put in our heads as we came up stairs that we could'nt say 'no'. That was on Twelfth night you are to understand – I didn't absolutely go into the dancing room — I stayed by the fire with Mr. Page & talked spiritualism, & about what was secular & not secular — we had a great deal of talk, and I a slice of cake, and then Robert who had been standing in the doorway of the quadrille-room, admiring the pretty women, & protesting that his own venerable age would prevent his dancing again — ("Said the Raven, Nevermore"!) came to remonstrate with me for staying so late – "Anybody like *me* for dissipation he never had to do with"! Robert is charmed, you know, when he can accuse me of "dissipation" before a witness – "He was dreadfully tired — but as for me I never was tired"– & so on. Its the only evening nevertheless I have been out in Rome, except now & then to the Storys to have tea in quiet, & once to Miss Blagden's festa when Penini & I went together. In fact the weather was cold here for one fortnight & I kept to the house faithfully – Now it is warm like May in England — only moist & given to showers. We are invited to the Clives on Wednesday – I shall not go, I think, but Robert will. I like Mrs. Kemble –[12] She comes here every now & then to spend the evening & has rather a leaning to me it seems to my vanity — certainly I like *her*. She made a curious sort of apology to us about coming to us — to knead cake[13] & tea — in a fine dress & white satin shoes. In the first place she liked fine dresses — & in the second, she wore her dresses in rotation & nothing ever induced her to put on the Monday's dress on Tuesday, or vice versa. If she stayed at home she wore the white satin shoes, supposing it was the day for white satin shoes. We said of course that she might dress as she pleased, as long as she permitted us the same license — for as Robert observed, "if *he* wore his dresses in rotation, he should be reduced to his shooting jacket tomorrow" – She came once or twice or thrice & looked beautiful – A noble-looking woman certainly, with splendid eyes & a voice full of soul – You may forgive to such a woman a hundred such gentle eccentricities — & fifty ungentle, even — I am told that she is quite a creature of habit — to the point of lighting fires & putting on flannel on a given day of the year when the cold weather ought to begin, whether it is as hot as a dogday or not — & of persisting to walk out at noon in Italy, when the very dogs creep into the shade, because she holds exercise to be better taken in the morning –

Penini has lost all his shyness — he goes here & there — to the Thackerays for instance — & lets Wilson leave him. He will go out in the Story's carriage without any of us. His Double, whom I told you of, turns out to have lighter hair & a darker complexion than he has — which leaves the advantage with Penini – The child is unique, I must say — a perfect darling. Within this month he has begun to write & his copybook is entirely miraculous to see – Also he has taken again to learning poetry — real poetry this time — ("I not like *Baa baa black sheep*, & those sorts of poems") — Alfred Tennyson's "Eagle," and Ariel's song in the Tempest, and Herrick's song to the "Blossoms" &c — & most beautifully he says them, with the right emphasis & expression, the infantine articulation making it all the prettier – He is rather flattered than otherwise when anyone asks him to repeat them, & performs directly with his usual vain-gloriousness. I was a little surprised to hear him at Miss Blagden's soirée giving a 'recitation' on the sofa with perfect presence of mind & calmness. He has as great a passion as ever for Ferdinando – The other day he (Ferdinando) complained of feeling unwell. "I hope," said the child (in Italian of course) "I hope, Ferdinando, you are not going to die — because I should be very sorry — (Molto dispiacente)". "Perhaps it would be better," replied Ferdinando, who seems to have been in a melancholy mood —'*forte meglio!* 'I should go to Heaven, you know — *in paradiso.*" "Well then"

— resumed Penini — "if you died, Ferdinando, I should do like Joe — eat a quantity of fruit & take no medicine, and then I should die too & go to you, & they would put wings on our backs and we should fly about wherever we like." – That's an agreeable scheme for *me*, George — isn't it? I didn't much like hearing of it, I assure you — Miss Blagden was showing him some of Flexman's designs for Homer.[14] On the design of the Dreams coming from Jupiter — fantastic figures, you remember — his observation was — "I think those must be God's *mitaines*" — very gravely –

Now I am going to tell you something – I hesitated whether to tell you, but Arabel at least will care to hear, & I should like to tell you besides – Wilson went with Penini the other day to dine at Miss Blagden's, where they go generally once a week — she is very kind. There was a great deal of talk of spirit-writing. Miss Hayes,[15] the translator of George Sand, & Miss Hosmer[16] the clever American sculptress studying under Gibson,[17] having both the faculty, & Marianne, Miss Blagden's maid, having just discovered that the pencil moved in her hand. Wilson, who had always laughed at these things & never thought of trying anything herself, said by a sudden impulse — "Give me the pencil & let me try" – In half a minute the pencil seemed to leap as she held it — & moved into intelligible letters though no legible word was made – When she came home she told me smiling – "But," said she, "I think there's something particular in that pencil of Miss Blagden's. I dont believe any other pencil would move so. Let me try." She took up a pencil – The end of it all is this, that the faculty has developped in her to an extraordinary degree – She has had communications purporting to come from her mother, containing allusions to family affairs with earnest advice & deep affection – You laugh, George – The mere physical phenomena are extraordinary – The hand in a moment grows cold & stiff, while the pencil vibrates & moves itself – The hand simply supports the pencil – She has not the least consciousness of what is being written – At the first intelligible sentence, at that first shock of conviction, she should have fainted she says, if many tears had not relieved her – Now she is in the steady &

quiet enjoyment of what she considers a great priviledge [*sic*] –
She said to me this morning —"I feel as if I could put off my
black"– Besides specific advice, such words were written as
"Dear Bessy". "Say if it is you mother," she asked – '*Mother*'
was written – "Are you happy?" *"Yes, very."* Now, for my part
— I sate down by her the day before yesterday, & asked "if any
spirit present would write its name"– Shall I tell you what happened? The pencil turned itself round in her hand & began immediately to *write backwards & upside down at once, presenting
the letters to* ME. She cried out —"Oh, its going backwards —
there's nothing written, is there?" "Yes," I said, "something is
written." I could read, though she couldn't – '*Mary*' was written
distinctly – I said "It is a christian name only – Will you write
the other name? – *"Barrett"* was written after – I commanded
myself & asked again "There are two bearing that name in relation to me – Will you write what relation?"— O George —
'*Mama*' was written under my eyes — turned to me carefully —
that familiar word from which we have been orphaned all these
years – I was very deeply moved — you will understand that.
Of course you will believe nothing, any of you, but I have made
up my mind to tell you whether you believe or not – You will all
believe some day, sooner or later, and I cannot make it sooner
than circumstances & the moods of your mind will facilitate –
The communication went no farther as we were interrupted — &
indeed for the moment I was so naturally overcome that I felt
inclined to think it was enough for once. Do you say are we going mad? "Not mad, most noble Festus,"[18] I never felt saner or
less excited. I have tried for a week together at fixed hours, holding a pencil in my hand for half an hour or more, & *always
failed,* & when I had seen Wilson write — I said —"I will try no
more. I am convinced that I am not fit to exercise the faculty.
There's some reason against it." Yesterday I sate by her again &
asked "if any spirit present would write its name for me"– The
pencil turned in the same way, wrote backward & upside down,
presenting the word written to me, till this phrase was legible —
"Write here alone"– "But" said I, "I cant write – I have tried
in vain very often. Is it 'possible' for me to write?" '*Yes*' written

clearly – "When shall I write?" *"Now"* "Who wants me to write?" – Then came a beloved name[19] — not the other – I took the pencil & sate down, feeling hopeless after all because of a supposed impotency or unfitness in myself. After five minutes, for the first time in the course of all my experiments I felt the pencil move in a spiral sort of way, the fingers growing numb at the ends — but the force was not sufficient to produce a stroke even, much less a letter. I was interrupted then– Still the movement was so clear to me, so unmistakeable, that I think it possible I may write still. It is just the same movement that comes into the tables when they turn. Rational people should not put away these things without examination, nor should Christian people decide the whole work to be of the devil, when there's no devil's stamp upon it – They should take heed lest they be found fighting against God. These things are no miracles, properly so called, but a new development of Law – I think Arabel had better not tell Mr. Stratton[20] or the Owens[21] — because of their preconceived opinions being too strong for the just reception of the facts — preconceived opinions of very opposite characters of course – That the Newman street churches[22] have been under the teaching of fallible spirits for years *I am convinced* — and they mistake it for the infallible teaching of the Holy Ghost, — while contrary (which it is in my mind on several points) to the infallible teaching of the Scriptures – No doctrine should be received from spirits, who are always fallible, but only from the Word – We should all be clear upon this –

Robert is hard at work with his poems, & I too do a little work most days – We are all very well – *I* am especially well & able to walk out most days.

[Around sides and top of first sheet]

I dare say Arabel is horribly vexed at my imputed opposition to the whole Christian Church! Why the man makes a sort of Satan of me — the presbyterian minister here does'nt think so badly of us — for having received us at the Lord's table both of us, & Robert twice, he asked him to write his name in a book of friends which he keeps.

Love to dearest Trippy – Ask Arabel what were the initials of Eliza Giles —[23] E.W. . what?

[On envelope] We were [torn out][24] through the Coliseum yesterday, the blue sky floating through the rifts of ruin. I have had a most interesting letter from Mrs. Gaskell (Mary Barton)[25] of which there's no room to speak. God bless you dearest dear George – Dont be vexed with me for anything in this letter, for love's sake! — & dont vex me by paying more postage, which we have to pay over again afterwards. So remember. [Think?] of dear Mr. Kenyon's kindness –[26] I told Henrietta – Speak of Papa – The galleries are said to be too cold in spite of the May weather. I wait for the spring & Vatican together. Did Arabel get my second letter. Robert's truest love to you, he says – What of Storm –   Your ever attached Ba

---

[1] Postmark: Rome, Jan. 10; Marseilles, Jan. 15; C. K., Jan. 16, 1854. Address: George G. Moulton-Barrett, Esq. 50 Wimpole Street, London, Angleterre Via France.

The house at the corner of "The Street of the Lion's Mouth" and "Wolf Alley," bears a marble tablet commemorating the Brownings' residence there. It is only a few steps from the house where Pompilia lived with Pietro and Violante and where all of them were killed. Browning had not yet come upon "The Old Yellow Book."

[2] Robert Hall (1764-1831), son of a Baptist minister, was one of the greatest pulpit orators of his day. His greatest sermon, *Modern Infidelity Considered with Respect to Its Influence on Society* was first delivered in Bristol in October, 1800, first published in 1801, and many times reprinted. The edition referred to here is that edited with an introduction by J. Newton Brown and published by the American Baptist Publication Society in Philadelphia, 1853.

[3] Armantine (Mercier) Soulé, wife of Pierre Soulé (1801-1870), United States Minister to Spain, 1853-54. The mention of her name here recalls a colorful incident in American diplomacy.

On November 15, 1853, the Marquis de Turgot, French Ambassador to Spain, gave an elaborate ball in Madrid, celebrating both the fête day of the Empress Eugénie and the baptism of the daughter of the Duke and Duchess of Alba, brother-in-law and sister of the Empress. The Soulés were present in spite of the Minister's well-known republican principles and outspoken antagonism toward Napoleon. The couple made a striking entrance, especially Mme. Soulé, a beautiful Louisianan, attired, according to the Paris *Siècle,* in "a robe of blue velvet, low in the neck, with flowers of lace and gold thread, and on her head a *torsade à glands d'or.*"

"As Madame Soulé passed the Countess de Montijo . . . the latter expressed to Turgot and her son-in-law, the Duke of Alba, rather stringent criticisms on the American lady's dress. Soon after the Duke . . . remarked in French, 'Here comes Marie de Bourgogne.' Someone whispered to him that the lady was French, and he turned away and changed the conversation. Young Nelvil Soulé [her son] had, however, overheard Alba and he now left the assembly, boiling with rage, and determined to make it a matter of life and death between himself and the Duke."

In the upshot Nelvil fought the duke with heavy Spanish swords. There was no damage beyond fatigue to either party, and a reconciliation was effected. Pierre Soulé, however, who had been ill since the ball, now challenged Turgot, his host. Turgot did everything to avoid trouble except apologize for what he hadn't done. They fought with pistols, and Turgot was wounded above the knee. The whole affair became a *cause célèbre* for the newspapers, especially in Paris where Soulé was very unpopular. Spanish opinion generally justified the son but condemned the father (see A. A. Ettinger: *The Mission to Spain of Pierre Soulé, 1853-1855,* Yale University Press, New Haven, Conn., 1932, pp. 225-40).

In spite of his inordinate pride and his sartorial excesses, Soulé seems to have been a man of unusual and various abilities. His main business as Minister was the acquisition of Cuba for the United States. When the Ostend Manifesto, to which he was a party, was repudiated by the State Department, he resigned.

⁴ Margaret of Burgundy (1290?-1315) was married in 1305 to Louis le Hutin, King of Navarre, later Louis X of France. She was convicted of adultery and died in prison, reportedly smothered by order of the king.

⁵ The "charges" in the Introduction (*note 2,* above) read:
The poetry of the Brownings has a Swedenborgian tendency; but the lady — a sincere friend of Harriet Martineau — was recently a liberal Unitarian. She turns from the whole Christian church. It has,
> "Too much of envy in its heart,
> And too much striving in its hands." (p. 24)
The article attacks practically all the leading writers of the day

and some earlier ones. Thackeray, Carlyle, all the Romantics, Emerson, Tennyson — all these and more are accused of heretical ideas. The general rendezvous of the new school of infidelity is the home of Leigh Hunt and the chief publisher is John Chapman, the "great infidel publisher," who published David Strauss.

[6] James Montgomery Stuart was lecturing on Shakespeare at Bagni di Lucca in 1849, where the Brownings met him. "He appears to be a cultivated and refined person," Mrs. Browning wrote, "and especially versed in German criticism, and we mean to *use* his society a little when we return to Florence, where he resides" (Kenyon, I, p. 422; see also DeVane and Knickerbocker, p. 106).

[7] Of Chapman and Hall, the Brownings' publisher.

[8] Daughter of William Wetmore Story (for her illness and her brother's death see Kenyon, II, pp. 152 ff.). She married the Marchese Peruzzi of the Medici family and Chamberlain to the King. Her brilliant social life came to an end with the involvement of one of her sons in a notorious scandal and his consequent suicide. After that she lived in seclusion and even experienced financial difficulties. Throughout her period of social ostracism Pen Browning remained her constant friend and to help her financially he bought from her La Torre all' Antella near Florence. This first expression of Pen's love for her is the place to recall that when he died, July 8, 1912, in Asolo, Edith Story, Marchesa Peruzzi, was at his bedside (Reese, p. 803).

[9] See *Letter 27, note 6,* p. 121.

[10] John Gibson Lockhart (1794-1854). A few days before this letter Mrs. Browning wrote to Miss Mitford: "if anybody wants a snow-man to match Southey's snow-woman (see 'Thalaba'), here's Mr. Lockhart, who, in complexion, hair, conversation, and manners, might have been made out of one of your English *'drifts'* — 'sixteen feet deep in some places,' says Galignani" (Kenyon, II, p. 154). Lockhart died at Abbotsford the following November.

[11] William Page (1811-85), "called 'the American Titian' by the Americans" (Kenyon, II, p. 128). Lived in Italy from 1849 to 1860; in 1854 occupied the apartment below that of the Brownings in Rome. In that year he presented Mrs. Browning with a "magnificent portrait" of her husband. Unfortunately, because of a mistaken theory of Page's concerning the fading of paints, the colors soon deteriorated.

[12] Fanny Kemble (1809-93), sister of Mrs. Sartoris (A. Kemble). The famous actress had been married to Pierce Butler in 1834.

After their divorce in 1849 she resumed her maiden name. Mrs. Browning referred to her as Mrs. Fanny Kemble (Kenyon, II, p. 16).

[13] Knead cakes were griddle cakes which were favorite fare with the Barretts and the Brownings for festive occasions (Huxley, p. 43).

[14] John Flaxman (1755-1826), English draughtsman and sculptor, famous especially for his monuments to the dead. He modeled for many years for Wedgwood, and in 1787 went to Rome where he directed the work of modelers for the manufacture there. During the seven years in Rome he executed many designs for poems, notably those for the *Iliad* and *Odyssey*, commissioned by Mrs. Hare Naylor.

[15] Matilda M. Hayes (1820-?), editor, actress, author, novelist, translator of George Sand's *Maufrat* and *Fadette*.

[16] Harriet Goodhue Hosmer (1830-1908), American sculptor. In 1852 with her friend Charlotte Cushman she went to Rome, where she lived until a few years before her death. Browning and "Hatty," as he generally calls her in his letters, finally fell out over the unfortunate incident of his proposal to Lady Ashburton (see Hood, pp. 325 ff.).

[17] John Gibson (1790-1866), the most distinguished English sculptor of the time. He rarely took pupils, but Miss Hosmer studied with him for some years. His pre-eminence is referred to in Browning's poem *Youth and Art*.

[18] Acts 26:25.

[19] Could this name have been "Edward" or "Bro"?

[20] The Reverend James Stratton of Paddington Chapel, the Barrett's London pastor (*Letters of R. B. and E. B. B.*, II, pp. 489-90).

[21] Unidentified, but obviously London friends and probably fellow parishioners of the Barretts.

[22] The significance of "Newman Street Churches" as a group is not clear. Irving's Apostolic Church (*Letter 43, note 13,* p. 183) was for a time located in Benjamin West's gallery in Newman Street.

[23] Unidentified.

[24] The word is torn out, but *nd* remaining under the seal suggests *wandering*.

[25] *Mary Barton: A Tale of Manchester Life* (1848) by Mrs. Gaskell (1810-65), author of *Cranford* and *Life of Charlotte Brontë*.

[26] Among so many this particular instance remains vague.

letter 48   [Summer, 1856][1]

My dearest George

Only late last night I remembered that by an engagement of a fortnight Penini was to go with Ferdinando & Wilson[2] to the Zoological gardens today with a ticket — I put them off last Saturday because of Peni's being unwell, & I have'nt the inhumanity to propose it again —

So I come to you — Now would you take Penini on any other day in change for this? and will you think me very ungrateful (& impudent besides) for making the proposal?

I hear your dinner was princely, George —

                                    Your ever attached Ba —

[1] The envelope to this note is addressed: George G. M. Barrett Esq., 50 Wimpole Street, and the note itself bears no date at all. It was probably delivered by hand, as the Brownings were in London this summer.

[2] Ferdinando Romagnoli and Wilson were married in Paris, July 11, 1855, while the Brownings were en route to England (Miller: *Browning*, pp. 183-84). "Wilson is married to a Florentine who lived once with the Peytons, and is here now with us, a good tender-hearted man" (Kenyon, ii, p. 207).

letter 49   [Marseilles]
                                                Monday
                                                [October 27, 1856][1]

My ever dearest George, As you wanted to hear from me here I am writing from Marseilles — In a horrible humour, however, for they ask so enormously for the land journey to Genoa, that we are deciding on going by sea — having missed the French post-boat besides — so that by land & sea there's failure. It seems really too much to give — twenty pounds only as far as Genoa, with the road before us to pay to Pisa over and above — whereas we go by sea to Leghorn for ten pounds — So I am disappointed.

Otherwise we had a most favorable journey, & drop into absolute summer here at Marseilles — windows open for air, & the whole southern sentiment everywhere, & my cough is in abeyance accordingly, & I slept from end to end of last night,— feeling only tired in a *healthy* degree, this morning. At Dijon we found our friend M. Milsand, at the station, & had the joy of a wringing of the hand from him — n.b. Robert had the embrace & double kiss all to himself. The weather has been beautiful the whole way, & the scenery of the southern half of France; never praised enough, to my mind – At Paris, we heard from Florence that all was right with Casa Guidi, which was prepared to receive us & so we shall be at home (if it please God) by Wednesday. Do let me have letters. Oh — I shall be so anxious to hear of the return from Ventnor & its results.[2]

Penini has been doing nothing except eat grapes since he entered France – I expect him to turn into a small Bacchus – Only they made him pay all the way as if he were a man (of full age) instead.

Oh — my visions of Hyeres,[3] Cannes, Nice & the rest.— never to be seen by my actual sight. For mark — as we dont go this time, with such weather, such a purse, & such desires — we never shall again – I blot it all out of my hopes, from this time.

Robert said he w^d do it if I liked. But then he said it *so,* that I plainly saw what his opinion was — and I suppose it would have been unwise, rash, unadvised,— find me all the epithets by which pleasant actions must needs be described in this cross-grained world,— use them all.

A really magnificent town is this Marseilles! — quite grand! We have been out walking — & I *sitting* on the boulevards at past six, & thinking how warm it was.

Dearest George, how good you were to me those last days — how I felt & feel the dear warmth of your affection — (not the sun here, more clearly) — but the love is more precious than any sun – May God bless you my dearest George. We sail tomorrow morning at eight by the — Durance, I think the name is — (at least is a new French steamer of some name –) Robert having gone out to take our places, I cant ask him.

Peni's best love – We've had a whole day of disagreeable —
"Shall I? Shant I? — ought I? — ought'nt I? — would you? —
would'nt you? –" and now the doubting's over to the hoping's
disadvantage. The boat goes at eight – Oh, I said that before –

Your ever attached Ba –

[1] Postmark: Marseilles, Oct. 28, 1856. Address: George G. M.
Barrett, Esq., 50 Wimpole Street, London, Angleterre. The sheet
is folded, sealed, and addressed on the back. It carries the stamp,
Affranchisement Insuffisant.

[2] The Brownings had spent the summer of 1855 in England, the
following winter in Paris, and the summer of 1856 in England
again. Immediately on their arrival in London —"the very day he
heard of our being in Devonshire Place" — Mr. Barrett had ordered
the "Wimpole Street people" to leave the city. They went to
Ventnor on the Isle of Wight, whither the Brownings followed
them (Kenyon, II, pp. 236-38).

[3] Hyères, which she was destined never to see, had long been
glamorous in the imagination of Elizabeth Barrett Browning. See
her letter to her grandmother of July 27, 1816, Appendix I, p. 336.

letter 50   September 18 [1858]
Havre[1]

My dearest George, Now I am keeping my promise about
letting you know our address in Paris, which I heard myself an
hour ago. Come & find us at RUE CASTIGLIONE 6. Sariana Browning undertook to get rooms for us, &, being exhorted to select a
central situation, she has done so, at the expense, I fear, of very
great incomodities, as we are to feel ourselves "in a box," she
says — meaning of course a pill-box. Arabel is "in for it" with
us — & the advantage remains, of our living or dying in excellent
society & neighborhood. Its the worst time possible for taking
apartments in Paris for a short time, seeing that the season begins, the town fills fast, and the landlords look forward with un-
slackened illusions to impracticable prices –

Let us all congratulate one another on dearest Storm's safe

return. Arabel had a horrible fright about the telegraph — & I for my part, wonder only that she could open & read it at all. You see if I had gone to England I should have seen little of Storm, — "so all is for best," as a poet says, nearly related to me – Its delightful to me to think of that dear Storm as near & well, — may God bless him! –

Meanwhile how are *you*, George – Have you amused yourself better at Heidelberg than was possible at Havre, *where* you could only get pleasure by giving it — dear dear George? How kind you were to me.— how kind & how tender! shall I ever, ever forget it? It makes the tears come, only to think of it all.

For the rest, I am quite pleased to go away from Havre, & so, I think, is Arabel. Wherever I may "go a-roaming, a-roaming, by the light of the moon"[2] again, it wont be to Havre. Come & help us at Paris, where we mean to do rather better.

Little Pen is 'in despair,' he says, "about his ships," and decides on carrying the man of war on his shoulder, for the great advantage of all fellow-passengers in the train tomorrow – He still wears on his finger the ring given to him by Mademoiselle Eisendecker, & wrote her an affecting letter on the morning of her departure, beginning "My dearest wife," & hoping to be married to her in Paris – Did Arabel tell you that *she* did not sleep, for her part, in Paris, till she had written a letter to Arabel[3] — full of all affectionateness? Really it is a pity that I should love her for a sister-in-law. What with her music, & her grace, her frankness & lovingness, she has caught me up a good deal.

Since she went, our chief business has been in photographing – Robert dragged me by the hair of my head to the jetty, and there I have been "done" over & over, & in all sorts of senses, till I was nearly out of mine. Just as he began to be convinced that nothing could be produced (upon the material) fit for anything but a frontispiece for the Woman's Journal,— representing all the wrongs of the sex by a face of exquisite misery — (& I thought of sending it to Bessie Parkes[4] the editress for that purpose) . . just at the moment of his "giving it up," a sudden success was attained,[5]— & you would be surprised how the sun has succeeded in glorifying me – *I* am, indeed surprised. It must have been a 'coup de soleil' & a 'coup d'etat' in one — Robert, in a state of ecstasy, has been having copies multiplied ever since, and if we did'nt go away tomorrow we should have to beg our way back to Florence. One photograph is already dispatched to America for engraving, to lose no time towards "the restitution of all things," Then Arabel has given me a most lovely portrait of Penini — looking like a Velasquez, Robert says. And even Annunziata has had herself photographed for her mother — an act of piety recompensed cruelly by the free gift of a pair of squinting eyes! [*On envelope flap*] Arabel & Robert send you their love — & Peni — dont let me forget

Your ever loving Ba

¹ Postmark: Paris, Sept. 20, 1858. Only the flap of the envelope bearing the postmark has been preserved.

During the nearly two years between the previous letter and this one the correspondence did not cease, but whatever letters Mrs. Browning wrote to her brother have disappeared. The most likely reason seems to be that they were destroyed in accordance with Browning's request (*Letter 79*, p. 309). It is clear from preceding letters that George certainly did not destroy or return *all* her letters dealing with spiritualism; nevertheless it is also clear from her published letters of this period that her mind was more than ever taken up with "spirits" and mediums. The events of the period were such as to turn her thoughts strongly in this direction. In December, 1856, a few weeks after the publication of *Aurora Leigh*, which was dedicated to him, John Kenyon died. He left the Brownings a legacy of eleven thousand pounds, which, welcome and gratefully received as it was, produced the painful situation that "we are overwhelmed with 'congratulations' on all sides, just as if we had not lost a dear, tender, faithful friend and relative — just as if, in fact, some stranger had made us a bequest as a tribute to our poetry" (Kenyon, II, p. 249). Then on April 17, 1857, Edward Barrett died suddenly, ending "all hope of better things, or a kind answer to entreaties such as I have seen Ba write in the bitterness of her heart" (Kenyon, II, p. 264). George had written "very affectionately" the sad news, and on July 1 Mrs. Browning wrote to Mrs. Martin: "This is the first letter I have written to anyone out of my own family" (Kenyon, II, p. 265). Her letters to her own family must have been very personal indeed. That summer the Brownings went again to Bagni di Lucca, only to have their stay marred by the serious illness of Robert Lytton and a subsequent fever of Pen's. During the summer of 1858, which the Brownings spent at Havre, they were visited by George as well as Alfred, Arabella, and Amelia, Henry Barrett's wife (DeVane and Knicker-bocker, p. 110).

[2] Characteristically misquoted from Byron: "So we'll go no more a-roving" etc.

[3] The name is puzzling because Mrs. Browning's only sisters-in-law were Elizabeth, wife of Alfred Barrett; Amelia, wife of Henry Barrett; and Sarianna Browning. The second *Arabel* is probably miswritten for *Amelia.*

[4] Bessie Raynor Parkes (1829-1925), poet, editor, pioneer in higher education for women with Barbara Bodichon, founder of Girton College, Cambridge. She edited *The Englishwomen's Journal, Victoria Regia,* and was a contributor to the *Eclectic Review.* She was an intimate friend of George Eliot and the Rossettis. She married M. Belloc in 1868, and was the mother of Hilaire Belloc.

[5] This photograph is reproduced in Plate IV, following p. 54.

letter 51   Wednesday — 28 Via del Triton
                                                [April 18, 1860 — Rome][1]

My dearest George,   Everybody holding up their hands against me in "deprecation," do you say[2]— You mean imprecation, I think. Such attacks as the Saturday Review's,[3] for instance, & Blackwood's,[4] almost overstep certain limits. They write to us from Florence that a Saturday reviewer, alive & in the flesh, has been there during three weeks. Certain of my friends who are furious at the criticism in question, reproached him with it,— on which he said he was "very sorry, & that it was a brutal article certainly." On which replied my friend properly,—"that he (the reviewer) should be most sorry, not for that particular paper, which was a consistent deduction from the general ideas of the journal, but for the general ideas themselves, & that such a line should be taken by a leading English newspaper —" Let me add that this said Saturday reviewer after his three weeks residence in Florence, avowed, "that his opinions on the French emperor were *modified* — though he still thought him *not good for England."*

What, in my mind, is still worse for England, is this ignoble madness into which you have all run. For it is not the "madness" of "great wits" — but the low consequence of some feline bite – You understand nothing – As for me, my dearest George, you rightly supposed me to be prepared for the reception of my book – If it had been otherwise received, its application would have been doubtful in my own opinion even.

Except for the Athenæum's mistatement,[5] I was prepared for everything,— & in fact, the weight given to the book, which besides the three columns of abuse for instance in the Saturday Review was referred to in three or four political articles of the same journal, has on the whole rather flattered me than otherwise. Odo Russell[6] observed to Robert yesterday that he (who by metier has to do with newspapers) saw the book everywhere struck at, & that "the sensation made by it was extraordinary –" Now, observe — there is no friendship between Mr. Russell & me, & no peculiar sympathy — he is very English and very *Russell* — only with keen perceptions & a wide experience – He added to Robert — "It is curious, the state of the English mind, just now. Monkton [*sic*] Milnes said a clever thing at Paris the other day, which was entirely true. Some Frenchmen exclaimed to him — "But what do you English want, after all"? "Why, we want," said Milnes, "first, that the Austrians should beat *you* thoroughly — then we want that Italy should be free,— and then we want that the Italians should be grateful to *us* for doing nothing towards it –"

Excellently seen & spoken, Monkton Milnes – But you wont have the courage & patriotism to repeat this clever & true speech from your place in Parliament – No – You probably belong to a rifle-club like the rest, & will hold up your hands in "deprecation" over 'Poems in Congress'[7]

Whatever may be the defect of that book, George, it is at least conscientious & honest — nor do I believe that it will fail to touch some generous chords in minds open to such an influence – Facts have been sacred things with me, & the very pressure of the time & the locality is on the verses. The heroine of the 'Dance' was the Marchioness Laiatico.[8] The Court Lady[9] was founded on the general fact of the ladies of Milan going in full dress & open carriages to visit the hospitals – Macmahon[10] did "take up the child on his saddlehorn"– Cavour did say, "It is the Emperor who *'did it all'* "– If my poetry falls below my own mark, it is strange. Never did I write anything with a fuller heart – Nor is your opinion my dear George, shared by some persons of considerable judgement in these things – Robert would not have let me print what he considered below my own mark — & I have letters from persons who pass with us as excellent judges in poetry, & who place these poems above anything I have written in their scale & proportion — that is, except Aurora Leigh. Do you not think that your distaste to the opinions, produced a repulsion to the medium? Anyhow I am very sorry, yes, vexed a little, at your thinking these poems unworthy of my reputation as an artist – Otherwise, I could not expect your sympathy & did not – It might be very difficult for any man who gets his views of Italian affairs from such newspapers as I read, to come to other conclusions than you have come to –

Only, if I were you & thought as you do in some respects, perhaps I might ask myself sometimes,—"What makes Ba hold these opinions so tenaciously, she who is honest, as women go, loves Italy & the people, & has peculiar opportunities of judging the real state of the case? May not, after all, these "political mistakes" of Ba's, as I call them, be nearer the truth than we fancy? May she not know the real colour of things better in Tuscany & Rome than Mr. So & So who sees them at Brompton? — or even than Mr. Thus & Thus, who takes a thousand a year from the Times to be its "own correspondent," at Florence,— & is *cut* by the Italian patriots in consequence of his amount of lying –? – And — if the Athenæum & a whole train of newspapers following its lead, makes a gross mistake about the reference of a particular poem, (which no one of common intelligence could read through conscientiously & mistake!) — what if it should be possible for the same persons to make a mistake about the bearing of an action —— such as the Italian war, for instance — or even the annexation of Savoy —"?! I believe I might ask myself such questions.

As to Savoy — annexing Savoy will make too long a letter — but I must ask you, as you say so much about it, why my Samaritan may not give away his "signet-ring" if he pleases, & without convicting his neighbors to whom he gives it, of a crime – If he gives it, does the neighbour "rob" him? Which however is considering the question according to your figure, & the red tape & this "legitimate" way of disposing of nations. For this signet ring has in it the right of *giving itself*, a right recognized on the present occasion, by both giver & receiver – If pressure were exercised on the populations, if their vote were not consulted, I should cry out loudly, I also — as loudly almost, as England ought to have cried when Austria swallowed Cracow – But what Victor Emmanuel parts with is simply his claim to the allegiance of the populations. Whatever that may be worth in the eyes of the old European governments — he frees them into the right of choice, to be expressed by a plebescito.

France has neither siezed Savoy, nor meant to sieze Savoy – There will be no troops on either side to exercise pressure – The peoples will vote as our Italians have voted – And why you should be pleased to represent them as *victims*, is only accountable on the principle upon which our Holy Father here & the Ex-Grand Duke of Florence go on to represent the oppression of the victim-voters in Romagna & the "beloved Tuscany"– I do consider that England may bestow her sympathy & compassion where they are more required than by Savoy. She may have been as loud in her pity for Florence, for instance, when Florence was under Austria – The hypocrisy of all this outcry would be ridiculous but for consequences & influences – The cession of Savoy is *not* the price of the war — it is the *condition* (a little prematurely arranged — but this will be obvious presently) of the ultimate re-constitution of Italy as a great nation – France never said that she required defences against 12 millions of Italians — she said "against a number *exceeding* twelve millions" — & the meaning of the phrase perfectly understood by us all here, pointed to Italy the nation, in respect to which & with reference to the future of the world the Head of the French nation had to think – He who had "done it all" had to be wise for France as well as Italy – There was no treaty nor family compact — but there was a "sous entendre" between the Emperor & the Piedmontese government that the *reconstitution of Italy* would involve the permitted return of Savoy to France in case the populations of that district preferred it so — and for years it has been difficult for Piedmont to rule them, so strong have been their straining & sympathy towards France. Cavour called Savoy, Piedmont's Ireland, from the disaffection there – For if there are no "natural frontiers" there are at least natural barriers, & the Alps are one of them, presenting impediments to direct trade & easy government.

It was understood therefore that Savoy should be permitted its choice, when Italy became a great nation — but, after the misfortune of Villafranca, Napoleon withdrew his claim, & was prepared to carry out the inferences of the treaty logically & in good faith – At the same time, they led *ad absurdum* — & he *knew it* – And now that a higher ground is attained by means of the constancy of Italy which he has protected all this while until she is able to protect herself, & will sustain to the end,— now it is the turn of Savoy – Nobody doubts what the decision of those peoples is & will be – After which the alliance is riveted – And the next moves will find King Victor Emmanuel still extending his territory. Cavour's eye is onward – The Neapolitan & the remaining Roman states will not remain as now – *Before a year we expect to have Venetia.* France will hold the shield — & perhaps the sword — but she will be true to her task to the end – The emperor has braved more than guns for Italy – Waleski[11] told him once he would sacrifice his dynasty for Italy, & he has certainly risked it. There is a coalition in France against him, (on the papal question) of the Orleanistes (more shame to them) & other opposing parties,— & if there is not yet a European coalition, it is'nt Lord Derby's[12] fault — at least — nor Mss. Kinglake[13] & Horseman's.[14]

What makes him hateful to all these fossil politicians is the fact which has recommended him to me — that he is the head in Europe of democratic progress & national ideas. 'Deep calleth unto deep' — yes, it is true – One ransomed people leads to the ransoming of another. But it is a great Head — it respects Law & Peace – War is a very unwelcome means to him.

Twelve months ago, when I was eager & sanguine, I did not expect that at this hour we should have such a consequence of the "war of liberation" as we see around us – The Italian people are grateful therefore — & they may well be –

My dearest George, the worst consequence to you of your letter, is this long one — for I must end by assuring you that I have not a touch of wrath against you — that, on the contrary, in venturing to give you my book, I might have expected a harsher reprimand, & that I feel through your reproofs the affectionateness behind them.

Also your good account of my darling Arabel would leave me your debtor,— & so much the happier, even if you had sworn at me — which you did'nt, you know – ! Let me tell you George I had a letter of "thanks" for my "courage & justice" from the editor of the Atlas[15]— who proved his sincerity by reviewing me. You are not *all* mad, poor people! – Then the Daily News from its point of view was very generous — Did you see that article. But I am enraged with the Daily News just now, who gave a shameful notice of Cavour the other day – That great & noble man! – Cavour, Azeglio, Farini[16] . . we have civic heroes here! Garibaldi is a hero of the camp only! – Let us honor him — though he *has no head* . . . between you & me. I am sorry for Garibaldi in the Nice question[17]— it seems hard – But not only the majority has rights,— but Italy goes before the noblest of her sons. And, be it known in England, where little is known, Garibaldi is *not* the noblest of those sons, though he is noble.

We leave Rome at the end of May I suppose, but we hear that the roads are not safe. So says Mr. Russell – A diligence stopped, & man killed, just now – We shall be cautious.

Mr. Chorley[18] has twice offended me by not putting in my letter. Now it seems as if I had taken fright & recanted meanly —

"My English readers will be glad." My English readers go to the D——l! I am

[*on side and top of first sheet*] very vexed with him for not printing my temperate letter. I dont want to please anybody — only
God, by speaking the truth as far as I can. I corrected the
Athenæum because it misstated simply. I have written my mind
to Mr. Chorley. I was more vexed as to his correction than the
first offence, for giving me an appearance of meanness before the
Eng & American public.

[*On envelope*] Poor darling Arabel – But dearest George I am
very sorry for her loss in Mr. Stratton[19]— very sorry for *him* too,
if the people have behaved ill to him, as I fear – Mr. Russell told
Robert he should cease to take in the Saturday Review, which
had become intolerable to him. Not for my sake, observe –

We have had no fires for a month, yet it is gloomy weather for
Rome.

Put in your head that Central Italy is only a *nucleus* of Italy
that shall be – Such letters from Florence describing the King's
entrance. Dearest George, we send you all our love, Robert, Pen
& your loving Ba.

[1] Postmark: Rome, April 19, 1860. Lon. Ap. 27. Address:
George Moulton Barrett, Esq., 2 Tanfield Court, Temple. Angleterre.

[2] Clearly the correspondence continued during the year and a
half between the previous letter and this, but the letters have
disappeared.

[3] The book in question is *Poems before Congress* (1860). The
review appeared in the *Saturday Review*, March 31, 1860, pp.
402-404. It begins by asserting the principle that, since all personal
opinions and sentiments in poetry serve a dramatic purpose, they
should always be given through fictitious characters and setting,
citing, of all poems, *Don Juan,* as an example of how it should be
done. It goes on to say that "the lounger of Paris or of Florence
adopts from fluent foreign teachers their opinions, first of their own
internal politics, and secondly of that very England which he ought
to have known better himself." Of the refrain "Emperor/Ever-

more" to *Napoleon III in Italy* the reviewer says: "Such is the refrain [of] a long dithyramb, and the words, though they have as little rhyme as reason, may serve to indicate an unbounded reverence for lawless strength and histrionic greatness." The rest of the review is an attack upon Mrs. Browning's coldness toward Britain and her lack of patriotism.

4 *Blackwood's* reviewed the book April, 1860, pp. 490-94, beginning: "We are strongly of the opinion that, for the peace and welfare of society, it is a good and wholesome rule that women should not interfere in politics. . . . The case is worse when women of real talent take part in political affray." They admire patriotism, "But cosmopolitanism is quite another thing, and so is identification with foreign nationalities." One cannot help remarking the present familiarity of this tune.

5 The *Athenaeum*, March 17, 1860, pp. 371-72, misread the final poem, *"A Curse for a Nation,"* as applying to England, calling it "a malediction against England,— infallible, arrogant; yet, nevertheless, 'with a difference', poetical."

6 Odo William Leopold Russell (1829-84) was a career diplomat who had served in Paris, Constantinople (before and during the Crimean war), and Washington, before being attached to the legation in Florence in 1858. He kept his residence in Rome from 1858 to 1870.

7 Mrs. Browning has misquoted her own title.

8 Marchioness Laiatico was the wife of Neri Corsini, who died in 1859 while serving as representative of the provisional Tuscan government in London. The poem recounts her invitation as "the noblest lady present" to the French officers to dance with the Florentine ladies. The *Blackwood's* review, quoted above, disparaged the poem on the ground of immorality and indecency. Mrs. Browning found the dance to be an inspiring example of brotherhood.

9 A poem in *Poems before Congress*.

10 Marie Edmé Patrice Maurice De MacMahon (1808-93), victor of the battle of Magenta (1859) and second president of France's Third Republic. The episode referred to is related in section XI of *Napoleon III in Italy*.

11 Alexandre Florian Joseph Colonna, Comte Waleski (1810-68); illegitimate son of Napoleon I and Countess Waleski. He became French minister of foreign affairs in 1855-60.

12 Edward George Geoffrey Smith Stanley (1799-1869), 14th

earl of Derby. He opposed Palmerston's foreign policy (1855-58) and as prime minister (1858-59) settled disputes with France and Naples. It was believed that he secretly supported Austria against France in 1859.

[13] Alexander William Kinglake (1809-91). He was in the Crimea at the start of the war and spent thirty-two years preparing and writing his *History of the Crimean War* in 8 volumes (1863-87).

[14] Edward Horseman (1807-76), English politician. After 1857 he occupied a seat in the Commons as an independent.

[15] Henry James Slack was editor and proprietor of the *Atlas,* a weekly review, from 1852 to 1862. The review of Mrs. Browning's volume was in the issue for Saturday, March 24, 1860. Complimenting the "poetess as the greatest our language has yet produced — a writer who unites the strength of a man's intellect to the largeness of a woman's heart," the editor goes on to display his regard for the poems as well as his political bias.

We know perfectly well beforehand what will be said of them by those who hate the cause they glorify — by deniers of popular rights, lovers of Austrian "order," scorners of sentiment, worshippers of aristocratical exclusiveness and petty international jealousies. They will assert that these songs of freedom are harsh and rugged, for they will make no account of that exaltation of the soul which may well cause a verse to stagger now and then, as it causes the human voice to break and fail when it should speak. They will talk of eccentricity and of obscurity; and they will raise the cuckoo cry which everyone whose sympathies are wider than the limits of his own land has to meet — the foolish cry that the authoress is anti-English simply because she is cosmopolitan.

With such an auspicious and eminently satisfactory introduction, it is not surprising that Mrs. Browning should feel herself vindicated by at least one journal's full appreciation, for the poetic side is treated fairly, calling attention to the grace and loveliness of lines and passages, particularly praising some of the very poems most open to attack by the other reviewers. But probably much less satisfying to the poetess was the final paragraph of the reviewer, who, like others, mistook the last poem "A Curse for a Nation" as being meant for England. The final sentence adequately sums up the editor's reason for later writing to Mrs. Browning personally. " . . . nothing will blot from the memory . . . a series of poems which will remain as an abiding contribution to an immortal cause." And perhaps that was as high praise as the author would want.

[16] Luigi Carlo Farini (1812-66). In 1859 he was Dictator of Modena. He secured the union of Parma, Bologna, and Florence

under Piedmont and served as Minister of the Interior in Cavour's cabinet of 1860. He was viceroy of Naples, November, 1860 – January, 1861, and prime minister, December, 1862 – March, 1863.

[17] Nice was Garibaldi's birthplace and, according to the agreement between Sardinia and France, Savoy, including Nice, was to be ceded to France on the authority of a plebiscite as the price for France's support against Austria.

[18] Henry Fothergill Chorley (1808-72), music critic of the *Athenaeum*. He also wrote reviews of literature and art, among them that quoted above of *Poems before Congress*. Instead of publishing Mrs. Browning's letter, the *Athenaeum* on April 7, 1860, ran the following paragraph in its column *Our Weekly Gossip* (p. 477): "Mrs. E. B. Browning wishes us to state that the verses in her 'Poems Before Congress' entitled 'A Curse for a Nation,' are levelled — not against England, as is generally thought — but against the United States; not on account, she now tells us, of any remissness on the Italian question, but on account of the Negro question. Every English reader of Mrs. Browning will rejoice in this assurance. We may be allowed to ask, in extenuation of our own hasty and incorrect inference,— why a rhyme on Negro Slavery should appear among 'Poems Before Congress.' "

[19] Minister of the Barretts' church in London.

letter 52   Florence, June 16
                                                              [1860][1]

My beloved George, I have an opportunity of sending to England in a stray Chapman (publisher) who comes here on business, to see after Lever's[2] affairs, whose books dont sell, & who will persist in keeping three carriages at the expence of his publisher. Dearest dear George, I have been thinking much of you lately, hearing from Arabel that the 'Dogs' of Law have been too much for your health lately & that you have given them all up & gone into seclusion – Dearest George, I dont like hearing of it at all – It may be well to give up hard work but I should like you to look about for some situation for which your legal ability would qualify you, & which would secure to you both comparative repose & moderate occupation. I fear that you who are used to work, will find the time heavy otherwise – Meanwhile, why not come abroad? I should say why not catch up Arabel on your back & bring her out here,— only perhaps during these troubled times it may seem a selfish entreaty – Like inviting a friend to take a cool place on the volcano beside one! – In fact, the probabilities are not favorable to peace even in Central Italy. I myself am far less anxious here than I should be at a distance,— but then I am peculiar it seems, & liable to mad illusions about peoples & their chiefs – Just now, we are full of Garibaldi — living & dreaming Garibaldi – My hopes are strong – There must be a struggle,— and then forwards for the unity of Italy – Meanwhile, be sure it is much more interesting here than at Budleigh Salterton,[3] in spite of the Volonteers, & the myth on which they are founded –

Chapman junior says that I have not hurt myself by the Congress poems which promise to go soon into a second edition, & which people praise for 'pluck'. Write to me George, & tell me what your plans are – We shall remain here till early in July, & then we go to Siena for the hot season – We could & would make ever so much room for you – We go to our villa of last year which is roomy & cool . . . for Italy. We should open our doors & arms to you — & have books for you from the Florence library, & you could go to sleep undisturbed when the sun was overhot — to say nothing of stray fans & water-melons – What could you want more?

And here are our photographs – Pen is Pen himself. I am rather black — but what then? Read the Mill on the Floss.

[*At side and top of first sheet*] Its better I think than Adam Bede – Read Anthony Trollope's books. They are admirable. I hear of the spirits in London doing wonders — Shall I complete my popularity by writing a work on them? May God bless you George – I cant write a word more today. Your ever loving Ba.

[*On envelope*] Roberts best love & Pen's. Pen is to have his Abbé at Siena & go on with Latin & poney [*sic*] The poney was rather overtired (like me) by a fifty miles journey in the sun one day, & from thirty to forty the two next until we reached the railroad.

¹ This letter must have been delivered by hand. The envelope bears only: "George G. Moulton Barrett, Esq."

² Charles James Lever (1806-72), Irish novelist. The Brownings first met him in the summer of 1849 at Bagni di Lucca (Kenyon, I, p. 413). An attempt to revive the acquaintance later in Florence failed. "I, who am much taken by manner," wrote Mrs. Browning, "was quite pleased with him, and wondered how it was that I didn't like his books" (Kenyon, I, p. 465).

³ A watering-place and coastguard station in East Devon at the mouth of the Otter River.

letter 53   Villa Alberti, Siena
                                                Sept. [6, 1860]¹

My beloved George. I thank God and thank you for the word of good — I take it with all the bitter. I had been in deep anxiety (to anguish) for three posts during which I had calculated on hearing — now the very coming of the letter is a good, & that she should be a shade better is a good — & the diminution of the pain, I do bless our God for! – The thought of that pain is the worst thought I have to bear – If anything here ever approaches with me to a pleasurable feeling . . if I look at the blue hills, or hear Penini's musical chatter, or get news even of our triumphant Italy,— instantly comes the idea . . . "My precious Henrietta is in great pain at this moment perhaps"– Be sure that, while I pass for being away from you all, I am with you in my soul; in my power of loving & suffering – Tell my precious sister this — that I am with her — with her — that I love her, not as much, but *more* than I ever did — & that I kiss her with an infinite tenderness, soul to soul, through this distance –²

My dear dearest kindest George, I will obey you in everything as far as I can. Let the next person who writes tell me whether *caustic* is used in any form, and also whether any of the pain has been produced by the remedies – I want to know also whether the sickness recurs. My dearest George, I like to think of your being there — and Storm, too, our dear dear Storm – So he goes back to Bryngwyn[3] this winter? What do you mean by Breconshire. Has any place been found out in Breconshire likely to suit him? Couldn't Devonshire or Cornwall offer anything? I fancied they might — and the climate there is so much milder than in Wales.

The country about us has been considerably agitated by the extraordinary movement of troops during the last few days – A pouring in of the national battalion from the north, & a carrying on with them all the troops in Tuscany, so that we are left simply with the national guard belonging to each city. Matteucci[4] (one of the deputation to Napoleon on behalf of Tuscany last October . . & a first rate man) lives in a villa near us – A telegram came to him the day before yesterday from Turin to enquire whether a second telegraph wire (in case of accident to the first) could be extended across Italy in five days. It looked much like war with Austria – But M^{dme} Matteucci came to me yesterday to say that we had not reached that point yet.— though everything might be *expected* – The present destination of the troops is to the frontier to be ready for contingencies — especially for the intervention of Lamoriciere[5] into the Neapolitan states, the consequence of which would be the intervention of Victor Emmanuel into the Papal. Also we shall occupy Naples, as soon as that government falls — the Mazzinians[6] are an insignificant party, but rampant for mischief — and to keep the national body a-head of all political sects is important to the health of the state. It is a moment of crisis, Garibaldi *is* a hero, & great is his work, yes, and single is his aim in doing it – But with all that, he is too easily influenced, & is too much surrounded with evil influences, for any of us *who know the circumstances,* to rest in him without anxiety. Observe. He will never be persuaded into a bad action – But into an action, the political consequences of which would be bad, he is capable of being persuaded — and for this reason, we fear sometimes.

I hope there will not be much more fighting in the Neopolitan States — therefore your volunteers are late – But they will be in time for the struggle with Lamoriciere, which sooner or later must be – The Neapolitans are not in a mind to fight — Marines & army dissolve before the patriots happily.

M^dme Matteucci gave me a most interesting account of the conversation between L N. & the Tuscan deputation . . Prince Corsini,[7] Matteucci & Peruzzi[8] . . about annexation & the restoration of the Gr Duke, last October – It lasted an hour & a quarter, & she waited in the carriage during that time – I can assure you my "August Voice" represents the significance of it – The emperor said he was bound at Villafranca & could give no other advice than &c &c – Also, he seemed seriously to think with regard to annexation that there *were* difficulties in the traditions of the country — (a great many Italians thought the same till quite the last moment) – He said, "Why how will your members attend a Turin parliament? They will have to go *by sea.*" As to the Tuscan princes — he was humorous about them – "Vous pouvez concevoir," said he "that I cant feel much sympathy with these petty princes. I care simply for the happiness of Tuscany. Ferdinando came to me here — *il a pleuré* — he offered everything in the way of promise & profession. I replied — *"Mais, mon cher, vous etiez à Solferino –"*

When the emperor had repeatedly told the deputation that he was not free himself to say what they would have him say, he added "that one thing I *can promise you"* — there *shall be no intervention –"* He repeated it with emphasis – Peruzzi, who is given to *push* and force entrenchments, looked into the emperor's face & said, "Mais, s'il n'y aura pas d'intervention, alors" . . . (*Then, then, we may do as we like,* implied in the pause.) The emperor threw up his hands exclaiming . . . . "Oh, oh, oh!" Meaning of course, "you must *not* force me to say what I will not."

The meaning of it all was clear. He could not protect the special choice of the Italians before Europe, but he would protect the Italians *choosing,* before Europe. Because observe,— his "No intervention," was not like yours in England . . . . a mere opinion . . He was prepared to hinder intervention from Austria, with the sword – All Italy understood & understands this. "It has been a real love for Italy on the part of the emperor" said M^{dme} Matteucci to me,—"quite a personal feeling." And at the end of twenty months, see what the effect is – Italy is a nation . . almost! — and there is almost a coalition of the old governments against France. I regard these facts with the mixture of wonder, scorn & melancholy, which is the frequent mood of thinkers on this world's affairs –

Whether you care to hear any of this I cant guess even — but little else moves in my life just now, except the private griefs heavy on you & all of us — I put down something, not to send you an echo of your own sadness — & nothing is at hand but this – Peni has had a cold, & we were half fearful of fever — but he is convalescent this morning. Someone gave him an Illustrated News – He is enchanted with it — has a plan of "putting his shoulder to the wheel," he says, "and buying it himself" – (For every successful lesson he is paid five centimes — a halfpenny.) He "knows the politics are wretched". (his own words). "Its too bad calling Napoleon *a tyrant!* Still, there's a *sympathy for Italy,* and Garibaldi is called our hero; — And the pictures are certainly most beautiful –" So Peni has been discoursing to me just now, trying hard to wheedle me out — of what he wont get. He is rather too much accustomed to have his fantasies pass into facts,— and this as he gets older, will grow more expensive — besides other objections. His Abbé has gone to Rome — so that I hold the Latin & other lessons — except arithmetic & music which Robert undertakes – I dont work him much just now, & he's quite good. Peni is never naughty, understand, in the naughty sense — he's only inattentive — which is a provoking kind of naughtiness, to be sure.[9] You would be amused to hear him talk Italian politics — he traces Garibaldi's advances step by step as the telegrams announce them — & he has all the names of Italian leaders on the tip of his tongue – I cant help smiling sometimes. But it ruffled me a little when on the Abbé coming to take leave of me, Peni, who had been joining in the conversation, observed very gravely that "We should be obliged at last to put the Holy Father into the castle of St. Angelo." (speaking Italian of course). I turned quickly to reprove him, but the Abbé with the most good humoured manner & smile

said — "I always tell you, Penini, that you are too little to talk so
much about politics. No grown up man would say so of the
Santo Padre — not even," he added to me slyly, "if he *thought*
so –" But the Abbé, besides being very liberal, has certainly one
of the sweetest tempers possible — and his presence & lessons are
a great loss to Peni.

The weather has been very hot – Today it is cooler, indeed
quite cool. Robert rides a great deal — for three or four hours
together sometimes. We stay here till the tenth of October — so
it was arranged at least.

Something was said about a governess for the dear children –[10]
Did the one thought of, answer? Are the children good, & not
noisy? Dear Surtees. Give him my true, sisterly love. How I feel
with him & for him – 'May God help us & hold us all — for we
need it indeed – Is Stone the first man? Was there not another,
famous in these special disorders? Mrs. Cust[11] was *kept* in London for months – Oh George — you need not fear that my spirits
go up too high – I suffer terrors sometimes. And, at all moments
— patience itself has the weight on my heart of a very heavy
stone – I know too that these cases must be long — yes, at their
best perhaps – And if that is hard for *us* what must it be for *her*
in her pain — poor precious thing ! – Oh — may God grant that
that acute pain may not return. I think at moments there may
be a turn in the case when we least expect it.

Remark George, that I have not even named my darlingest
Arabel – Tell her that I hold her fast notwithstanding, & that
she must do so by me . . We want one another just now. She is
happier than I am in being where she is — & I ought to be satisfied with just that — only I keep worrying & teazing everybody
just because I can do them no good –

As to you, George — if you knew how I feel to you — but
you dont — I hold you in true love & true honor too

[*on envelope*] & all your words are dear to me. Our kind love to
Occy & Charlotte[12] — & a kiss to the babe. To all the children
besides. Robert's love to everyone of you with your attached

Ba's –

[*On side and top of first sheet*] If I had not recd your letter yesterday, I could not today. Railroads all occupied by troops – No passage for anybody, or for newspapers or letters. It is said that we are to have fighting directly — but there's mystery.– May God save Italy.

[1] Postmark: Siena, Sept. 7, 1860; Taunton, Sept. 12. Address: Angleterre via France, George Moulton-Barrett, Esq., Stoke Court, Taunton, Somersetshire.

[2] Henrietta suffered from cancer. Her painful illness and her death, November 23, 1860, put a severe strain on Mrs. Browning's failing strength.

[3] Storm's home, located 28 miles east of Llanfyllin, Montgomeryshire, Wales.

[4] Carlo Matteucci (1811-68), a professor of physics who in 1860 became an Italian senator and inspector-general of the Italian telegraph lines.

[5] Louis Christophe Léon Juchault de Lamoricière (1806-65), French general and, during the second republic, a member of the Chamber of Deputies. He vigorously opposed the *coup d'état,* and was exiled in 1852. Refusing to accept Napoleon III, he took command of the Papal army in 1860 and in September was defeated at Castelfidardo, the battle which permitted Garibaldi to enter Naples.

[6] The followers of Giuseppe Mazzini (1805-72). They opposed the formation of a Kingdom of Italy, holding out for a republic.

[7] Husband of Marchioness Laiatico (see *Letter 51, note 8,* p. 231).

[8] Ubaldino Peruzzi (1821-91), director of the railways of Livorno 1850-59; later senator, and minister of public works and of the interior under Cavour 1861-64.

[9] An early indication of Pen's later career as a student.

[10] Henrietta's children.

[11] The name is almost indecipherable. It is probably Cust, referring to the lady identified in *Letter 43, note 8,* p. 182.

[12] Charlotte was Occy's wife. He was the fourth of the Barretts to marry, but only after his father's death.

letter 54   Florence, Oct. 12
                                                      [1860]¹

My ever dearest George, I had your letter on the morning of
our leaving Siena — which accounts for this two days, no, three
days silence on my part. I travelled, dear, dear George in the
shadow of your letter – There was nothing new, & something
welcome — and yet it cast on me a sort of sadness! — which
wears off — perhaps through the unconscious influence of the
change of air & scene, or perhaps, as Robert thinks, in a more
reasonable appreciation of what you wrote. Our dearest tenderly
beloved Henrietta seems to suffer less acute pain – That is all
mercy – And that she should not be forced to *increase* the
anodynes a good symptom in itself — I try to gather up the
crumbs of comfort, you see – Indeed I do not vex myself beyond
what is necessary,— I shut my eyes on no ray of light — "As
those who wait for the morning" I look for it on all sides – You
were very dear, George, to write so soon — for it was before my
time of expecting a letter – Thank you, dearest George –

Believe me, I have had time too for thinking of you lately.
You will know *that* by my impertinent remarks on your rural
schemes, when I wrote of them to Arabel – I admire & love you,
George . . *more than you have an idea of* . . and I cant hear
of your taking to infinitesimal farming in a country seclusion
(sewing up your life in a bag) without much heart-burning &
groaning. Dear, dear George, dont do any such thing — especially in a hurry — & before you have taken a wider look at the
world and its various highways – Surely there are positions open
to you, with your legal antecedents, where you might do moderate & useful work with satisfaction to your country & yourself –
I tell you clearly — Only one fact could reconcile me to your
country retirement, & that is — forgive me — your marriage – If
you mean to take a companion with you into retirement,—well
— then I have no more to say – Otherwise, I do protest — the
louder too that I have your promise, (& when we are all somewhat happier I shall dun you upon it) to pay a visit to me in
Italy – Oh — it makes me sigh now to think of any pleasant

thought – It hurts me — when my precious Henrietta is bearing pain – To hear of her being a little, a little satisfactorily better would make the thought of a pleasure *possible* — but now, as it is,—*"may God save her"* seems the end of all wishing — the extreme point, I mean – So, may God help us all –

As to Garibaldi, George, I would indeed have willingly hindered much you have read of. Bid Arabel observe that the fear I expressed some time ago *is only justified.*– He is a hero and loyal — honest — true to the truth — but easily influenced & exposed to the worst influences,— not strong – Col. Peard[2] ("Garibaldi's Englishman") writes to Florence in a private letter, that Mazzini's people cling about him day & night poisoning his mind too successfully – Among the rest, my unlucky friend Jessie Mario,[3]— who "pretends to be busy at the hospitals" but is busy instead with Garibaldi.– Such decrees! — confiscating property & the like! The fleet unmanned — troops melting away — popular disaffection alarming. Still, the resolute & united sentiment of the national party throughout Italy, & the largeness & energy of the mind at Turin[4] have produced their effect, we hope & trust — and the king is likely to be received at Naples with open arms – True, that Mazzini, who was civilly requested to go at once, refuses – But we shall see the last of him presently.

At this moment I am more "put out" by Viterbo, & the French letting in the Pope's people after dispossession, (if they have done it) – "Napoleon cant do wrong," you say, with me.– Yes, he *can*, George, *if he does* — only it is not proved till then. He has hitherto done so admirably well, produced such great results at so small an expence of human suffering & destruction, & shown throughout these Italian movements, together with surpassing ability, so unimpeachable a degree of sincere desire to attain the best for Italy, that it is reasonable as well as just to give him the benefit of the doubt in any doubtful case – The direction of his troops on Viterbo, Velletri &c &c has been understood to be the occupation of certain points for temporary strategical purposes — & also perhaps to make as much noise & smoke as he can, in order to keep the Pope quiet, & the powers from intervening –

It is even said by some persons that after Warsaw, Austria will be down on us, & that the French are preparing for that movement. And General Goyon[5] is apt to do good things badly — besides having a secret sympathy for the cardinals, which makes him very unpopular in the French army – At last we shall see the road clear. I *believe in Napoleon* – I know too much of him in fact, not to believe – He is the man of the time, & at the head of all progress. In return, the reactionary governments are getting up a Holy Alliance against him . . in which England has her finger – I am sorry England should have her finger in it – Prussia is simply contemptible – Germany acts after her kind — (that is, the petty princes do). Russia might have done better — (considering some noble efforts about the serfs) – Austria does the best for her corruptions. But I am sorry England should have her finger in it – I wish that finger were burnt rather –

When the secret history of this Italian revolution shall come to be read, students will turn in their chairs & say, "Curious" – It is very curious –

We still intend going to Rome — unless disturbances increase – The danger to *me* is rather in the cold than in the revolution — but I dont think of it — we leave the point undetermined for a few weeks – In Rome, the Romans are preparing flags to welcome Victor Emmanuel — so I heard a few days since from a safe source – At that time, the Pope's fugitives (Lamoriciere's) were disarmed by the French as they entered the city — & the populace assembled in the streets in a manner unknown to Rome hitherto.

Let me tell you – There is an ancient prophecy in Italy,— old by hundreds of years – "The Cross will perish by the cross –" Nobody knew what it meant till lately, when the whole world finds out that it indicates the destruction of the church's temporal power by the cross of Savoy –

Then there's another prophecy – *"When a battle shall be fought on the mountain of the crosses, monte delle crocette,"* (a place near Loretto — the very place where Cialdini[6] gained his fight against Lamoriciere, *"Italy shall be one."*

So speak the prophets here & Frederick Tennyson writes to

me from Jersey that Napoleon is the number of the Beast 666 –
So you see he does'nt take my view exactly of Imperial merits –

I have not been out since we arrived here – Yesterday we had
a visit from Anthony Trollope the clever novelist, who is at
Florence visiting his brother. I like both brothers – The novelist
is surpassingly clever as a writer — dont you think? And he has
a very kind feeling for me, I understand from those who bear
witness. Mr. Landor came with us & was deposited at his house –
He is crossing Robert just now by insisting on translating into
Italian & printing ("for the benefit of Garibaldi"!) certain of his
Imaginary Conversations – His Italian is not up to the mark, &
the proceeds are likely to be considerably behind hand with the
expenses – He is so selfish, so self-adoring, and so little earnest,
that I cannot pretend to like him much – I am simply kind out
of humanity, & for Robert.

We have had an offer from America lately – If either of us
will give a "scrap" of verse "ever so short," every week for a
year to a periodical in America, five hundred pounds English
shall be his portion – I am offered, too, six hundred pounds for
a novel on Italian affairs – These brilliant offers however are not
accepted – I couldn't bind myself to work of that kind, which
would exclude work more after my own desire. They pay well
in America – For five short lyrics about Italy, I have a hundred
pounds — as much as they sent me for Aurora Leigh – "The
forced Recruit"[7] had ten guineas – You see literature is not such
a bad trade after all — though one works for it in the nervous
system, and the returns fluctuate. Also you know, they pay *me*
a good deal in England with mud & eggshells – One must remember that.

Robert is going to write to ask you to be our trustee in place
of the Indian Judge Arnold,[8] my dearest George – He wishes it
much, & of course I should like it — but dont be drawn to engage in anything too uncomfortable or troubling to your dear
self.

I am afraid of naming Arabel – *Tum charum caput*[9] is sacred
— *but take care of it* — DO. I almost wonder you dont *see* me
walking about the rooms! — I think so much of you all – May

God love you & help us all — & love & bless that precious Henrietta of ours who is first just now with every one of us – Arabel will let me know when you hear of Sette's arrival in Jamaica. I hope he may be qualified to manage the estates[10]— dearest George's most attached Ba –

[*On margin and top of first sheet*] Love to dear Surtees & the children. Tell Arabel to remember about Miss Sewell's[11] books — "Ursula" for instance. Let Henrietta feel how closely my heart is with her – And *never* let her write to me.

. . . .

[*On inside of envelope*]

Dear George – Ba leaves me little space enough to say more than a word about the trusteeship: the whole matter was put into Mr. K's[12] hands who appointed Chorley & Arnould, my friends: I don't know what the provisions of the deed were, it having been purely a matter of form — consequently for fourteen years neither trustee has had to do anything,— but they *may* have,— so that Arnould, being too busy and distant, we must replace him — I *suppose* — for the words of the *solicitors** are 'We presume you will have to appoint a successor, and if you will instruct your solicitor to prepare the necessary deed, we will attend to it immed[y] on behalf of Sir Joseph. If we can really go on with one trustee only — *good* — so much expense and trouble will be saved — but if a new one is necessary — will you not gratify me by being that one? I think or am sure that the trust only concerns what takes place in the interest of Ba and our child after my death — so that it is really *your* affair.

For the rest, Ba's & your sympathy with dear Henrietta are wholly shared in by

Yours affectionately ever RB.

[*At top of flap*] * Murray, Son & Hutchings, 11 Birchin Lane

[1] Postmark: Firenze, Oct. 13, 1860; Taunton, Oct. 17, 1860. Address: George G. Moulton-Barrett, Esq., Stoke Court, near Taunton, Somersetshire.

[2] John Whithead Peard (1811-80), Oxford M.A. and barrister of the Inner Temple (1837). He joined Garibaldi in his Sicilian expedition, commanding a company of revolving-rifle soldiers.

[3] An Englishwoman, née Jessie White, married to Alberto Mario, an "honest man around Garibaldi." T. A. Trollope called her Garibaldi's Englishwoman. She accompanied the general in all his campaigns as a hospital nurse, and later published a life of Garibaldi. Both Marios were followers of Mazzini and therefore, disagreed with the Brownings by favoring a republic for Italy. There are frequent references to her in Kenyon. (See T. A. Trollope: *What I Remember*, 3 vols., London, 1889. II, pp. 227-29.)

[4] Cavour.

[5] General Goyon, commander of the French occupation forces in Rome.

[6] Enrico Cialdini (1811-92), victor of the battles of Castelfidardo and Ancona, and director of the siege of Gaeta. Ancona is only a few kilometers from Loretto.

[7] Included in Mrs. Browning's *Last Poems* (1862), published after her death.

[8] Sir Joseph Arnould (1814-86), one of Browning's oldest friends. He was born in Camberwell and was associated with Browning and Alfred Dommett (*Waring*) in the days of their greatest intimacy. He was one of the trustees of the Brownings' marriage settlement, but asked to be relieved after being appointed to the Supreme Court of Bombay in 1859.

[9] The writing seems to be *tum*, but must be *tam*, an echo of Horace's phrase *tam cari capitis* (for a head so dear), Odes I, 24, l. 2. *Charum* a familiar spelling for *carum*, showing the influence of Greek.

[10] He was not. It was during his management that the circumstances developed which later forced "Storm" to liquidate the estates.

[11] Elizabeth Missing Sewell (1815-1906). The novel *Ursula*, 2 volumes, was published in 1858. Miss Sewell was much interested in the education of girls and wrote many religious and educational books, as well as fairy tales and books for children.

[12] John Kenyon.

letter 55   Nov. 1, Florence
                                                            [1860][1]

My ever dearest George, I have Arabel's words at the back of
Mrs. Martin's letter, to give me courage & heart to write — for
ah, 'dearest George, your last news saddened me much again'—
Somehow & in spite of advice & intention, I had got up too high,
& expected to be lifted higher yet when your hands next touched
me. But no – That is not God's will so soon – We must humbly
thank him for what He gives — diminution of pain – I bear
everything better than to hear of her suffering so. Also, as far as
it goes, the evident reduction of inflammatory tendencies must be
a progress — & must at least, prepare the way for a progress.
Dear Darling thing – My tender love to her — it is with her
always – I yearn after her, & hold her name before God when
nearest to Him in prayer – May He show mercy to us by restor-
ing her to us –

You are very kind, dearest George, as to the trusteeship, &
Robert, who is *anxious* to have you, bids me to be sure to thank
you on behalf of us both. The only doubt is . . . would the expence be great of naming another trustee since you say it is not
necessary? Perhaps we had better wait till we shall be in England
next year & if, meanwhile, your fine defences dont nibble away
all the money there is to take care of — Spain is going to establish a system of defences, it seems, now! – What a madness!
Everybody defending himself from everybody — & nobody intending to attack –[2] Not even Austria, if the word of an Austrian
government could be taken for anything – Here we are prepared
for war. I dont suppose that Rome will be less exposed to the din
of it than Florence is – Anyway I am indifferent as far as we are
personally concerned — & nobody need fear for us –

You are not to imagine that I named Miss Sewell's novels for
their literature – In fact I never read but one of them — they are
scarcely in my way – Only Arabel told me that our precious sufferer liked religious reading in that form, & I knew that the
colour of the opinions would please her – They are popular books
— many people like them much – I agree with you in adhering
to Anthony Trollope — & indeed Robert & I both consider him

firstrate as a novelist – Framley Parsonage is perfect it seems to me – The writer is just now in Florence, & came to see us yesterday for the second time – I like both brothers[3] very much. Anthony has an extraordinary beard to be grown in England, but is very English in spite of it, & simple, naif direct, frank — everything one likes in a man – Anti-Napoleonist of course, & ignorant of political facts more than of course, & notwithstanding that, caring for *me* — which is strange, I admit –

I saw a German lady two days since who came from Garibaldi — an old friend of his – She found him worn to the bone & in the worst spirits,— torn to pieces by his "friends"– Also it was depressing, she said, to hear him spoken of on all sides with a sort of affectionate contempt . . . "il est trop bon enfant, ce pauvre Garibaldi!" In Naples there was no government, no police, no order,— & everybody intriguing against everybody – After the vote, will enter the king & good government – In the meanwhile all Italy is delighted with the noble manifesto expressing Napoleon's policy, in the Constitionnel – The emperor's hand is unmistakeable under the signature of *"Boniface"*. My poor Italy – The Marchesa Torrearsa,[4] a very interesting Sicilian, called on me yesterday – She said the deliverance was so great & sudden that she "felt like one just recovered from an illness — scarcely strong enough or certain enough to be joyful –" That was striking — was it not?

It is true — is it not? that Mrs. Orme is dead – I have thought so for long – This morning I had a note from Mrs. Robson[5] to announce that she & Charlotte had come to Florence for a year — not greatly to my satisfaction – Only we are going away — and next year shall probably — certainly if we live[6]— be in England & France.

I wish you would always mention dear Uncle Hedley – Mrs. Martin seems unwell, & doubtful whether she may not be prevented from leaving England — which I shall be very sorry for – The weather you have had must be bad for everybody — though my comfort is that the object of our especial care is not likely to be affected by climate to any great degree – We have seen no fire yet — & I cant wear anything warmer than silk, though I tried for a day – Peni is well – I do hope & trust that the governess has acceded to terms, & has arrived – Let Arabel write & tell me about her & how Henrietta likes her – It will be a relief to Henrietta to feel a reliable person at hand.

Answer the question by message or otherwise about the expences of renominating the trustee. Sir Joseph Arnould wrote in reply to Robert's letter of condolence,[7] that he had taken another wife "young & pretty"! Also, that the distance obliged him to give up the trusteeship. I want to know, George, whether it is lawful for trustees to permit us to [on top of first sheet] transfer our funded money — in case we chose it — in case you "defend" any more & increase the income tax. May one ask also whether you quarrelled with Mr. Chorley about me at all? May God bless you & love you – I love you all as a human being may. Oh, for a letter of encouragement –

[On envelope] Will Arabel forward this little note to Mr. Chapman after reading it to ascertain whether Henrietta has seen the two books mentioned? Dearest George I accept your resolution about the house – Your own Ba
[Torn] send the books to Arabel for Henrietta.

Robert's & Pen's true love –

[1] Postmark: Firenze, Nov. 6, 1860. Address: Angleterre., George G. Moulton-Barrett, Esq., Stoke Court, Taunton, Somersetshire.

[2] The situation is familiar.

[3] The other brother was Thomas Adolphus Trollope (1810-92). He spent most of his life in Italy, chiefly in Florence. Like other members of his family, he was a voluminous writer. What I Remember, his autobiography, was published in 1887.

[4] Marchesa Torrearsa, wife of Fardella Vincenzo Torrearsa (1808-89), Italian Marchese and Florentine official (McAleer, p. 127).

[5] Unidentified and apparently unwanted.

[6] After twenty years of thinking in these terms the phrase now becomes prophetic.

[7] Robert's letter of condolence had been occasioned by the death of Sir Joseph's first wife (see Miller: Browning, pp. 213-14).

letter 56   Florence
                                                [Nov. 11 ?, 1860][1]

Beloved George,

We are going to Rome tomorrow morning – Robert thinks it best that I should not wait for more letters good or evil, lest I should be prevented by the weather from going at all – So I shall find your next word at Rome – As for me I do as he likes – It is better perhaps – I told him to decide,— it was the same for *me*.

I have your two dreadful letters. Of course I feel as you know I must — feeling sure too that you state everything as often to me as you can – May God help us all – There is a ray in your postscript — which will do to try to travel on – And you say she is not weaker than when you wrote before – But I am very frightened — & it is perhaps better to wait for news in a carriage than sitting here in this chair — which makes one mad almost.

Anyway Robert says its a duty for me to go to Rome — & if we *are* to go, the only chance for it seems to go at once –

We shall find your letters waiting for us, if you wrote in the time you said —"again that week"–

Write straight to Rome (poste-restante) after receiving this.

May God be with you all – My whole heart is — dear dearest George –

                                                Your Ba –

Roberts eyes were not dry over your letter — feeling for me & with me. His love.

                                                Nov. 19
                                                Florence

[1] Postmark: Firenze 19, Nov. 60; (Taunton) November 23, 60. The Brownings reached Rome on Friday, November 17, after a journey of six days. (See below, *Letter 56a.*) Address: Angleterre, George G. Moulton Barrett, Esq., Stoke Court, Taunton, Somersetshire. This was Henrietta's home.

letter 56a[1]   Rome, via Felice, 126
                                                  Dec. 3, '60.[2]

My dear George,

   I give you the first moment I can take from Ba to tell you the
few words that you must be anxiously waiting for. Your last
letter, of the 24th came this morning. Ba has been suffering for
the last fortnight just as much as she could bear, so that the last
news finds her in a fitter state to receive it than she might have
been had the calamity befallen her without notice. You will have
been apprehensive or alarmed, perhaps, at receiving (if you did
receive) a telegram I sent last week. On getting yours a fortnight
ago, Ba's distress was so acute that I thought of no better resource
than to hurry our journey at once. We were to have taken advantage of a break in the cold weather & started on Monday —
but I prevailed on her to let me get her off the very next morning
— & she suffered it to be so: I believe the step was the best we
could take — for it secured to her six days respite at least from
the sad announcement of which I knew your letter was the immediate herald[3]— besides which, the change of scene and necessity for exertion would do good, and the reaching Rome and receiving the shock in a milder climate than at Florence was most
important. So we got off, and after a wretched journey arrived
at Rome on Friday, the 17th. I had prepared everything, arranged for receiving the letters which must have preceded us —
more were waiting! Then followed four or five days of suspense
till it became unbearable, and I sent telegrams to Florence &
Taunton on the Wednesday. From Florence came the result of
your last note thither — and, afterwards, the five notes that had
been kept back thro' the infamous negligence of the officials —
the notes to Rome reached me duly, I believe. Of course I had
all along to do my utmost in breaking the contents of your letters
to Ba. indeed that has been my business since the beginning:
even at Siena I was forced to get & inspect all letters before they
got to Ba – She had the firmness to desire me to do so. Let me
say, however unnecessary, my dear George, that I, for my part,
cannot express to you my grateful sense of all your considerate-
ness, and affection,— out of which it arose: I understood what

you would imply thro' all the kind keeping back — and yet was able to use it so as to give hope enough to help her to bear up. She has borne it, on the whole, as well as I should have thought possible — but the wounds in that heart never heal altogether, tho' they may film over. God bless her.

I will write again — do not alarm yourself. The worst is over — the suspense having been as hard to bear as the ending of it. I just write this in utmost haste to save the post — wishing if possible to write a word to Arabel — but I am well spared any attempt to speak to all of you, or to poor Surtees. Ever affectionately yours, my dear George,

Robert Browning

[1] This letter of Robert's is so intimately connected with the preceding that it has seemed best to detach it from the body of his letters and include it here in its chronological position among the letters of his wife.

[2] Via Felice is now Via Sestina. No. 126 bears a plaque which recalls that from 1835 to 1842 it was the residence of the Russian poet and novelist, Gogol.

[3] Henrietta died November 23, 1860.

letter 57
Rome 126 Via Felice
April 2 [1861][1]

Ever dearest George – I dont like putting in my line about business to you, when there are things nearer to speak of — but Robert says he must write today on this deed question & so there's really a necessity on *me*, I feel (poor She of a Ba as I am) to write a word too.

Dearest George, you know I dont care much about these things — but on this particular point of throwing back our last money into England, I have a strong opinion. It would be an inconvenience to us in various ways, & objectionable in some others into which there is no use entering. When the first Deed was made fourteen years ago, I protested strongly, and yielded only to a representation of dear Mr. Kenyon that I had no right to put my husband into a false position & to expose him to the shadow of a suspicion even for a limited time.[2] I yielded — agreeing that the advantage we lost by the Deed, (being simply a money-advantage) was not worth that other risk – I point out to you, however, that we suffered for a great many years pecuniary disadvantage from the restrictions of the Deed. We had to live on half the small income at best possible to us — & how much we were pinched & ground down through Robert's resolution to keep out of debt, none of you perhaps ever knew – If Mr. Kenyon had not forced on us his hundred a year after three years, when Pen was born, the straight [sic] would have been increased –

Since his bequest, all this is of course altered – Through our prudence in not increasing the circle of our expences in proportion to the enlarged income, we never want to think of money, which is an infinite blessing to people like us – We are free to move our hands, & to please ourselves.– And to suppose that, being still in our right mind, we ever would consent to being tied up again to a post, is really out of the question my dearest dear George – The six thousand pounds in England, I considered sacrificed. Between income-tax & minute percentage, its scarcely worth counting in one's resources.[3] We can make as much by passing a few stanzas through an American newspaper in two months, as what we draw from England.

Then — after fourteen years, we are above suspicion. Agreed that Robert will probably survive me,— agreed even, on my side, that he may remarry . . being a man . . nay "being subject to like passions" as other men, he *may* commit some faint show of bigamy — who knows? But what is absolutely impossible for him is that under any temptation or stress of passion, he *could* sacrifice what belongs to Peni to another.– Draw up the strictest legal document by the help of a confederation of lawyers, and I would rather trust Robert. Your deed may have a flaw in it after all – "You can drive a carriage & four through any Act of Parliament!" But for Robert to fail *here* is IMPOSSIBLE. He has that exaggerated idea of virtues connected with money, which distinguishes the man from the woman. He is *rigid* about such things

— I know him. He is far more capable of committing murder, than of the slightest approach to pecuniary indelicacy. That is beyond the circle of his temptations, be sure.

The end of all this is to prove to you how entirely motiveless it would be as an act of folly, if *I* consented to restrictions of the kind you hint at.

If you have the goodness, dearest George, to accept any trust for us, you will find everything laid as straight, & smooth for your hand as you could desire,— poets though we be – Property in Italy as in England, will be left clear – The worst we do is to add to the principal – We had a temptation towards buying an exquisite villa close to Florence last autumn, but resisted on the ground of the doubt whether the winters there were not overcold for me – To resist, on the ground of the money's being tied up, would have been considerably more mortifying.

Ah, dearest George – May peace & joy sit at your hearth! I dont like your scheme of living alone in that way! You shall tell me how it turns out when you come with Arabel to meet us in France –

No — you did not think that I *could* have the heart to go to England this year –⁴

May God bless you, beloved George –

Love & thanks to Dear Henry –

> Your grateful & affectionate
> & selfwilled Ba

¹ The envelope has not been preserved.

² The suspicion to be avoided was that Browning, being in his own right penniless, had married Miss Barrett for her money, which under English law immediately became his. That this suspicion was held in some quarters, especially by her brothers, is evident from Elizabeth's letters immediately after the marriage.

³ The interest rate must have been low indeed to render a principal of about $30,000 so contemptible.

⁴ The absence of Henrietta, who died the preceding November, would have made England unbearable.

letter 57a   Rome, Via Felice 126, Apr. 2d. 61[1]

My dear George,

I think, or am sure, that you cannot misunderstand me when I say that it will be far better for us to give you no more trouble about the Trust-deed,— thanking you heartily for all you have taken & are ready to take. I will write by this post to Arnould, & beg as a favor that he continue his Trusteeship. As for the Deed & original provisions of it, relating to the money of Ba as I found it,— the whole thing was quite unnecessary — as my executing it many months after our marriage proved — but Mr. Kenyon suggested it and so it was done. As for engaging to take "any property Ba might afterwards acquire" out of her hands and send it to invest in England,— that, indeed, never entered my head. The claim to which you refer was meant to apply to a very different contingency — as Mr. Kenyon particularly stated to me more than once. I use the phrase "take the money out of Ba's hands" very advisedly, because were I inclined to really advise her giving it up for any such purpose, she would refuse, pointblank; — but this time[2] I entirely agree with her as to the impossibility of any step of the kind. Our money is invested here entirely to our satisfaction,— the loss at selling out, re-investing, differences of interest, and fresh expence of receiving every payment of the same from England would be extravagant. We shall live in Italy always, and the convenience of our present arrangement causes us to bless ourselves every quarter day at least. On what principle of justice to Ba *would* I advise that she forthwith deprive herself of some £150 a-year — for what? All that we save, after necessary expenditure, I invest and add to our capital, from which in fifteen years not a sixpence has been subtracted. The whole of this will go to Ba and her child after my death. I will make a fresh will[3] (you may see the old one, which I made to supply the inadequacies of the deed, and which the subsequent birth of Peni rendered inoperative: I will appoint *you,* dear George, if your goodness will permit me, *executor* — and you will see for yourself, I repeat, that I leave Ba & my child not only all *her* money proper, in the law's eye, but all that I have got or saved or (in the exercise of an economy I pride myself upon) shall save or get: nobody else in the world has a fraction of a claim to it, and — for other causes or of incitements to injustice in testamentary dispositions, I shall only say that Ba and I know each other for time and, I dare trust, eternity: — We differ *toto coelo* (or rather, *inferno*) as to spirit-rapping, we quarrel sometimes about politics, and estimate peoples' characters with enormous difference, but, in the main, we *know* each other, I say.

All this was unnecessary to say except in explanation due to your affectionateness — to anybody else I should reply "suppose Ba made a present of the £4 000 to Mr. Hume,[4] the day after receiving it,— what then? Could *I* prevent her, and could she consider herself bound, on receiving a present, not to make any use of it during her life-time beyond receiving a yearly trifle by way of interest: and further, ought she to deal in the same way by every pound she receives from America (for instance) for poems delivered? When does the "property" *begin,* with sums received? Only with the thousands and not with the Hundreds nor the Tens?

I shall always be sure — as I will tell Arnould — that you will be at hand to help and administer the Deed, should I die first: Let what is done be done — but the subsequent proceedings are to be free, and I promise you we all shall be the better for it.

I wont add — that is, can't add a word — time pressing — it is a good thing this hitch has stopped the trouble and useless expence — for, I suppose, the deed would have needed our signatures,— bless us all! I wish you all joy and prosperity in your new domicile. "Luck to your roof-tree"— and love to you and yours from

> Yours affectionately ever
> Robert Browning.

[1] This letter from Robert was enclosed with the preceding.

[2] Suggests other times when, perhaps, the well-known difference between their attitudes toward England may have produced different ideas on the subject of investments.

[3] Whether or not Browning made a new will immediately, it was

superseded by that made on February 12, 1864, and published in the London *Times*, February 22, 1890. This will was witnessed by "A. Tennyson . . . F. J. Palgrave." George Barrett was appointed executor along with John Forster. The latter died during Browning's lifetime, and in 1876 George "renounced probate." Letters of administration were then granted to Robert Wiedemann Barrett Browning "by whom the gross value of the personal estate and effects in the United Kingdom has been sworn at £16,774 19s 4d."

⁴ Daniel Dunglas Home (Hume), the medium. Browning could think of no sillier or, to him, more objectionable thing for Mrs. Browning to do with her money. For Browning's contempt for this "unmitigated scoundrel" as well as Home's own account of a seance with the Brownings, see DeVane and Knickerbocker, pp. 198-200. Home, of course, was the original of *Mr. Sludge, "The Medium."*

letter 58   [Rome]
                                        [April 30, 1861][1]

My ever dearest George,   Indeed you mistake if you suppose we supposed — or suspect we suspected — no, indeed – You spoke of course as to the point of law, or result of a legal expression — and I, for my part, said so much because I wanted you to see and understand that the serious objection to making a certain knot stronger, was at least as much mine as Robert's — in fact, even more mine than Robert's. I hope Sir Joseph Arnold will be good natured for old friendship's sake, & that we shall not [have had our pain for nought][2] or rather for a good deal worse than nought – It is a great convenience in many ways to have our chief resources in Tuscany, and although we look disturbed at a distance, we feel very safe — also I would rather pay for a war for Venetia than for fortresses on the Thames, if the question falls into the alternative –

My dearest dear George, I thank you for all your cordial words — better to me than if said of me – You are very kind, very generous,— & we will use you, & not abuse you, whenever your valuable services can be made available.

Only you wont come to France – You cant afford it? Ah George, when you say such a word, it does not reconcile me to your beautiful new house so high up that nobody can get at you. The first thing people do with liberty seems to me to tie themselves up to a post. I thought when you gave up the bondage of the law, you meant to come to Italy, where you have never been, & see us a little – And you cant even come to Fontainbleau – Arabel too says that though she will come to Fontainbleau, she wont come to Italy — which all turns me to a black humour. Well — I dont give it up – There is time for teazing & converting her – Just now it is enough for me to gather together my courage for the journey to France — which seems to me very, very far. I feel more fit for going to Heaven sometimes — and yet there's great lacking of justification for that even, let me say, hastening to agree with my friends – It isn't merely or so much the bodily effort. I am stronger, & have been out driving several times — went to see Mr. Story's new statue of the African sybil — a very good work. Pleasant, to see men grow so perceptibly! & I never supposed him equal to this height.

We go to Florence in the latter part of May — & shall remain to rest there. Three months in France will be enough I fancy,— two in the country, one perhaps (at the end), in the city – But I keep it out of my head – I should prefer vegetating here in Italy among the hills — I am really fitter for it in body & soul — only there's a clear duty in the case –

Work, work, work — is the best we can get at in this world, we sons & daughters of men — I keep on sending to America, lyrics on Italian subjects — with all drawbacks – For five or six, in this dreary spring, there are a hundred pounds for result,— which considering the expenses I cause is no more than I owe our household — & the advantage is that these poems are left to the English public as fresh as manuscripts –

All these Italian poems are about to be translated I believe by my friend Dell'Ongaro,[3] the Venetian poet – He is a poet, but has the disadvantage of not understanding much English – So I shall translate the text literally into Italian, line by line — which will give me some *pedestrian* work (as opposed to the flying imagination) this summer — that is, if we keep to our plan. It seems to please Dell'Ongaro so far, & does not displease me – He is very competent as far as lyrical command of his own language goes — & I am the more inclined to him, as I have heard of a Sicilian poetess (of very unequal power of course) attempting the same thing.

Dearest dear George, your house must be very pretty, though you hang me up in it – That's kind. Have you books enough? Do you subscribe to Mudie?⁴— Do you take in many papers –? You will see that our Garibaldi has been Garibaldizing a little in the Chambers,— but that it is over now, & he & Cavour are reconciled – I thank God.

[IV] Have you seen dear Mr. Martin's photograph which they had the goodness to send me? It gave me a true pleasure. The likeness is perfect — and what extraordinary youthfulness! Looking back to the beginning of time I really see little difference between what he was & is – It is most remarkable – And these photographs spare no man in their scrupulous veracity,— no man, nor (which is worse!) woman, George!

Have you any society near you,— anybody you can talk with, exchanging thoughts, as well as words? The worst of those country places is, that even if you get, by good luck, intelligent neighbours, you miss the new intellectual blood,— the fluctuant society with which (under obvious disadvantages) you yet arrive at fresh openings into civilization. Here, in Rome, the river passes, — & very interesting people from all countries are met by turns – This winter of course I have seen nobody except such as made their way up these stairs for a morning visit,— though Robert has been out a good deal – Among the persons most interesting to me, who came to see me, has been Mr. Severn,⁵ the new English consul, who was here with Keats, you remember & in whose arms the poet died – I make him tell me the most minute details, — some very painful — Keats revolted against death, on that deeply tragic ground (always so affecting to me as an artist) of his gift being undevelopped [sic] in him — of having a work to do in his right hand, which he must let fall. "In ten years" said he, "I should be a great poet — and now, I have not even philosophy enough to die by —"

There would be no answer to such "divine despairs", if it were not in the facts in which I deeply believe, that life and work, yes, the sort of work suitable to the artist-nature, are continued on the outside of this crust of mortal manhood, & that the man will be permitted to complete himself, if not *here, there* – Mr. Severn is a simple man — who wont be distinguished much as a consul, I fancy – The other person I liked to see, & wanted to see more of, was Sir John Bowring.[6] [V] He brought a letter of introduction to me – Both in poetry & politics we had sympathies – But, poor man, after one visit here, he had an attack of illness, & was suspended between life & death for weeks, till he was carried away the other day at considerable risk to Civita Vecchia on his way to the north. He had a mission from the English government to Turin, on commercial affairs, & meant to do his best to get there – Lady Bowring came the last day to tell me how disappointed he was in having our intercourse cut short — and *I* was, very much! There were various points on which I wanted to hear him talk – He suffers the reproach of having drawn us into a bad war with China, but he is a man of excellent sympathies, & very advanced opinions. Knowing Napoleon well by personal relation, I should have liked you to hear him talk on that 'Head'– Napoleon is perfectly misconceived of, he told me, in England — the Emperor was thoroughly liberal in his views, & only desired to give liberty, & to be the occasion of giving it, at the least cost of instability of institutions – Frank & loyal he (Bowring) believed Napoleon to be — & full of great ideas for the world.

It is my view – The fault *I* find with the emperor is, that he conceives himself to be immortal — he calculates on having too much time – He was *really* regretful of the hurried invasion of the Neapolitan states by Garibaldi, & of the intervention of Piedmont . . though (as a *necessity he certainly admitted both*) while diplomatical arrangements between Francis II & Victor Emmanuel were going on. He wanted to wait for six months – Hence, the term "unjust aggression" in his letter to Francis – Also he has protracted the situation here, and other Italian "situations",— to avoid convulsion & dangers from without – Hitherto all has ended well — but he was wrong in calculating on his own life so surely – If either he or Cavour had died suddenly within the last year or so, all would have ended for Italy — the event would have been awful.

Our dear Storm wrote a precious little note to me before leaving England,— & I shall be much smoothed down at hearing of his safe arrival in Jamaica –

May God bless you, my dearest George. I hope your headaches have left you with the Law – Penini's love with mine –

And I am yours in truest gratefullest love –

Ba –

[*Single sheet, unnumbered*][7]
coaxed it out of his father.

He has got up — what he calls a *"sort of interest"* (when accused of a love-affair) towards the pretty sad queen of Naples, who shakes her parasol at him & admires his poney.– She is very pretty, & Pen's politics swerved under a distinct compliment to the "bellino caballino"; swerved enough to admit of his galloping after her carriage on the Pincio, & calling her, *"Oh, so* pretty, mama! much prettier than your photograph of her"![8]

Pen is getting on with his Latin & will find his Abbe here next winter, when our plan is to return. Then, he is to begin Greek too – He sleeps in my room still, & says "Good night, Darling", before he goes to sleep — but all this must end as other sweet things do, for he is twelve years old, & fencing & sleeping in "Mama's room," dont go well together. He looks younger than he is, with the same infantine face — and yet he grows both tall & fat together — which is satisfactory – The Duchess de Grummont (French ambassadress)[9] has just sent him a card for her *"Matinée d'enfants"* which is to be something magnificent – Robert will go with him for escort & come away when he's tired.

[1] Postmark: Tiverton, May 6, 1861. Address: Angleterre, George G. Moulton-Barrett, Warnicombe House, near Tiverton. Mourning envelope. The heading of this letter has been cut off.

[2] Part of the line has been cut out. "ght" at the end is legible. The reading is a conjecture.

[3] Francesco Dall'Ongaro (1808-73), Italian poet. He founded the revolutionary journal *La Favilla* in Trieste, 1836, and organized the first Italian legion for Garibaldi in 1848. He directed revolutionary journals in Venice and Rome and wrote many political and patriotic lyrics.

[4] Mudie's Lending Library, founded and carried on with great success by Charles Edward Mudie (1818-90), English bookseller and stationer.

[5] Joseph Severn (1793-1879). In spite of Mrs. Browning's prediction Severn served as British Consul in Rome until 1872. Although he survived Keats more than fifty years, he is buried beside him near the Pyramid of Cestus.

[6] Sir John Bowring (1792-1872), an extraordinary man with an enormous variety of interests. He published books on the poetry of Russia, Poland, Serbia, Hungary, and others, translating from all these languages. In 1825 he became editor of the *Westminster Review* and by his articles developed quite a reputation as a political economist. Besides serving as governor of Hong Kong he also served on numerous commercial missions, was for a time a member of Parliament, and after he left the British service negotiated treaties as minister plenipotentiary of the Hawaiian government to the courts of Europe. When he died, he left to the British Museum a fine collection of coleoptera. It is not remarkable that Mrs. Browning should have found him interesting.

[7] As indicated, parts of this letter are numbered I, II, IV, V. This half sheet is unnumbered and may be the second half of the missing part III.

[8] A precocious example of what later became a habit.

[9] Wife of Antoine Agénor Alfred Duc de Gramont (1819-80), later foreign minister in the last days of the second empire.

letter 58a   Rome, April 30 -'61[1]

My dear George,

I shall only write one word — no more can be necessary – to acknowledge your truly kind & good note & to say that I never for a moment was vexed at your suggestion or supposed it to imply anything but the admirable precision & probity which characterise you — on the other hand it would not be paying the unfeigned respect I have for your sense & power of observation if I supposed you could suspect me to be capable of any negligence or indirectness in such a matter as the future comfort of Ba & her child. Indeed, I profit by the good opinion which you make me proud (or something better) by avowing, to act on my own knowledge as I am sure yourself would do, had the peculiar circumstances under which we have lived for the last fifteen years, given you the like experiences. I invested our money on the soundest advice I could get, and the ultimate disposal of it has been a settled thing from the beginning. Of course I shall always look to you for advice on the many other points I may need it upon — ex.gr — Look at Lord Kingsdown's bill[2] and tell me, *when it is carried,* what its provisions enjoin or allow — for this reading his speech gives me the pleasant assurance that no will made in or out of England at this present time by a man who has any likelihood of staying six months and dying in a foreign country is worth a farthing — this wise, necessary measure, if adopted, will cure an anomaly of which (for my peace of mind's sake) I have been happily ignorant hither to. Do pray keep your eye on the results.

I will only repeat my truest wishes for your fortunate housekeeping and general welfare. Ba writes the rest, and for me, no less than herself, whenever she writes affectionately — as, I dare say, is sometimes the case!

Ever yours heartily
Robert Browning

----

[1] This note of Robert's accompanied the preceding letter, and serves to date it.

[2] Thomas Pemberton Leigh (1793-1867) was created Baron Kingsdown in 1858. He was enormously wealthy and highly respected in the legal profession. The bill in question was entitled "Wills of Personality by British Subjects Bill" and its basic objective was to establish the principle that a British subject who made his will abroad could conform either with the English custom or

that of the country in which the will was made. Lord Kingsdown's main speech was made on the second reading of the bill, April 23, 1861. The bill was brought back for a third reading and passage on August 6, 1861 (*Hansard's Parliament-Debates* for 1861 in various places in volumes 162, 163, and 164).

Letters of Robert Browning to George Barrett

letter 59   Tuesday E[g] [1]

My dear George,

What can I say to you, for Ba & myself, or how thank you for
this beautiful present? You know, I hope, that nothing was less
necessary than such a gift to convince us of your entirely affectionate feeling towards us both — of *that* your whole demeanour
since your return has been a most gratifying proof. Be assured
that I rejoice in the hope, nay the conviction, that the union
between us will only grow closer with time, and that I shall ever
feel it, as I do now, a great pride & privilege to be known as
    my dear George, Yours most affectionately & gratefully,

                                                    R. B.

[1] It is impossible to date this note precisely. The contents suggest
that it was written in the summer of 1851 shortly after the reconciliation between brother and sister. The Brownings arrived in London
toward the end of July and remained through September. In a
letter to Mrs. Martin, September, 1851, Elizabeth wrote: "After
Robert's letter to George had been sent three times to Wales and
been returned twice, it reached him, and immediately upon its
reaching him (to do George justice) he wrote a kind reply to
apprise us that he would be at our door the same evening. So the
night before last he came, and we are all good friends, thank God"
(Kenyon, II, p. 19).

letter 60   Rome, Via Felice, 126
                                                Jan. 15, '61.[1]

My dear George,

Our recent troubles[2] had put out of my head that matter of
the substitution of your name for that of Arnould in Ba's mar-
riage-settlement — which you were kind enough to allow. The
solicitors, "W. Murray, Son & Hutchins, 11 Birchin Lane" — are
pressing for an answer — may I beg you therefore to undertake
the troublesome business?

The deed is in the keeping of Mr. Hawthorne, — I accompany
this by a note which will request the transfer of it to yourself. I

also furnish you with a pro forma note to Chorley — to apprise him of my application & your consent. I have only further to beg that you will furnish me as soon as possible with the note of expenses.

Ba writes to Arabel who will send this to your address of which I am ignorant. She is in improved health — having suffered much.

This is not the place to recur to your own kindness, old or recent — be sure I remember it all, however.

Ever very affectionately
R Browning

¹ The sheet is folded over the text and sealed and addressed on the back to Geo. Moulton Barrett, Esq.

² Henrietta's death and the precarious health of Mrs. Browning.

letter 61   Rome, Via Felice 126.
                                            Feb. 12. '61¹

My dear George,

Arabel asks for information on a point or two concerning the business of the Trust-deed which you have so kindly taken on yourself. I have no attorney (here you may imagine an internal thanksgiving of mine) in London nor elsewhere – I did not know Mr. Hawthorne was one,— simply that he is Mr Kenyon's executor who, in that capacity, wrote to me mentioning that he had the Deed in his keeping and asking what I wished him to do with it — he offered to be of any possible use, I remember — and if he still officiates as Drawer of Deeds, you can use your discretion in applying to him now — but, understand, that I leave the matter wholly in your hands, with entire confidence.

I have received no answer from Chorley which may cause a new embarrassment — he says he will do exactly as I wish "*but* — he *must* say — he had already written to Arnould to suggest that somebody else should be substituted as Trustee for himself, Chorley, seeing that his inexperience of business, his uncertain health &c &c made him a sorry help in need"– I don't know how much of this is real diffidence & how much pique — but I am bound, I suppose, to tell him politely that if he really wishes to rid himself of the trouble he would better mention it *now* — when the deed is being concocted — as there will be a saving of as much again trouble and expense at some future period if his apprehensions fairly get the better of him – So I shall direct him to give a decisive answer to *you,* (care of Arabel) and on that decision you can act. I need not say that yourself, sole and absolute disposer of Ba's & Pen's belongings after my death, would suit me *most* — but you are delicate,— which I understand, and may insist on a coadjutor — in that case,— dear George, *pray* press into the office anybody whom yourself would trust in a like matter. You must be able to find such an one, and I intreat you to do so — it being altogether an arrangement for the convenience of your sister & her child.

I never did more than "skim" the Deed in question,[2] having merely begged Mr K. to prepare one which should secure the whole of Ba's money to herself in case of my death,— and this was done,— as an outward & visible sign rather than for any good, since I knew what course I should take then, & hereafter by my will. I say this to show that you will have *no* trouble during my life,— you must not be more than amused, for instance, by Ba's unpatriotic proposals to sell out & transfer stock,— *hers* will always yield the respectable 3% less income-tax — my own (i.e. that portion of hers which comes to me nominally) I deal with after my own fashion,— (and have invested a trifle, a month ago, at 6% which I have no kind of fear about, I would have you to know!) Seriously, you will do all this, troublesome as it is, for the love of Ba, and in consideration of the entire love & trust she has in you,— impulses which I cordially approve of & sympathize with. I write therefore to Chorley by this post, and you can act upon his answer at once. Take my truest thanks beforehand, and believe me, dear George, Yours affectionately ever

R Browning

[1] No envelope.

[2] Mrs. Browning also said that she had only glanced at the deed and recalled only that it provided for "all 'future husbands' and an unlimited number of children" (Huxley, p. 31).

letter 62   Florence
                                        Tuesday, July 2 [1861][1]

This is in answer to your
letter received yesterday[2]

Dear George, You must not hate me for giving you any pain anybody else might have spared you,— tho' I am too stupid to tell how. She was never "ill," arrived "*well*," had the news of Cavour's death next day and was prostrated by it—recovering, I suppose, only partially when she caught cold "the usual attack, no worse," was never in bed in the day time, till the last day, and then by a combination of circumstances which kept her from going into the drawing room, and kept assuring us that the doctor was wrong in his serious view of the case until the end came. The last evening Wilson (the maid) came to see her & went away satisfied nothing would happen. My instinct knew better, all the while, but my reason[3] was justified in believing her assurances that she would "certainly soon be well again." The last evening she wanted me take & furnish a Villa for three years. Thro' the night she repeated she was better, "comfortable," "*beautiful*" — bidding me "only come to bed now — why stay up now?" I knew the worst was impending by some instinct, I repeat — for I could explain away every ill symptom,— a little wandering, after a weeks absolute refusal of solid food, and a (prescribed) slight addition to the morphine dose, what was in that? The frightful thing, really, was only the vehement expression of her perfect love for me when, if nothing was to happen, there would be nothing to account for it in my simply standing beside her — but I will say, in profound gratitude, that her last words were bidding "God bless me" in tones and with what never accompanied any words of hers to me before. She laughed with pleasure and *youth*, and I believe in some perfectly gracious way allowed by God suffered no pain whatever, even as she averred. Had you been in the next house I don't think I should have called you in — but I sate up myself every night but one — unknown to her, who supposed I slept on a sofa, to please my inward misgivings, for the most part, rather than satisfy any so apparent need. The best Doctor we have, stayed with us till morning the first night and supposed the difficulty was over and that "sleep now" would mend all: then he found out that one lung was solidified — the right. "The *left*, Dr. Chambers would have it" — she replied — "it's the old experience I've had in plenty — they don't understand &c" and I was bound to hope they did not: the worst he remarked was — "If I were not assured this is a very exceptional case, and did I not know that there are such cases, I should suspect an abscess on the lungs. She is however certainly better today, better again this evening — and so on. The last night she sate up by herself, cleaned her teeth, washed her face and combed her hair without the least assistance — and she took two servings of jelly from me spoonful by spoonful and drank a glass of lemonade not a quarter of an hour before the end:[4] this is all I can bear to tell you now of it, and I bear so much only to be relieved of your just reproach if my silence to you had arisen from disregard of an obviously impending calamity. She was buried yesterday — with the shops in the street shut, a crowd of people following sobbing, another crowd of Italians, Americans & English crying like children at the cemetery, for they knew who she was — "the greatest English Poet of the day, writer of the sublimest poem ever penned by woman, and Italy's truest and dearest of friends" — as the morning & evening papers told them, "calling on the friends of Art & Italy, of whatever tribe and sect, to go & pay a last homage" — & so they did, I am told, for I saw nothing but for one minute a flash of faces — noble, grateful Italians.[5]

I have nothing more to do with Italy for many a year, however. I shall at once go to England, or rather Paris first, and then London:[6] I shall give myself wholly up to the care & education of our child; I know all Ba's mind as to how that should be, and shall try and carry out her desires – I have formed no particular plan as yet, but am certain enough of the main direction my life will take: but there is much to wind up here before I can go away with the relief of knowing that I need not return in a hurry. Penini is like an angel to me — inspired all at once: he is quite well and so am I,— I assure you, and beginning to get rid of the business already (the business of arranging affairs).

Wednesday. Dear George, I must write no more letters like this. I propose to go to England the moment I can wind up my affairs here, and to see Arabel for a few days: I shall then be able to say as much as I ought to say & no more — which I cannot manage now. For the last time, all brothers & relatives *must* forgive my not attempting to write to them – I am absolutely alone, — with much help of another kind, and every sort of offered assistance, but I cannot yet go over this again & again in letters. I hope I shall see you in England. Peni is quite well and very perfect in his goodness. I hope to get off in another week. I will write to Arabel of course.

Ever yours affectionately,
Robert Browning.

[1] Address: Angleterre. George Moulton Barrett, Esq., Warni-combe House, Near Tiverton, England. R.B. in lower left corner. Postmark: Firenze, July 3, '61; on back, Tiverton, July 7, '61, also pencil note in another hand, R.B./61.

[2] This sentence was added in the small hand in which the last paragraph, beginning "Wednesday," is written. The rest of the letter is written in an unusually large and unsteady hand.

[3] This sentence sets a tone of self-reproach which persists throughout the letter. Browning's instinct told him that his wife's condition was more serious than usual, but his natural optimism combined with his long experience of her relapses and recoveries and her own confidence allowed him to be "convinced" that all would be well.

[4] Mrs. Browning died at 4:30 in the morning of June 29, 1861. On the same day Browning wrote a note to Sarianna (DeVane and Knickerbocker, p. 131). Another and longer letter to her on June 30 is published in Hood, pp. 58-63. (See also letter to Miss Haworth, July 20, Orr, p. 239; also in Hood, pp. 64-65; and see James: *Memoirs of W. W. Story*, II, pp. 64-66.)

⁵ The funeral is described again in a letter to Sarianna, July 5 (DeVane and Knickerbocker, pp. 131-34).

⁶ Browning and Pen, accompanied by Isa Blagden, left for Paris on July 27. He spent some time near St. Malo and, as the next letter states, arrived in London September 29. He never returned to Florence.

letter 63   7 Delamere Terrace
                                               Saturday Mr.
                                               [September 30, 1861]¹

My dear George.

I feel your goodness deeply — do believe it: to have you & Arabel together caring for me *so* — is precious indeed to me. But see if I came to you, I won't say I should weary you just now — your sympathy prevents that — but certainly I should only half enjoy your society, half benefit by my visit. Now, one day — at no very distant day — I shall hope to go & see you and get the full advantage of your kindness. Will you let it be so? I have a restless anxiety, besides, to begin with Peni — there is much to be done & no time to lose: it will be best then to settle at once, to get to work at once — and whenever I can breathe freely and feel the first difficulties over, what dearer holiday can I give my-self than such as you propose? Meantime, thank you from my heart.

We arrived yesterday and were pleasantly smothered with Arabel's hospitality:² she finds Pen much grown, and healthy-looking. Yes, I am resolved, after much turning over the matter in my mind, that the only proper course to be taken with Pen is that in which you concur. I fully believe that he will do well,— best of all, indeed — with an English education. He has the spirit of emulation singularly strong — accompanied, as it is, by no drawback such as envy or vanity: his abilities are consider-able & various, and he has a happy, social temper that makes him friends everywhere. My plan is to begin with a good tutor for the purpose of initiating him into the English ways of study: I am not sure whether in another year there might not be added with advantage an attendance at one of the Junior Schools of King's College or the London University where there is a gradual introduction to be got, to the difficulties of a public school, mitigated by the residence at home and superintendence there. I should like him only to go to Eton or Harrow when qualified for the Upper forms, thus saving him many of the early troubles; he would then be prepared to work in right earnest, with a full sense of the advantages of so doing — and proceed to the University with a reasonable prospect of success. This is rather an ambitious programme of mine[3]— but I believe I am in possession of all the means, and my own wants will be moderate enough. He is anxious, himself, to do whatever I want, & satisfies me greatly thus far.

My dear George, I hardly know what you mean by explaining so proper and necessary a step as that which you took, to my great pleasure: (I was sure *you* had taken it.) It was hardly in my competence to speak with authority on matters so far back — moreover I was away, as you observe, and the foolish, blundering article required prompt correction. The writer, is, I think, the unhappiest nature I ever had to do with — such an union of self-conceit, irritability, and rashness, accompanied by a real kindness which must suffer on reflection from these sallies of ill-temper, or whatever causes them. He complains that his friends fall off! And takes no measure to rid himself of the miserable susceptibility that sees offence in everything & nothing. So he will live & die, poor fellow! I am puzzled to know how to act about him.[4]

Do you know what an escape we had on Thursday? I was informed by a timetable & the railway official that a train would leave Paris for Boulogne at 6. in the morning to arrive at 1½; (any other train would arrive too late for the customhouse, without a permission from which Pen's pony could not be embarked — I should therefore be delayed 36 hours at Boulogne.) on the faith of this information I brought the horse to the station at 5. a.m. — & found no train was to go: the next *available for horses* would start in the afternoon & I must wait till then — horses on no account could go by the "express" which alone would arrive in time. I reasoned with the officers for above two hours, declaring quietly I would prosecute the company — they admitting the blunders and calling them inexplicable. At the last minute (there was no time even to pay for him) they gave in. The horse was attached to the express ("for the first time") to the wonder of everybody along the line. So I gained my point and got off by the boat at 2 past midnight. Had they persisted, I should have been forced to go by the 8. p.m. train, arriving at 12: and, as you see by the papers, at 11 there was the dreadful accident & loss of life on the line at Amiens.[5] Strange to add, while on the train, I was thinking of the meeting we had with Tennyson ten years ago on our first return to England — catching a glimpse of him at Paris, and looking out of the window, there *was* Tennyson again entering the carriage! I could not believe my eyes: at Boulogne, I went with Pen to the quay — the Folkestone boat was about to leave. I said, "I will show you Tennyson": We went close — he was there with his wife & two children. I would not be recognized, but stood looking for a quarter of an hour till they left.[6] He, too, therefore escaped the same danger. I leave myself room only & hardly to thank [*on envelope*] you once more for your true kindness. It is as useless to try & say a word about dearest Arabel & *her* kindness. God bless her & you.

Ever yours affectionately
R Browning –

Writing in almost darkness, I made the confusion you will have seen in the sides of my letter –[7]

[1] Address: George Moulton-Barrett, Esq., Warnicombe House, near Tiverton, Devon. Postmark: London W.C. 4, Sept. 30, 61. Mourning paper. R. Browning in lower left corner.

[2] Arabella Barrett was living at 7 Delamere Terrace. According to the next letter Browning did not remove to his lodgings in Chichester Road until after October 7.

[3] The letters which follow contain many references to the successive failures of this "plan of mine." It clearly was never Pen's, and Browning seems never to have recognized that there might be

a difference. Such obtuseness is all the more surprising in view of his own educational experience and his psychological insight. Robert Browning, Senior, had been a wiser and much less egotistical father, not even complaining when his son, after a short trial, found it impossible to continue in London University. Certainly he had had a different son, one equipped with boundless curiosity and intellectual energy and not in the least "emulative." Perhaps it was Pen's amiability, which he never lost, that permitted his father so easily to deceive himself. Of course, one could never expect a father's psychological insight however brilliant into figures of the imagination to operate successfully in reference to his son, but one can hardly avoid speculating upon what the great special pleader, in that clarifying reincarnation which Browning so hopefully contemplated, might say of the son whom on earth he never understood.

[4] The identity of this unhappy gentleman remains a mystery. The blunders, however, seem clear enough. In a notice of Mrs. Browning's death in the *Guardian,* a London newspaper, for July 10, 1861, the statements concerning Mrs. Browning's background — her father a merchant, a Dissenter, and "her early education . . . of that austere and somewhat narrow kind which often cramps, but if it cannot cramp, sometimes, by its very resistance, stimulates genius." — were all of the type that plagued Robert for years afterward. The next week, July 17, 1861, a few corrections were made by one signed "Long Ago." But by the next week, evidently the matter had been called to George's attention and the following letter signed "G. G. Barrett" appeared in the *Guardian* for July 24, 1861. "Her father was at no period of his life a merchant; but soon after he left Cambridge he purchased a property in Herefordshire, where he resided many years. In regard to my sister's early education being cramped, I may state that, on the contrary, it was of a singularly enlarged and comprehensive character. Her great love of literature, in every language and in all ages, being quite unchecked even when quite young in life. Her education was entirely self-regulated."

These same notices were copied in several journals including *The Critic* for July 20, 1861, and July 27, 1861.

[5] Although Browning's escape was the result not so much of chance or forewarning as of his characteristic persistence, one cannot help recalling Mr. Sludge's example of "interpositions":

How yourself
Once, missing on a memorable day
Your handkerchief — just setting out, you know, —
You must return to fetch it, lost the train,
And saved your precious self from what befell
The thirty-three whom Providence forgot.

Mr. Sludge, "The Medium" was published in *Dramatis Personae* in 1864. The incident is retold from *Memoirs of W. W. Story*, ii, p. 100, in Griffin & Minchin, p. 225, without reference to Sludge, to show that in spite of his years abroad, Browning "remained an Englishman."

[6] The sight of Tennyson is also retold in the same place as the preceding incident with the added detail that Browning "pulled his hat over his brows."

[7] Sheets two, three, and four are reversed — bottom of sheet treated as top.

letter 64

7 Delamere Terrace
Monday Mr.
[October 7, 1861][1]

My dear George,

You will be anxious to know how dearest Arabel bears this fresh affliction. The anxiety she was under for the last two days was hardly bearable — and now that the worst has befallen her,[2] bitter as her grief is, I hope & think that the need of helping & comforting others comes as a beneficial diversion to it. She is a Christian and will bear up where unsupported human nature would fail altogether. I was going away to-day, with a heart full to the brim of her kindness, to an apartment only a few doors removed: I shall have the joy of being at hand, and trying to be of use in never so poor a degree. Till she can herself write you, I will keep you informed of her state of health. You will of course absolutely command me, — you or anyone of the family, — should you imagine I can be of the least assistance.

Ever affectionately yours
Robert Browning

[1] Address: George Moulton-Barrett, Esq. Warnicombe House, nr

Tiverton, Devon. Postmark: London, Oct. 7, '61; Tiverton. Oct. 8, 61. Mourning paper. R. Browning in corner.

² Serious as the catastrophe seems to have been, its nature remains obscure. One conjecture is that the aged Barrett housekeeper, Minny, who made her home with Arabella, had died. Mrs. Robinson had been in the household since Hope End days.

letter 65   1 Chichester Road, Upper
                                                Westbourne Terrace
                                                Dec. 21, '61¹

My dear George,

It only this moment strikes me that you may have wondered at hearing nothing from me about the investment of the proceeds of the sale of the "David Lyon"² on Peni's account: The reason is that I have not got, nor am likely to get, a farthing of it for some time to come. The estimable "Boddingtons" who sold the shares on a mere verbal assurance (quite warranted of course) from Chorley that Arnould³ would agree to the measure,— on the presentation of Arnould's *written warrant* to that effect, almost three months ago, first of all kept silence for six weeks till I wrote to ask the meaning of it: they then replied, that they returned me "the paper purporting to be signed by Sir J. Arnould" & would pay the money (and last year's dividend) when duly authorized by him. I answered this pleasant charge of felony (is it not that?) by sending the letter which had conveyed to me the warrant in question, about the genuineness of which there could be no possible doubt: at the same time I congratulated Boddingtons on having been able to get that money on no sort of authority at all, which, on being asked to account for, they could not give up on a signed written authority: they returned to this, in a modified tone, that they would send the Bill of Sale to Bombay⁴ at once, and on its return, properly signed, would pay the money and dividend to Chorley: the object being clearly to keep the said money & take its interest as long as practicable, for had they told me *at once* that they objected to the written authority I gave them, it would have saved six weeks: & what is the use of

Arnould's authorising the "Sale" which *has taken place* as they now admit, without his permission? The ground of demurring, I believe, was that Arnould had added "(signed)" to his signature — but by sending the letter which accompanied the paper and gave a reason for its detachment, all doubt was dissipated, as I said. I shall have to wait at least another month or two, & then, probably some other excuse will be found for touching the interest a little longer.

If I get it, & when I get it, I will consult with you as to the investment to be recommended to Chorley: were the money *mine* nominally, I need hardly say Messrs Boddington should not have treated so familiarly — choosing what should be authority enough, for their advantage, & no authority for mine — but it is the Trustees' business, & Pen must suffer accordingly. By the way, can you tell me who has the Trust-deed, — did you see it at Mr. Hawthorne's? I should much like to see under what conditions I lie in other respects. Can you give me Mr. Hawthorne's address, if he has the Deeds — or is it still as it used to be? I ought to observe that I never applied, or dreamed of applying to "Boddingtons" for the money — only begged that they would pay it to the Trustee — with the effect that you have heard. (Had the House been an Italian one?)[5]

I have scribbled this in a few disengaged minutes, & leave myself no time to add a word besides — yet a word *must* be added to thank you most heartily for your beneficence to Pen: he has fared sumptuously every day since, & never forgets the founder of the feast.

Arabel & Octavius are very well, you know — tho' Arabel is *not* so well, having a severe rheumatic affection, — you may imagine how invaluable her goodness is to me — I see nobody else. But my arrangements for Pen's education are getting completer, & I shall soon have a little more time. Pen is quite well, at his German lesson, a few door's off, or he would add his truest love to that of

Yours affectionately ever
Robert Browning –

Does the addition "signed" really invalidate a document the signature to which is indisputable? I thought the maxim in Law was "*plus* non vitiat" – But my attack had I been Trustee, should have gone on the sale without even oral authority, since they stood upon "authority."

P.S. On turning the page I discover that I have been writing on a piece of Pen's music — I despair of finding time to copy on a fair sheet & can only beg your indulgence!

[*On envelope*] Send Locke to this Station on Tuesday for a basket. RB

¹ Address: George M Barrett, Esq., Warnicombe House, near Tiverton, Devon. Postmark: London, Dec. 21, 61; Tiverton, Dec. 22, 61. Mourning paper. R Browning in corner.

² Among Mrs. Browning's assets at the time of the marriage was a share in the "David Lyon," which was one of Mr. Barrett's ships in the West India trade (Marks, p. 479). At that time it paid just under £200 (Hewlett, p. 199). By the time the Brownings had settled in Florence this income had been "reduced by £100 a year" (Hewlett, p. 246).

³ Trustees of the marriage deed.

⁴ Arnould had been appointed to the Supreme Court of Bombay in 1859.

⁵ The inference remains conjectural. It could be: 1) "I shouldn't have been surprised at its action"; or 2) "It would never have acted so"; or even 3) "I should have been able to deal with it more easily."

letter 66   1 Chichester Road, Upper W'bourne
                                                                    Terrace
                         Jan 2, '62¹

My dear George,

Thank you heartily for your letter — which I take the first minute's liberty to answer, so busy is the time with me. The sequel to the Boddington affair is characteristic. You will remember I was hurt (& much hurt) at the impertinence & want of feeling to me under the circumstances in which, for the first time after fourteen years' acquaintance, I was forced to have to have to do with them. Had they simply & politely said that the legal formality was imperative, you may judge whether I should have objected the least in the world: but after writing for *our* leave (not the Trustee's) to sell the shares,— acting forthwith upon that leave & the bare assurance that Arnould *would* not refuse leave,— it seemed too bad to begin professing scruples when the money had to be accounted for, in face of a document which no sane man could doubt the authenticity of, and which was all they had required (for they never said a word about sending the Bill of Sale for signature till the last moment) — and the delay (of six weeks) in even signifying that they *did* doubt its authenticity (& then only in reply to a pressing demand of mine) — & more then [*sic*] all, the studied impertinence of their letter — gave me a very decided feeling about those gentlemen. When your opinion concerning the right of Chorley to receive the dividends without his co-trustee's help reached me, I saw my advantage. I instantly wrote to B.s that I had "taken legal advice on that point" — & with what result, adding that I directed them to pay Chorley the money forthwith or be prepared for the consequences — using the curtest and least palatable expressions in my power, precisely in order to get them to remonstrate with me for such discourtesy & so enable me to reply *"You* talk of discourtesy, you who &c &c &c —" & in short, tell them my whole mind on the matter. No such chance! Here is the answer to a kick, from those who kicked me in return for a bow! "Sir — we have rec^d your note of yesterday & are much surprised at the tone of its contents, particularly as we have had a great deal of trouble with the "T.d." Not wishing to put the Estate to the expense of counsulting our lawyers, as to the disposal of the proceeds, we have not done so. We shall therefore pay the dividend from the last voyage when settled, for security's sake to Mr. Chorley as a Trustee, who will no doubt hand it over to you. The shares will be transferred to the purchaser on receipt of the Bill of Sale from Sir J.A. & the proceeds sent to Mr Chorley. We are Sir &c &c." So, they knock under! I think it will not be worth while to carry on the warfare a point further with such people:[2] but when they *do* pay the principal I shall consider whether your notion of *interest* may not be urged with advantage. (You see, they say they have *not yet* transferred the shares — a Boddingtonianism, no doubt.) Mark, I never asked them to pay *me* from first to last — & in the note used such an ambiguity in the language as might lead them into the belief that *Chorley* would act in the matter: they would have laughed at *me* except as behind him: and *your* "legal advice," no doubt seemed fresh from some sharp attorney both of us had first feed! Such terrors are in a Boddingtonian conscience!

All best wishes to you, from Pen &

Yours affectionately ever
Robert Browning

¹ Address: George Moulton Barrett, Esq., Warnicombe House, near Tiverton, Devon. Postmark: London, Jan. 2, 62; Tiverton, Jan. 3, 62. Mourning paper.

² Browning is generally least attractive when he has a real or fancied grievance. He can be at once petulant and truculent, and, taking his stand on courtesy, glories in his own offensiveness.

letter 67

19, Warwick Crescent,
Harrow Road.
Dec. 22. '62¹

[*Crest*]

My dear George,

How good & kind of you to remember us! Though a less substantial assurance of it than your presents would be quite enough: Pen writes (or wrote last Saturday) for himself, though we were prevented sending the letter: your *Brawn*² is a wonderful success: it is superior, to my taste, to the Cambridge productions I used to enjoy now & then at Christmas-time in old days.

Harry³ called here on Friday afternoon — most unluckily I was out of the way – Pen came down from his lessons, however, & told me all about it, increasing my regret at having been absent: he left early next morning — & no doubt was greatly disappointed at finding Arabel away. You may imagine whether we residents sympathize with him or no.

Dear George, I want to tell you that at the beginning of last October the Tablet & Inscription were placed over the entrance door of Casa Guidi: it is described to me as the largest tablet in Florence: & they were four days putting it up: I think the last tribute of the kind was that placed similarly on the House wherein Alfieri lived & died: I surely gave you a copy of the inscription: but as there may be some minute corrections, I repeat it as transmitted to me last week —[4]

Qui scrisse e mori
E. E. B.
che in cuore di donna conciliava
scienza di dotto e spirito di poeta
e fece del suo verso aureo anello
Fra Italia ed Inghilterra.
Pone questa memoria
Firenza grata
1861.

I can't help the descent from this to saying that they publish to-day a little selection of my things,[5] containing nothing new, but a pretty little book enough: I send it by this post, if you will accept it.

Please give my love to Harry whenever you see him and tell him how sorry I was at missing him.

Ever yours affectionately
Robert Browning.

[1] Address: George G. Barrett, Esq., Warnicombe House, near Tiverton, Devon. Postmark: London, Dec. 22, 62; Tiverton, Dec. 23, 62. Crest on paper. Browning had moved to 19 Warwick Crescent in the spring of 1862. Miller says June, but DeVane and Knickerbocker include a letter from Warwick Crescent dated May 23, 1862 (see Miller: *Browning,* p. 221, and DeVane and Knickerbocker, p. 145). The location was close to Arabella's house where

Browning called every afternoon. A notation on envelope reads: "Florence memorial" and "R.B. to GGMB" in another hand, probably George's and referring to content of letter.

² Boar's flesh boiled, pickled, and pressed.

³ Henry Barrett.

⁴ The inscription was written by the poet, Tommaseo, and is echoed in the last lines of *The Ring and the Book:*

> Thy rare gold ring of verse (the poet praised)
> Linking our England to his Italy.

It reads in English: Here wrote and died/ E.B.B./ who in the heart of a woman united/ the knowledge of the learned and the spirit of the poet/ and made of her verse a golden ring/ between Italy and England./ A grateful Florence placed this memorial/ 1861.

⁵ Probably *Selections from the Poetical Works of Robert Browning,* London, Chapman and Hall, 1863, described "[1862] 15.6 cm., pp. xii, 411. Edited silently by John Forster and Bryan W. Proctor." (*Robert Browning: A Bibliography, 1830-1950,* Cornell University Press, Ithaca, New York, 1953, p. 31.)

letter 68

19 Warwick Crescent,
Upper Westbourne Terrace, W.
Oct. 19. '66.¹

[Crest in black]

My dear George,

I feel very grateful indeed for your letter, and all the kindness it is replete with. For the monument, I am simply rejoiced that you like it.² You know it was just what I was able to accomplish in that direction, and no more: I mean,— that had it been of pure gold it would have gone no farther in the way of being a *fit* offering,— and, on the other hand, if my circumstances had only allowed me to put up a wooden cross, *that* would have sufficed. But I was fortunate in the sympathy of Leighton,³ and so, I hope, have been able perhaps to manage that the little which *is* done, is on the whole well done. I could not be on the spot and care for the execution personally — and mistakes were made at first which have been rectified since:⁴ but, by the photographs, I judge that Leighton's work is adequately rendered,— and we must be content.

I am really rejoiced that you, of all others, should be content. It was right that in a city where so many beautiful monuments are to be found,— whatever was intended as *this* memorial should try, at least, to be beautiful. I hope to see it one day: and, although I have no kind of concern as to where the old clothes of myself shall be thrown,— yet, if my fortune be such, and my survivors be not unduly troubled, I should like them to lie in the place I have retained there. It is no matter, however.[5]

Well, as to the Bust, I cannot but be touched (I won't descend to being "honored") by your thought about a companion head: Story has all the photographs necessary besides a good memory of his own,— I shall like the idea of his making *this* portrait also from memory. I hardly recollect the bust already made,— but quite agree with you that an altogether new one would be preferable: so, do just as you like; and may the result please you at least![6]

I have returned lately from Bretagne — and a place I much enjoyed, Le Croisic. It is wild and solitary enough, with good bathing and wonderful air scented with the salt-pits which fill the country. We stayed there two months — my sister and Pen, with me — and come back the better for our journey: You are lucky indeed to be able to see — what surely cannot be much longer deferred — the break up of things at Rome; you will find plenty of company there — all lovers of "a sight" are starting or about to start. Pen thanks you immensely for all your kind messages and enquiries,— also for the very welcome newspapers, with which he regales Italian friends. He is very well,— working very hard, poor fellow, for the awful matriculation "soon after next Easter," according to the official notice I have received. I hope — earnestly pray, he may be successful,— but am not sure. They require real proficiency in Greek & Latin at Balliol, and the examination is in no sense a sham. I lose him at Michaelmas. Arabel is very well, and bids me give her best love to you — she will write immediately, I am also to say. Occy, his wife, and the boy have just left her, and she feels such separations keenly. My sister thanks you exceedingly for your kind remembrance of her — and Pen sends his most affectionate regards.

Goodbye, dear George: We were often anxious about you,— pray take care of yourself. You may see Leighton — who is at Rome *now:* He would be gratified by a word from you, should your ways meet; a dear good fellow I have always found him.

Ever most affectionately yours
Robert Browning

[1] No envelope. Mourning paper.

[2] The Monument erected over Mrs. Browning's grave in the English Cemetery in Florence. For a view as it appears now, see Plate VI, following p. 54.

[3] Frederick Leighton (1830-96), President of the Royal Academy (1878), created Lord Leighton, 1886. His youth and years of instruction in art had been spent on the continent, and he did not settle in England until 1860. He had met the Brownings in Rome in 1852 in the circle of artists in which they moved. Leighton designed the monument for Browning. He was a brother of Mrs. Sutherland Orr.

[4] The execution of the monument was left under the supervision of Count Cottrell. (For the early mistakes see Hood, pp. 74-76 and 80-81.)

[5] It is hard to see where the "place . . . retained there" might have been. Certainly there is none adjacent to the grave of Mrs. Browning. By the time of Browning's death in 1889 the English Cemetery in Florence had been closed to further interment. He was buried on December 31 of that year in Poets' Corner of Westminster Abbey.

[6] W. W. Story's bust of Browning had been made in 1861. After Mrs. Browning's death he made one of her from memory. George commissioned one of each in marble; the "companion bust" here referred to must be Browning's, and his desire is that it, like his wife's, should be made "from memory." It must be his own that he "can hardly recollect." George presented the busts to Pen.

letter 69   19 Warwick Crescent, Upper Westbourne
                             Terrace, W. Jan: 28. '67.[1]

                             [Crest]

My dear George,

I was very sorry indeed to get your letter two days ago; the proceeding of Mr. Forster in the matter of the book,[2] I was quite ignorant of — but, unluckily, so well informed of certain circumstances, apparently unknown to Mr. Locker,[3] which would influence Mr. Forster in such a proceeding, that my first notion was to mention them, in reply to you, at once & without addressing him at all. However, not to throw away a chance of help, I did address him yesterday, with just the result I expected. The case is briefly this. Last October Mr Payne,[4] under no matter what impression of wrong received, insulted Mr. Procter[5] and Mr Forster grossly — to that degree that it is inconceivable how he could suppose that Mr Forster would do him the minutest favour even should Mr Payne bring himself to ask it. He ought to have warned Mr Locker – "There must be a mistake, Mr Forster cannot have allowed a line of his property to appear in any publication of mine — who have just chosen to suppress a few words of grateful dedication to him in Mr Procter's book,[6] on the ground that, being *my* property, it should not contain any mention of Mr Forster." – Through whatever blindness, he has omitted this, and must take the consequences — I hope & trust, *not* involving Mr Locker therein: Forster told me he was very sorry at Mr Locker's likelihood to suffer for Mr Payne's fault, but that nothing should alter his resolution, and probably nothing will — certainly no proposal of money-indemnification; either Mr Payne will have, *this day,* engaged to withdraw all the copies at the booksellers', as well as to cancel the offending sheets in any future editions, or an injunction will be applied for; and assuredly obtained, since Forster's right is unquestionable.

I don't moralize on all this: we say, and not in church only, "and forgive us as we forgive those &c" — and in the same breath, declare that there is to be *no* forgiveness for trespassers. But, once leave Gospel and go to Law — even social Law —

and, in this instance, Forster is blameless. But that is what I don't feel disposed to say of Chapman,[7] if I at all understand what he has said and done, or rather left undone. He knew nothing of the quarrel, I believe, and may have acted in a careless, irregular fashion, which by no means surprises me. Mr. Locker will have difficulty in getting an explicit acknowledgement of the statement, which amounts to a permission, out of *him*,— if it is Frederick;[7] he had no sort of right to make it. And now I come to the end of what I can say about this regrettable business; the end of all, like the beginning, being true sorrow for and sympathy with Locker — so tell him, however unnecessarily: Lady Charlotte,[8] too, will know that could I hope to do the least good in the matter, I most joyfully would.

There is little home news: Arabel, Ocky, his wife, and children,— Pen — all are well. Pen has skated diligently while skating-time was: to-day we have a sickly *mild* day, better for peoples' lungs and worse for their spirits — if they resemble mine, at least. It is good, and too good of you to expend gold for ugly marble;[9] but there is no hindering your kindness. Give my love to the Storys. Oh, my book,[10] that you enquire about, is in the main *done* — and, I hope, will be off my mind and out of my hands before long. By the bye,— should you happen to come across any old postal map of the road between Arezzo and Rome, via Perugia,— containing the names of *all* the little [*margin of first sheet*] villages by the way,— of the year 1700, a little earlier or later,— I should be glad to have such a thing — *not* glad to make you hunt for it; because it is not of much importance; but only glad, as I say, should such a thing turn up without trouble. With Pen's best love, dear George, ever affectionately yours

Robert Browning

[1] Address: George Goodin Moulton-Barrett, Esq. Reform Club. Not posted. R. Browning in corner.

[2] *Lyra Elegantiarum* (1867), an anthology compiled by Frederick Locker-Lampson, which included forty poems by Landor. It was published by Moxon's without permission of John Forster, who held the Landor copyrights.

³ Frederick Locker-Lampson (1821-95), a writer of light verse of which he published a volume entitled *London Lyrics* (1857). His friendship with Browning seems to date from about this time. Through a mutual interest in old prints he also became associated with the poet's father and sister. He added Lampson to his name in 1885 from that of his second wife, Miss Hannah Jane Lampson, whom he married in 1874. Augustine Birrell, his son-in-law, edited his memoir, *My Confidences* (1896), and published *Frederick Locker-Lampson: A Character Sketch*, London, 1920.

⁴ James Bertrand Payne, manager of Moxon's. In a letter to John Forster, July 16, 1866, Barry Cornwall characterizes him as "one of the evils which a poor author cannot avoid," and adds:

> Payne! Payne!
> Never complain!
> All we can say or do is in vain!
> In youth, in manhood, in life's sad wane,
> Our verse must have ever the same refrain,
>   in   in   in
> Of Payne, Payne, Payne!

(Richard Willard Armour: *Barry Cornwall*, Boston, 1935, p. 311.)

⁵ Bryan Waller Procter (1787-1874), poet and biographer, who wrote under the name of "Barry Cornwall." He knew intimately Hunt, Lamb, Dickens, and many others of the literary world. Browning had a standing engagement every Sunday afternoon at the Procters' home in London. *Colombe's Birthday* is dedicated to him.

⁶ *Charles Lamb: A Memoir*, London, 1866. Procter's letter to Forster, August 9, 1866, is headed with a transcript of the dedication and continues: "The Life of Charles Lamb was dedicated to *you, in the above words.* I received a *proof* — and also a *revise* of the Dedication which I returned to Payne's house. I knew nothing of the omission (or rather the supression) *until* this morning . . . This seems to me the most impudent fraud upon an author which a publisher can be guilty of" (Armour, *Barry Cornwall*, p. 313).

⁷ Frederick Chapman (1823-95). He was a nephew of Edward Chapman and associated with the firm of Chapman and Hall. For the story of Browning's break with Edward Chapman, his publisher, see DeVane and Knickerbocker, Appendix C, pp. 393-400. The whole Payne episode is also referred to in a letter to Isa Blagden. (Hood, p. 110; see also McAleer, p. 253).

[8] Lady Charlotte Bruce, daughter of Lord and Lady Elgin, married Frederick Locker (later Locker-Lampson) in 1850. She died in 1872.

[9] The bust referred to in the preceding letter.

[10] *The Ring and the Book.*

letter 70   Tuesday, July 28. '68.[1]

My dear George,

I believe we (my sister & I) shall leave London on Thursday, for the usual two months' travel in France, Brittany — probably.[2] I wish with all my heart I could know you also were about to allow yourself — I wont say, a holiday, but rather the necessary relaxation from so much painful trouble.[3] I hope earnestly you are through the worst of it. I have not been in a condition to render any service,— but I have sympathized with you however fruitlessly. If now, by any of the strange chances of the world, I still can be of any service, you will count on me, I think. I just write this to give you a day in case there is anything you would say: in any case, it is equivalent to a good shake of the hand, if I don't find you at the Club presently. God bless you — it is unnecessary to say that Pen, in his last letter to me, bade me remember him kindly to you,— and that my sister joins with me in every affectionate feeling.

Ever yours

RB.

I must be back by the beginning of October.

[1] No envelope. Mourning paper.

[2] A letter to Isa Blagden (McAleer, p. 299) relates the travels before settling in an inn at Audierne on the western tip of Brittany.

[3] The "painful trouble" was probably incident to the death of Arabella Barrett on June 11. "George, the useful brother, was away touring it in Ireland, nobody knew where." He could not reach London until June 20, and Browning writes apprehensively: "He is alarmingly susceptible, and may find the blow too much" (McAleer, p. 298).

letter 71   19 Warwick Crescent,
                                                 Upper Westbourne Terrace, W.
                                                 Nov. 13. '69.[1]

[*Crest*]

My dear George,

I am *just* on the point of setting out for a visit to friends in Norfolk; friendship apart, I could wish myself at home, this cold week that is likely to be: I will however answer your kind letter at once. I think you will give the greatest pleasure to the most people by bequeathing — at least *one* of the Busts[2] as you generously propose. You don't know, probably, that Miss Heaton[3] has already presented her chalk drawing by Talfourd, that which was exhibited at the National Portrait Exhibition two years ago,[4] — to the Natl P^t Gallery: they wished me to inspect & pronounce upon a certain very indifferent portrait, and, on hearing this, Miss Heaton at once proposed to *give* her picture and to prevent an unsatisfactory purchase: there was a sitting of the Committee on the subject, and the offer was accepted very gratefully — making an exception,— they said,— to a rule as to the proper time that should elapse before a portrait could be admitted. Miss H. is, at this present moment, having two copies made, (for herself and for me) before she finally consigns her gift. Meantime — and long before your legacy be receivable, I hope,— always remember that the Busts are merely *here* till you require them.

The portfolio shall be at once sent to Ocky at the Hall: it is safe in my keeping.

I am very sorry for my own part, that you mean to domicile yourself anywhere but in London,— still you know best, and London will not be out of reach. I grieve to hear of Mr. Martin's illness — his advanced age gives it too much importance. Still, the wonderful old man may fight out another battle. All kindest [*top of first sheet*] remembrances & thanks from my sister: Pen is away, of course.[5]   Ever, dear George, yours most affect^y

                                                 R. Browning

292 LETTERS OF THE BROWNINGS TO GEORGE BARRETT

[1] Address: George Moulton Barrett, Esq., 8 Spa Building, Cheltenham. Postmark: London, Nov. 13, 69; Cheltenham, Nov. 14, 69.

[2] See *Letter 68, note 6,* p. 286.

[3] Miss Ellen Heaton of Leeds is mentioned several times in *Letters of R. B. and E. B. B.* and always as a pressing bore. She first met Mrs. Browning in May, 1846. The association continued and Mrs. Browning's tolerance grew. In 1859 Miss Heaton commissioned Field Talfourd to do a portrait, resolved with "her singular want of refinement and delicacy to 'have the only portrait in the world of Mrs. Browning' " (McAleer, p. 31).

[4] The National Portrait Exhibition of 1868, consisting of some 600 portraits from the Gallery and some 300 loaned, was made up of nineteenth-century celebrities. An insertion, labeled National Portrait Exhibition, in the *Times* for Tuesday, April 14, 1868, at the bottom of col. f, p. 5 states: "We are requested to correct an error in the catalogue of this exhibition. Elizabeth Barrett Moulton Barrett was not, as described, 'the daughter of a London merchant,' but of a private gentleman." This must be the correction referred to below in *Letter 79,* p. 308. The portrait is reproduced in *Works of Elizabeth Barrett Browning,* 6 vols., London, 1890, as frontispiece to vol. 5, where it is stated that it was done in Rome in March, 1859. It also appears in Griffin and Minchin along with Robert's by the same artist, pp. 216-17.

[5] Pen matriculated at Christ Church, Oxford, October, 1869.

letter 72   19. Warwick Crescent,
                                       Upper Westbourne Terrace, W.
                                       June 17. '70[1]

My dear George,

Pen has failed again: he did his best in the country, I believe, — but two months of labor were not enough to overcome nine years of idleness. He is obliged to take his name off the books at Ch. Ch,— and, though I might possibly get him yet another respite, I shall not dream of doing so: his expenses for the last term of residence (scarcely five weeks) were about £170. He cannot be made to see that he should follow any other rule than that of living like the richest and idlest young men of his acquaintance, or that there is any use in being at the University than to do so: and if I tried the experiment for the fiftieth time the result would be the same. You see that all my plans are destroyed by this double evil — the utmost self-indulgence joined to the greatest contempt of work and its fruits: how should I be justified in proposing to introduce him to a diplomatic career, wherein his temptations to spend would be far more numerous, and his incitements to study infinitely less?

So, dear George, *what do you advise?*

I am ready to make all possible sacrifice that may end in something like success: I can hardly make a greater than I have done — of the last nine years of my life, which have been as thoroughly wasted as if they were passed in playing at chuck-farthing.[2] All I can do, — except to give money, — is *done* & done in vain. What do you think of the army? Or will it all end in my pensioning off the poor fellow to go & rot in the country? I have no sort of influence over him: but something must be decided on at once for a young man in his twenty-second year, who told me just now, in Ocky's presence, that he would not have consented to be at Ch. Ch. at any less expense than he had been incurring, and that he considered getting a first class no brilliant thing at all.

Ever affectionately yours
Robert Browning.

---

[1] Address: George G. Moulton Barrett, Esq., Reform Club, Pall Mall S.W., Immediate: to be forwarded. Postmark: London, Jun. 17, 70. R. B. in corner. The succeeding letter, which goes over the same matter, indicates that this one was not delivered so promptly as desired.

[2] Browning must mean that the nine years have been wasted so far as Pen's education is concerned. Otherwise, he must have forgotten *Dramatis Personae* and *The Ring and the Book* besides certain reprints of his own and his wife's verse during those years. He was, however, prone to speak violently about his wasting his time. When Julia Wedgwood, apropos of *The Ring and the Book,* suggested that he might have spent "all these years on a mistake," Browning replied: "I have given four full years to this 'mistake', but what did I do with my fourteen years in Italy?" (Miller:

Browning, 245). Here is not the place to try to analyze the reasons for this attitude, but important among them must have been that confidence in his powers which he retained in spite of clear evidence that much of it was misplaced. It is precisely this confidence that, for some reason or other, Pen lacked. The whole relation of father and son has been treated by Gertrude Reese in "Robert Browning and His Son," *PMLA,* LXI (September, 1946), 784-803.

letter 73

19, Warwick Crescent
Upper Westbourne Terrace, W.
July 1. '70.[1]

My dear George,

You might be sure that my very first proceeding, after the result of the examination became known to me, was to write to you,— I directed the letter, by Ocky's advice, to "the Reform Club to be forwarded," and some time or other it will reach you. Well,— the poor boy failed again. He had made a real and important effort for the previous ten weeks,— I believe, *working,*— so as to deserve the expression,— for the first time in his life: his tutor, a very competent one, and successful in immediately obtaining that influence over his pupil which I could never obtain, wrote to me regularly every fortnight: he found no sort of disqualification for study in Pen, admitted none of the foolish excuses for idleness & inattention under the pretence of want of memory &c, but said from the beginning that the only difficulty was in a mistrust of the boy in his own power of learning: and at the last, he reported him to me — and to Jowett also — as "quite able, should he do his best, to pass: but fluctuating in his performances, now exceeding and now falling below the mark." So he came up, passed one day here, went to Oxford, did well the first day, and badly — in arithmetic! — the next,— he consequently has failed, and it is to little purpose that I hear how near the mark he came in other respects. The fact is,— two months' serious labour could not altogether do away with the effect of nine years indolence,— it comes *too late* — the saddest word in the language. His case seems to be very well understood, and sympathised with at Oxford,— and the Dean intimated that should Pen apply for leave to try again, he would give the application every attention: but, to what use? The stay at Ch.Ch. is enormously expensive, and Pen's outlay impossible to be sustained: his expenses for the last term, of some five weeks barely, were something like £150 or 160 — multiply that by 4, add seven months of holidays to be provided for, and you will judge whether I am justified in trying to go on with the experiment. On the other hand, I am quite at my wits' end and hopeless of doing anything to the boy's advantage. He is unfit for anything but idleness and pleasure,— each as harmless, as such indulgences can be.[2] The diplomatic service is out of the question now: nobody *in* it but wishes he were out of it, as a *profitable* career: and all Pen's notion of the proper behaviour in any career or position whatever is — simply to live as expensively as the richest of his companions, and do no sort of work that is not forced upon him,— as for any ambition to distinguish himself *at the price of work* he is — at present at least — quite incapable of it: therefore you may imagine what would be his requirements for the next five or six years as an *attaché* at Paris or Vienna in the company of the sons of men of fortune. This exquisite stupidity being unconquerable, applies even in greater measure as a disqualification for the only other career that he would like,— that of a "cavalry officer": I will not hear of a life,— first of all, hateful to his Mother: next, as hateful to me,— finally, involving all the worst temptations to every sort of weakness. It is all miserable to contemplate. The poor boy is simply WEAK — not bad in any way,— clever, quite capable of doing all I ever had the hope he would do, singularly engaging to his friends with whom he is as popular as possible, and quite docile and amenable to reason with a comparative stranger: I believe were he with *you,* he would conduct himself with the utmost propriety, even self-restraint: but I am merely the manger at which he feeds, and nothing is more certain than that I could do him no greater good than by dying to-night and leaving him just enough to keep him from starving: I believe it will end in my making him an allowance, going abroad, and so doing the next best thing. There is something infinitely pitiable in this butterfly-nature with no fault in it but what practically is the worst of all faults,— weakness: a restive horse may be broken of his vice and made win a race against his will,— but how can you make a butterfly cross the room to his life, much less yours?[3]

Tell me, my dear George, anything that occurs to you: had you been still a barrister,— to give you an instance of the influence *anybody but myself* can exercise over him — he would have cheerfully worked under your eye, had you allowed it, and *worked well,*— I, at least, would have made the experiment. What do you suggest? I know your kindness, to me, to him, to his mother: help us all if you can — indeed, I know you will,— BUT! —

Ever yours affectionately

R Browning.

[1] Address: George G. Moulton Barrett, Esq., Queen's Hotel, Aberystwith. Postmark: Paddington, Jy., 1, 70; Aberystwith, Jy. 2, 70: R.B. in corner.

[2] Not always so harmless, according to Frances Winwar, who states that before Pen was nineteen "he had two illegitimate daughters by different mothers, peasant girls of Brittany" (*The Immortal Lovers,* London, Hamish Hamilton, 1950, p. 306). Does Browning's judgment express his ignorance, his disbelief, or his complaisance?

[3]

And, Robert Browning, you writer of plays,
Here's a subject made to your hand. — *A Light Woman.*

letter 74   Monday[1]

[*Crest*]

Dear George,

I have been thinking over that notion of Pen becoming a barrister: I am not likely to indulge in too lively hopes, but in some respects it seems a promising scheme. The advantages would be, — a position, admitting of the chances of any windfall or godsend in the future: while such a poor clerkship as would be

within Pen's reach at present would not only lead to nothing but
stand in his way hereafter, should any ambition ever spring up
and inspire the poor fellow: I hear such phenomenon does sometimes occur at four or five and twenty. At worst, there remains
the *position,*— quite as good a one as he would get in diplomacy: while my expenses of supporting him would be less: I
speak on the too-well grounded expectation that he will never
work in either or any case: but if by miracle he *should* so incline,
I don't see why he might not cut a respectable figure as a pleader
under certain conditions: I am told that nothing could exceed
his coolness and readiness at improvising in the charade at L^d
Houghton's,— himself remarking that he felt no embarrassment
at all. He is really shrewd, quick enough at rendering a reason,
and able to take his own part volubly when it would seem a
difficult matter.[2]

I have said *nothing* on the subject to him,— but would it not
be worth while for you to see how the ground lies and question
him a little about his likings and aptitudes? I am profoundly
ignorant as to what steps should be taken, should the plan be
feasible, and your advice would be invaluable to me, of course.

My sister, with whom I have talked this matter over, thinks
very favorably of the scheme: I have been too often disappointed to be sanguine But I think there are more chances of
success in it than in any other that occurs to me. I am convinced
that Pen would not keep a Government London situation for six
months — or three — supposing he got it: monotonous work
would — perhaps really — affect his health: and we should end
just where we began — but with a bar to our trying anything
else: whereas decent attention to work, under a competent in-
structor, even if it ended with the call to the bar, would have
given him a *status* in the world of service in all his after life. You
will kindly think this over a little and act upon it as you judge
best. He will be with you at 7.[3]

Ever affectionately yours   RB.

[1] This letter, undated and for which no envelope has been pre-

served, clearly follows the preceding by no more than a few days. Paper stamped with the crest of the Athenaeum Club.

[2] Browning's humor is likely to be heavy-handed and not always unmistakable in print; nevertheless a bitter humor seems more credible here than the astounding naïveté required to advance seriously to George such criteria for success in his profession.

[3] Unfortunately there is no reference to what transpired at this meeting.

letter 75   19, Warwick Crescent, W. Jan. 20. '75[1]

My dear George,

You will certainly have wondered at the delay in replying to your kind letter: it was occasioned by the necessity of consulting with Leighton about the proper course to take in a matter which concerned him so much. I am deeply obliged to you for informing me about what I might else have long remained in ignorance: and the particulars of the damage, as well as the estimates of needful repair & expenditure are just what I should have desired. I wish every fit measure to be taken, and leave the whole in your most capable hands: but there is this difficulty,— Leighton is very averse to the destruction of his design by the substitution of black marble: he would prefer the renewal of the old work, even if one needs to begin again in another eleven years. Cannot this be managed? I wish it were as easy to replace the coarse nature of the relic-mongers by some more human and decent stuff, but *that* is impossible. Would a more effectual railing be of any use? or would a cover, such as you mention as being made for the Demidoff monument, answer the purpose here? You have such an advantage over me who never *saw* the Tomb, that I accept your judgment, whatever it may be. Leighton said he should prefer letting the ornaments quite go, in process of time, and *then* renewing them — that is, prefer this to substituting the black stripe.[2]

Poor Wilson is — not figuratively, but, in sad earnest, *insane,* — subject to delusions which are dangerous. I have known this for many a year: the jealousy of all & every body leaves no

doubt about *that*. Last year, she wrote to me that poor Isa
Blagden had helped "a lot of women" to seduce Ferdinando,—
"she would not call her a *Lady!*" &c. She writes to me most dis-
tressingly about her poverty; and at this moment I have on my
desk an application — which I shall answer presently — for the
advance of the money which I ought to send in March: and
there are not wanting examples of positive craziness in the letter.[3]

It will be more pleasant to tell you that Pen has indeed done
capitally,— made remarkable progress for a student of less than
a year's standing.[4] Millais[5] came to see his pictures last week,
and said all we could hope or wish: there wants nothing but a
continued application — such as he has shown he can easily
manage. We (my sister & I) visited him in Antwerp & made
acquaintance with his admirable master, Heyermans, to whom
we owe everything. Millais said — under *nobody* in England
could Pen have made such progress. I bought a little picture,
which Pen had seen him paint,— most charming, "perfect in its
way," declared Millais. Pen came here at Christmas and left on
the 12th to return in some six months, I trust.

I wish you all joy of the new year, dear George! — all pleasure
in your southern dwelling — different enough from the dull
scenes about us here! My sister sends her best love. You will let
me know, with your usual kindness, what is determined on about
the monument. I enclose the Estimates which you may require.

Ever affectionately yours
Robert Browning.

---

[1] Address: George G. Moulton Barrett, Esq., Hotel Splendide,
Menton, Alpes Meridionales. Postmark: Paddington, Jy. 20, 75;
Marseilles, Jy. 25, 75. R.B. in corner.

[2] Leighton's advice must have been taken, since there is no "black
stripe" on the monument. The lettering, however, is in black, and
there are some black ornaments on each side of the medallion.

[3] When in 1887, Pen settled in the Palazzo Rezzonico in Venice,
he brought Wilson and Ferdinando into his household. Ferdinando
died in 1893. Wilson, her mind long enfeebled, lived on with Pen
until her death in 1902.

⁴ Pen's childhood interest in drawing had been given a serious turn by the influence and encouragement of Sir John Millais. Early in 1874 he had gone to Antwerp where he studied under the tutelage of Jean-Arnould Heyermans.

⁵ Sir John Everett Millais (1829-96). Along with W. Holman Hunt in 1848 he began the Pre-Raphaelite movement, which with the joining of Rossetti and others grew into the famous brotherhood. He became one of the most distinguished painters of his time and President of the Royal Academy. He painted portraits of Occy's children (see below, *Letter 78*, p. 307).

letter 76   19 Warwick Crescent, W.
                                                 May 25. '75.¹

My dear George,

Thank you — but your information is quite needless. Whenever there is a funny piece of raving against me in a newspaper you may be sure my little bug of an Austin² is biting his best: this is the third instance within as many weeks — and I suppose he has written above a dozen such things. "Dwarfs," Dickens tells us, "are mostly sarcy –" and if this particular Quilp gets any good, beside the penny-a-line, out of his "sarce," he has my full leave: but even dwarfs need not be blackguardly: and this one has a trick of "giving an instance of Mr. Browning's unintelligible stuff" which he makes so indeed by altering my words to his own,— leaving out a whole line, for instance, and joining two broken ends! He did this in the "World" a fortnight ago. In the same article he said "my whole poem³ was a transcript from Jowett"— whom I have not seen these four years, and who never opened his mouth on that, or any other subject of the same sort, in his whole life:⁴ All this bug-juice from a creature *I* never saw in my life, and whose scribblings, except when they related to myself, I never read a line of!⁵ But — as the poet⁶ sings –

　　　　Who would be satirical
　　　　On a thing so very small?⁷

Not, assuredly, yours ever, my dear George,

　　　　　　　　　　　　R. Browning

¹ Address: George G. Moulton Barrett, Esq., Reform Club, Pall Mall S.W. Postmark. Paddington, May 25, 75.

² Alfred Austin (1835-1913), appointed Poet Laureate in 1896.

³ *Aristophanes' Apology* (1875).

⁴ In a letter to John H. Ingram, February 11, 1876, Browning wrote: "Last year I wrote, and published, a poem about Aristophanes, and somebody, wholly a stranger to me, reviewing it in *The Athenaeum,* observed (for fun's sake, I suppose) that it was 'probably written after one of Mr. Browning's Oxford Symposia with Jowett.' Whereupon half a dozen other critics reported the poem to be 'the transcript of the talk of the Master of Balliol'" (Hood, p. 171). The review is to be found in the *Athenaeum* for April 17, 1875, pp. 513-14.

⁵ In 1870 Austin published *The Poetry of the Period,* containing an article on Browning originally published in *Temple Bar* for June, 1869 (vol. xxvi, pp. 316-33). On March 22, 1870, Browning wrote to Isa Blagden, "it 'riles' such a filthy little snob as Mr. Alfred Austin to read in the Morning Post how many dinners I eat in good company." As the letter continues, he refers to Austin as, "this literary 'cad' ", "the little fool", "the 'blighted being'" (Hood, pp. 135-36).

⁶ The poet is Jonathan Swift in *Dr. Delaney's Villa.*

⁷ Here appears the famous attack on Austin *one year before* it was published in *Pacchiarotto* (May, 1876). The concluding lines of section xxvii of *Pacchiarotto and How He Worked in Distemper,* as printed, run:

> While as for Quilp-Hop-o'-my-thumb there,
> Banjo-Byron that twangs the strum-strum there –
> He'll think as the pickle he curses,
> I've discharged on his pate his own verses!
> "Dwarfs are saucy," says Dickens: so sauced in
> Your own sauce, (1) . . .

at the foot of the page:

> (1) No, please! For
> "Who would be satirical
> On a thing so very small?" – *Printer's Devil*

Hood in his note, p. 363, points out that these lines "do not appear in the MS." and "were certainly introduced while the poem was in press." It may be, as the same note suggests, that the poem originally ended with "Goodbye!" at the end of section xxiii. The question then arises: How did this insult, thought up and cast off a year before, come to be included in *Pacchiarotto?*

It seems certain that the dance of the chimneysweeps (critics) was not the starting point of the poem; in fact sections xxiv-xxix have only the loosest mechanical connection with the preceding story. The tale of the painter who foolishly tried to reform the world and, fleeing from his assailants, was forced to take refuge in a vault beside a cadaver, which taught him not to try to make a heaven of earth, enforces a familiar Browningesque theme. This time, however, it is set forth in a style deliberately and humorously capricious and rhyming notably fantastic even for Browning. Neither the painter nor the cadaver nor the abbot is subjected to any psychological analysis. Browning turns from the finished story in xxiv with:

> I have told with simplicity
> My tale, dropped those harsh analytics,
> And tried to content you, my critics,
> Who greeted my early uprising.

Though not immediately apparent, it becomes clear that Browning already has Austin in mind when one recalls that in the 1870 article Austin had written: "Browning is a mere analyst . . . pottering about among the brains and entrails of the souls he has dissected" (McAleer, pp. 332 ff.). It seems likely that Browning having finished the poem, conscious of unusual simplicity of matter and deliberate grotesqueness of style, was reminded to pay his respects to his critics without regard to the fable. The reviews of *Aristophanes' Apology* were, of course, fresh in his mind as is shown by the last line:

> We'll up and work! won't we, Euripides?

They rekindled his contempt for Austin, and the "witticism" he had written a year before to George recurred to his mind.

Hood's note, pp. 358-63, gives a detailed account of the whole unpalatable mess of Browning's attack upon Austin including the latter's vehement disclaimer of the *World* article referred to at the beginning of this letter. "I have never," he wrote, "reviewed any book in that paper, whether of verse or prose, from the day it was started to this hour."

According to DeVane, "His disclaimer was not generally believed" (DeVane: *A Browning Handbook*, p. 396, n. 5).

letter 77   Blairbeg, Lamlash, Arran.
                                                                N.B.
                                               Aug. 12. '76[1]

My dear George,

Your most kind & valued letter has followed me hither — and
comes in pleasant harmony with all the good influences of this
charming place. I am glad indeed that you care at all about
anything in the new little book.[2] It was not worth while, perhaps,
even to amuse myself for once (first time and last time) with my
critics – I really had a fit of good humour — and nothing worse
— when the funny image of Austin, "my castigator," as he calls
himself, struck me in a vision of May-morning: a "castigator"
should be prepared for an appropriate reception from the "cas-
tigated" one.[3]

I make great haste to say this poor little word of a very real
gratitude, because I may be too late for your stay at Engelberg
should I delay a minute: to-morrow there is no post, and *this*
post is just about to leave: leave, however, it shall not — without an assurance that Pen is doing excellently well — working
hard, and sure — if he may but preserve his health — of succeeding admirably. What a joy this will be to you, dear George,
whose affectionate interest in him has been hardly second to my
own. Let me add, we — (my sister & myself) are here till the
end of next month. *You* need not envy us — and I, & my sister
also, rejoice to think that you are in so delightful a place as you
describe, and with such memories of travel too! The letter is all
but snatched from my hand by the necessities of the quarter of
an hour. Let me cram as much good will & love as can go into a
mere adieu from

                                               Yours affectionately ever,
                                                       R.Browning.

My sister will make me send her
very kindest regards!

---

[1] Address: George G. Moulton Barrett, Esq., Hotel Sonnenberg,

Engelberg, Switzerland. Postmark: Lamlash, Au. 12; Engelberg, 15, viii 76. R.B. in corner.

² *Pacchiarotto.*

³ This seems to confirm the suggestion that the passage was an afterthought. Also one senses a slight feeling of chagrin without any apology to Austin. Browning's amusement at Austin's deformity is completely Aristophanic.

letter 78   19 Warwick Crescent, W.
                                                May 2. '82.¹

My dear George,

Pen is here; a week now; very well, though he has been much affected by his hard two months' study of modelling & anatomy in Paris, and was obliged to recruit, under a doctor's hands, in the Ardennes; all which exertion has got its reward. A Bust in bronze of a Velletri girl, and a statuette (two-thirds life-size) in bronze also, were "cast" by the desire of his master and other judges — the former has arrived; the latter is to be here in a week: and the former really deserves — considering it was begun after one month's study — what Prof. Legros² says of it — "C'est étonnant." It is the first success in a quite "new departure" towards the "Charming". One of his pictures is at the Academy, another at the Grosvenor. So much for him,— dear good and absolutely satisfactory fellow, as I most thankfully as well as truthfully can declare him to be.³

But my immediate business is about another matter — that mentioned in a letter to him which is now before me, and which gives me the opportunity of saying what has long been much on my mind.

Your remarks refer to the inaccuracies in an article published by a magazine.⁴ As they are merely inaccuracies and no worse, I leave them unnoticed as on other similar occasions, from a determination not to be drawn into furnishing any biographical details on any pretence whatever. What a pressure has been put upon me to break my determination you do not imagine, I am sure: even *threats* have been tried (years ago, I was informed that unless I furnished these details for a memoir in the *Revue des Deux Mondes,* the writer's *friend* would certainly print — for instance that my wife had been a governess — "in vain do I tell my friend it is untrue; I cannot remove the conviction, unless &c." all which I stopped by myself appealing to the Editor. The applications have generally been for a publication of the Letters I may possess or have a control over — or at least for leave to inspect them for the sake of what biographical information they might contain. I have once, by declaring I would prosecute by law, hindered a man's proceedings who *had obtained all the letters to Mr Boyd,* and was soliciting, on the strength of that acquisition, letters in all the quarters he guessed likely. The only instance in which I departed from my rule was that of Horne — who, poor, old and pitiable, saw a golden resource in the publication of the correspondence which began and, in the main, ended before I knew the writer.[5] I found he would not take money for giving up these, and, on the whole, in my confidence that nothing but literature could have been discussed in them, I acted as I conceive her generous spirit would desire. It would be a long affair if I troubled you with my troubles of this nature during the last twenty years: I shall just enclose,[6] as a sample, a letter I received a few weeks ago — the proposal mentioned in it, and my refusal to accede to it, having ended, I believe, in the estrangement of the lady intended to be employed in the business — a very estimable and kind as well as clever friend of mine, and who, could I have brought myself to oblige her, would have been the least objectionable biographer as the most under my management: still, the difficulties were *insuperable.* We are all of one mind here, I, you,— no doubt, the Brothers,— and assuredly the One whose feelings we know and respect.

Now, I possess hundreds of letters — besides those addressed to me,— those to the Martins, Miss Mitford, Mr Boyd, Chorley, Kenyon, Miss Blagden — and others: and moreover am promised the reversion of other collections when their owners die. I religiously abstain from reading one line of these — as I never was in the habit of doing during the life of the writer,— both

of us being determined that a full liberty of speech on paper
should be maintained — as would hardly be possible were things
to be spoken *with a witness*. While I live, I can play the part of
guardian effectually enough — but I must soon resolve on the
steps necessary to be taken when I live no longer — and I complete my seventieth year next Sunday. I shall soon have to pass
in a very superficial review all these letters, just inspecting so
much of them (and a mere dip into each will suffice) as to
ascertain what should be destroyed, what preserved as containing nothing to hurt the living or the dead: it is an immense
sacrifice — but one that must be made, and I shall not for a
moment consider anything but what I know would be the desire
of my wife in the matter. So much for my part of the duty. There
is however a danger which I apprehend, and cannot be responsible for. The letters to Arabel were deposited in security somewhere: I suppose that the copyright of them belongs to me — so
that, if by any accident publication was attempted, I could prevent it: but if I am off the scene, if you, and the Brothers, in
due time follow me, *who* is to be the keeper of what must inevitably be the most intimate and complete disclosure of precisely
those secrets which we unite in wishing to remain secret forever?[7] Are the young people likely to be interested in this as we
are, or certain to be as able to withstand literary cajoleries — or
such representations as the example I enclose — as I have been
and shall be? The same danger is to be apprehended from any
publicity given to the letters to Henrietta — which I am altogether powerless concerning: as indeed I probably am in the
case of the letters now in question. So, dear George, I do all in
my limited power by bringing, once for all, this state of things
under your notice. There will not be found in the whole of the
correspondence one untrue, ungenerous word, I *know* — but
plenty of sad communication which has long ago served its purpose and should be forgotten. Unfortunately the unscrupulous
hunger for old scandals is on the increase — and as the glory of
that most wonderful of women is far from at the full — I cannot
help many forebodings — which you share with me, I know.
Why are you not here — a resident, and not — as you almost

threaten — a confirmed stay-away? I could talk to you and have your advice so much more easily than by the way I am forced to take.

Pen & my sister are away – I know what affectionate message either would charge me with were they in reach. Millais' portraits of Ocky's children is his best picture this year, and greatly admired. Pen's portrait of myself, painted last year, was sold, "without the frame" which was a favorite one, for a hundred guineas. a few weeks ago. The two pictures sold to America[8] have had great success there, and a project exists there for acquiring two others! You well know whose heart would have been rejoiced at this besides mine.

Ever, Dear George, affectionately yours
Robert Browning.

[1] Address: George G Moulton-Barrett, Esq., Cercle Masséna, Nice. Postmark: Paddington, May 2, 82; Nice, May, 82.

[2] Alphonse Legros (1837-1911), painter and etcher, settled in London in 1863, naturalized, 1881. He was Slade Professor of Fine Arts, University College, London, 1876-93.

[3] Browning's worries about Pen are over and all past disappointments forgotten.

[4] This may very well be the article referred to in Browning's letter of May 22, 1882, to John H. Ingram (Hood, p. 211). If so, it appeared in Tinsley's Magazine for May, 1882, and did, by Browning's report, contain some glaring "inaccuracies." For instance, not only is Mrs. Browning listed as having been born in the "ninth year of this century," but also in "Ledbury in the County of Durham"!

[5] See DeVane and Knickerbocker, p. 228, letter to S. R. Townshend Mayer, who edited Letters of E. B. B. Addressed to R. H. Horne, which appeared 1876, title page dated 1877.

[6] No enclosure has been preserved with the letter, but see Hood, p. 210, for Browning's letter to Ingram, May 5, 1882.

[7] First among these secrets, as a later letter specifies, must have been Mrs. Browning's interest in spiritualism and her comments upon it. Another, perhaps, was that, except for a few periods in her life, she was a constant user of morphine.

[8] See DeVane and Knickerbocker, pp. 269-71, concerning the purchases of Mrs. Bloomfield-Moore.

letter 79   29 De Vere Gardens
                                                     Nov. 5, '87[1]   W.

My dear George,

   In reply to your letter — for which, as for every token of you,
true thanks — I have to say that I trust you will never believe
for a moment that any species of "biographical memoir" of our
beloved Ba, long or short, important or trifling, can appear "with
my knowledge and sanction" — or rather, "with my sanction,"
for unfortunately I have a quarter of a century's experience of
the indelicacy with which the writers, male and female, of such
things will in all cases try hard to get information, and, failing
that, tell you with the utmost impudence, that, "after all, such a
life is public property and must be given to the public somehow —" this last intimation being in the nature of a threat. I
have but one answer to make on these occasions — that my consent is impossible. How otherwise, when I am intimately in possession of my wife's feelings on the subject?[2] The last (repeated)
application to me was made respecting a series of "Lives of
eminent Englishwomen" — now in course of publication[3] — and
the rejoinder to my reply was just what I have told you — that
"something must be done." One is powerless against this "something" — but I have thought it best never to interfere and correct
any particular misstatement, lest by so doing I should appear to
be silently approving of all I left undisputed. Once however, —
on the occasion of a notice in the "Times", many years ago, of
the new pictures in the "National Portrait Gallery," the likeness
of Ba had, appended to the catalogue, quoted in the "Times,"
the information "Daughter of &c West India Merchant." I at
once wrote to the editor of the Catalogue, and to the "Times,"
correcting the error just as you have done, and for the same
reason, — that a fact is a fact.[4] Perhaps the statement recurs in
a shameful reprint of as many of Ba's poems as are no longer
copyright[5] — and as subsequent corrections continue to be protected, *these* are left out, and the passages given precisely as their
author wished them no longer to be: besides which, all the ju-
venile and immature poems she was so anxious to suppress are
fully reproduced. I believe Smith[6] is going to make an announce-

ment of this abomination,— but it will only make the edition in
the greater request. All I can think of doing is to bring out a
complete edition, in a cheaper form (the reprint, a thick closely
printed volume, costs 1ˢ) and add a few notes, to give it distinction. This will keep the copyright in our hands *so far* — for I
cannot imitate the cunning of the bookseller who has picked up
carefully whatever was deliberately rejected. Of the genuine
biography I know next to nothing: Ba had the greatest disinclination to refer to it, and I was careful to avoid giving her pain.[7]
If you can furnish me with any particulars — dates &c — which
you judge necessary for insertion, they may be helpful in this
way: but I shall do as little as I possibly can. While on the
subject, let me repeat — for probably the last time — how much
it is on my mind that, when I am no longer here to prevent it,
some use will be made of the correspondence not in my power:
all in my power is safe, and will ever remain so: and I shall
enjoin on Pen, with whom will remain the property allowed by
law in the manuscript letters — *not* in the writings themselves,
but in the publication of them,— to hinder this by every possible
means.[8] The letters to the sisters,— of which I never read one
line, but their contents are sufficiently within my knowledge,—
these unfortunately contain besides the inevitable allusions to
domestic matters, all the imaginary spiritualistic experiences by
which the unsuspecting and utterly truthful nature of Ba was
abused: she was duped by a woman[9] through whose impostures
one more versed in worldly craft and falsehood would have
clearly seen at once,— and the discovery of this came too late to
prevent disclosures which will never be properly accounted for
by the careless and spiteful public, only glad to be amused by
the aberrations of a soul so immeasurably superior in general
intelligence to their own. I have done all I can do,— you have
naturally influence where I am helpless, and so I leave the
matter — with grave forebodings.

And now,— to more pleasurable matter. My young couple[10]
arrived here, from Venice, a week ago,— spent a happy week
with me, left yesterday for Liverpool, and this day — nearly at
this hour (12.) sail for New York in the "Aurania." They stay

till the beginning of next year, then return — but what their ultimate settling-down may be,— where they mean to reside,— I leave to their good sense and kind feelings. I am more and more satisfied with the match,— indeed no one least drawback to my satisfaction is discoverable. Fannie is thoroughly good, affectionate, full of ambition for Pen, to whom she is devoted — and he is fully aware of his good fortune in obtaining such a wife. They may possibly — probably — live — for a while at least — in Venice — for which Pen's passion is strong as ever: but he will have a studio permanently in London, and spend much of the year there — and eventually — will, do for the best, I hope and trust.[11]

[The rest of the sheet is torn off.]

[1] No envelope has been preserved.

[2] Reference to *Letter 41*, p. 162, will show that Mrs. Browning's "feelings on the subject" were less pronounced than her husband remembered.

[3] *Elizabeth Barrett Browning* by J. H. Ingram in the Eminent Women series was published in 1888.

[4] See *Letter 71, note 4,* p. 292; also *note 6* below.

[5] J. H. Ingram: *The Poetical Works of Elizabeth Barrett Browning from 1826 to 1844,* edited with a memoir; 1877. The publisher was Ward, Lock & Co. A note in the *Athenaeum* for December 10, 1877, p. 782, remarks that the poems "are those of which the copyright has expired. The chief value of the edition lies in a brief, but accurate biography prefixed by Mr. Ingram." Another edition of the sort deplored by Browning was *The Earlier Poems of Elizabeth Barrett Browning, 1826-1833* by R. Hearne Shepherd, London, 1878.

[6] George Smith (1824-1901), head of the publishing house of Smith, Elder & Co., Browning's publisher after the break with Chapman in 1866. In a letter to Pen and Fannie, December 17, 1887, Browning wrote: "I have condensed some facts furnished by George Barrett into a prefatory note — to be printed along with the little edition of E. B. B.'s collected poems — correcting the mis-statements in a recent memoir: we dined with Smith yesterday, — he thinks it will have an useful effect. I have sent proof to George to add to, if he thinks fit" (Hood, p. 278).

[7] Plenty of circumstances might be cited which could have made it painful for Mrs. Browning to contemplate the past, but they seem rather to sharpen the "disinclination" than to explain it totally. Both her poems and her letters show her to have been a person who lived vividly in the present. It may be remarked that Robert, for all his imaginative absorption in the past, was quite as reluctant to speak of *his* past as she was of hers.

[8] It is clear from many of his remarks that Browning, understandably, wanted at the same time both to publish the letters and not to publish them. Pen quotes him as saying of the love letters: "There they are, do with them as you please when I am dead and gone." *Letters of R. B. and E. B. B.*, I, *NOTE.*

[9] Mrs. Sophia May Eckley. David Eckley and his wife Sophia were Bostonians of considerable wealth who became intimate and generous friends of the Brownings in Italy. The story of this friendship and its collapse has been frequently told, notably in DeVane and Knickerbocker, p. 153, and McAleer, p. 31. Suffice it to say here that Browning is referring particularly to Mrs. Eckley's activities as a medium and her possession of letters from Mrs. Browning which dealt with spiritualism. For Browning's anxiety concerning these letters and their subsequent history see DeVane and Knickerbocker, pp. 187-89. Browning was much more cordial to Mrs. Eckley in the letter there printed of December 4, 1869, than he feels in November, 1887.

[10] Pen and his wife (Fannie Coddington). They had been married in September and had spent their honeymoon in Venice.

[11] This is, of course, more wishful and, one may say, selfish thinking on Browning's part. Pen clearly never had any intention of settling in London.

letter 80   29 De Vere Gardens,
                                                             W.
                                         March 28. '88.[1]

My dear George,

Pen and his wife returned from America last week. Their visit was sadly affected by the illness of Fanny, who having suffered much from sickness during the passage, remained so thor-

oughly week [sic] that the result was a premature confinement:
fortunately at a very early stage. This of course interfered greatly
with what otherwise would have been a very pleasant occasion
of travel, among the wife's friends and in scenery Pen had long
wished to see. As soon as her health permitted, they left — just
escaping the terrible storm of which the newspapers have informed us: their own experience of the sea, this time, was altogether favourable. I am happy to say, Fanny is returned to
her usual condition of health and strength: Pen however is
troubled with an ugly and teazing cough,— from which I think
he is slowly getting rid. They leave next week for Venice,—
where Pen is bent upon settling for some months, in order to
paint certain aspects of the city and its inhabitants which he
fancies have never been made use of before. He will go first, for
a short stay, to Paris where he wants to finish a picture still at his
studio there. His purposes "in the rough" are to return to London, and at least spend part of every "Season" there — first
ascertaining how he may like a partial residence abroad. All this
apparent vagrancy is induced by very real and reasonable con-
siderations,— and completely sympathized in by his wife — of
whom I will merely say in the fewest words possible, that we
love her and esteem her more and more as day by day we (my
sister and myself) become acquainted with her qualities: as for
Pen, he quite realizes his supremely good fortune, and I am certain that his Mother would have agreed with us in every respect.
And now to the immediate business of your letter: Pen knows
very well the ability of Mr. Joy,[2] and will call on him at his
studio in a day or two, as the easiest method of complying with
what is so kindly desired. Pen sends his true and grateful love to
you: on his next visit to England he will assuredly manage to
see you and his other relatives — he had hoped to do this, and
much beside even before leaving — but his earnest desire to resume work has hurried his departure — which nobody regrets
more than we do: but we *must* let him distinguish himself if he
can.

I suppose you saw the letter of Mr. Ingram to the "Athenaeum."[3] I had no mind to be drawn into a controversy with

him,— and the Editor, whom I wrote to on the subject, helped me well enough.

Yes, the new Edition[4] promises to be successful. Smith interests himself greatly in the affair, supplies illustrations liberally, and is all zeal in my behalf. I do my part and correct what little I can, — but there will be no material change anywhere.

My sister's best love goes to you with that of

Yours affectionately ever
Robert Browning.

[1] No envelope has been preserved. There are, however, in the collection two envelopes for which there are no letters. The first is postmarked Kensington, Dec. 3, 1887, and addressed to George G. Moulton-Barrett, Esq., 3 Frederick Place, Weymouth. The second is postmarked London 3, March 12, 1889 and Ilfracombe A, March 13, 1889. It is addressed to George G. Moulton-Barrett, Esq., 2 Runnacleave Crescent, Ilfracombe. On the front is marked in pencil, 292/295, and on the back "Memoir and c — , 1889. — ," probably referring to content of the letter concerning Browning's memoir of his wife.

[2] Mr. Joy seems to have been an artist, but has remained otherwise unidentified along with George's "kind" desire.

[3] Because so much has been said in these letters concerning the facts or lack of them in memoirs of Mrs. Browning and since the discussion illustrates the confusion which existed twenty-seven years after her death and persisted for many years more, it seems justifiable to quote here at length from both Ingram and Browning. Ingram's letter is in the *Athenaeum* for February 4, 1888, p. 146. It follows:

To a volume of poems by Mrs. Browning recently published by Messrs. Ward, Lock & Co., I contributed a short memoir of the poetess. Mr. Browning has since published a memorandum in correction of certain mistakes he deems I have made in this memoir of his wife, and sums them up in four paragraphs.

Firstly, I say Elizabeth, the eldest daughter of Edward Moulton-Barrett was born in London on the 4th of March, 1809. Mr. Browning says: "The eldest daughter died in childhood. Elizabeth was born at Carlton Hall, March 6th, 1806." In November, 1866, in kind response to my inquiries, Mr. Browning then wrote of the memoir of Mrs. Browning by Mrs. Ritchie, in the Dictionary of National Biography: "I engaged to verify any dates she had furnished, and I did so. *Only those are to be depended upon.*" Mrs. Ritchie writes that Mrs. Browning "was born at Burn Hall, Durham, on

March 6th, 1809." Both Mr. Browning's verifications cannot be correct. It is certain that Mrs. Browning was not born at Burn Hall, Durham, nor on the date first given. I cannot discover any Carlton Hall in Durham, nor any record of Mrs. Browning's birth in that city. A contemporary journal, however, announced for "March 4th, 1809, in London, the wife of Edward M. Barrett, Esq., of a daughter." [The birth referred to above was that of Mrs. Browning's sister Henrietta. The paragraph concludes with a justification of his statements of the early age at which Mrs. Browning wrote her first published poems, all based on the "fact" that she was born in 1809.]

The second paragraph is a flimsy defense of Ingram's "suggestion" that Hugh Stuart Boyd was Mrs. Browning's tutor. The third sustains his misstatements about Edward's age and death "on the faith that Mrs. Browning was born in 1809" and "the deposition of witnesses at the coroner's inquest."

Fourthly, it is alleged I am mistaken in saying Mr. Barrett's property was augmented by his accession to his only brother Richard's property. Mr. Browning states Mr. Barrett's only brother was Samuel, that the Richard referred to was merely a cousin, and that "by his death Mr. Barrett did not acquire a shilling." Again I must cite Mrs. Browning's words. Writing to Miss Mitford in 1837, she speaks of having "heard from the West Indies of the death of poor papa's only brother"; and Miss Mitford refers to the deceased gentleman as Speaker of the House of Assembly at Jamaica, which Richard Barrett was, styles him her friend's uncle, and says that owing to his decease childless "his property came to our friends," the Barretts.

Thus Mr. Browning and my readers will see that my statements have not been made carelessly or without good authority.

John H. Ingram

Browning's reply to this letter appeared in the *Athenaeum*, for February 11, 1888, p. 179. It follows:

In reply to the letter of Mr. Ingram, I have only to say that every fact which he questions was recently furnished from a source the authority of which is indisputable, and must override the loose and vague impressions of any mere acquaintances or even friendly memories impaired by the lapse of time. For myself, I have always disclaimed any pretence to certitude in the matter from knowledge of my own.

A single point in my notice requires correction, however; the sister who died in childhood was the elder in birth, I now find.

Robert Browning

The "memorandum" referred to by Ingram was included in the Prefatory Note to the *Poems of Elizabeth Barrett Browning*, 1887, being a reprint of Mrs. Browning's two-volume *Poems*, 1844, in one volume. This same Prefatory Note is reprinted with the 1887 date in the final authoritative edition of *The Works of Elizabeth Barrett Browning*, 6 vols., London, Smith, Elder & Co., 1889, reprinted 1890.

The memorandum states that:

1. Mrs. Browning was born March 6, 1806 at Coxhoe Hall, county of Durham;

2. Hugh Stuart Boyd was her friend, not her tutor;
3. Edward was "younger by nearly two years", was drowned in Babbi-
come Bay, and that the body was recovered after three, not twenty-
four days;
4. Mr. Edward Moulton, by the will of his grandfather, was directed to
affix the name of Barrett to that of Moulton, upon succeeding to the
estates in Jamaica. Richard was his cousin, and by his death Mr.
Barrett did not acquire a shilling. His only brother was Samuel, some-
time M. P. for Richmond. He had also a sister who died young, the
full-length portrait of whom by Sir Thomas Lawrence (the first
exhibited by that painter) is in the possession of Octavius Moulton-
Barrett at Westover, near Calbourne, in the Isle of Wight. [This is the
famous "Pinkie" now in the Huntington Gallery, San Marino, California.] With respect to the "semi-tropical taste" of Mr. Barrett, so
characterized in the "Memoir", it may be mentioned that, on the
early death of his father, he was brought from Jamaica to England
when a very young child, as the ward of the late Chief Baron Lord
Abinger, then Mr. Scarlett. . . . He was sent to Harrow, but received
there so savage a punishment for a supposed offense ("burning the
toast") by the youth whose "fag" he had become that he was withdrawn from the school by his mother, and the delinquent was expelled.
At the early age of sixteen he was sent by Mr. Scarlett to Cambridge,
and thence, for an early marriage, to Northumberland. After purchasing the estate in Herefordshire, he gave himself up assiduously to the
usual duties and occupations of a country gentleman — farmed largely,
was an active magistrate, became for a year High Sheriff, and in all
county contests busied himself as a Liberal. . . .

Many other particulars concerning other people, in other "Biographical Memoirs which have appeared in England or elsewhere" for
some years past, are similarly "mistaken and misstated"; but they seem
better left without notice by anybody.

29 De Vere Gardens, W. December 10, 1887.   R.B.

⁴ This is probably *The Poetical Works of Robert Browning,*
"Fourth and complete edition," Smith, Elder & Co., 1888-94. The
edition includes seventeen volumes. Browning edited all but volume
17, which was edited by Berdoe. The first eight volumes appeared
in 1888.

letter 81   29 De Vere Gardens
                                                  Apr. 24, '88.   W.[1]

My dear George,

Pen sends the enclosed letter[2] for me to forward, and I take
the occasion of adding a word of my own to whatever it may
contain. He suffered much during his stay in London from *lar-
yngitis* — and was forced to keep not merely in the house but in
his bedroom for nearly a week. As soon as the Doctor would

allow, and profiting by the fine weather, he left last Saturday week for Paris — where he stays to finish a picture,— interrupted in its progress by the manner matters [*sic*] that took up his attention before and after his marriage,— and to be present at the opening of the "Salon", where two pictures have been received "avec numero"— that is, special commendation to the hangers: besides a bust — a portrait of myself.[3] He is well now, — and his wife — whom we love the more as we know her the more — is quite well also: they will get you to know them some day.

Yesterday, Pen was elected a member of the "Athenæum." His proposer & seconder being Locker-Lampson and Leighton. I never solicited a single vote: and was pleasantly surprised by seeing what influential names were spontaneously appended to his nomination Card,— no better names in the Club. He was elected almost without opponents,— 4 only,— against 173. supporters. I heard of his success at a great dinner given to Pender[4] last evening (where I was merely a guest) — for though I passed the Club on my way to the house, I chose not to enquire — for I am hardened now against any such merely spiteful attacks as this would have been,— seeing that Pen can have no "enemy" but *perhaps* an Academician or two, or even four![5] The privilege will be useful if Pen eventually settles in London, as possibly he may do: he goes now to Venice — on trial of it.

Dear George, I trust you continue well, and that all goes well with the Brothers. My sister sends her kindest love: and I am ever yours most affectionately

Robert Browning.

[1] Address: George G. Moulton-Barrett, Esq., 3 Frederick Place, Weymouth. Postmark: London, April 24, 1888; Weymouth, April 25.

[2] The enclosure has not been preserved.

[3] There is a photograph of the bust in Hood, facing p. 282. It was then in the possession of Thomas J. Wise.

[4] Sir John Pender (1815-96). He was a pioneer in submarine telegraphy, suffering heavy financial losses and disappointments in

the laying of the Atlantic cable before finally offering security for
the successful cable in 1865. He was also instrumental in the laying of eastern cables and worked on the electric lighting for London. He was made K.C.M.G. in 1888, when Lord Derby presided
at a banquet in his honor.

[5] It is perhaps gratuitous to call attention to the many facets of
Browning's personality revealed in this paragraph.

letter 82   29 De Vere Gardens, W.
                                                        Dec. 21, '88.[1]

My dear George,

On returning home, after a four months' absence,[2] I find your
letter of so long ago as Oct. 3. You will have easily conjectured
the cause of the delay in acknowledging the news of you — always a great pleasure. One or another reason induced me to pro-
long my stay far beyond what I had counted upon. If one could
but see you occasionally to talk over what needs to be written![3]
I don't think I have told you what an advantageous bargain Pen
has made in acquiring his huge Rezzonico Palace,— the finest
now obtainable in Venice. He was most efficiently helped by his
kind and clever friend Mr. Malcolm, a thoroughly business man,
— and he possesses a magnificent property worth more than
double what was paid for it: he could sell the mere adornments
of the building,— its statues, pillars (internal decorations) and
painted cielings [sic] (two by Tiepolo) for the full prize of the
palazzo itself. He is full of energy, and superintends all the restoration work, (all that is requisite, and not much of even that)
and may safely be considered "the right man in the right place."
Far from neglecting his art, he has every motive for devoting
himself to it: and there seems only one circumstance likely to
overcloud the sunshine of his life — the uncertain health of his
wife. The two would otherwise really seem perfectly happy in
every condition of their fortunes here below. Pen has painted a
whole-length portrait of myself[4]— with other works, which you
will see, I hope, in the course of the spring.

I have not been able to do more than examine the outside of

the great pile of books and letters which have accumulated during my absence, I know nothing of various articles relating to matters interesting to us both — Ingram's book &c. I believe he has avoided giving annoyance unnecessarily. My own "Edition,"[5] about which you kindly enquire, is doing very well, I hear: we print every month 2000 copies for England, 1000 for America, and a large paper edition of 50 for special subscribers. It is nicely "got up" and Smith, always my energetic helper, has done his best in its behalf. Our house here proves warm and comfortable, and in that matter also we seem to have succeeded beyond our expectations. The weather was appalling enough when, last week, we exchanged three months of glorious sunshine and cloudless sky for the fog which met us at Dover. I suffered not a little and expected to undergo much more, but the last couple of fine and mild days are consolatory. Do, my dear George, look in upon us some day. It is long since we met. And why not run over, in the spring, to Venice — when Pen and his wife will be installed in their palazzo and not let you get out of it, once inside. He intends to fit up "some Bachelor rooms": he himself will occupy the Pope's[6] old apartment — the snuggest: and quietly wait till, bit by bit, he "furnishes" the whole of his domain — which he does not find at all too vast. He reminds me of the mouse (in a poem of Donne's) who got into the trunk of an elephant — "wherein, as in a gallery, this mouse walked and surveyed the rooms of this vast house."[7] But in reality there was only two or three "vast" rooms; — those habitable and not for mere passage or receptions, are quite moderate in size. Good bye, dear George — my sister (at my side) sends her best love with that of yours affectionately ever

RB.

[1] Address: George G. Moulton-Barrett, Esq., 2 Frederick Place, Weymouth. Postmark: London, Dec. 21; Weymouth, Dec. 22, 1888. Pencil note on envelope: "Some of R.B.'s letters. Most of them I burnt — March 1892."

[2] Browning and his sister had been visiting with Pen and Fannie in Venice.

³ Probably another reference to "misstatements" in the memoir of Mrs. Browning.

⁴ Browning was greatly pleased with the portrait which was exhibited at the Grosvenor and later in Paris and New York. It now hangs in the Armstrong Browning Library, Baylor University, Waco, Texas.

⁵ Described above, *Letter 80, note 4,* p. 315.

⁶ The Rezzonico Palace had once been occupied by Cardinal Rezzonico, later Pope Clement XIII. For a view of the palace, see Plate VIII, following p. 54.

⁷ The lines occur in *The Progresse of the Soule,* stanza XL, ll. 391-92.

letter 83   29 De Vere Gardens. W.
                                             Jan. 21. '89[1]

[*Top of sheet*] I send this for Pen's perusal. I have others like it—

My dear George,

I am greatly obliged by the loan of the letters and piece of poetry,[2] which I return with truest thanks. I feel deeply indeed the interest which attaches itself to the merest scrap of that beloved handwriting, and am perfectly aware of a very general desire on the part of the Public to possess such a collection of letters as you suggest might be made,— and some collection of what may be procurable will be one day made, I have no doubt, when matter over which I lose control becomes, by accident or otherwise, the property of the collector. But there seem to me insuperable obstacles to my taking on myself such an office: not so much,— strange as that might appear,— from the repugnance of the writer to any publicity of the kind, as from certain unfortunate circumstances connected with the case. I could disregard perhaps a feeling caused simply by the modesty and avoidance of notoriety which were conspicuous in the writer, and which I have on occasion been forced to withstand: but the difficulty is that if once a beginning is made there will be no power of stopping there: we cannot pick and choose what portions of a life may be illustrated and what left obscure — and it is precisely upon what is so left that the public curiosity would be exercised. I could perhaps see my way to presenting just so much of the correspondence as merely relates to literature, politics, theology, description of persons and things: but if once matters of a personal and more intimate nature were ventured upon, every endeavour would be made — eventually — to supply the gaps: and, you will believe me, it is not for my own memory, once safe out of this gossip-loving and scandal-hungry world, that I am at all apprehensive. Two years ago, I spent more than a week in destroying my own letters to my family, — from my earliest days up to the death of my father they had all been preserved.[3] But I possess hundreds of letters of the most interesting kind — addressed to Mr Boyd, Mrs Martin, Miss Mitford, Mrs Jameson, and others — which I could not bring myself to do away with, — whatever may be the ultimate disposition of them. As for the letters to myself, — and for months before our marriage I received one daily, — these which are so immeasurably superior to any compositions of the kind I have any experience of, — would glorify the privileged receiver beyond any imaginable crown in the world or out of it — but I cannot, any more than Timon, "cut my heart in sums — tell out my blood."[4] Notwithstanding all this, my dear George, you may be assured that the responsibility attending my ownership of letters and other documents is never absent from my thoughts, and I remain open to any conviction which may result from circumstances that have not as yet taken place. The unhappy letters which concern spiritualism I wish with all my heart could be eliminated from those out of my hands, and burnt forthwith — as they ought to be.[5]

I leave myself no room to say more — of Pen and his wife, for instance, who are just on the point of inhabiting their great house — the lady in excellent health, I am glad to say. You *must* go and see them, and delight them, as you would. I suffered from the fog, and keep house of an evening all this current month. My sister sends her true love with that of Yours affectionately

ever RB.

[1] No envelope has been preserved. The note at the top of the page is in pencil and appears to have been written by George.

[2] The materials concerning Mrs. Browning which are spoken of in this and the three following letters were furnished Browning for the purpose of preparing the Prefatory Note quoted in *Letter 80, note 3,* p. 313, probably in an endeavor to make any necessary changes to the 1889 note. None was made.

[3] Robert Browning, Senior, died in June, 1866. Browning's passion for destroying all evidence dealing with what he considered his personal life is well known. Other Victorian writers, notably Tennyson, Thackeray, and even, at times Dickens, show the same characteristic but with less violence of both statement and action. In Browning it extended to the length of, as he constantly maintained, never inquiring into the circumstances of Mrs. Browning's life, and even sometimes attributing to her the same attitude. She, on the other hand, seemed to be concerned only that her privacy be respected while she lived. Browning's habit of dramatic composition was fundamentally a projection of this personal reticence. In one of his early letters to Miss Barrett (January 15, 1845), he wrote: "your poetry must be . . . infinitely more to me than mine to you — for you *do* what I always wanted, hoped to do . . . You speak out, *you,* — I only make men and women speak — give you truth broken into prismatic hues, and fear the pure white light, even when it is in me." *Letters of R. B. and E. B. B.,* I, p. 6.

[4] *Timon of Athens,* III, 4, l. 93.

[5] George clearly did not share this attitude; at least he did not accede entirely to his brother-in-law's wish.

letter 84   29 De Vere Gardens, W.
                                         Feb. 24, '89.[1]

My dear George,

   Thank you exceedingly for the Packet — the contents of which I will not say "interest me" — no such word will serve. I cannot bring myself to do more than very cursorily examine them now, — they will wait with the abundance of similar documents I have till I can resolve what is fittest to be done with them —

always wholly with regard to what I conceive would be the wish of the beloved author — whose mind indeed I sufficiently know as regards many matters in their connection.[2] Since I wrote to you I have seen Ingram's book: one has to make allowance for the necessity (as he esteemed it) of somebody's bookmaking in the case: and, barring the silly occasional criticisms, he has been, I believe, anxious to give as little offence as possible. I hardly conceive it is worth while to go into the question of the date and birth place now — as it is of little importance to the general readers of her poetry — and regardless of her life with the appropriate feeling. One day — perhaps! — I may attempt, as I may be able, some sort of statement.

I hear from the couple at Venice constantly — from Pen yesterday. They are, within the last few days, lodged in their fine Palazzo: they gave two modest entertainments there by way of house-warming, and were congratulated by everybody on what they had done for Pope Clement XIII, — whose apartment they occupy: and it is pleasant to hear how grateful the old Venetian families are at the palace having fallen into such reverent hands (I will get a photograph of it for you when I can) — not being destined to vile uses, turned into an hotel, or the like. It is really, on the whole, the best palace in Venice, and has never been modified in the least — except in the trifling business of blocking up windows &c — all which Pen has carefully restored. I am particularly happy to know that his wife, — a woman of whom I can imagine no greater praise than I imply when I say Pen's Mother would have thoroughly loved and esteemed her, — *she* is as satisfied with her new conditions as Pen's self. And now it will be for Pen to show he is worthy of his belongings. He is sending over his very striking Portrait for exhibition here, and will make a considerable show at the Paris grand affair. There is a funny circumstance connected with the "Rezzonico." There is — was — a family down in the Golden Book of the old Republic — that of "Widmann" — very wealthy, owning many palaces still bearing the name, but now (lately however) extinct. The last of the Rezzonico family was one Widmann Rezzonico, nephew of the Pope: he died at the beginning of the present century. Now, my mother's maiden name was "Wiedemann"— and Pen was named after her — Robert W. B. B.— which name he mispronounced as "Pennini"— hence his old and customary appellation. He was not aware of the last of the Rs being so called till after we had bought the property: and the Venetians account for his getting such a bargain by thinking there was something more than natural in his ability to do so! As for what Burke wrote of Venice and its manners before the Revolution,— I am pretty sure,—from what knowledge I have from no few sources, memoirs, &c — that he was in the right:[3] but all that is as thoroughly changed now as the form of government and all else: I fancy few cities are — at least outwardly — so decorous. It may come of the universal poverty, too probably.[4]

Have I tried your goodnature? I rejoice to hear that, at least two days ago, you could "sit at an open window": it is bitterly cold here, and snowing at intervals while I write. Will you never come our way? You *must* go Pen's way at some time or other, and see his achievements: and when you have had enough of such vanities, here is our small quiet but comfortable house, with a room for you, and a welcome to make all insufficiencies disappear!

My sister sends her kindest love: she continues in excellent health: and I am, dear George, always

Very affectionately yours
Robert Browning.

[1] No envelope has been preserved.

[2] Browning's confidence in this respect was not completely justified.

[3] Compare *A Toccata of Galuppi's*.

[4] This judgment is in accord with Mr. Bernard Berenson's comment that Venice is "the richest and most exquisite artifact in the history of civilization, because she has been spared by the great and beneficent goddess Poverty" (*New Yorker*, October 20, 1951, p. 40).

letter 85   29. De Vere Gardens.
                                                              W.
                                                   March 29. '89.[1]

My dear George,

You need no assurance of how deeply I feel your kindness in all
you have said and done. The MSS[2] are precious,— and, with the
many others I possess, may be used perhaps, at some future time,
for an illustration of their authors. Whatever is undertaken will
be directed by the knowledge, that is as fresh in me now as years
ago, of what would be her wish that the public should be made
acquainted with — supposing that it had a right to *some* acquaintance with anything but her poetry.

Since we must suppress "Carlton Hall"[3]— (however did the
mistake arise?) I should be very desirous of giving a drawing of
Hope End, if such a thing is obtainable. I was about to give a
photograph made at my request and that of dear Arabel just
before the house was pulled down: it was the work of a local
photographer,— a poor performance, and already very indistinct
in parts,— besides being more dreary looking through the wintry
aspect of the leafless trees beside it: I should be glad indeed to
give a more favourable view. The dates you furnish oblige me
greatly: I daresay I could supplement them by referring to
papers and letters: but I think of the business with a heavy
heart.

I got yesterday a courteous letter from the Editor of a magazine who had published a depreciatory notice of Ingram's book,
— to which Ingram had replied by a letter in which he more
than implied that *I* myself had furnished him with the facts:
the Editor wished to know what was the truth.[4] I have just told
him that I never gave — but distinctly refused — all "sanction or
assistance" to the work — and only, when its writer assured me
it *must* be produced, remarked that he would do it in as kindly
a spirit as anybody — which has probably been the case. He had
evinced, on various occasions, a desire to treat me civilly —
though I never saw him, that I remember, in all my life. I shall
give an engraving from the pretty picture given to me by Miss

Tripsack — the childish full-length by Hayter.[5] Any illustration that occurs to you shall be given most gladly, of course.

I believe that Pen's most happy marriage is mainly attributable to his being the son of his mother — whom his wife from her girlhood has all but worshipped. They are actually going to dedicate to her memory the little chapel in their palazzo — once a witness of the daily devotions of Rezzonico — Pope Clement XIII.*

All thanks and love to you, dear George, from yours ever affectionately

Robert Browning.

*The inscription on Casa Guidi will be placed there in letters of gold: Tommaseo, its author, was a Venetian, and is honoured by a statue.

[1] No envelope has been preserved.

[2] In a letter to Pen, March 30, 1889, Browning wrote: "I have a letter from George, giving me a few dates and facts. . . . He has sent me many interesting MSS: poetry written at eleven years of age, and diaries &c" (Hood, p. 306). In the Browning papers at the University of Illinois are several early poems, mostly birthday greetings to members of the family. The earliest, however, is dated March 8, 1819, when Elizabeth was 13, and describes a day at Hope End. See Appendix I, p. 338.

[3] See *Letter 80, note 3,* p. 313. Carlton Hall was "Occy's mistake" (Hood, p. 306) for Coxhoe Hall, where Mrs. Browning was born.

[4] Anyone not yet worn out by the Ingram affair must feel a certain sympathy for the luckless biographer. Browning's first refusal of his request for information is dated March 21, 1880 (Hood, p. 188; see also other letters, Hood, p. 210 and p. 257).

[5] This portrait is reproduced as the frontispiece to volume I of the six-volume edition of Mrs. Browning's works (1889); also in Miller: *Browning,* facing p. 36.

letter 86   29. De Vere Gardens.
                                                              W.
                                               Apr. 8. '89.[1]

My dear George,

The drawing is charming, just what was desirable: it does justice to Hope End, as my poor photograph fails to do. Did not Mr Barrett build it? Could you give the date of its erection? I want to make the edition as good as possible and shall contribute other illustrations: I grieve at the mistakes about the birthplace. Yes,— by the kindness of Ocky I received and acknowledged the receipt of her miniature[2] some days ago: it is interesting in the highest degree — and, to my fancy, represents much of the features I remember. In all cases, be quite certain that every imaginable care will be taken of these precious objects so kindly entrusted to me: George Smith,[3] into whose hands I shall deliver them with an earnest caution, is to be wholly relied upon: I have no doubts respecting their safety — any more than that of the pictures I myself put under his care: and the engravings once made, the originals shall be immediately returned to the respective owners: but I cannot promise that the operation will be immediate. Any fresh *dates* or *facts* that subsequently occur to you, will be valuable if you supply me with them in time.

You will like to know that a portrait of myself painted by Pen[4] and sent to London from Venice has met with a very gratifying approval from the few friends who have seen it,— Millais, Alma Tadema,[5] Joachim,[6] Boughton[7] and a few others have been — I may really say enthusiastic in their appreciation, and Leighton, whose duties all this last week at the Academy occupied him exclusively, told me yesterday that he was informed that Pen's picture was exquisite. It goes this morning to the Grosvenor Gallery — they having asked for it. Pen figures very well both in painting and sculpture, at the Paris Exposition.

With renewed thanks, dear George, believe me ever affectionately yours

Robert Browning.

[1] No envelope has been preserved.

[2] The identity of the miniature is undeterminable since, as the following letter states, it was rejected in favor of the Hayter portrait. This suggests that the miniature may have been a childhood picture. It may, however, be the one reproduced in Miller: *Browning*, facing p. 52, or the one reproduced in Plate II, following p. 54 and referred to in *Letter 8*, p. 57.

[3] The publisher.

[4] The portrait referred to earlier (see Hood, pp. 305 and 307).

[5] Sir Lawrence Alma-Tadema (1836-1912) was born in Holland and settled in England after his marriage in 1871. He was made a member of the Royal Academy in 1879 and knighted in 1899.

[6] Joseph Joachim (1831-1907) was Browning's favorite violinist and is described in *Grove's Dictionary* as the "greatest master of the violin in his generation." Browning was present when Oxford conferred on him the degree of Doctor of Music, March 8, 1877 (see DeVane and Knickerbocker, p. 238, note 4).

[7] George Henry Boughton (1833-1905), painter, was born in England but taken as a child to the United States and was brought up in Albany, New York. After 1863 he spent most of his life in London. He was elected to the Royal Academy in 1896.

letter 87   29, De Vere Gardens.
                                                                 W.
                                        Apr. 16. '89.[1]

Thank you yet again, my dear George, for your very interesting letter – I shall make use of its information certainly, but, at present and for the especial purpose in view, I shall write no sort sort [sic] of regular memoir — only give, as I said, the facts — with certain corroborative notes — enough to show the untrustworthiness of the current accounts.[2] Hereafter — who knows? – I may attempt a fuller account, and, in that case, put in evidence what her feelings were on the point you mention,[3] and others: but what I now do will be quite enough to show that Ingram had no sort of knowledge respecting the matters he took in hand to exemplify, and the "taking in hand" was the consequence of his being simply a literary *hack* — bound to get a livelihood by scribbling about what might lend himself importance — not derive any from his treatment. Of course, in a series of "Celebrated English Authoresses" it was impossible to do altogether without some notice or other: and you know the old story of the stage manager who, when his white paper snow-storm was exhausted, resorted to *brown*.

The miniature is precious: but unfortunately Smith thinks it a superfluous illustration — preferring the equally charming likeness in the portrait by Hayter given me by Miss Tripsack: I am greatly obliged by Ocky's trusting it to me, and, should I require the loan hereafter, I hope he will again indulge me with a sight of it. The views of Coxhoe are all I could wish.

We have a letter from Venice to-day: all well and in high spirits: the owners of the Palazzo do its honours in high glee — and have visitors in abundance, whom they entertain hospitably — the last being my friends Ld Arthur and L^r Russell.[4] It is agreed on all hands that the treatment of the grand old pile is just what it should be: and, from particular and private accounts, I hear that, as a mere investment, the purchase money could not have been more profitably employed. With my sister's love, I am ever Dear George, affectionately yours

Robert Browning.

[1] No envelope has been preserved.

[2] Browning actually printed only the Prefatory Note dated December 10, 1887.

[3] The "point" is obscure and, therefore, the "feelings" also, but the remark indicates that George was not altogether sure that Browning always knew how his wife felt on certain points.

[4] Lord Arthur Russell was the brother of Odo Russell (see *Letter 51, note 6*, p. 231) and son of Lady William Russell. All of them were old and dear friends of the Brownings.

letter 88   Asolo, Veneto, Oct. 22. '89.[1]

My dear George,

It was a great pleasure to get your kind letter,— though after some delay. We were not in the Tyrol this year, but have been for six weeks or more in this little place which strikes me,— as it did fifty years ago, which is something to say, considering that, properly speaking, it was the first spot of Italian soil I ever set foot upon — having proceeded to Venice by sea — and thence here. It is an ancient city, older than Rome, and the scene of Queen Catherine Cornaro's exile,[2] where she held a mock court, with all its attendants on a miniature scale,— Bembo,[3] afterwards Cardinal, being her secretary. Her palace is still above us all, the old fortifications surround the hill-top, and certain of the houses are stately — though the population is not above 1000 souls: the province contains many more of course. But the immense charm of the surrounding country is indescribable – I have never seen its like — the Alps on one side, the Asolan mountains all round,— and opposite the vast Lombard plain,— with indications of Venice, Padua, and the other cities,— visible to a good eye on a clear day: while everywhere are sites of battles and sieges of by-gone days, described in full by the historians of the Middle Ages. We have a valued friend here, Mrs. Bronson,[4] who for years has been our hostess at Venice, and now is in possession of a house here (built into the old city wall) — she was induced to choose it through what I have said about the beauties of the place: and through her care and kindness we are comfortably lodged close by.[5] We think of leaving in a week or so for Venice,— guests of Pen and his wife: and after a short stay with them we shall return to London. Pen came to see us for a couple of days: I was hardly prepared for his surprise and admiration which quite equalled my own and that of my sister. All is happily well with them: their palazzo excites the wonder of everybody — so great is Pen's cleverness, and extemporized architectural knowledge, as apparent in all he has done there: Why, *why* will you not go and see him there? He and his wife are very hospitable and receive many visitors. Have I told you that there was a desecrated chapel which he has restored in honor of his Mother — putting up there the inscription by Tommasei now above Casa Guidi? Fannie is all you say; and most dear and precious to us all — if her health will but allow the consummation of their happiness, I don't know what else to wish in their behalf.[6] Pen's medal,[7] to which you refer, is awarded to him in spite of his written renunciation of any sort of wish to contend for a prize — knowing how such distinctions are awarded. He will now resume painting and sculpture[8]— having been necessarily occupied with the superintendence of his workmen — a matter capitally managed, I am told. For the rest,— both S.[9] and myself are very well: I have just sent off my new volume of verses[10] for publication. The complete edition of the works of E. B. B. begins in a few days.[11]

I would gladly say nothing more of a repulsive incident,[12]— but perhaps a word or two may be not uncalled for. I felt and expressed my horror and disgust at finding that a man, who had never seen my wife, nor been heard of by her, could not record his dislike of her Poem without coupling it with a satisfaction at her death: The brutality of this equals its stupidity,— because the publication of "Aurora Leigh" preceded by five years the death of its writer — who was never likely to produce such another work. Had he disliked the novels which Dickens and Thackeray left unfinished,— the brutality of being "relieved by their death" would have been simply brutal, not stupid, since certainly nothing but such an accident would have stopped the continuance of their work. In this case, there was no effect deducible by cause; and only a cur could couple them as did this fellow. I did not read any more of his book, though I ran my eye afterwards through the proper names occurring therein — to see if any more wanted notice. In an extract elsewhere, I observe that, having to find fault with Wordsworth's sonnets he needs must "wish old W. had his sonnets fastened round his neck and was pitched into the Duddon," or a similar bestiality — in the true Celtic strain: cruelty and fun together. I was blamed for "striking a dead man": was the person he insulted alive? And when was he ever alive *to me* until I got this token of his existence? Meanwhile I am content that my "blow" should be felt in its rebound by all and everyone of his enthusiastic friends who sympathize with the man living or dead — above all, those who had the perusal of the letters before publication and were too much taken up by the flattery of themselves and their friends to think the offence to my wife of no importance. I had a proper apology from the Publisher Craik (Mac M. & Co.) a public one from the Editor,— and, best of all, the approval of my own conscience. Mere literary criticism, however inept and even malicious, I should have left alone: "The wild ass o'er her head/ stamps with his foot and nought disturbs her sleep:"[13] but to couple *that* with any satisfaction at the greatest calamity of my life,— no, indeed!

You will forgive all this, Dear George,— you cannot but have heard of it, and I am unwilling you should not hear me also. Let us forget it if you can. I am glad to hear all the Brothers are well: my best regards always go to them. My sister, always happy to hear from you, charges me with her love — and you must always remember me as

Ever affectionately yours

Robert Browning.[14]

[1] No envelope has been preserved. Most of the text of this letter was published in Orr: *Life and Letters of Robert Browning*, rev. ed., London, 1908, p. 394.

[2] Caterina Cornaro was a Venetian lady who in 1468 was married to James II of Cyprus, the last active ruler of a line of kings who had ruled the island for nearly three centuries. She was only fourteen at the time and was married by proxy. In 1472 she joined her husband in Cyprus, but he died after a few months leaving her pregnant with a son who died in infancy. Beset with palace intrigue and external threats from the Turks, she was forced in 1489 by the Republic of Venice to abdicate in its favor, and was given the township of Asolo. Her small court there was a center for artists and writers, and her own charities made her universally beloved. Until her death she signed herself Queen of Cyprus, Jerusalem and Armenia, and Signora of Asolo (Thomas Okey: *The Story of Venice*, London, 1931). She is, of course, "Kate the Queen" of the song in *Pippa Passes*.

[3] Pietro Bembo (1470-1547), a Venetian, distinguished for his learning and the purity of his style. His dialogue, *Gli Asolani*, praises Platonic love in terms at considerable variance from his own conduct. In the dedication to *Asolando* Browning recalls that to him was attributed the coinage of the word *asolare:* "to disport

in the open air, amuse one's self at random," admitting, however, that the word does not appear in Bembo's writing.

[4] Mrs. Arthur Bronson with whom and her daughter Edith, Browning experienced the happiest friendship of the last decade of his life. Every biographical notice of Browning tells how he finished *Asolando* in her house La Mura, built into the walls of Asolo. There is a plaque on the wall of the house and the street has been renamed Via Robert Browning. The best account of Browning's visits in Venice, where also she was his hostess, is Mrs. Bronson's "Browning in Venice," *Century Magazine*, LXIII, 578 ff.

[5] Browning and his sister had rooms across the street from the Bronsons.

[6] The part of this sentence following the dash was deleted in Orr.

[7] "In 1889 he [Pen] was awarded a third medal at the Paris Exposition, which would automatically give him the right to exhibit his pictures at the Paris Salon without the usual required permission" (Reese, p. 797).

[8] As a matter of fact, Pen did nothing of the kind.

[9] Sarianna Browning.

[10] *Asolando*. The first volume of the first edition was received by Browning in Venice a few days before his death. The date of publication was the day of the author's death, December 12, 1889.

[11] The remainder of this letter was not published in Orr: *Life and Letters* "by desire of Mr. Browning's sister and son."

[12] The "incident" is the subject of two letters in Hood (p. 311) and of a copious note (ibid., pp. 377-88). According to the first of these letters Browning came upon the following passage in *The Life and Letters of Edward FitzGerald,* edited by William Aldis Wright, on July 7, 1889.

"Mrs. Browning's death is rather a relief to me, I must say. No more Aurora Leighs, thank God! A woman of real genius, I know; but what is the upshot of it all? She and her sex had better mind the kitchen and the children; and perhaps the poor. Except in such things as little novels, they only devote themselves to what men do much better, leaving that which men do worse or not at all" (Wright, I, pp. 280-81 in a letter to W. H. Thompson).

Browning's reaction was expressed spontaneously in the following lines:

> I chanced upon a new book yesterday:
> I opened it, and where my finger lay
> 'Twixt page and uncut page, these words I read

> — Some six or seven at most — and learned thereby
> That you, Fitzgerald, whom by ear and eye
> She never knew, "thanked God my wife was dead."
> Ay, dead! and were yourself alive, good Fitz,
> How to return you thanks would task my wits:
> Kicking you seems the common lot of curs —
> While more appropriate greeting lends you grace:
> Surely to spit there glorifies your face —
> Spitting — from lips once sanctified by hers.

One is reminded of Caponsacchi's characterization of Guido, had the priest killed him at the inn, as

> A spittle wiped off from the face of God!

The Ring and the Book, vi, l. 1454.

The storm aroused by the publication of these lines in the *Athenaeum,* July 13, 1889, p. 64, accounts for Browning's still writing so vehemently about the incident in October.

[13] The lines are from FitzGerald's *Rubáiyát,* no. 17 in the first edition, later no. 18:

> They say the Lion and the Lizard keep
> The courts where Jamshyd gloried and drank deep:
> And Bahrám, that great hunter — the Wild Ass
> Stamps o'er his Head, but cannot break his Sleep.

[14] No later letters to George survive, and there are few Browning letters of later date. Miller: *Browning,* quotes from two to George Smith of November 6 and 30 (p. 280, 281). According to Griffin and Minchin, p. 282, Browning went to Venice on November 1. Though he was not aware of it, his heart was showing weakness, and a cold contracted late in the month brought on bronchitis from which his heart did not recover.

APPENDIX I

Life at Hope End

I

The following letter was written by Elizabeth Barrett to Mrs. John Graham-Clarke, Elizabeth's maternal grandmother. It presents a vivid picture of the children's games at Hope End and bears witness to Elizabeth's physical vigor at the age of 10. The ages of the other Barrett children at the time of writing were: Bro (Edward) 9, Henrietta 7, Sam 4, Storm (Charles John) 1½. The "sweet little boy" is George, born July 15. Marks lists George as having been born July 15, 1817. This letter is clearly dated, so that unless the ten-year-old author had lost a whole year — at that age an eternity — Marks must be in error. Granting that the birth dates for the other children are correct, the most likely spacing points to 1816 as George's year. Charlotte, Jane (Jenny?), Fanny (Frances) and Bum (Arabella) are, of course, the Graham-Clarke daughters, Elizabeth's maternal aunts. Law-

son and Smith remain unidentified, but the surnames suggest
that they may have been employed in the Graham-Clarke household.

July 27th 1816

My dearest Grandmama

I am very glad to tell you, dear Mama is getting quite nicely,
she can walk a *little* now, and the sweet little Boy improves every
day. Indeed we want nothing to complete our happiness, but to
have the pleasing gratification of seeing you, dearest Grandpapa,
Charlotte, and Jenny not forgetting Lawson, & Smith &c as you
know I wish for *Bum,* Fanny &c I need not say *"Not forgetting"*
over again – Oh but I forget [*sic*] must to tell you we have got
grapes now but remember not ripe, and we have pineapples, also.
Oh what am I thinking of! Mr Somebody, or Mrs Somebody gave
them to us. But really the grapes are ours – Oh dearest Grandmama, Hope End is so beautiful, Nature here displays all her art,
the ivy that droops upon the ground, she fastens up to some
majestic tree without the aid of nails, or the active gardener. We
have played at a new game lately, we have each been Queen, or
King of some country, or island, for example, I and Arabella are
the empresses of the Hyeres, Bro and Henrietta are the emperor
and empress of Italy, Storm is the Prince of Rome, and Sam is
Emperor of Oberon. Pray dear Granny, beg Grandpapa, Charlotte
and Jane to be on my side, for we sometimes have Battles, the other
day Henrietta and I fought. I conquered, took her prisoner and
tied her to the leg of the table. And pray ask Lawson and Smith,
to be on their *pet* Sams side. Hoping this and loving you all very
much, I am

Always
Affectionately
Your child
Eliz. otherwise, signed,
Empress of the Hyeres

An answer as quick as time will permit
"Time" alias *distance.*

Pray tell Sunny James we send him a thousand kisses Pray ask
him to be on my side. We have heard the melancholy news from
Garyhunden of Miss Butlers death and are anxiously awaiting a

letter to hear how long it will prevent their coming. You must excuse this bad writing for I have been working in the hay till I am
quite tired & not likely to appear to advantage either on paper or
on my legs.

II

The following letter was addressed to Elizabeth by her paternal grandmother, Mrs. Elizabeth Moulton. It is undated,
but it must have been written before July 1818; i.e., before
George reached the age of two. In fact it may have been written
a year earlier since it suggests that "Dr [Dear] George Goodin"
may be running about and should soon talk. Grandmama's concern for the propriety of Elizabeth's dress and conduct confirms
the future invalid's tomboy reputation as a child. "Harry," who
is "a dear, good girl" is Henrietta, two years younger than Elizabeth. Brother Henry was as yet unborn.

Thanks My Beloved Ba for your kind and charming letter, it was
read over two or three times – I have sent you six slips to wear
under your frocks, you are now too big to go without them & they
will also keep you warm — if they are too long or want any other
alteration Dr Mama will let *Maddox* do them for you also two
frocks one for Harry, 7 India Handkerchiefs for *Dr* papa, My love
to him tell him I hope he does not expose himself to this damp
Weather if he does he may depend his pains will be as violent as
ever – Our sweet Storm is ever in my thoughts, Dr George Goodin
& himself must be a charming pair. the latter must now run all
about. I shd think begin to talk — pray how comes dr BRO &
Sam — You my sweet Ba dont say a word about your Musick —
Harry I know is fond of it & therefore must in time play well, *she
is a dear good Girl.* — Your friend Trip is now writing you, you
must write her & explain what you want, & you will have it —
Now my darling Child you must allow me to say I think you are
too BIG to attempt fighting with Bro, He might give you an *unlucky* Blow on your NECK which might be serious to you. He is
strong & powerful – I have seen him very rude & boisterous to you
& Harry. He is now a big Boy fit only to associate with Boys, NOT
GIRLS – Give my love to him & all our dear pets. Kiss & love Storm,

George Goodin for me – Trip joins me in love to dear Mama, papa –

> Dearest Ba — your truly
> affectionate GrdMama
> EM —

III

The following poem, written at the age of 13, relates with charming detail and characteristic classical "machinery" the story of a day at Hope End.

Ye Muses warbling in melodious spells
Near resting Helicons immortal wells
And bending graceful o'er the sacred spring
Rouse all your powers and aid me as I sing
And thou Apollo patron of lost wits
The glaring sun and rise of verse by fits
But when that sun! alas thy votaries mourn
And call in vain deserted and forlorn
Their dull thoughts stop for want of custommed fire
And critics rage & talk in endless ire
In vain they call & critics rage about
Thou seldom reigns within scarce e'er without
Be merciful for once — for once agree
To lend thy succour and to pity *me!*
First e're the gentle moon desert her sway
Ere rosy morning blushes into day
Pillowed with pillows snug in bed reclined
With Nodkin wisdom I refresh my mind
Then swift Time in open daylight flies
I read a page from scripture ere I rise
Till the loud clock seven — fatal number tolls
And strikes all terror on our fainting souls
We rise and dress then thank the almighty power
For all his mercies and our God adore
In haste we fly to school and half asleep
On tiptoe up the creaking staircase creep
Arrived — one instinct all our souls inspire

At once we crowd around the ready fire
Till at the door we hear the fatal tread
And fancy sees the ruler near our head
Quick to our seats we run while open flies
The door! and M^r — stands before our eyes
What we have learnt we say — the clock strikes nine
And all our thoughts to breakfast straight incline
Down stairs we clamourous rush to break our fast
On lasting bread & milk — no "rich repast"
To school again till twelve then glad we run
To seek the glories of a midday sun
Till dinner — then immerging from the air
At home again, to dine, we then repair —
Roast mutton smoking on the board we view
In a cracked dish theres mashed potatoes too
O'er joyed and hungry to our seats we haste
And bless the cook who served the rich "repast"
And then we guess what pudding shall arrive
Some hope tis tart & on that hope they live.
One says "Its bad *I* know" — another "nice"
One bread — one suet — lo! it comes — 'tis rice!
Oh fatal pudding! At that hated sound
Fierce Discord spreads her jealous wings around
On every side despair & murmurs rise
And Nursery Hall resounds repeated cries
Not half such grief in Hectors bosom sprung
When Troy in ruins jaws tremendous hung
Not half such cries nor such resounding ire
The Trojans uttered with their towers on fire
But midst such horrid woes to mortals due
Time does not flag the fatal clock strikes two
To school till five! — & then again we fly
To play & joy & mirth & pleasures ply
Some dance, some fight, some laugh, some play — some squall,
And the loud organs thunder circles all
And then at tea we snatch a short repast
As long as one large plate of toast doth last
At nine fatigued upon the grateful bed
We stretch our weary limbs & rest our head

A gentle night succeeds & silent peace
Infolds our bodies in the sweets of ease
So pass our days so pass our happy hours
Our time may well be said to glide in flowers.

E. B. Barrett

Monday evening March 8th 1819.

APPENDIX II

Diagnoses of Elizabeth Barrett's Physicians

These letters from three doctors should settle some of the arguments about the nature of Elizabeth Barrett's illness. It has been generally known that she become seriously ill at the age of fifteen, and the explanation persisted that it was due to an injury to the spine incurred while saddling her pony Moses. Elizabeth herself seems never to have given her support to this story, and these letters — especially Dr. Coker's — specifically eliminate any injury to the spine. The late Dr. D. J. Davis, then Dean Emeritus of the University of Illinois Medical School and familiar with the sort of diagnosis here presented, assured the editor that both symptoms and treatment indicate clearly a diagnosis of "general tuberculosis from girlhood." All the Barrett daughters seem to have suffered in the same way in 1821, although Elizabeth's illness was the most severe. All three cases seem to have been arrested, but Elizabeth's recurred with shorter intervals of decreasingly vigorous health between until her death.

As late as 1938 her niece, Arabella Moulton-Barrett, "Storm's" daughter, attributed her aunt's illness entirely to the pony episode, aggravated by deliberate malingering. The article ("The Barretts of Wimpole Street," Kingston, Jamaica *Daily Gleaner,* June 13, 1938) was called forth by Miss Moulton-Barrett's understandable anger at the characterization of Edward Barrett in the play *The Barretts of Wimpole Street.* Her defense of her grandfather, however, takes the form of a vicious attack upon her aunt. Since she never knew her aunt, the information must have come to her from family talk, especially from Charles John (Storm) Barrett. The reader will have noticed that several of the early letters clearly indicate that George had accused Elizabeth of malingering in Torquay. Also, it will be remembered that at the time of Elizabeth's marriage all the brothers sided with their father in condemning her. Nevertheless, this medical diagnosis, subsequent events, and all the testimony of others, as well as Mrs. Browning's letters confirm the reality of her illness. Tuberculosis, though very common in the mid-nineteenth century, was not well understood, and it is well known that victims of the disease experience periods of what seems to be good health and generally seem to think that they are getting better. Miss Moulton-Barrett's letter, however, indicates that at least Charles John and perhaps others of the immediate family never forgave Elizabeth for what appeared to them to be gross ingratitude to her father.

The "bark" in Dr. Carden's letter refers, of course, to quinine.

Letter from Dr. Carden, May 8, 1821

Dear Sir

Your clear detail of the symptoms of the disorder still affecting your daughters, though considerably mitigated, induces me to entertain the same opinion of the nature & treatment of the malady as I form'd on witnessing it for the first time. The only variation I am inclined to suggest in the medicine, is to make the Bark draught a little stronger with Bark & add to each dose half a teaspoonful, a little more to the eldest & rather less to the youngest, of the volatile Tincture of Valerian. The cold shower bath for Miss B I entirely approve of. The system of exercise in the open air must be pursued as much as possible & if the rides could be varied the advantage w^d be greater. In this way I hope & expect you will see a progressive amendment in their complaints, & that in a few weeks I shall have the pleasure of hearing of their being free from this harrassing malady. Should it prove however more tedious than I anticipate, an entire change of air would be desirable, & the choice of place, if dry, would be less material than the change itself. Before I conclude I would suggest the trial of a *tight* flannel roller around the abdomen by day only. With cordial good wishes to Mrs Barrett & your young people I remain

My dear Sir
Yrs faithfully
I Carden
May 8 1821

Worcester

Letter from Dr. Coker, June 24, 1821

Sir,

You will probably have been prepared by your friend Mr. Barrett to expect a letter from me, which in the hope of soothing a highly interested, and interesting family I gladly undertook to write to you – The subject on which I have to communicate upon, is not new to you — the case of Miss Barrett — that prodigy in intellectual powers and acquirements! — I saw her in consequence of some of our mutual friends having known that I had been successful in removing some painful affections of the nerves which assume the intermittent shape – This case unfortunately differs materially from them and is one of essential importance, both to the lady herself and to her friends – Though you have had a description of it from her own eloquent pen, I shall, as briefly as I can recapitulate it's history and state its present symptoms — It began with pain in the head, which continued at intervals for seven weeks – The pain then attacked various parts of the body, for a considerable period — and for the last month it has permanently seated itself on the right side, that is about the center of the angle formed by the greatest projection of the ribs, the umbilicus, and the anterior superior spinous process of the ischium – The pain commences here is carried to the corresponding region of the back, up the side to the point of the right shoulder, and down the arm. The suffering is agony — and the paroxysms continue from a quarter of an hour to an hour and upwards — accompanied by convulsive twitches of the muscles, in which the diaphragm is particularly concerned – The attack seems gradually to approach its acmé, and then suddenly ceases – During its progress the mind is for the most part conscious of surrounding objects but towards its close, there is generally some, and occasionally very considerable confusion produced by it – There are generally three attacks in the day and none during the night – Very considerable debility and consequent nervous irritation, producing smallness and feebleness of the pulse — pain, and weakness in the back, which will not allow her sitting up, without support by pillows, and she is always rendered worse by exercise – The feet are generally cold – The pupil appeared much dilated, but contracted on the stimulus of light – She sometimes awakes in the night in great fright; and says that in the morning there is a sensation as though a cord were tied round the stomach (i.e. the part affected) "which seems to break") to use her own expression. She is unable to rest on the right side — the tongue clean, and the stomach and bowels (aperient medicine is required) seemed to be so little affected, as to have excited my surprise, though she has only a relish for highly seasoned food — She has shrunk so much as to have produced in the minds of her friends great anxiety, though her countenance does not indicate to a stranger any cause for alarm – The mind has ceased in a great degree to engage in those investigations and pursuits which formerly constituted its greatest delight, and there appears to be a degree of listlessness perceptible to those around her, even where the affections are concerned –

I understand she has taken a variety of powerful medicines without any permanent benefit – Opium at one time relieved the spasms but it has ceased to have that effect – I examined the side, and spinal column as accurately as I could – In the side I should have remarked that she feels the sensation of its being swollen, which by no means appears to be the fact. There is too great irritability in the abdominal muscles to allow of much pressure being made upon them — but nothing like visceral accretion is to be inferred from the case itself or from the best examination I could make, nor could I detect any thing obviously wrong about

the spine – I should state that two of the sisters of this young lady
had some time since, the same kind of pain, or nearly so, which
occupied the *second* stage of this malady. They were all suffering
at the same time, which created a suspicion that they had taken
something deleterious – They both however soon recovered, without much, if any, medical treatment – For what remains for me to
add, I shall have to make some apology – I trust you will excuse
my giving you the views I entertain of this case, and, I hope you
will with the same candour give me yours – I am greatly assisted
in this subject, by having witnessed some years since in a young
lady, a strikingly similar, though much more aggravated case,
which terminated at length in decided affection of the spine —
from which she has recovered and is the mother of three children –
When I first saw this lady in Hampshire, she was suffering from
the same kind of spasms, as I observed in Miss Barrett (the left
side being here affected) and they were most vividly recalled to
my recollection on this occasion – She was at this time relieved by
bleeding &c, though her debility was infinitely greater than Miss
Barrett's. I did not see any reason at this period to imagine there
was disease of the spine, nor had it entered into the contemplation
of the physician and surgeon who attended her – After some three
or four weeks, she was enabled to travel home to Salisbury a distance of 40 miles, where I again saw her in consultation. I had no
doubt the vertebral column was now affected. The surgeon who
attended her concurred with me in opinion, and she ultimately
recovered – You will agree that it is difficult to remove the effect
which an impression of this kind, must make upon the mind of a
medical man – Keeping therefore this case in view, and for reasons
which shall be stated below, I should recommend, generally, the
treating Miss Barretts case as for diseased spine, upon the plan
recommended by Baynton — giving only such medicine as might
assist the operations of nature or as its exigencies would require —
bleeding might also be employed if necessary to mitigate the
spasms, and the Unguentum Antimonii Tartarisate applied to the
side, would prove some counter irritation — proper attention should
be paid to the ingesta – Medicine seems to have, and to have had
no effect, and the worst as it appears to me that can result from the
adoption of this measure, will be the loss of time if it should even
be proved to have been injudiciously recommended — The reasons
I alluded to above, are the history of the case – No relief having

been obtained from the variety of well directed attempts to re-move its influence. The increasing debility — loss of locomotive power — pain in the back — its requiring support in the erect posture — no attack during the night — constant inconvenience from exercise, together with the state of the nervous and sanguif-erous systems, indicating a high degree of sympathy, and most probably referable to derangement in some highly important organ – The uterine system is not materially affected – At the same time that I confess, the positive proofs are wanting of the existence of diseased spine, I must say that this is the best inference I could draw of Miss Barrett's from the opportunity I had of enquiring into its nature and of witnessing her sufferings – Being more anxious for the welfare of the sufferer, than for the fate of my own opinion, I shall again request you to use every freedom in commenting upon this communication, and beg to remain, Sir, Your most obedient servant.   Wm. Coker

N.B. You will probably have thought me tedious but it is impos-sible to see such a patient without feeling a lively interest in her recovery.

. . . .

Dear Sir – I have thought you might derive some satisfaction from knowing what communication I made to your friend Dr. Nuttall. I have therefore taken the liberty of sending you a copy of it — any mis-statement or omission which may have inadvertently occurred you will be enabled to correct and supply — that the Doctors mind may not be misled in its conclusions by a want of precision and fact, in the details of this interesting case — for the removal of which you have my most hearty wishes. I am Dear Sir,

Your most obedient servant
William Coker

N.B. I trust Mr. S. Barrett will excuse my
sending this under cover to him – June 24, 1821.

Letter from Dr. Nuttall

I take it kind, my dear Elizabeth, in you, to deliver so clear a description of the symptoms which necessarily obtruded themselves on your observation, but before I can advance any opinion further, than that, already in the possession of your Father, there are other symptoms of which I wish to be apprized, of the existance [*sic*] or modification of which you could not be aware unless your attention had been attracted to them, & there are a few more besides which are obvious to none but the practised eye & touch. Under the last class the pulse is to be ranged, & also the action of the Heart, as to number of strokes during the minute, their regularity, or otherwise; their force compared with that of others; at the present time, as well as during a paroxysm. Under the former class are to be included sensations arising from pressure on a part &c. Having offer'd these general remarks allow me to request that you will answer the following questions as early as you shall have gained the necessary information.

What is the state of your pulse, and Hearts action, during the *advancement* of a paroxysm? What, when you do not suffer? If you apply moderate pressure to your sides, below the short ribs, pit of stomach, or bowels, what sensations arise? does pain ensue? or does a positive sense of uneasiness? When actually, or passively suffering. Are your bowels distended more than before your complaint began, or has your appetite vacillated? food oppressed, bowels torpid, or irregular in their action? At the time you suffer so much commotion, & distress, when rising do you suffer much distension from wind, & does it escape when the "tendons & lineaments break"? How long after breakfast is it before the agony begins, & what do you take for breakfast? Does any one part of the bowels seem more tumid, at one time, or constantly, than another, & *harder,* as if distended with air or even something more solid? The severe pains you experience about the chest & right side, proceeding towards the back, are in all liklihood owing to irregular, or spasmodic action, then occurring in the Heart; arising sympathetically from some disorder advancing in the alimentary canal, generating flatus, which pressing *in* the midrif, or internal boundary of the chest, & consequently impeding the Hearts free action renders it for a time irritable. Your active turn of mind, & *inactive state* of body, together with your age &c incline you, as well as other young ladies under similar circumstances to dyspeptic complaints. It not unfrequently happens, that the Bowels become loaded with vitiated matter, which does not sometimes become obvious, notwithstanding the best means have been adopted to remove it, for 10 days a fortnight or three weeks, nay more. The sure criterion that all is not right there, is the appearance of clay-coloured, or greenish, of blackish, or frothy, or mucous, or yeasty motions, foetid in character, but sometimes these conditions do not occur till the disease is about to be removed.

You have too much good sense, my dear Elizabeth, not to be candid with me, on a point, of so much moment to yourself, & those who love, & value you. In matters of this kind, false delicacy might, & have, often lead to the most ruinous consequences; therefore scrupulously attend to all I have suggested to you, for observation. Get the following prescription made up directly & take the two pills the same night . . . [*piece torn out*] they shall cause to be dislo[*dged*] from the [*bow*]els next morning. Give my best love to Father, Mother, Brothers & *sympathetic Sisters*.

Yours truly
G. B. Nuttall

Rx

Extracte Jalapae	gr. v [*torn and indecipherable*]
Extracte Aloes	gr. ii
Hydroxgyn Aub-mur	gr. ii

Bene contumde, & divide in pilutas duas. nocte sumundas hora somni.

G B N

APPENDIX III

The Reverend George Barrett Hunter

Miss Hewlett refers to this letter as one which "might by inference be attributed to Hunter," the signature of which is said to be "indecipherable" (p. 58). The latter phrase indicates that Miss Hewlett got her information of the letter from the Maggs Brothers catalogue (1937). Actually the initial *G.* of the signature is perfectly clear, and the contents make it quite certain that the letter was written by the Rev. Mr. Hunter shortly after Elizabeth's departure for Torquay. The combination of intense feeling with the evasiveness and circumlocution of the style bears out Elizabeth's comment on Mr. Hunter, written four years later: "He wants abstracting by the exertion of an outward-working energy. The very owl leaves its ruin sometimes or would hoot out its own knell — & a self-conscious heart is a ruin, if old enough" (*Letter 16,* p. 82).

"The Romaunt" is "The Romaunt of Margaret."

"Christopher's Cave" refers to a review by James Wilson

(Christopher North) entitled "Christopher in His Cave" which appeared in *Blackwood's Magazine*, August, 1838. The section devoted to *The Seraphim* covers pages 279-84. Wilson clearly knew nothing of the author, whose name he gives as Elizabeth Barnett. He is not too kind to "The Seraphim" but expresses warm admiration for some of the shorter poems, quoting "My Doves," "The Deserted Garden," "The Sleep," and "Cowper's Grave" entire.

Miss Barrett
Hedleys Esqre
Braddon's Hill Torquay

Axtr Sept 26th/38

Dearest & ever dearer Friend – If I thought you would be grieved by telling you that I am, I would not tell you so. In every other case than this, I believe I know that your kindness & sympathy would make you sorry with me in my sorrows — but in this case let me presume that you will not be grieved, because I am so, for having GRIEVED YOU. To give you any pain at any time, is a thought exceedingly distressing — how much more exceedingly so, must the thought be of, in the least degree grieving you NOW! Be most assured my dearest Friend that I was most utterly unconscious of having written in my last anything unkind — and I am at this moment quite unable to remember or imagine to what you refer by "hard thoughts" and "silence" called "ingratitude." Dearest Friend there *must* be some mistake here. Have I left out, in hurried writing, some word or words, and by such an omission, entirely altered the intended expression — or did I write so unintelligibly that you have mistaken some word, for its very opposite?– I beseech you to tell me from *what* you derived the impression that I had "hard thoughts" — and was "angry" — and deemed your silence "ingratitude" — for my most laborious recollections do not furnish me with the slightest surmize. All was the contrary! As to *silence* there was *none* — and if there had been, I should have ascribed it to your fatigue & feebleness — and to your kind effort to comply with a repeated request of mine *not* to write, when doing so would in the least degree fatigue you — and for such a silence (out of its cause) I should have been *grateful* — as one wh. spared you from an in-

jurious exercise. O my ever kindest & dearest Friend! how COULD
I ever associate "ingratitude" and YOU? It is in *many* ways *utterly*
IMPOSSIBLE — and I am altogether bewildered & astonished. Had I
ever made such an association my very consciousness would become
a shuddering self disgust — and I should wear away in the
wretchedness of having impaired — yea, of having deservedly & for
ever forfeited a regard wh. is dearer to me than that of all the
world besides. Did you think me angry when I was but joking about
the *Dr.* or at least very nearly joking? The only expressions wh. I
can remember as giving occasion perhaps to the view you took of
my temper in my last letter, are those about *"Aristocracy."* Could
my dearest Friend, imagine that they referred, even in the remotest
manner, to *Her?!* Does She remember having once jocosely but
truly applied the term to the moral or mental temperament of a
certain friend of Her's? He took the application, as he felt it, to be
a true one — and regard[d] it as one proof that She knew him – And
the knowledge wh. it intimated, from some cause or other *pleased*
him. He does not know that he ever referred to the matter, before
he did so in a late letter, in wh. he saw something wh. some foolish
sensitive imagination suggested, but wh. could not in any possibility refer to *Her.* – But after all I do, on several accounts, most
sincerely & painfully regret that I ever used those expressions —
and I do most anxiously & affectionately ask Your forgiveness. I
assure You — that I had no feeling while writing them that suggested they would grieve You — if I had had, would they have been
there! O no! Will you pardon them, for the MOTIVE's sake? *I
wanted to see You.* I fully understood, just as I do now, the suggestion about delaying a certain journey – I fully understood it in
all its gentleness & kindness — and it was as *wise* as it was kind &
gentle — but if it were so, that I foolishly imagined an obstacle
(altogether apart from Your own wishes) and wrote nonesense [*sic*]
Aristocracy — forgive it, my dearest Friend — for *I wanted to see
You.* – But I am sure You will wish me to leave this subject, and I
will do so. I need not inform you that I received Your parcel this
morning. I cannot tell you, therefore imagine, how I thank you, —
and prize the unwearied kindness wh. sent it. I am almost reluctant
to touch on its contents now I have so little room left. That *"Sab-
bath on the Sea"* is most beautiful & dear — and *it* too is *mine*. I
cannot, may not tell you how & what I intensely feel of your kindness — while I call that and others — *Mine* — and the feeling is so

intense as it is because *you* taught me to call them *so.* – *"The Romaunt"* — if there could be brighter & warmer and purer tears than Miss Mitford's — or admiration more worthy than that of Walter Scott's most intimate friends — it is worthy of them — and would give more honor than it would receive. (Do expressly and affectionately thank dear Henrietta, for me, for having written out the former) *The Reviews* – It was like Bulwer to perceive "sublimity" "natural grace" and "etherial beauty" — and to tell of "pure & lustrous gems" and "perfect models." – "Christopher's Cave" was a little too glomy [*sic*] when he wrote of "OUR ELIZABETH"!!! Critics of Her Seraphim should be judges in *Eyre* (I appeal to the Templar). To write of Seraphim in a *Cave!* (i.e. in one, perhaps the least correct etymology of the term) I am vexed to find that Christopher uses some expressions like — nay the very same as those of the Atlas. Yet he has written some things truly & beautifully. His productions *have now* their beauty — may the future give them *truth.* You know *what* productions I mean – *One* of them is of *"conspicuous splendour."* Besides he writes with a certain devoutness wh. the rest of your critics want — (by the way — the sprit of *our* poor "Sea-men" will be jealous of "The Doves."

—— This is Wed^dy evening and it is probable that I shall see your Brother. Yet I fear the probability is not much for there will be no coach from Exeter till 1/2 past eleven. I shall meet it however. How glad I shall be to meet *him*. I heard from Mary to day. You shall *see* her letter. She says *"Papa* is going to Newcastle" &c. and talks about the house being "turned onto its chimneys" before he comes back again. She tells me of "a BEAUTIFUL *Polar Bear"* in the Z. gardens — and asks permission to *ride on the elephant* the next time she goes. She says of Miss Trepsack that she likes her (Miss T.) very much indeed — and that she is "a kind *lovely* old lady." She has a very poetical passage about the Harrow cemetary [*sic*] — part of it runs thus. "I wish Carissima-Ba could see it. I am sure she would write such eloquent Poetry — as well as YOURSELF." I commend the compliment & the Grammar to your especial admiration.– "The dear little Doves have had a young one — and all are doing well." She speculates about coming back in *May!!* Her epistle contains Latin, French & Italian — so you see what Carissimabella is making of her.

I thank you for transcribing so much of dearest Bella's account of Mary — but have I written thus far without a word about your

health — my dearest Friend? – I fear the best news only amounts
to — much as usual. I have constantly hoped & prayed that the
change of climate might prove decidedly beneficial before this – I
yet hope & pray — and feel the consolation of commending you to
the tenderest care — and the recovering mercy of Him who so
mercifully cares for You. Dont dont I beseech you give way to
anxieties & regrets about leaving your beloved ones in London.
Their beautiful & precious love! I thank you for the view you
have given me of it. O! how could it be but what it is! Do let the
cheerfulness & gratitude wh. such love demands prevail over the
painfulness of being removed for a while from the scene in wh. its
fulness gathered round you . . . May you my most beloved Friend
soon be restored to all its endearments — in health — happiness and
all the blessedness of *His love* who "giveth His beloved sleep." – As
you love *them*, try to make us cheerful by your cheerfulness. Forgive me if I have written to you in some cases too cheerfully — but
our darling Bella charged me to be very cheerful with you. How
could I — how *could* I be *angry* and have *"hard thoughts"*. – *Tell*
me that it is *not* — that it *never can be so.* – I wrote yesterday to
your Brother — for I was very anxious to hear of you. I am almost
fearful lest I should have said anything to grieve you. Give to him
& Mr. Geo. and to dear Henrietta my kindest regards. Dr. Smith
said nothing whatever to me in his letter that could unfold the
secret — but of course I know or conjecture *now* what it is. By the
way how surely *Woman can* keep a secret! How glad I shall be to
hear that you have entered on your own cottage. Regard it as a
temporary & merciful *Home* – May it abound with mercies in the
fulness of wh. you shall return to your own dearer home.

Your ever most affecte. friend G.B.H.

1/2 past 12. I have been to meet the coach, but I found no one in
it who had seen you a few hours ago. It would have been a great
pleasure to have seen them — but it is a greater to think they are
with you. I prophesy that your beloved Bro will be appointed your
guardian at Torquay. It *should be so.* It is more than midnight and
my thoughts remind me that you have never told me whether you
sleep well at night. –

[*Across sheets 1, 2, 3*]
Thursday Morng. 27th
I have a few minutes this morning to add a few lines. Neither my
waking nor dreaming thoughts during the night have dissolved

yesterdays mystery and yet I rose with a surmize that my dearest Friend must have absolutely mistaken my *jocoseness* for *Anger* (about the *hard thoughts* I can win no hint either from light or darkness). Is it possible that my abruptness in some sayings about the Dr was mistaken for snappishness and anger, when positively it was my object to make you laugh at them. By the way I do think that there were some criticisms of a similar character in my last letter to Bro. — criticisms on a critic of yours — and I fear that you will become still surer than you were before about my having turned to a sad ill natured mood since my Guardian Angel left me. Well, I will give up this trying to make you laugh. I am the *beautiful White Polar Bear* trying to dance & sing for your amusement — and you take it for a growling passion. Ah my Friend I assure you that mine is no mood of merriment — a far other mood is mine. Well forgive it all. Mary tells me that you go on to the sea every day almost. And she says too (Wh. I pray you observe) that you have not yet granted her request to be made Lady of your study chamber. After writing a letter fuller if possible than this — she hopes in the *last line* that I will excuse her for not writing any *more* as she was going to write you. There is *such* a passage about Mr. Boyd. She says that great Greek scholars can talk a great deal of nonsense (pray observe that) and that as for Mr. Boyd he does not know where Madagascar is! Good bye again.

APPENDIX IV

Letters to Henry Moulton-Barrett and to
Henrietta Moulton-Barrett Surtees Cook (Altham)

The two following letters of Mrs. Browning's, one to her
brother Henry and one to her sister Henrietta, are included here
because they are hitherto unpublished items in the Browning-
Barrett correspondence and because they point up certain aspects
of Mrs. Browning's personality already apparent in the letters to
George.

The letter to Henry is chiefly interesting for her enthusiastic
approval of marriage thirteen years after her own courageous
venture.

The letter to Henrietta points conveniently the difference
noted in the *Introduction* between Mrs. Browning's letters to her
sisters and those to George. The comments on Pen show again
that her maternal possessiveness by no means blinded her understanding of the masculine nature and that she saw what was to

come with no more than a natural regret for something dear which must pass. Pen was at the time ten years old.

Harry M. Barrett, Esq'ʳᵉ
4 Darlington St
Bath
Angleterre via France.

Florence, January 9, 1858

My dearest Henry – I cannot express to you what deep joy your letter has given me, and I answer it directly that you may have some idea. May God bless you and *yours,* my very dearly loved Brother — and may God be thanked that he has blessed you already by giving you a *"yours",* something to love you & to be loved by you in that closest of relations which (when a true marriage) lasts beyond this world. I am very happy for you – Often and often have I wished lately that you could marry, — but it never once struck me that you had an undevelopped angel over your head, on the point of dropping by your side. Your letter made me cry out — Amelia! – Amelia Morris! – Nobody had I heard of with such a pretty name as 'Amelia' and belonging to a friend of yours. We exiles are at a great disadvantage, you see, — and before I was an exile from England, I was an exile from society, so that I knew nothing even of Amelia Holland — did I? Could I? — no, indeed. But now the veil is lifted up, and I know her, or seem to know her – I know at least that you love her, — which is enough for me; and besides that knowledge, I have your charming description of her, however brightly coloured in the colours peculiar to your position, Harry. (You will forgive me for making some deductions) & I have her over again unmistakeably, in her sweet, natural, touching letter to Henrietta – Oh, that letter quite touched me! – Will you tell the person who wrote it that I will love her, if she will let me, and that I believe in her fully from this moment, and have a great prejudice in favor of this marriage as if she was sure to be an affectionate sister to me, and a tender, true wife to you, my dearest Henry –

Let me tell you. Not only Robert was sitting by the fire when your packet came, but Mrs. Jameson, — and I assure you, I was kissed and congratulated again and again on both sides, for I cried out, and could not conceal my ecstatical state of mind.

Dearest Henry, may you both be very happy. She is right in trusting you, as she says, for I, who know you, know that you will not fail,— that your good kind heart and upright and manly nature will expand and give joy (as well as take it) in a genial home. May you be happy, *Dear* – And a happy marriage is the best form of happiness which is granted upon this earth, be very certain. –

I shall be eager to hear more of your plans; when the great event is likely to happen,— & where you are likely to go & settle afterwards. Send me little bits of your dreams as they turn up. Penini hears with great interest of Uncle Harry's being about to present him with another aunt. He is always interested in marriages, and hopes to be married himself "in about twelve years", though the object is not yet decided upon – The other morning, he suddenly broke out with —"Is it against the law to marry one's own mama?" And when I said 'yes',— he gravely exclaimed . . "Oh, I do hope, *that* law may be broken before I am grown a great boy!" He had thought of doing me the honor of selecting me . . .

But more than of marrying & of giving in marriage, just now, Peni thinks of the carnival, and of how he is to mask and in what colour he is to wear his domino. I hear of nothing but masks & dominos between the sentences of Grimm's German stories and 'L'ami des enfants'. In spite of this he gets on, and is much more good and attentive than he was when you knew him — quite as high-spirited but more gentle & reasonable,— in fact, a very good child — grown too, but quite unaltered, except that he has a rounder rosier face than he wore in London ever.

Yesterday I had a visit from the celebrated Improvisatrice who has been filling the theatres here with enthusiastic crowds, the Signorina Milli. I who could not go to hear her on account of the cold, happened to say that I wished she would come and see *me*. Instantly somebody said, "But, if she knew you wished it she would be pleased to come – I will enquire". Whereupon she was made to know, and immediately & very graciously, though she had refused every invitation pressed upon her in Florence, except the Princess Corsini's, she acceded, and came here yesterday with her mother & brother; yes, and recited two poems with a musical voice & articulation worthy of Italy & her fame. She has beautiful eyes, and spoke with much eloquence, and without the slightest affectation. Robert ran out to fetch Mrs. Jameson — otherwise, we were alone. It was very interesting & characteristic.

Who knows but that some day you and your Amelia will come & see our Florence. Was she ever in Italy? — and dont you dream (in those dreams) of marriage-tours across the Alps and the sea? –

I am happy to think of them all at Bryngwyn and of that dear kind Storm's kindness to everybody.

And now, once more, and always, may God bless you! Try to persuade your Amelia to be prepared to love me a little, & promise her, from me the right true sisterly feeling – Robert's best love & congratulations & a kiss from Peni.

Your ever attached

Ba –

Mrs. Surtees Cook
Stoke Court near Taunton, Somerset.
Angleterre

Casa Guidi Saturday
[November 5, 1859]

My ever dearest Henrietta, Though I have just written to Arabel, I cant put off any more sending you the letter which is to express my true sympathy in dear Surtee's & your own & the childrens great loss & grief – I heard of it with a deep regret & full sense of how you must all have received the sudden a blow, of the removal of a person so much beloved & venerated by you – Such griefs do however bring their own counteraction – The more you have lost the more he has gained – I did not know him, nor did I agree in certain of his views as you are aware, but this does not hinder my appreciation of a devout & holy life, & my assurance that having entered here into the service of his Lord, he has entered there into His joy – Our love, Robert's and mine, to your dear Surtees. Let him accept the loving sympathy of both of us.

Now, you will write to me soon, dearest Henrietta, & tell me all about you all. I have been full of thoughts & pity for you on another ground — that is, your parting from Altham for his school-days. You are probably quite wise about it — & by this time, I trust, the natural pain both his & yours is merged in the satisfaction of a strong sense of advantage. Unless you had a tutor at home for your boys it would be imperative on you to send them to school of course — & perhaps the sooner you break certain home-habits the better in the long run — though it *did* seem to me that you were rather in haste to begin the classical part of Altham's education. Pen has not learnt a word of Latin yet, observe. But he will run where others walk, on account of his knowledge of Italian, so that we dont lament it much. We mean to have a master for him presently, our time being valuable beyond money – It wont do to give up our art for teaching — it is not good even for Peni — and I, for one, have not strength, for the systematic instruction which is necessary for boys as they get older, even if I had nothing else to do. Robert is perfect in his regularity about the music lessons. Even at Florence, where Signor Del Bene gives one hour a day, Robert gives his hour — & at Siena, he sate by Peni full two hours as surely as the sun rose & set. The pupil does him great honor I must add. He has just learnt, or is finishing to learn rather, Schuloff's Carnaval de Venise — & will play it really brilliantly. The way in which those small fingers dart & leap on the piano with combined accuracy & rapidity, is considered & may well be considered quite remarkable — "quite amazing" said Mr. Russell. I am very proud of his music — and Robert, who taught him, may well be, therefore. Indeed Penini doesn't do ill in his general lessons — he is more attentive, less volatile — and he begins to spell rather less outrageously badly. His spelling in Italian is a great improvement on the English. For instance he wrote more than half a copy-book page of Italian diction in close lines and small running hand the other day; with only two faults in it. He couldn't do that in English — more's the shame to us. Still he makes progress even on this ground of spelling & generally, as I said, he applies better. The poney & the riding go on capitally. The poney, from change of diet & care & rubbing down since he came to us, grows prettier than ever with a beautiful, glossy coat — of what colour is Altham's poney? And what height? And where do you put him? in stall or in field? Pen looks lovely on his poney, I must admit, & is said to ride with a most perfect grace. Annunciata & I have been providing his costume for the winter, & she has made blouses of various sorts, green, blue & other, to be worn with short & very full cloth trousers, trimmed up the sides with buttons & velvet. They wouldn't do for school, but presently you will like them for little Edward – People admire them here. We have just bought, too, one of the fashionable felt hats (black) turned up — have you seen them — with a large plume of the black-green cock feathers (and white swan feathers laid on it) falling behind. The effect is peculiar, but altogether it is becoming to the child. Tell me, Henrietta, if you make your children wear flannel next their skin. Peni has very fine merinos shirts (rather than waistcoats) as soft as silk, which he does not object to wearing, he who is difficult in such things. And do you know, I wear the same in scarlet merinos, of a still finer wool — buttoned up to the throat & extending to the hips — with long sleeves. I think they will be very useful to me, &, ever since I put them on last week, I have been wishing & wishing that our Arabel could be persuaded to wear the same. The simple expedient of keeping an equal warmth on the surface of the skin, & of not exposing herself in the evening after your barbarous English fashion, would do more for her general health than she has any idea of. But no, she wont yield on this point. Tell her that my Paris flannel jacket (trimmed with red) will serve me again this winter. I have bought a fine flannel skirt (grey) to wear with it. You see my *idée fixe* just now is rather to be warm than beautiful. Peni who likes bright colours, "really wonders" at Mama's bad taste. I am going however to have a Zouave jacket — much worn at Paris just now — with the waistcoat under — a very pretty costume, besides being very convenient. I saw one made of black lace (both jacket & waistcoat) yesterday, just arrived from Paris & quite beautiful. The jacket is loose & short — closes at the throat, & leaves the waistcoat exposed lower. Thus — [*drawing*] (No, that looks more like a grate.) One of the advantages is that a small quantity of stuff makes the jacket. But my jacket will be made not of lace, but of cloth — & the waistcoat shall be velvet. Then I am to have a new black silk dress, because one can scarcely see a ceremony at Rome, without being dressed in sables for it. But I hope that the ceremony I shall be called to see, after all, may be the Pope's expulsion, — for which no particular costume is necessary! Prices are so low in Rome that we are offered apartments at twelve pounds the month, for which friends of ours paid forty and fifty last year. Nobody from England goes.

Wilson has removed to her new house, & Mr. Landor follows her tomorrow. The rooms are very nicely furnished — but I hear of a plague of mosquitos — which is an intolerable nuisance, of course. It is difficult here to have a *garden* without that nuisance. Tell me more of your new residence & how you continue to like it. It must be delightful, I should think. Tell me, too, of the children. I have not had *details* of them for a long time, it seems to me. How is my

pet Mary, whom I envy you for so much? What would I give to
have a little girl, to stand by me when Pen sits at the other end of
the room, absorbed in ponies, & the things which succeed ponies.
Not that he is far from me yet, poor darling. He is quite a child still,
and a very loving one — and this may last my time perhaps – But
the young man (when *he* comes) will have, I suppose, the young
man's ways. And the curls & the cuddling will be clipped one day.
Mr. Chorley has written a novel called Roccabella which I forgot
to mention to Arabel. It is dedicated to me — so you must all read
it (if the opportunity occurs) out of gratitude. By the way, Mr.
Chorley writes to tell me that, English though he be, he does not
share the Atheneums [*sic*] politics or sympathize with the Times. He
approves therefore of my poem.

[*At side and top of first sheet*]
Do you see much of the Hedleys? My love to them. What is the
distance? I am well now. The weather is almost too warm, but
there must be a change soon. You would call it summer and the
green peas we have every day w^d keep up your village. We have
not had a fire yet, nor [*on envelope*] could bear a fire. I can drive
out & have the windows open. It cant last long, though – I want
to hear of George. And nobody mentions Storm. Now write, my
beloved Henrietta, & believe how I love you.

Your ever attached
Ba –

Sophia Cottrell enquires after you. She has a fine fat little girl.
Tell me how is Mrs. Cook? I fear she has suffered much.

APPENDIX V

Letters from Cornelius Mathews

The first of the two following letters from Cornelius Mathews to Elizabeth Barrett is the one referred to by her in *Letter 18* (p. 90). It reached London by packet March 13, 1843.

The second and longer letter reached London January 30, 1843. It is included here for its picture of the state of publication in the United States as well as for its evidence of the popularity of Miss Barrett's poetry at the time. Her first letter to Mathews published in Kenyon, I, pp. 132-35, is dated April 28, 1843. This is clearly not the letter to which she was replying, but the two are closely complementary.

14 Pine Street
New York, 21st Jan. 1843

My dear Miss Barrett:

I write, in haste, just as the packet is casting her cable to say that if you have determined to write for Graham's Magazine, you are at liberty to draw on Wiley & Putnam, Booksellers, Paternoster Row for £10 – I sent you through this firm the parcel to which I referred in my last letter: a letter by the way marked to go by Brittania Steamer, but which somehow or other loosing its channel, was clumsily re-sealed and sent by the "Stephen Whitney" Packet. I have asked you to write for Graham's Mag^e not because I regard it as by any means the highest medium through which good Poetry should reach the world — but with the hope that its circulation, which is very great, might extend your reputation in this country & because I had a notion that even so trifling a tribute as you would get in the way of money, might be looked upon as a levy from one of the Provinces, having so much of grandeur even in its smallness.

Believe me
Yours most Truly
Cornelius Mathews.

P.S.

I imagine you may be in the way hereafter of all kinds of applications from the getters-up of Magazines in this country & may be pardoned for suggesting a caution to the effect that some of these have character & some *not*.

New York, Dec. 28th. 1842

Dear Miss Barrett.

Dear Madam, I should say, but friendliness conquers form — I owe you sincere thanks for the generous eye with which you are inclined to regard the imperfect and unfinished Poem "Wakondah" – I sent it to you with doubt and trembling, casting my bread upon the waters, and after many days it has returned to me with a better and higher character. Your kind approval has given it a new interest in my eyes and when I return to it, as I shall in a good season of propitious thought, it will be with new strength and spirit. – What you say of our American Poetry and its imitative character is true enough: our Poets are not Men but Echoes. An European looks to America, naturally, for strength and vigour of conception and execution, and not for the last refinements of Literature which belong to older countries. If the First Pilgrims and settlers had been thrust forth into the wilderness with no other knowledge of the other world but Homer and Shakespeare, it strikes me, America would have furnished much better and nobler additions to Literature than she can claim to have yet furnished. And this brings me to say that although you sympathize with us in our strong desire for a Law of International Copyright, you can scarcely have a conception of the hardship of the present state of things as it bears upon the American writer. He has in truth and in effect no paymaster — no Publisher — no Public. He may at times make his voice heard but it is in the midst of so great a din and clashing of, what is here called, the Mammoth Press — in venting of ill-gotten gains — the pluckings and plunderings of British Literature — that it perishes almost instantly. There are two re-publishing Establishments in this city, which (to give you a notion of the Extent of this system) pledge themselves to issue a new work complete, every week: upwards of 100 novels or other British productions a year for which the British author is not only to have nothing, and the American still less — that is not even the privilege of appearing in print on any terms whatever. - As to periodical literature, to which you refer, it is, with us, just now taking the shape of Fashionable Monthly Magazines, with plates of costumes and borrowed engravings of other subjects. These at present absorb the enterprize of Publishers and the subscription-money of the Public. There are a few of a different kind — but they languish and live by permission and not subscription. Elevated standards of opinion and criticism are among the great wants of this country. The question you ask and which you seem to think is put across the Atlantic as if you were at one side of a great table and I at the other — How I was pleased with Mr. Dickens' judgement? — can be safely answered, Displeased? not at all. I regard it, with errors of fact and opinion as might be expected from his hasty travel, as an eminently sincere and honest book. He has written in a fair spirit, meaning well by us, and in points where most fault has been found with him, should be regarded as yielding — where he speaks gravely — to the impulses of a fresh and generous nature: in others, where his tone is lighter, as indulging, not censurably, his genius for sportive comment on life and manners. - For the Poets — whose names occur in your note — Tennyson, Browning and Horne — I have in part and am still more inclined from your kind mention of them — to encourage a true regard. Of Mr. Horne I happen to know less than the others, because, perhaps, his writings have appeared in less accessible shapes; Browning fixed my at-

tention at the start in the Extracts from Paracelsus in the 'New-
Monthly', which has followed him since, in his various advances,
through the "Examiner" – The true Poet is in him breaking his
bonds, and I hope to live yet to see him standing forth, in the
disencumbered attitude, which his friendly critics, think he should
assume. Tennyson's two volumes have been read in this country
with great pleasure: A slight evidence of the esteem in which he
is held you will find in a couple of newspapers one of which, if you
think it worth the conveyance, belongs to Mr. Tennyson himself.
Due allowance must be made for sundry transpositions of awkward
printers blunders. [An] ungenerous word in the North American &
one still more so in the Christian Examiner — he need not heed
a jot: Ten chances to one they spring from some of his many
imitators in this country, who may think to escape the punishment
that belongs to "children's sins" by a long score on the back of the
"father." – I am glad that anything of mine is going into the hands
of Miss Mitford — a name thronged with kindly associations in
America — and whose "Rienzi" shows a spirit capable of entering
the stronghold of passion & expression when it chooses. In a small
parcel which accompanies this, I have sent you "Grahams Magazine" & the "Boston Miscellany"— containing sonnets by Miss
Barrett & "The Cry of the Human." Reperusing the last in print,
I cannot avoid saying, that I concur in the general verdict that it
is one of the most successful poems you have written. You must
know that you are in some request when I tell you I had a message
from Boston soliciting the original MSS. as something more than
commonly valuable. If agreeable to you the Conductor of "Graham's
Magazine" would be pleased to have from you such future Poems
as you might find it convenient to contribute. The money-part I
could arrange for you — but as this is so mere a trifle (2 guineas
for a poem of even the breifest [sic] length & 1 1/2 guineas for anything longer) you may not think it worth your while to trouble
yourself with the undertaking. In the event of any arrangement I
would endeavour to fix it so that you could draw on Wiley &
Putnam, Paternoster Row for, say £10 — at once.

Yours, with sincere regard,
Cornelius Mathews

P.S. After wavering back & forth half a dozen times, I have thrust
into the bundle a newspaper containing a few lines on "The Death

of Channing"—which may be almost said to have been written or spoken aloud to myself over the paper where I first met the annc[t] of his death. The Articles on Tennyson are by a friend, whose judgements on most literary questions go abreast with mine: if I had written them they would have been in some passages worded otherwise.

The Family of Elizabeth Barrett Browning

The following list contains the given name, nicknames, and other titles of the relatives so frequently mentioned in the Browning-Barrett correspondence. The list is arranged by the family groupings to which each individual belongs.

Graham-Clarkes

Maternal ancestors of Elizabeth Barrett

John Graham-Clarke — Grandfather of Elizabeth from Newcastle, Northumberland.

Arabella Altham Graham-Clarke — Grandmother of Elizabeth.

Mary Graham-Clarke — Mother of Elizabeth (1781-1828).

Uncle John Graham-Clarke — Mrs. Barrett's brother, Elizabeth's uncle of Kinnersley Castle, Herefordshire.

Aunt Arabella — Mrs. Barrett's sister, Elizabeth's maiden aunt referred to as "Bell" or "Bummy."

Aunt Jane Hedley — Mrs. Barrett's sister, Elizabeth's aunt, married to Uncle (John) Hedley.

Aunt Charlotte	Mrs. Barrett's sister, Elizabeth's aunt, married to The Rev. Richard Pierce Butler.
Aunt Frances	Mrs. Barrett's sister, Elizabeth's aunt, married to Sir Thomas Butler, referred to as Aunt Fanny.
Leonard Parkinson Graham-Clarke	Elizabeth's cousin, son of Uncle John of Kinnersley Castle, later married to his cousin Isabel Butler.
Arabella Hedley	Elizabeth's cousin, daughter of Aunt Jane and Uncle John Hedley; later married to J. J. Bevan.
George Robin John	Sons of the Hedleys, and Elizabeth's cousins.
Ibbet Fanny	Daughters of the Hedleys, and Elizabeth's cousins.
Charlotte (Arlette) Butler Cissy	Daughters of The Rev. R. P. Butler and Aunt Charlotte. Arlette married C. W. Reynolds. Cissy died in May, 1843.
Uncle James Hedley	Brother of Uncle John Hedley; no relation but a good friend of the Barretts through the Hedley family connection.
Barretts, later Moulton-Barrett	**Paternal ancestors of Elizabeth**
Elizabeth Moulton	Grandmother of Elizabeth (*d.* January 15, 1831).
Edward Moulton-Barrett	Elizabeth's father, Papa (*b.* May 28, 1785; *d.* April 17, 1857).
Samuel Moulton-Barrett	Mr. Barrett's only brother, a bachelor, and Elizabeth's favorite uncle in youth (*d.* in Jamaica, December 3, 1837).

Mrs. Browning's Brothers and Sisters

Edward Barrett Moulton-Barrett	Elizabeth's eldest and favorite brother, "Bro," whose death by drowning at Torquay was the one inconsolable grief of her life (*b.* June 26, 1807; *d.* July 11, 1840).
Henrietta Barrett	Elizabeth's sister who later married William Surtees Cook (later Altham), a distant cousin, in 1850 and suffered the same paternal ostracism as her sister. In her childhood she was called "Harry" (*b.* March 4, 1809; *d.* November 23, 1860).
Samuel Barrett	Elizabeth's second brother, whose premature death by fever in Jamaica, February 17, 1840, greatly agitated the recuperating Elizabeth in Torquay (*b.* January 13, 1812; *d.* February 17, 1840).
Arabella Barrett	Elizabeth's maiden sister, her favorite, and Robert's devoted friend after his wife's death (*b.* July 4, 1813; *d.* June 11, 1868).
Charles John Barrett	Elizabeth's third brother, born during a Hereford storm and called "Stormie" most of his life; a lifelong stutterer (*b.* December 28, 1814; *d.* January 21, 1905, in Jamaica where he was the last proprietor of the original Barrett estates).
George Goodin Barrett	Elizabeth's favorite brother, who remained a bachelor and was Elizabeth's closest family counselor, after the death of Bro (*b.* July 15, 1816; *d.* August 11, 1895).

Henry Barrett	Elizabeth's brother referred to as "Harry" (*b.* August 19, 1818[?]; *d.* May 17, 1896).
Alfred Price Barrett	Elizabeth's brother who won his sister's support by marrying in 1855, though he too was disowned by Mr. Barrett (*b.* May 20, 1820; *d.* May 24, 1904).
Septimus James Barrett	Elizabeth's seventh brother, referred to variously as "Set," "Sette," and "Septim" (*b.* February 22, 1822; *d.* March 17, 1870).
Octavius Butler Barrett	Elizabeth's youngest brother referred to variously as "Occy," "Oc," "Ocy," "Jocy," and "Joc" (*b.* April 12, 1824; *d.* November 11, 1910).

Barrett Household

Mrs. Robinson	Hope End housekeeper who was still in the family and lived to a great age, dying at Arabella's, 7 Delamere Terrace, possibly in 1861 (see *Letter 64, note 2,* p. 278). She is almost always referred to as Minny.
Mrs. Mary Trepsack	Loyal servant of Grandmother Barrett who lived on in the Barrett service and company, remembered in Edward Barrett's will, though she died a few months before him at her home in Welbeck Street. She is usually referred to as "Trippy" or "Treppy." While she was not actually a servant in the household, she was a devoted regular visitor (1768?–1857).

Chronological Listing of Letters

ELIZABETH TO GEORGE

For other letters from and to Elizabeth, see Appendixes.

INDEX

Names and places are identified by notes on their first appearance in the text. All index entries refer to the text except in cases where the pertinent matter occurs only in the notes.

Members of Mrs. Browning's immediate family are listed under Barrett. In 1798 the family name was changed by royal permission from Moulton to Moulton Barrett. Members of the family did not generally hyphenate the name, but the usage in the text, especially on envelopes, is inconsistent.

386 LETTERS OF THE BROWNINGS TO GEORGE BARRETT

132, 133, 134, 137, 139, 141, 146, 152, 158, 173, 215, 305; on Eliza-
beth's poetry, "The Dead Pan," 81, 91, 92, 93, 95; "A Drama of
Exile," 113, 116, 117; and Browning, 81, 82, 130, 152; urged trust
deed, 245, 253, 268-69
Kinglake, Alexander William, 228
King's College, 274
Kingsdown, Lord, 263
Kinnersley, near Hereford, 74, 76, 101, 120, 128
Kinney, Elizabeth Stedman (Mrs. William B.), 27, 188
Kinney, William Burnet, 188, 192, 193, 196

Laiatico. See Corsini
Lamartine, Alphonse, 174
Lamoricière, General Louis Christophe, 236, 243
Landon, Letitia Elizabeth, 9, 72
Landor, Walter Savage, 95, 244, 288, 360; *Imaginary Conversations,* 244
Landseer, Sir Edwin H., 142
Langley, Henry G., 122
Lawrence, Sir Thomas, painting of "Pinkie" (Sarah Goodin Moulton),
315
Lawson (servant), 335, 336
Leader, The (newspaper), 173
Ledbury, Herefordshire, 92, 96, 307
Leghorn, Italy, 137, 219, 242
Legros, Alphonse, 304
Leighton, Lord Frederick, 326; plans for Mrs. Browning's monument,
284-86, 298; seconds Pen's nomination for Athenaeum Club, 316
Lever, Charles, 233
Lewes, George Henry, 104
Locke (George's servant), 280
Locker, Frederick (Locker-Lampson), 182, 287, 288; proposes Pen for
Athenaeum Club, 316
Lockhart, John Gibson, 209
London University, 75, 274, 276
Longfellow, Henry Wadsworth, 91, 171; *The Golden Legend,* 171
Longmans (publishers), 141
Louis Philippe, King of France, 173
Lowell, James Russell, 91, 119
Lyndhurst, Lord, 104
Lytton, Robert ("Owen Meredith"), 184, 189, 201

Macarthy, Dr., 171
McCarthy, Barbara, *Elizabeth Barrett to Mr. Boyd,* 1
Macgregor, John, 193
Mackenzie, Mrs. Stewart, 174
Mackintosh, Collin, 105
Mackintosh, Emily, 124
Mackintoshes, the, 48, 88, 96
Maclean, George, 74